Jus Gentium in Humanist Jurisprudence

History of European Political and Constitutional Thought

VOLUME 9

The titles published in this series are listed at *brill.com/hepct*

Jus Gentium in Humanist Jurisprudence

On Justice and Right

By

Susan Longfield Karr

BRILL

LEIDEN | BOSTON

Cover illustration: *Emblem* 39 ('Harmony') from Andrea Alciati, *Andreae Alciati Emblemata cum commentariis Claudii Minois I.C. Francisci Sanctii Brocensis, & notis Laurentii Pignorii Patavini. Novissima hac editione in continuam unius commentarii seriem congestis, in certas quasdam quasi classes dispositis, & plusquam dimidia parte auctis. Opera et vigiliis Joannis Thuilii Mariaemontani Tirol ... Accesserunt in fine Federici Morelli ... Corollaria & monita, ad eadem Emblemata. Cum indice triplice* (Patavii: Apud Petrum Paulum Tozzium, 1621).

Library of Congress Cataloging-in-Publication Data

Names: Longfield Karr, Susan F., author.
Title: Jus gentium in humanist jurisprudence : on justice and right / by Susan Longfield Karr.
Description: Leiden ; Boston : Brill, [2022] | Series: History of European political and constitutional thought, 2589-5966 ; volume 9 | Based on author's thesis (doctoral - University of Chicago, 2008) issued under title: Nature, self, and history in the works of Guillaume Budé, Andrea Alciati, and Ulrich Zasius : a study of the role of legal humanism in western natural law. | Includes bibliographical references and index.
Identifiers: LCCN 2022029785 (print) | LCCN 2022029786 (ebook) | ISBN 9789004523661 (hardback) | ISBN 9789004528451 (ebook)
Subjects: LCSH: Law–Europe–Roman influences. | Jus gentium (Roman law)–History–16th century. | Humanism–Europe–History–16th century. | Natural law–Europe–History–16th century. | Budé, Guillaume, 1468-1540–Influence. | Alciati, Andrea, 1492-1550–Influence. | Zasius, Ulrich, 1461-1535–Influence.
Classification: LCC KJC431 .L66 2022 (print) | LCC KJC431 (ebook) | DDC 340.5/4–dc23/eng/20220831
LC record available at https://lccn.loc.gov/2022029785
LC ebook record available at https://lccn.loc.gov/2022029786

Typeface for the Latin, Greek, and Cyrillic scripts: "Brill". See and download: brill.com/brill-typeface.

ISSN 2589-5966
ISBN 978-90-04-52366-1 (hardback)
ISBN 978-90-04-52845-1 (e-book)

Contents

Acknowledgements

This book would not be possible without the generous support of the University of Chicago Department of History, the German Academic Exchange Service (DAAD), Herzog August Bibliothek, Max Planck Institute for Legal History and Legal Theory, the Max Weber Fellowship Program at the European University Institute, the Mellon Foundation, the Law and Public Affairs Program at Princeton University, and the University of Cincinnati, especially the Department of History and the College of Arts and Sciences.

Nor would this book exist without the generosity of a vast array of mentors, scholars, friends, and colleagues, who, in seminars, symposia, workshops, conferences, research venues, coffee breaks, and hikes, have not only shown great interest in the project but have also encouraged me to make the story of how *ius gentium* was transformed at the hands of the 'fathers of legal humanism' accessible to a variety of audiences that all too often do not intersect. To that end, I am incredibly grateful for the insightful questions, invaluable feedback, and generosity of Constantin Fasolt, Martin van Gelderen, Anthony Grafton, Michael Geyer, Tamar Herzog, William J. Novak, James Hankins, Annabel Brett, James Tully, Quentin Skinner, Brian Cummings, Lorraine Datson, Kim Lane Scheppele, Marie Theresa O'Connor, Stephen Porter, A. J. Aiseirithe, Daniel Gullo, Peter Brooks, Elizabeth Mertz, Gordon Silverstein, Janet McLean, Michael Lobban, Erika Gasser, Laura Culbertson, Tracy Teslow, Janne E. Nijman, Chana Baron, Katherine Sorrels, Robert Stern, Sigrun Haude, Ethan Katz, Maura O'Connor, Douglas B. Klusmeyer, Steven Gill, Theo Jung, James Murray, and, of course, Abigail Laura Karr and Ingo Trauschweizer. All of whom gave freely of their time to discuss the nuances of the argument, pushed me to clarify concepts, and challenged me to be a better writer. Special thanks are also due to the editors of this series and to those who carefully reviewed the manuscript, their comments and suggestions have undoubtedly made this a better work. And, to William Barker, who graciously shared the images of Alciati's *Emblems* that appear in this volume from his private collection.

I owe an enormous debt to Constantin Fasolt, James Hankins, Daniel Gullo, Cameron Hawkins and James Murray for their Latin expertise and advice that helped me (over the life of this project) render the meandering prose of Guillaume Budé and the technical vocabularies of Ulrich Zasius and Andrea Alciati into accessible English. Naturally, all errors remain my own.

Finally, I wish to thank Janne E. Nijman and Anthony Carty, co-editors of *Morality and Responsibility of Rulers: European and Chinese Origins of a Rule of*

Law as Justice for World Order, and Paul du Plessis and John W. Cairns, co-editors of *Reassessing Legal Humanism and its Claims: Petere Fontes?*, for the opportunity to explore and develop some of the ideas that shape this book. I am grateful to Oxford University Press and the University of Edinburgh Press for permitting me to use some of that material in this volume as well.

Figures

Introduction

Historical Imagination, Collective Memory, and the Historicization of Roman Law

In the wake of the Italian Wars that involved all the significant powers in Europe (in various permutations from 1494 to 1559), the emergence of the early modern state—demarcated by territorial boundaries and delimited by legal jurisdictions, rather than merely by dynastic claims and religious ties—challenged the stability, universality, and utility of the *ius commune*. The latter was the case, in no small part, because the *ius commune* had stemmed from an eclectic combination of customary practices understood to be shared among peoples across the European continent and islands, which were explained, underpinned, informed, and legitimated by Roman and canon law, and with it an immense body of medieval university-based jurisprudence. All of which came increasingly into question over the sixteenth century in response to (1) the overall impetus towards legal reform to help effect political and economic stability within discrete communities, (2) the breakdown of Universal Latin Christendom with the advent of the Protestant Reformation in Europe, and (3) the direct confrontation with the brutality of European incursion and excursion into the Atlantic. Combined, though not necessarily contingent, these three (nearly) simultaneous processes illuminated the limits of the *ius commune* tradition and the necessity to rethink aspects of it to address new local and European-wide problems. The turn to *ius gentium* at the start of the century and the articulation of the theory of sovereignty by Renaissance jurists as the century unfolded, essentially offered an alternative means to ground universal and civil jurisprudence that could bypass, and even overcome, the limits of the *ius commune*. This book aims to demonstrate how the fathers of humanist jurisprudence contributed to this process, by focusing on their discussions of *ius gentium*—and its relation to justice and right—as the common law not simply of Europe, but of all mankind.

In the opening decades of the sixteenth century, the fathers of legal humanism, Guillaume Budé (1467–1540), Ulrich Zasius (1461–1536), and Andrea Alciati (1492–1550), deliberately set out to offer alternative interpretations of ancient Roman law, and therefore civil jurisprudence, from their scholastic predecessors and contemporaries.[1] It was necessary to do so, they held,

1 This book follows the most common forms in the existing literature, and thus uses Budé instead of Budaeus, Zasius instead of Zäsy, and Alciati instead of Alciato (granted, neither Alciati nor Alciato are used more frequently than the other).

 | DOI:10.1163/9789004528451_002

because law and justice had fallen out of joint; lawyers and jurists had managed to corrupt both the law and legal interpretation not only as a result of their own ambitions and the desires of their patrons but also as a consequence of what Budé, Zasius, and Alciati argued was a grave and grievous error at the very foundations of university-based jurisprudence: the misinterpretation—and misunderstanding—of the underlying relationship between justice and right, as expressed in law—customary, natural, and civil—over time. These errors, they contended, extended directly from the *Gloss* of Accursius (1182–1263), wherein definitions of the basic categories within Roman law, such as *ius* (the art of what is good and fair) and *ius gentium* (the law of nations) as well as explanations concerning the relation between natural law, *ius gentium*, and civil law set the parameters for legal interpretation and practice in Europe for centuries.

Convinced that errors in the *Gloss* had led to faulty interpretations by lawyers, jurists, advisors, and diplomats, Budé, Zasius, and Alciati argued not only for the necessity to restore ancient Roman law to its original but also for using humanist methods and sources to teach and interpret law in universities. Only when the *Digest* and the *Institutes* were returned to their original form (*ad fontes*)—before they were glossed, commented on, and changed by medieval jurists—would it be possible to understand the extent to which they embodied and reflected the principles of justice and right. The latter required, in turn, the ability for professors and students alike to understand the fragments and excerpts of ancient law that had been long since removed from their proper context by Byzantium compilers. It also required the capacity to interpret these fragments in historical and comparative perspectives. Upon acquiring an extensive knowledge of the sources and methods of the *studia humanitatis*, viz., history, moral philosophy, grammar, rhetoric, and poetry, students would realize that the foundational and fundamental principles embodied in and expressed by the language of Roman law were the same principles that underpinned all bodies of laws—both written and unwritten—across time and space.[2] Armed

2 See Paul Oskar Kristeller, *Renaissance Thought: The Classic, Scholastic, and Humanistic Strains* (New York: Harper and Row, 1955); and Kristeller, *Renaissance Thought and Its Sources*, ed. Michael Mooney (New York: Columbia University Press, 1979). However, there has been much debate concerning Kristeller's emphasis on the formal qualities of humanism, see especially Kenneth Gouwens, "Perceiving the Past: Renaissance Humanism after the 'Cognitive Turn'," *The American Historical Review* 103, no. 1 (1998): 55–82. See also Christopher Celenza, "Late Antiquity and the Florentine Renaissance: Historiographical Parallels," *Journal of the History of Ideas* 62, no. 1 (2001): 17–35; and Celenza, *The Lost Italian Renaissance: Humanists, Historians, and Latin's Legacy* (Baltimore, MD: Johns Hopkins University Press, 2004); Riccardo Fubini, *Humanism and Secularization: From Petrarch to* Valla, trans. Martha King (Durham, NC: Duke

with this knowledge, jurists, lawyers, professors, statesmen, and chancellors could carefully and deliberately reform laws and institutions which had hitherto missed the mark of justice, thus restoring the rule of law that had been diminished by those more interested in serving power than justice.

In an era already rife with calls for legal reform, most notably those initiated by Maximilian I (r. 1486–1519) in the Holy Roman Empire and by Louis XII (r.1499–1512) in France, Budé, Zasius, and Alciati set out—albeit in radically different ways and addressing different questions—to provide tools, resources, and training for lawyers and jurists across the continent so that they could participate in the ongoing process of purging errors and corruptions from civil jurisprudence.[3] Given that so many of the corruptions that needed to be addressed extended from misinterpretations and misunderstandings—and even the intentional twisting—of foundational principles and categories of Roman law by medieval jurists, it should be of no surprise that a common feature among their works was a full-scale attack on traditional, university-based jurisprudence. Their attacks were quite bitter, brutally direct, and, in some cases, exaggerated to the point of diminishing the import of their own arguments. Nevertheless, their works left little doubt as to how dangerous they regarded the errors within scholastic jurisprudence to be, especially long-held understandings of *ius* and *ius gentium*.[4]

University Press, 2003); Charles G. Nauert, "Humanism as Method: Roots of Conflict with the Scholastics," *Sixteenth Century Journal* 29, no. 2 (1998): 427–38, and Nauert, "Renaissance Humanism: An Emergent Consensus and Its Critics," *Indiana Social Studies Quarterly* 33 (1980): 5–20; Ronald G. Witt, *"In the Footsteps of the Ancients:" The Origins of Humanism from Lovato to Bruni* (ACLS Humanities E-Book: Brill, 2000); and Witt, *The Two Latin Cultures and the Foundation of Renaissance Humanism in Medieval Italy* (Cambridge: Cambridge University Press, 2012).

3 The call for reform was not limited to jurisprudence, see Brenden Bradshaw, "Transalpine Humanism" in *The Cambridge History of Political Thought 1450–1700*, eds. J. H. Burns and Mark Goldie (Cambridge: Cambridge University Press, 1991), 95–131; William J. Bouwsma, *The Waning of the Renaissance 1550–1640* (New Haven, CT: Yale University Press, 2000); Charles G. Nauert, *Humanism and the Culture of Renaissance Europe* (Cambridge: Cambridge University Press 2006); and John Witte, Jr., *The Reformation of Rights: Law, Religion, and Human Rights in Early Modern Calvinism* (Cambridge: Cambridge University Press, 2007).

4 For a discussion of the major contours of the historiography, especially at the intersections of legal humanism and the history of rights, see Susan Longfield Karr "'Often we are deceived, and we suffer glaucoma': Rethinking Legal Humanism in the History of the Western Rights Tradition." (European University Institute Working Paper, 2010). For a discussion of the intersections between rights and *ius gentium* in the early modern era see Janne Nijman and Anthony Carty, "Introduction: The Moral Responsibility of Rulers: Going Back Beyond the Liberal Rule of Law," in *Moral Responsibility and the Rule of Law: European and Chinese Origins of a Rule of Law as Justice for World Order, eds.* Janne Nijman and Anthony Carty (Oxford: Oxford University Press, 2018), 1–52; especially 1–25.

Their attacks also reflect their concern that those trained only in the methods they deemed responsible for the mess in the first place would be given the authority to fix it. Hence, their calls for reform in legal education, interpretation, and practice were urgent: if the errors of the scholastics were sanctioned by being reproduced and extended, the opportunity to improve the laws and restore justice might be lost altogether. If faulty interpretations were confirmed and perpetuated through the process of systemization and codification, then customary practices and universal rights that stood at the very core of social, civil, economic, and political institutions across Europe could be further diminished, violated, and even abolished.[5] If left in the hands of traditional jurists, the already dangerous rule by lawyers could be extended. Rather than restoring civil jurisprudence, and thus a rule of law based in universal jurisprudence, these jurists might continue to use their expertise to extend power rather than ensure justice.[6] This could magnify the very types of legal and political authority that Budé, Zasius, and Alciati were explicitly questioning, critiquing, and attempting to limit through their restoration—and redefinition—of fundamental terms within Roman law, such as justice (*iustitia*) and right (*ius*).

Deeply concerned with the meaning and significance of words in context, they knew that restoring the language of Roman law was no mere academic exercise. In a world in which Roman law served as the common denominator that tied jurists and lawyers together across Europe and as the foundational text of civil law, restoring the basic terms and categories within the Roman *Digest* would provide those charged to reform unjust laws as well as the codification of local laws with an understanding of universal jurisprudence. However, through the application of their humanist methods, Budé, Zasius, and Alciati ultimately reinterpreted the law that they set out to restore. In the process, they used the categories of *ius* and *ius gentium* to defend universal rights and obligations that reached beyond the *ius commune* in the face of the creation of new forms—and the expansion of older forms—of legal and political authority.[7]

5 It should be noted that even while Zasius and Alciati made such claims, they did not fundamentally break with traditional jurisprudence, despite their frequent use of Bartolus and Baldus as straw men to highlight their own arguments.

6 As will be shown below, Budé, Zasius, and Alciati's rejection of universal monarchy was not equivalent to a rejection of universal jurisprudence; indeed, the latter required the former.

7 Joseph P. Canning has recently argued that "Medieval jurist used the term *ius commune* to describe the Roman law as the law common to the Roman Empire; in the *corpus iuris civilis*, the law of peoples, the *ius gentium*, was referred to as the *ius commune* of all mankind." (102). Yet, by the turn of the sixteenth century, the term *ius commune* had a much broader meaning

They did so in their capacity as councilors and advisers, as lawyers and jurists, and, most importantly, as professors in the universities, where they were responsible for training those who would be expected to administer and reform local laws in Germany, France, and northern Italy.[8] Only through careful attention to changes in the meaning, language, and interpretation of Roman law—both in relation to particular contexts and in response to particular problems—would it be possible for their students and readers to grasp the universal principles such as justice and right that underpin it. Thus, rather than study the *corpus* of Roman law as fixed or unchanging and attempt to extract universal principles from it as many of the scholastic civil jurists had done, Budé, Zasius, and Alciati historicized (viz., placing it in time and place) Roman law and its sources in order to observe the moral principles upon which it was based.[9] In so doing, they shifted their attention away from the *ius commune*—that is, the amalgam of civil and canon law grounded in the authority of emperors, princes, popes, and lesser feudal lords that permeated

---

insofar as it encompassed an amalgamation of Roman, canon, and customary law as well as statutes and feudal laws that served as the endoskeleton of university-based jurisprudence within Latin Christendom. Cf. Joseph P. Canning, "The Medieval Roman Law and Canon Law Origins of International Law," in *Medieval Foundations of International Relations*, ed. William Bain (London: Routledge, 2017), 102–16, with Manlio Bellomo, *The Common Legal Past of Europe, 1000–1800* (Washington, D.C.: The Catholic University of America Press, 1995). In many respects, Zasius and Alciati ultimately rejected the European *ius commune* as Bellomo defines it by turning to the medieval *ius commune* as Canning defines it. Yet, in the process, they also broke away from the medieval conception of *ius commune* when they re-defined *ius* and *ius gentium*.

8 Jospeh Neff, *Udalricus Zasius: Ein Beitrag Zur Geschichte Des Humanismus Am Oberrhein: Als Beilage Zum Programm Fur Das Schuljahr 1889/1890 and 1890/1891. 2 vols.* (Freiburg i. B.: Universitats-Buchdruckerei von Chr. Lehmann, 1890); and Neff, *Ulrich Zasius: Ein Freiburger Humanist* (Freiburg i. B.: Stoll & Bader, 1890); Paul-Émile Viard, *Andrea Alciat, 1492–1550* (Paris: Société anonyme du Recueil Sirey, 1926); Harold J. Berman, *Law and Revolution I: The Formation of the Western Legal Tradition* (Cambridge, MA: Harvard University Press, 1983); Donald R. Kelley, *Foundations of Modern Historical Scholarship: Language, Law, and History in the French Renaissance* (New York: Columbia University Press, 1970); Steven W. Rowan, *Ulrich Zasius: A Jurist in the German Renaissance, 1461–1535* (Frankfurt am Main: V. Klostermann, 1987).

9 John W. Baldwin, *The Scholastic Culture of the Middle Ages, 1000–1300* (Lexington, MA: Heath, 1971); Neal Ward Gilbert, *Renaissance Concepts of Method* (New York: Columbia University Press, 1960); A. S. McGrade, ed., *The Cambridge Companion to Medieval Philosophy* (Cambridge: Cambridge University Press, 2003); Norman Kretzmann, Anthony Kenny, and Jan Pinborg, eds., *The Cambridge History of Later Medieval Philosophy: From the Rediscovery of Aristotle to the Disintegration of Scholasticism, 1100–1600* (Cambridge: Cambridge University Press, 1982); and Katherine Park and Lorraine Daston, eds., *The Cambridge History of Science: Volume 3, Early Modern Science* (Cambridge: Cambridge University Press, 2006).

university-based jurisprudence—and towards a conceptual understanding of the foundations of law and society grounded in the attributes and actions of man, wherein natural law, *ius*, and *ius gentium* were central.

Key to this transformation was the use of—and appeal to—historical imagination and, by extension, historical authority. For example, Budé, Zasius, and Alciati each revisited the origins of law and society by drawing on Cicero's description of the founding of civil society in his *De inventione*, which they then used to construct a distant past that reached far beyond recorded history.[10] In so doing, they attempted to explain man's pre-political condition, which could account for how and why the rights and obligations and the customs and conventions that man shared in common before he quit his original condition to enter civil society could still be used to hold political and legal authorities to a higher criterion of justice within it.

They also applied their understandings of a distant (and imagined) past as well as a recent one to explain why and to what extent the relations between societies mirrored the relations between individuals, families, and primordial communities before the emergence of modern territorial states and oversea empires. Exercising their historical imaginations and placing laws and customs into historical perspective, they effectively infused political and legal institutions with a moral authority that was anchored outside of traditional jurisprudence, and thus could effectively bypass it.

By appealing to their own and their readers' imaginations, both historical and critical, Budé, Alciati, and Zasius also called on and contributed to a historical fiction—or, rather fictions—that could then be used as a measure of man's ability to live in and govern civil society. In the process, they helped to lay the theoretical groundwork for a historical fiction of the "state of nature" or man's condition outside of states, which has permeated modern legal and political

10 Marcus Tullius Cicero, *De inventione, de optimo genre oratorum, topica. Trans.* H. M. Hubbell (Cambridge, MA: Harvard University Press, 1949). The literature on the impact of Cicero and Stoicism on Renaissance thoughts is far too extensive to do justice by citing here. As such, readers would do well to explore the nuanced and detailed discussion of this influence provided by the following texts: James Hankins, *Virtue Politics: Soulcraft and Statecraft in Renaissance Italy* (Cambridge, MA: Harvard University Press, 2019); William J. Bouwsma, *The Two Faces of Humanism: Stoicism and Augustinianism in Renaissance Thought* (Leiden: Brill, 1975); Gerhard Oestreich, Brigitta Oestreich, and H. G. Königsberger, *Neo-stoicism and the Early Modern State* (Cambridge: Cambridge University Press, 1982); Quentin Skinner, *The Foundations of Modern Political Thought. Volume 1: The Renaissance* (Cambridge: Cambridge University Press, 1978); Richard Tuck, *Philosophy and Government, 1572–1651.* (Cambridge: Cambridge University Press, 1993); and Witt, *"In the Footsteps of the* Ancients."

thought so thoroughly since at least the sixteenth century that it stands as a fundamental characteristic of the modern Western legal tradition itself.

Moreover, the historical fiction of the state of nature, or man's pre-political state, that man quit when he entered civil society served as a collective memory—or at least a common trope—that humanist jurists could employ to respond to contemporary issues and problems. Appealing to a distant and imagined past also injected discussions by and among humanists with an ersatz nostalgia of sorts. This was not a nostalgia for the ways things were before man entered civil society but rather a nostalgia for man's original intent in creating it; that is, they conjured a nostalgia for what could have been to offer a critique and an alternative to what was and is.

Reaching beyond recorded history to show how and why a specific law, practice, or claim was out of joint with—and even directly violated—justice could serve a fundamental purpose that written sources could not. Indeed, appealing to moral philosophy, and thereby universal norms of justice and right among individuals and communities, helped to transform civil society from a mere artifice to a work of art. By infusing the state and those who helped to govern it with moral authority, civil laws and political powers were necessary attributes and components for the pursuit of justice, security, and a common good.

Written sources and recorded history—including discussions of the origins and ends of legal, political, and religious institutions by the Ancients—filled out, and even gilded, the artifice to be sure. Yet, without the ability to ground it in universal norms that transcend the confines of time and place, it remained a structure without a blueprint, foundation, or buttress. What is more, focusing on man's informed choice—that is, a choice effected as a result of reason and deliberation, not impulse or emotion—to place his neck under the yoke of civil law and thereby live under the jurisdiction of states and empires served to transform these states and empires into moral persons who stood as equals vis-à-vis one another. Not only were there rights and obligations that predated states but there were also rights and obligations between states.

Even though the moment when man first made the choice to found civil societies, states, and empires was lost to time immemorial, the historical fiction of man's pre-political state was a product, for many, of history and experience and of collective memory. The fact that this imagined history did not reach back to the origins of man but instead focused on a time when man already lived in mutual company—ranging from families to primordial communities—made the theory seem more plausible or, at the very least, made it a far more useful metaphor than if it had been rooted in creation. This was especially the case given that the latter would necessarily invoke theology, and therefore revealed and institutionalized religion. As such, focusing on this period of human history, even if it could not be confirmed by extant sources and historical evidence, enabled humanist jurists to step outside of and away from one fundamental aspect or frame of traditional jurisprudence, namely a detailed engagement with God's eternal will and plan and how these were revealed to man in and by civil laws over time.

This appeal to an imagined past (or founding moment) allowed the so-called fathers of legal humanism to do two things. First, to bracket, or at least try to circumvent, religious dogma, even as it took on a new urgency from the onset of the Reformation. Indeed, it is essential to remember that attempts to bracket or circumvent disputes over sacred rites and prerogatives—as part and parcel of early-modern state-formation—helped create the powder keg that the religious Reformations set ablaze in the first place. Second, by invoking this metaphor to reimagine the past and to create a kind of ersatz nostalgia to address problems in their present, the fathers of legal humanism were able to offer a vision for the future which required the return to a time when natural law, *ius*, and *ius gentium*—not civil law or canon law—mediated and moderated the actions of man. It was inconsequential that the vision of the past summoned to do this work likely never existed. What mattered most was that the idea of that past and the rhetoric used to present it could be used to suggest—and even effect—change in the present.

By stepping outside of, bypassing, and even dismissing aspects of traditional jurisprudence, Budé, Zasius, and Alciati were able to demarcate the limits of legal and political power vis-à-vis those who were subject to their jurisdictions as well as in relation to those who were not. They did so in a myriad of ways, ranging from offering an explanation as to how and why *ius gentium* was the source of universal rights and obligations to a discussion of the basic rights among all peoples—rights that, if violated, could serve as a justification for the passive (and active) resistance of persons, peoples, and princes. To explore how and why they did so, this book is divided into three distinct, yet inter-connected parts, wherein their foundational and fundamental re-interpretations of terms within first title of the *Digest*, *De iustitia et iure* (*On Justice and Right*) are central.

The fact that each part of this book focuses on the same title of the *Digest* does not, however, mean that Budé, Zasius, and Alciati covered precisely the same ground, or even attempted to treat the same definitions. In fact, (borrowing from Guido Kisch) it is fair to say that each of the humanist jurists under examination projected onto the term *ius gentium* his own idea of *ius*—as justice and as right—"in order to create appropriate ways and reliable means for the practical application of the law" in very different yet overlapping contexts.[11] In so doing, Zasius and Alciati adopted and developed Budé's definition of *ius* at the same time as they departed from his understanding of the relation between *ius* and *ius gentium*. Likewise, while Alciati shared Zasius' understanding of *ius gentium* as a source of universal rights and obligations, he appeared to reject wholesale the idea that *ius gentium* was a form or quality of natural law. Even so, their re-interpretations of basic categories within ancient Roman law shared an emphasis on the dignity of man *qua* man (across all time and place) as well as on the necessity of rulers (no matter the political constitution of the state) to respect it.

What's more, Zasius and Alciati offered their students a theory of universal jurisprudence, whereby the political and legal authority of sovereigns (no matter what the political constitution of the state in question) rested in their ability to protect (with law and by force), to enforce (with punishment and by war), and to respect (with law and by restraint) the universal rights and obligations that extended from *ius gentium*. Indeed, they put forth theories of universal jurisprudence—extending from punishment to war and grounded in right and dignity—that might well remind modern readers of the ideas found in the works of the so-called fathers of international law, namely Francisco de Vitoria (c. 1483–1546) and Hugo Grotius (c. 1583–1645), as much as ideas in the works of some of the most (in)famous theorists of sovereignty and right in the early modern period, such as Jean Bodin (c. 1530–1596) and Thomas Hobbes (c.1588–1679), even though the fathers of legal humanism were writing in the context of the re-reformation of Europe—from dynastic and feudal kingdoms to modern territorial states—in the early-sixteenth century rather than in the wake of religious, civil, and international wars that dominated the late-sixteenth and early-seventeenth centuries.[12]

•••

11 See Guido Kisch, "Humanistic Jurisprudence," *Studies in the Renaissance* 8 (1961): 71–87; 79.

12 The term re-formation draws out the changes that encompassed legal reform within states, as much as the negotiation of boundaries and borders between them, as all the major powers and significant political entities in central and southern Europe came into conflict—first over Naples and then over Milan—in the early decades of the 16th century. The use of the term re-formation of Europe is not meant as either a play on, nor an alternative to, the religious changes of that followed from the (Protestant) Reformation or the (Catholic) Counter-Reformation.

Unlike students and readers five hundred years ago, we are neither acutely trained to read texts through scholastic methods nor able to directly access and engage with the worldview that those methods reflect and embody. As such, we might find it difficult to appreciate Guillaume Budé's, Ulrich Zasius', and Andrea Alciati's criticism of these methods or the world that shaped them as innovative, exciting, and, in some cases, even dangerous. Moreover, we are so accustomed to reading the sources associated with the *studia humanitatis* and to employing the critical and historical methods humanist scholars, jurists, and theorists used in constructing them, that we risk not appreciating how original their ideas and insights were, especially concerning *ius*, natural law, and *ius gentium*. Hence, if we wish to grasp fundamental shifts in legal and political thought that humanist jurisprudence amplified in the early-sixteenth century, then we need to tend carefully to how they distinguished themselves from their scholastic predecessors and contemporaries. The latter task, in turn, requires an understanding of how and why the texts of Roman law were at the center of sixteenth-century legal education and application in the first place.

Given that Guillaume Budé—whose 1518 *Annotationes* stand at the center of the first case study presented in this volume—never completed his formal legal education and indeed had little patience for university-based jurisprudence, the scope of Chapter 1 is relatively limited insofar as it neither focuses on nuanced aspects of medieval jurisprudence (e.g., Thomism) nor on specific debates that were at the center of scholastic political and legal thought by the turn of the sixteenth century. Instead, each section within Chapter 1—whether read selectively or as a conglomerate whole—provides overlapping and episodic histories to help set the scene for Budé's treatment of the foundational categories and idioms within the first title of the *Digest, De iustitia et iure*—precisely because he was convinced that he was simply restoring Justinian's *Digest* to its original before it was misinterpreted by Accursius in the *Gloss*. To that end, Chapter 1 lays out some of the essential aspects of the compilation, transmission, and recovery of the Justinian's *corpus iuris civilis*. It also offers a brief account of the quest for legal precedents that led to the recovery of the Roman *Digest* and a short narrative of scholastic teaching and interpretative methods both before and after the founding of universities in post-Roman Europe. The broader aim of the episodic histories is to make the present work accessible to a variety of audiences, ranging from scholars who focus on Renaissance humanism proper to those who are deeply entrenched in the history and development of Western legal—and rights—traditions.

Beyond its content, the ways in which the episodic histories in Chapter 1 are arranged stand as exemplary of the structure of the volume. Just as the four sections within the first chapter intersect and overlap, so too do the three parts of the book. Indeed, the goal of each part is to offer readers overlapping and comparative histories rather than a linear account of the history and development of European legal thought or, more specifically, an intellectual genealogy of the fathers of legal humanism and how they reinterpreted the foundational terms within the *Digest*. The latter, in fact, would be an insurmountable task given that each of the humanists featured here focused on the interlocking aspects of *ius*, natural law, and *ius gentium* for very different reasons and to effect different ends. With that in mind, it is essential to note that the aspects of traditional jurisprudence that informed interpretations by Budé's peers, rather than his own, are folded into subsequent chapters when appropriate. As such, the last section of Chapter 1 focuses on the teaching and interpretive methods developed during the Quattrocento, some of which Budé employed in his attack on university-based jurisprudence.

Chapter 2 focuses on Budé's wholesale rejection of traditional jurisprudence in his 1508 *Annotationes*. After placing Budé in his specific historical and local contexts, the remainder of the chapter offers a close reading and analysis of his scathing attack on scholastic jurisprudence, his serpentine restoration of *ius* as the art of what is good and fair conjoined, and his treatment of *ius* as an inherent characteristic of man *qua* man. The chapter concludes with Budé's distinction between natural law and *ius gentium* and with his link between *ius* and *ius gentium*. Regardless of his acerbic attacks on lawyers and jurists in universities, Budé's work proved useful for his humanist peers teaching in Southern Germany, in particular Ulrich Zasius (Part 2) as well as in Northern Italy and France, namely Andrea Alciati (Part 3).

Although the first title in the *Digest* was relatively short and consisted of little more than a collection of definitions of justice, right, and categories of law compiled from the works of ancient jurists, Zasius used it to present a nuanced and complex theory of universal jurisprudence, wherein the relation between natural law, *ius*, and *ius gentium* was central. He did so by organizing the lecture into a series of interlocking questions: "What is justice; what is *ius*? In what manner is justice divided? And, what follows from *ius*?" Addressing each in turn, Zasius ultimately offered his students an innovative understanding of *ius gentium*, which not only fundamentally departed from his scholastic predecessors and peers, but also from the Romans (Byzantine and Ancient), when he argued that *ius gentium* was a form of natural law, an expression of justice, and a source of universal rights and obligations shared by all humankind across time and place. Moreover, none of these rights and obligations could be fully demolished or abrogated by civil laws, institutions, and authorities. In so doing, Zasius adopted aspects of Budé's definition of *ius* as an objective standard of justice and as an inherent characteristic of man, and thus as a signifier of human dignity. At the same time, however, Zasius made it abundantly clear to his readers and to his students that the relationship between *ius* and *ius gentium* had implications that extended far beyond Budé's limited understanding, given that he lacked both a proper education and practical experience in law.

In addition to placing Zasius in historical and local contexts, Chapter 3 focuses on how he presented his *modus docendi* to prospective students before turning to his lecture on the first title of the *Digest*. After drawing his students to his lectures with the promise that if they studied with him, they would gain not only an understanding of the law but also of justice, in his oration/declamation *In Praise of the Law* (*In laudem legum oratio*), Zasius' opened his *De iustitia et iure* lecture with one fundamental question, initially presented as two related ones: namely, 'What is justice; what is *ius*?' For Zasius, understanding why this was a single question that required a single (albeit complex and nuanced) answer was not only necessary for acquiring a proper understanding of justice but also foundational to his overall theory of universal jurisprudence, wherein the universal and inherent rights and obligations that followed from *ius* were essential. After he refined Budé's definition of *ius* as both the art of what is good and fair conjoined by emphasizing that *ius* was effectively justice in action, Zasius then turned his attention to how and why justice had been divided. To explore the latter, he invited his students to exercise their historical imaginations in order to consider the relationship between public and private law and, by extension, between public and private interests—as presented by the excerpts from Ulpian and Gaius preserved in the *Digest*. In so doing, he explained the moral necessity for, and the historical authority of, jurists to mediate conflict within and between societies.

After explaining *ius* as justice in action and complicating his students' understanding of the relationship between public and private law, Zasius offered a substantive and nuanced answer to the final question that framed his *De iustitia et iure* lecture: "what follows from *ius*?" In response to this question, which serves as the focal point of Chapter 4, he provided his students an organic account of three universal and interlocking qualities of natural law that were shared among humankind across time and space and without distinction. Zasius articulated how and why each quality of natural law was rooted in man's inclination to satisfy his selfish interest and his propensity to pursue a common good in tandem. He then explored the fourth quality of natural law, which he asserted was *ius gentium*. Arguing not only that *ius* was justice in action but also that *ius gentium* was natural law in action, Zasius presented his students with an innovative understanding that fundamentally rejected aspects and distinctions within traditional jurisprudence, namely, that *ius gentium* and natural law were understood to be two distinctly different things that, without reference to the *ius commune*, were not related. Zasius did not stop there. Within his lecture on the first title of the *Digest* as well as in his remarkable 1518 *Preface* for his *Lucubrationes* ("night musings"), Zasius presented a theory of universal jurisprudence wherein *ius gentium* could be invoked to reform civil laws, institutions, and authorities that attempted to demolish, rescind, or destroy the universal rights and obligations of man *qua* man that extended from *ius gentium*. The latter is especially apparent in his critique of slavery and serfdom, an examination of which concludes Chapter 4.

While Zasius' interpretation of *ius* as justice in action and *ius gentium* as a source of universal rights met the calls for legal reform and codification within an empire made up of different states with discrete legal traditions and norms, his emphasis on *ius gentium* as a source both of universal obligations and universal rights was neither suited to nor directed at questions of authority that reached beyond the Germanies. In fact, as useful as linking *ius gentium* to natural law—thus infusing it with moral authority—was for settling conflicts of law between different entities subject to the same superior ruler (*de iure*), such an understanding of *ius gentium* could not address the conflicts between empires and kingdoms under their own discrete rule. Exploring the relationship between *ius* and *ius gentium* in the realm of emperors and kings required a decoupling of *ius gentium* and natural law, and thereby justice and right, in the realm of sovereigns. This was something Zasius' Italian counterpart, Andrea Alciati, was particularly well-suited to explore given his more immediate context of the Italian Wars, which had commenced in 1494 and continued until 1559.

Although Alciati shared Budé's understanding of *ius* as the art of what is good and fair (justice/natural law) within civil society as well as Zasius' interpretation of *ius* as justice in action (right/*ius gentium*) among persons, he approached his lecture on *De Iustitia et iure* from a wholly different perspective than the other two members of the so-called "le grande triumvirate" of humanist jurisprudence. This is not surprising, given the fluidity of categories and idioms within the first title of the *Digest* and the volatility of Northern Italy, especially his native Milan. What is surprising, however, is how he used the opportunity to explain the first title of the *Digest* in a way that had little to do with Roman Law as the Romans had known it or, for that matter, how it had been interpreted by his scholastic predecessors. In essence, Alciati used his *De iustitia et iure* lecture to explain why and how *ius gentium*, although related to natural law, was not merely a quality or expression of it. This required him to disrupt the narrative, that is, to arrange his lecture thematically rather than following the order of the definitions set out by Byzantine compilers and repeated by his humanist and scholastic peers and predecessors.

Rather than begin by defining *ius* as the art of what is good and what is fair conjoined, for example, he organized the discussion around three discreet, but analogous, comparable, and familiar scenarios, in which *ius*—as the right to meet force with force—was exercised. These scenarios were homicide (self-defense and commissioned), war (defensive and offensive), and dueling (recompense and satisfaction). Alciati's choice to interpret foundational categories of Roman law through the lens of force rather than of justice enabled him to articulate a theory of universal jurisprudence in which the category of *ius,* as a criterion of justice and inherent right, remained a distinguishing characteristic of man *qua* man, and thus a marker of dignity and equality. At the same time, however, exploring *ius* through the lens of force allowed him to decouple *ius gentium* from natural law and to offer a theory in which *ius gentium*—and the practices that fell under it—delineated various kinds of rulers (e.g., kings, emperors, princes, dukes, and republics) as equivalent in the realm of rights, even if they retained markers of difference in the field of politics. Moreover, his understanding of *ius gentium* reverberated from his lecture to his treatise on dueling and in select *Emblems* so to reach audiences well beyond the universities at which he taught. Together, these works reveal that Alciati's illumination of the limits of majesty (*majestas*; *majeste*) and the attributes of *imperium* anticipated some of the most salient features and principles of modern sovereignty (*sovereinete*) bounded by, and grounded in, the moral authority of *ius* and *ius gentium.*

The first half of Chapter 5 places Alciati's academic life into the broader context of the Italian Wars, given that local and international conflicts profoundly informed his interpretation of the relation between *ius gentium*, *ius*, and natural law. Doing so provides readers with a sense of why Alciati—despite his promise to do otherwise—interpreted the first title of the *Digest* through the lens of recent events that shaped politics across the Italian peninsula rather than the more distant histories of Rome (Ancient and Byzantium). It also helps to illuminate the concerns on the minds of his students in Northern Italy whose fortunes were directly impacted by the territorial ambitions and dynastic claims of the Sforza, Valois, and Habsburgs in Milan. Tending to Alciati's context offers readers the opportunity to think about the relationship between the Italian Wars and the history and development of *ius* and *ius gentium* from an underemphasized (and undervalued) perspective, namely, the instability and conflict that permeated Southern Europe for the first half of the sixteenth century. All too often this context is elided by explorations centered almost exclusively on European expansion into the Atlantic world or on religious wars, revolts, and rebellions in the wake of the Reformations across central and northern Europe.

Emphasizing the ways in which Alciati's uncertain career was directly affected by the conflicts between the Holy Roman Emperor and the King of France also reveals how rapidly the categories of *ius* and *ius gentium*—and the broader theories that underpinned them—could be reinterpreted and redeployed to affect different ends at any given time, even by those who were drawing on the same methods (*studia humanitatis*), reading the same texts and sources, and even attacking the same enemy, (viz., traditional university-based jurisprudence). It also amplifies the extent to which a nuanced study of the ways in which the fathers of legal humanism approached the first title of the *Digest* serves as a narrative of the transformation of *ius* and *ius gentium* from a relatively unimportant category to an immensely important one in a distinctly local European context, well before these categories were deployed to challenge or legitimize imperial expansion beyond Europe.

The second half of Chapter 5 explores Alciati's orations in praise of the law that were delivered at Avignon and Bologna. In both, he called students to study with him and levied criticisms against his scholastic and humanist peers. These orations also stand as examples of Alciati's methods in action, especially his emphasis on the power of eloquence in the founding of civil societies and his appeal to and use of history to demonstrate the utility of Roman law among Germanic tribes in Europe. Within these orations, Alciati likewise made clear to his potential students that under his direction they would not only be invited to think about law in new ways but would also be expected to travel meandering and uncertain paths, sometimes arriving at dead ends, if they wished to reach an understanding of jurisprudence. In this respect, his orations informed his students that the journey they were about to undertake with him would be as important as the destination given their potential—upon completion of their studies—to help avert wars and maintain peace. Caught between duchy and city-state, emperor and king, persistent war and intermittent peace, the fact that Alciati effectively offered students who attended his *De iustitia et iure* lecture a critique of just war theory rather than an explanation of the *Digest*, also serves as a reminder that the task of defining and understanding *ius* and *ius gentium* always carried risks, and therefore required meticulous modes of argument. As such, the lecture often implied more questions than Alciati answered directly.

Alciati's brief lecture on *De iustitia et iure* is the centerpiece of Chapters 6. Within it, Alciati made good on his promise in his orations that he would help students, no matter their previous experience or natural talent, acquire a practical and pragmatic understanding of Roman law by drawing on the methods and sources of the *studia humanitatis*. He also fulfilled his pledge that, no matter what aspect or text of the *corpus* they studied, they would not move on until he made it accessible to all. Aware that many of his students approached the study of law as a means to an end, rather than an end unto itself, he invited them to question the suppositions and assumptions underpinning traditional jurisprudence that—without much critical reflection—they might have otherwise accepted wholesale. This manner of teaching required a great deal of exertion on Alciati's part and a fair amount of effort (and patience) on the part of his audience, especially when it appeared that he was repeating points rather than building on them to arrive at a novel interpretation. Indeed, Alciati made a careful and nuanced argument, framed by Hermogenian's definition of *ius gentium* preserved in the first title of the *Digest*, whereby he slowly led his students through a series of interlocking examples to demonstrate how precarious—and even futile—some of the distinctions and categories that structured traditional jurisprudence were, especially those touching on the rights of war and peace. As such, the lecture is often reminiscent in form, albeit not in content, of Francisco Petrarca's (1304–1374) letter describing his *Ascent of Mont Ventoux* (1350).

Chapter 6 explores Alciati's definitions of *ius* and *ius gentium* among persons, his distinction between legitimate and illegitimate violence, his rejection of just and unjust wars, and his rejection of pure and mixed *imperium*, including the distinction between inferior and superior rulers. In each case, Alciati pushed aspects of humanist jurisprudence into new—and even dangerous—directions. In so doing, he effectively severed *ius gentium* from natural law in his discussion of *imperium*. This did not mean, however, that Alciati severed *ius* from justice altogether. Rather, he distinguished between the relation of *ius* and *ius gentium* and *ius* and natural law to make an argument about the limits of sovereignty and the inviolability of rights. The chapter concludes with a discussion of the significance of Alciati's re-interpretation of *ius gentium* during the Italian Wars and a suggestion as to why his work accents a fundamental principle of early humanist jurisprudence, namely *ius* as a marker of equality among all mankind prior to and within civil society as well as of equality between all rulers (and states) regardless of their size or their history in the realm of *ius gentium*. Such an understanding of *ius gentium* was, moreover, key to rethinking the distinction between mixed and pure *imperium*, along with the hierarchy of sovereignties that permeated medieval political and legal thought.

Given the extent to which the rule of law set out to limit the power of rulers vis-a-vis their own subjects, it is not surprising that the distinctions attendant on *imperium* were so entrenched in the institutions and practices of European political and legal thought that it would require new conceptions of *ius gentium* to fundamentally challenge its underlying assumptions. Perhaps what is surprising is that such challenges came from jurists in contexts that were neither driven by religious Reformation within Europe nor by imperial expansion beyond it. Even more striking, such challenges did not come from the margins, nor did they remain buried in academic circles and texts. Instead, they were made by those who—like Alciati, Zasius, and Budé—not only had the attention of some of the greatest rulers of the age but also—in the case of Zasius and Alciati—were charged with training those who would be expected to reform and maintain a rule of law in a world fraught with rapid economic, social, and political transformations amid the persistent violence, insecurity, and uncertainty of the Italian Wars (1494–1559) in the first half of the sixteenth century.

Since the overall aim of this book is not to fold the early legal humanists into existing narratives that attempt to trace the overall development of the history of political and legal thought from the late-medieval to the modern period, the conclusion offers observations as to the significance of the turn to *ius gentium* as part and parcel of the re-formation of Europe within a more modest time span, viz., the early decades of the sixteenth century. It also draws out comparisons between the theories of justice and right explored in this volume as well as those that have dominated the scholarship on political and legal thought for decades, namely the so-called modern theories associated with Grotius and Hobbes, among others. The latter is meant to invite readers to reconsider the value of modest case studies in understanding the diversity of ideas that contributed to the changes within European political and legal traditions more generally; these changes are often elided by depictions of the ideas and jurisprudence associated with northern (Protestant) Europe as modern, innovative, and even marking a revolutionary break with the past, whereas the ideas and jurisprudence associated with southern (Catholic) Europe are often characterized as traditional, static, and even resistant to change. In essence, this volume invites readers to consider what the historiography might look like—and how much more nuanced our understanding of the shifts within the Western legal traditions might be—if we followed ideas as they traveled across Europe from the north to the south, and west to east, rather than merely from south to north and east to west. And further, how our understanding of the history and development of both *ius* and *ius gentium* might change if we broadened our inquiry to include how and why these categories were re-imagined and re-deployed by humanist jurists to address problems and conflicts associated with and attendant on early modern state- and empire-state formation in the early sixteenth century.

PART 1

Guillaume Budé: Jus, *Justice, and Dignity*

CHAPTER 1

Setting the Scene

Justinian's Digest and University-Based Jurisprudence

This chapter consists of four overlapping sections designed to provide readers with a sense of what Budé was departing from when he offered his readers an alternative understanding of fundamental categories of Roman law in his 1508 *Annotationes* (the focus of the next chapter). As such, the primary goal of this first chapter is to illuminate the backdrop against which he unfurled his acrimonious attack on the glosses and commentaries on Justinian's *Digest*. To that end, each section offers readers a short episodic history—rather than a linear narrative—centered on discrete actions, conflicts, or complex processes that either served as the catalyst for or bore the weight of the imposing edifice of jurisprudence that dominated law faculties by the turn of the sixteenth century. The aim of what follows is not to provide a comprehensive history of the Western legal tradition, but to bring together and illuminate various aspects of the university-based tradition of legal teaching and interpretation as it stood when Budé published his critique of it. Given that Budé never completed his legal training (indeed, he effectively failed out of law school), the episodic histories that follow are presented in broad strokes, whereas the features within scholastic jurisprudence that Zasius and Alciati rejected or reinterpreted are discussed within parts two and three of the volume.

Each part of this chapter draws on expansive, complex, and nuanced historiographies that explore: the creation of the Roman *Digest* by and for Byzantine jurists; the context in which the Byzantine *Digest* was recovered in Latin Europe; the way it was studied, interpreted, and deployed upon its recovery; and the development of education in monastery and cathedral schools as well as at universities and, with it, the methods of teaching (*modus docendi*) law developed by the scholastics and humanists. This is necessary because each of these aspects illuminates what Budé deemed as the original intent within ancient texts and informed what he regarded as inexplicable, and unforgiveable, errors by lawyers and jurists. Finally, the episodic histories presented here often overlap and repeat, even as they cover different ground, precisely because there are so many different strands and contributing factors that produced a tradition of jurisprudence steeped in things lost, found, reformed, restored, and reimagined through the study, interpretation, and the commentaries dedicated to the *corpus iuris civilis*.

 | DOI:10.1163/9789004528451_003

1 *Corpus iuris civilis:* Composition and Transmission

Shortly after becoming Byzantine Emperor in 527, Justinian I (482–565) commissioned a series of juridical reforms aimed at replacing an unwieldy Roman legal tradition—one that reached as far back as the Twelve Tables (451–450 BCE) and included a sweeping array of laws, imperial decrees, and jurisprudence produced by an empire that stretched from the Mediterranean to the Near East—into a manageable one.[1] Although Justinian's project to reduce, clarify, and systematize discrete parts of law was not without precedent (the Theodosian *Code* attempted to do something similar in 438), the sheer scale of the legal reform—and the speed at which it was accomplished—was. Indeed, within six months of his coronation, Justinian commissioned a panel of ten men to review all previous compilations of imperial laws with the directive to eliminate anything that they deemed obsolete, unnecessary, or redundant.

Despite the enormity and complexity of the task, the resulting *Code* was first promulgated in April 529, and then again in 534. The first edition, which has not survived, included legislation that spanned from the reign of Hadrian (r.117–138) through Justinian's coronation, whereas the second was amended to include imperial decrees and laws passed during the early decades of Justinian's reign. In each instance, the *Code* replaced all previous constitutions, reducing not only the sources of law but also their form. For example, after selecting which imperial constitutions should be preserved, the "preliminary statements that explained why the text has been drawn up as well as its particular scope" were omitted when they became part of the *Code*.[2] These abridged forms—wrested out of their historical, political, and juridical contexts—not only served to limit speculation about why such constitutions had been created but also forestalled debates as to the original intent and meaning of the laws that were preserved by contemporary jurists as well as by generations of lawyers and scholars who followed them.

Encouraged by the swift success of the compilers, Justinian commissioned what became known as the Latin *Digest*, or Greek *Pandectae*, in 530. Completed under the direction of Tribonian (500–527), the *Digest* was promulgated into

1 The general narrative that follows in this section is informed by Mario Ascheri, *The Laws of Late Medieval Italy (1000–1500): Foundations for a European Legal System* (Leiden: Brill, 2013), Berman, *Law and Revolution I*; Bellomo, *The Common Legal Past of Europe*; James A. Brundage, *The Medieval Origins of the Legal Profession: Canonists, Civilians, and Courts* (Chicago: University of Chicago Press, 2008); and Peter Stein, *Roman Law in European History* (Cambridge: Cambridge University Press, 1999).

2 Ascheri, *The Laws of Late Medieval Italy*, 11.

law in 533. Over the course of merely three years the commission had, according to Justinian, "collected in a well-arranged and perspicuous compilation, a multitude of opinions of the ancient founders of the law, which were distributed through almost two thousand volumes and three million sentences."[3] Then, "with the assistance of heaven," they compiled the law into a mere fifty books by "accepting everything that was useful, rejecting all ambiguities, and retaining nothing which was contradictory."[4] Although the *Digest* was arranged in the same manner as praetorian edicts, and thus made some organizational sense, the fragments and opinions collected within the titles of each book, were arranged far less systematically. Indeed, Peter Stein suggests that in some instances they seemed thrown together haphazardly.[5] The latter resulted, at least in part, from the sheer number of jurists helping complete an enormous task over such a brief period. It also resulted from the fact that the compilers were authorized by Justinian to collect opinions, laws, and procedures that preserved the wisdom of the ancients and "expressed the law of the sixth-century Byzantium."[6] As such, they adjusted, and even recast, the opinions of ancient jurists to suit their purposes.[7] Thus, they were not only allowed to omit materials they deemed as irrelevant, outdated, or contradictory, they were also authorized to bend the materials to match the task at hand.

When completed, the *Digest* was, despite the claims of Justinian, an immense and unwieldy text. Not least because it contained more than forty-thousand passages drawn from about forty jurists, nearly all of whom lived during the peak of the "golden age of Roman law," which had been reached, as far as Justinian was concerned, about three centuries prior. Had the compilers included annotations or commentary to convey why a particular opinion was selected, or even to explain the original context of a fragment or the excerpt they chose to include, the jewel in what would eventually become known as the centerpiece of Justinian's *corpus iuris civilis* would have likely been far more accessible and useful to those who were required to use it. What the compilers produced instead was far too cumbersome and archaic for most lawyers and students to access without a great deal of effort and additional resources.

---

3 Confirmation of the *Digest*, c533, in *The Digest of Justinian*, trans. Alan Watson, 2 vols. (Philadelphia: University of Pennsylvania Press, 1998). Note: all excerpts from the *Digest* included in this book are taken from Watson's translation.

4 Ibid.

5 Stein, *Roman Law in European History*, 34.

6 Ibid.

7 By the sixteenth century, humanist and scholastic scholars had identified several instances in which the original words of the Ancients had been changed by the compilers of the *Digest*. See Ascheri, *The Laws of Late Medieval Italy*, 13; and Stein, *Roman Law in European History*, 34.

One such resource was the Greek *Paraphrase* of the *Digest*, created by Theophilus (n.d.) shortly after the *Digest* was completed. The translation was necessary because while Latin was the official language of the law and administration within the empire it was not the most common language of the lawyers, administrators, or scholars within it. A second resource that students and lawyers had at hand to help them understand the *Digest*, or at least access it more efficiently and effectively, was the *Institutes*. Issued with the *Digest* in 533, the *Institutes* had been commissioned by Justinian "for the benefit of those who have recently begun the study of the law, and who are unable as yet, to understand the more advanced principles of that science."[8] This textbook was based on a work of the same title by Gaius (d. 180), which had been written more than three centuries prior and had connected the golden age of Roman law to Justinian's rule, while at the same time it served to structure the study and practice of law in sixth-century Byzantium.

Just as in the case of the *Code* and the *Digest*, once the textbook was completed Justinian set the text in stone, forbidding its revision. However, unlike the *Digest*, which was almost exclusively dominated by the ancient opinions, the compilers of the *Institutes* could "make mention of the Constitutions which We promulgated for the amendments of ancient jurisprudence."[9] Allowing it to be amended in this way made it a more practical text for those who completed their legal studies as well as those embarking on them. As for its use, first-year students were expected to master the four books of the *Institutes* relatively quickly, enabling them to dedicate the remaining three years of their study to the *Digest* "with an emphasis on the problems of private law and thus also to juridical practice."[10] Although the size, form, and content of the *Institutes* was far more accessible, intelligible, and relevant for students and jurists than the *Digest*, it too was written in Latin. Hence, just as he had for the *Digest*, Theophilus created a Greek paraphrase of it shortly after its completion.[11]

The completion of the *Institutes* and the *Digest*, both of which became law on 31 December 533, paired with the revised *Code* in 544, were monumental achievements. After 544, they were supplemented by Justinian's *Novels*—a collection of all new laws modifying the *Code*, but not replacing it—that he had decreed up to his death in 565. Although Justinian "never did issue an official compilation of these new constitutions," they were collected and published in several unofficial forms so that lawyers and jurists could more readily have

8 Confirmation of the *Digest*, c533.

9 Ibid.

10 Ascheri, *The Laws of Late Medieval Italy*, 14–5.

11 Ascheri, *The Laws of Late Medieval Italy*, 36; and Stein, *Roman Law in European History*, 35.

access to them, and thus stay up to date on changes made to the laws.[12] Unlike the *Code*, *Digest*, and *Institutes*, most of these *Novels* were originally written in Greek, which made them more immediately intelligible to Byzantine lawyers. These *Novels* constituted the fourth part of what became known as Justinian's *corpus iuris civilis*, viz., the body of civil law. As important as the revised *Code* and *Novels* were, however, it was the Latin editions of both the *Institutes* and *Digest* that became the focal point of scholars within post-Roman Europe. Such interest in these texts among scholars, however, did not emerge in earnest until about five centuries after Justinian had originally commissioned them.

Indeed, before the "rediscovery" of the *Digest* in the eleventh century and the subsequent "recovery" of Roman law over the course of the twelfth, "Justinian's legislation found life impossible everywhere."[13] Not only because the texts, once completed, were, as Manlio Bellomo put it, "like a jewel case guarding precious gems and removing them from use," but also because the *corpus* was, for the most part, "extraneous to local customs and even the ideology of the empire."[14] In the east, for example, the *Digest* was replaced by the Greek *Ecloga tōn nomōn* in 740; a compilation, that attempted to clarify, streamline, and update law just as the *Digest* had, but tended to emphasize Byzantine law and jurisprudence more so than an Ancient Roman tradition. In the west, the impact of Justinian's *Digest* was, in his own lifetime, negligible. It was unknown to the Germanic Kingdoms, who had taken possession of much of the Western Roman Empire during the previous century, and its influence in the Italian peninsula, when it arrived with conquering armies in 553, was minimal.

Even after Justinian issued a "pragmatic sanction"—at the request of Pope Vigilius (r. 537–555)—enabling the "extension of his compilation to Italy," the reception of the *Digest* among lawyers, jurists, and scholars was tepid.[15] Most of those who remained loyal to Byzantium, even after the Lombard invasions and occupations began in 568, spoke and read Greek rather than Latin, thus making the *Digest*, as well as the *Institutes* and *Code*, as difficult to understand in the West as it had been—aside from the Greek paraphrase—to lawyers and jurists in the East. Interest was slim even among those scholars and lawyers who could read Latin. Indeed, Justinian's laws invited as much hostility as it did curiosity since it harkened back to the golden age when the capital

---

12 Timothy G. Kearley, "The Creation and Transmission of Justinian's Novels," *Law Library Journal* 102, no. 3 (2010): 377–97; 379–80.

13 Bellomo, *The Common Legal Past of Europe*, 39.

14 Ibid.

15 Ibid.

was in Rome—an age that was remembered by many as especially harsh and unforgiving.[16]

Nevertheless, the fact that some areas remained in contact with Byzantium ensured that the *corpus* was never quite lost to post-Roman Europe, even though much of it fell out of use. For example, an abridged copy of the *Novels*, translated into Latin and known as *Epitome Juliani*, survives from the sixth century, so too does a reduced version of the *Code* (the last three books, viz., *Tres libri*, which dealt with the administration of the empire, were not included).[17] The *Institutes*, thanks to its brevity and style, fared far better. As the official textbook used in Rome—after Rome was briefly reunited with the Eastern empire and, thereby at Ravenna, when the law school was relocated there during the Exarchate (584–751)—it not only remained relevant to jurists within and bordering Byzantine territories, but it also continued to draw the attention of scholars from across the *Regnum Italicum*.[18] In addition to the few copies that survive from sixth-century Italy, mention was made to it and excerpts were reproduced in documents and texts from other legal traditions. Indeed, the most significant conduit of the ideas and categories of Roman civil law beyond six-century Byzantium was the *Institutes*; aspects of it were not only preserved within and transmitted by canon law but were also folded into customary, or tribal, law across post-Roman Europe.

The *Digest* on the other hand, thanks to its complex form and archaic content was neglected, and indeed nearly lost to the West altogether, before it was "found" to be of interest and gradually "recovered" by medieval scholars in the late eleventh century. To understand why there was an interest in ancient Roman law—an interest that led to the "rediscovery" and "recovery" of the Byzantine *Digest* within Latin Christendom—it is worth acknowledging the extent to which aspects of Roman law shaped medieval legal traditions that reached beyond (and stood outside of) the direct cultural and political influence of Byzantium. Not least because it reminds us of both the appeal and durability of Ancient Roman law as a source of legitimacy as well as its flexibility and mutability in the hands of those who, although they might appear or claim to be merely preserving it, ultimately transformed it to suit their purpose (in the eleventh century, as much as in the sixteenth). It also helps to illuminate why legal texts that had no authority in post-Roman Europe nevertheless helped to shape, and indeed serve as the foundation for what set the

16 Ibid.

17 Stein, *Roman Law in European History*, 44.

18 Ascheri discusses this in numerous contexts in "Chapter Two: The Multi-faceted Eleventh Century" of *The Laws of Late Medieval Italy*.

parameters for an emerging legal tradition across Latin Europe by the end of the eleventh century.

2 Law before Lawyers

Before the late-eleventh and the early-twelfth centuries, there was no legal system to speak of in post-Roman Europe.[19] While there were of course laws, most of them were distinctly local in scope. As such, the law in which institutions were enmeshed was largely customary, held in common among those who shared conceptions of morality and religion more generally, or between those who shared the same geographical space and rulers. In this context, discrete bodies of customary law—paired with the law of the church, viz., canon law—served as the sinew that bound communities together, underpinning everything from marriage to inheritance, from labor to property, from power to diplomacy, and from punishment to war.

The validity of customary law extended from—and was confirmed by—the collective memory of the communities it bound together. Notwithstanding the fact that customary law changed over time, such changes were gradual, and as a result customary law seemed as if it was immutable and perpetual, a perception which ultimately infused it with both historical and moral authority. Put differently, long-held customs were perceived as good and fair by those who shared them precisely because they had been passed down over time; if customary laws and uses were bad or unfair, then it stood to reason that they would have been rejected or changed by previous generations or by contemporary rulers. Despite its pedigree and importance, customary law was never systematized and rationalized in the same ways that Roman law was, or, as it turned out, the way that canon law would be.[20]

---

19 The general narrative that follows in this section is informed by Ascheri, *The Laws of Late Medieval Italy*; Berman, *Law and Revolution I*; William J. Bouwsma, "Lawyers and Early Modern Culture," *The American Historical Review* 78, no. 2 (1973): 303–27; Brundage, *The Medieval Origins of the Legal Profession*; Stein, *Roman Law in European History*; and Witt, *The Two Latin Cultures.*

20 For a general overview of the development and systemization of canon law, especially under the guidance of Gratian, see Anders Winroth, *The Making of Gratian's Decretum* (Cambridge: Cambridge University Press, 2004); Berman, *Law and Revolution I;* Wilfried Hartmann and Kenneth Pennington, eds., *The History of Medieval Canon Law in the Classical Period, 1140–1234: From Gratian to the Decretals of Pope Gregory IX* (Washington, D.C.; The Catholic University of America Press, 2008); Stein, *Roman Law in European History*; and Tamar Herzog, *A Short History of European Law: The Last Two and a Half Millennia* (Cambridge, MA: Harvard University Press, 2018).

Although there were discrete traditions of customary law that were transformed from oral to written traditions and expanded over the course of the early medieval era, these laws were not arranged systematically, nor were they the purview of professional lawyers or jurists, as in Byzantium and ancient Rome. Even in the case of early church laws and dictums, for example, to decree a standard or rule for the church at an ecumenical council or synod was one thing, but to enforce it was quite another, especially as the latter depended on cooperation with local—and in some cases tribal—leaders bound by and enmeshed in long-held practices and traditions throughout post-Roman Europe.

The fact that much of this customary and tribal law was developed outside the confines of Byzantium does not mean that these laws—and the codes that contained them—were devoid of any trace of Justinian's *corpus*, but rather that the surviving traces tended to be "simplified, popularized, and corrupted" in order to fit the needs of the time.[21] Nevertheless, the inclusion of fragments of "vulgar" Roman law adopted from Byzantine or older Roman sources into customary legal traditions ultimately "helped preserve the idea that law should play a role in the ordering of political and social relationships."[22] Moreover, the preservation of specific terms and categories of law, especially those that remained in Latin, helps to account for how and why Roman law would later become such an important aspect of—and indeed the foundations underpinning—the Western legal tradition by experts who shared a common second (or perhaps third) language between them.

Customary legal traditions, written and unwritten, also provided fertile ground for the creation and acceptance of new laws crafted to clarify or expand existing customs or to establish and commemorate a major change—most notably, within the history of western Europe, the transliteration and promulgation of legal traditions into written form in the wake of a ruler's conversion to Christianity. When a Germanic tribal leader converted, for example, he would order customs and norms—previously passed down through use or speech—to be transcribed into written form as part of bringing his territory and people into Christendom. The earliest surviving examples of this process from within Western Europe fall under the rubric of *leges barbarorium*, viz., the laws of the barbarians, and include the *Lex Salica*, issued by the Merovingian King Clovis shortly after he converted to Christianity in 496, and the *Laws of*

21 Berman, *Law and Revolution I*, 53.

22 Ibid.

Ethelbert in England, commissioned by the titular ruler of Kent when he converted to Christianity around 600.[23]

Beyond such ceremonial compilations, there were many instances when rulers, in their attempts to solidify their power or to establish peace, promulgated legal codes that preserved both tribal customs and aspects of vulgar Roman law. The *Lex Burgundionum* promulgated after 500, the *Edictum Rothari* promulgated in 643, and the *Lex Visigothorum* promulgated in 654 all serve as apt examples not only of the transformation of oral traditions into written ones but also of shared categories and practices across these kingdoms. They also contained, to a lesser and greater degree, customs shared among peoples across and around the Adriatic and Mediterranean seas. The most notable example of the latter was perhaps the *Breviary of Alaric*, promulgated in 506 by Alaric II, King of the Visigoths, to preserve—and congeal—customary traditions (tribal law) with Roman law. This law applied to those living south of the Loire, and thus his Hispano-Roman and Gallo-Roman subjects, rather than his Visigoth ones.[24]

As a consequence of transforming oral legal traditions into written ones—whether originally rendered into the vernacular or Latin—as well as creating new codes to reflect changing authorities, local, tribal, and regional customs were added to a growing cache of practices, uses, and rules embedded in the *ius commune*—in this context, the customs and laws shared across post-Roman Europe. The *ius commune*, the common language of which was Latin, enabled aspects of vulgar Roman law and customary traditions to be preserved in word as well as in practice. The most influential and vast component of the *ius commune* within medieval Europe was canon law. Indeed, canon law was laden with ideas, terms, and categories adapted from Roman law, Ancient and Byzantine, that reached back to antiquity. Yet, before the twelfth century, there was no systematic compilation or study of canon law.[25] Instead, it consisted of a vast array of rules and decrees—written in multiple languages, viz., Greek, Syriac, Armenian, Latin, and Coptic—issued by ecumenical councils, synods, and bishops, that bore witness to theological disputes. Each set the parameters for subsequent disputes and decrees, and many bore the mark of Byzantine/Roman culture, helping to preserve legal categories and terms in written form, just as customary legal traditions had.

---

23 Ibid, 53–4; and Stein, *Roman Law in European History*, 29–32.

24 Stein, *Roman Law in European History*, 31.

25 For a comprehensive history of the first compilation see Winroth, *The Making of Gratian's Decretum*.

Although the meaning and significance of Roman terms, whether adapted by the Christian church and thus preserved in canon law or accommodated by tribal traditions and thus ensconced in customary law, changed over time, even among scholars the *corpus iuris civilis* drew little attention. After the connection and affinity between the Catholic church and Greek Orthodox church was severed in 1054, however, the shared ideas and vocabulary of Roman law as preserved in Justinian's *Institutes* became increasingly important. Cut off from their Greek counterparts, and their Byzantine past, renewed interest in legal texts, which extended back to the ancient Roman empire as well as to a unified church, proved decisive. So too did the practical applications of Roman law, embedded in formularies and contracts by notaries.[26]

Before and after the rediscovery and subsequent recovery of Justinian's *corpus* in Latin Christendom, notaries provided essential services for both secular and sacred rulers as well as for emerging and growing cities and trade networks that spanned medieval Europe. In so doing, notaries preserved, passed down, and expanded formularies preserved by Roman law to mediate economic, social, and political interactions among individuals as well as kingdoms. Precisely because Roman law was "the 'fixed' or established law at the basis of every legal enquiry," Mario Ascheri reminds us, it was "not only the most comprehensive, but—being written in Latin—also offered a common technical language to all," for secular and sacred governance and administration.[27]

Roman law, in other words, was the common language shared among notaries and scribes well before it became the centerpiece of legal studies in the late-eleventh century. Indeed, the sheer volume of legal instruments that notaries produced not only demonstrated but also created a demand for their expertise in Roman vocabularies and procedures, which helped to create a demand for more notaries and scribes more generally. Even so, notarial "record-keeping was mostly reserved for decisions of some significance, and thus (apart from legislative and judicial acts), tended to concentrate on juridical provisions concerning private individuals that would have enduring effects."[28] For example, emperors and popes commissioned public notaries to prepare documents

26 See especially Ascheri, "The Multi-Faceted Eleventh Century," in *The Laws of Late Medieval Italy;* Brundage, *The Medieval Origins of the Legal Profession*, 61–3; James M. Murray, Walter Prevenier, and Michel Oosterbosch, *Notarial Instruments in Flanders between 1280 and 1452* (Brussels: Palais des académies, 1995). See especially Witt's distinction between a documentary and book culture, and with-it different forms of production and learning, in *The Two Latin Cultures*, 59–68.

27 Ascheri, *The Laws of Late Medieval Italy*, 42.

28 Ibid, 65.

"that were often critical for a successful outcome in contested matters" and courts "operated on the assumption that notarial documents were authentic reports of the transactions they recorded."[29]

In addition to the legal terms and technical forms of the Roman legal tradition that such notarial documents preserved and passed on, they also reflected contemporary customs and practices like those embedded in Lombard law. Indeed, according to Ascheri, some notarial documents "illustrate just how much Roman and Lombard law was being subjected to change at a local level."[30] By the turn of the twelfth century, some notaries sought to expand their expertise and utility by joining with others in cities, especially in the *Regnum Italicum*, to acquire formal instruction in formularies. Equipped with a pragmatic understanding of the language of law, ensconced in vulgar Roman law, as well as customary and canon law, these notaries were also joined by scholars and students from monastery and cathedral schools across Europe, who brought their understanding of antiquity—acquired through their study of grammar and rhetoric—and their methods of interpretation—dominated by logical exegesis—with them. This combination of practical need, antiquated interest, and instrumental interpretation set the parameters for, and ultimately produced, scholastic jurisprudence, and with it, the founding of the first universities in Latin Europe. What made the latter possible, however, was not existing expertise or increasing demand for notaries, nor was it merely the interest in ancient ideas and texts, but a political conflict that came to a head over the conflicting claims of authority by popes and emperors, and within the broader context of institutional reform. Its manifestation was the Investiture Controversy, which, as Harold J. Berman argued, was nothing short of a revolution, the roots of which can be traced back, as the story goes, to a monastery founded in southern Francia, viz., *Regnum Francorum*, nearly two centuries prior.[31] It was revolutionary, in no small part because the contest between popes and emperors inadvertently led to the rediscovery, and the subsequent recovery, of long-lost parts of Justinian's *corpus*. Indeed, it was the recovery of the *Digest* that led to the founding of university civil (Roman) law faculties in northern Italy in the first place.

---

29 Brundage, *The Medieval Origins of the Legal Profession*, 4.

30 Ascheri, *The Laws of Late Medieval Italy*, 67.

31 Berman, *Law and Revolution 1*, 88–94. Following Witt, the term "Francia" is used "to describe those lands held by the king of Francia and his feudatories as well as Provence." *The Two Latin Cultures*, 13.

3 Reform, Revolution, and Rediscovery

"The creation of modern legal systems," and with it professional and university-based jurisprudence, "was, in its first instance, a response to a revolutionary change within the church and in the relation of the church to the secular authorities."[32] Although the origins of this revolutionary change can be traced to the founding of the Benedictine Abbey at Cluny in Southern Francia in the early-tenth century, its fundamental impact on the legal and political landscape of Latin Christendom did not become fully apparent until the late-eleventh century. To understand the latter, however, requires attention (albeit brief) to some of the most noteworthy features of the former.[33]

With its founding, the Abbey at Cluny became the seat of a reform movement aimed at purging the Latin church of the vestiges of temporal influence and corruption. The genesis of such a movement stemmed from Cluny's unique charter, which was, in turn, informed by those who wished to return to the practices ensconced within the original Rule of St. Benedict of 516. Among the most significant aspects of the latter from the perspective of legal history was the fact that it not only outlined a clear structure of governance within the monastery, with the Abbot at its head aided by Deans, but also outlined the consequences for violating the Benedictine Rule, including private admonition and excommunication, for offenses ranging from disobedience to the possession of private property. It was, in short, a rule of law, whose authority stemmed from one's full and voluntary submission to the Abbot's authority, who, in turn, provided all necessities and oversaw the spiritual and physical work of the community. By the ninth century, however, the Rule designed to create, regulate, and insulate monastic communities from worldly temptations and concerns in the sixth century had been so thoroughly bent—and even broken—by temporal authorities who endowed them (especially when feudal lords who made such bequests imposed their wishes on them) that some monasteries hardly looked Benedictine at all. Abuses in some places were so

32 The general narrative that follows in this section is informed by Ascheri, *The Laws of Late Medieval Italy*; Berman, *Law and Revolution* I; Brundage, *The Medieval Origins of the Legal Profession*; Herzog, *A Short History of European Law*; and Witt, *The Two Latin Cultures*. Quote from Berman, *Law and Revolution I*, 87.

33 A focus on the relation between Cluny and rediscovery of Roman law does not, by any means, diminish the emphasis on law as the 'rightful order' in monastic reforms, or eschatological approaches to reform more generally. However, the latter is beyond the bounds of this brief background chapter precisely because the goal of this chapter is to merely set up and provide general background for Budé's, Zasius', and Alciati's departure from traditional jurisprudence and the ideas that underpinned and framed it.

pronounced that they triggered calls for reform aimed at reaffirming the Rule for the community and the independence of the Abbot to oversee and enforce it without interference from secular authorities.

The charter for Cluny, which was confirmed at Bourges in 910, served as a direct refutation of lax practices and as a model for establishing independence. Indeed, William I (875–918), the Duke of Aquitaine, relinquished all his rights—and those of his successors—over the lands, revenues, and inhabitants of the regular monastery at Cluny in the hopes of insulating it from worldly corruption and politics. The charter also declared that "the monks shall congregate and live according to the rule of St. Benedict," under the direction of Abbott Berno (850–927), and after his death "have power and permission to elect any one of their order whom they please as abbot and rector" without "the intervention of our own or of any other power."[34]

Placing the monastery in the hands of the first Abbot and, upon elections, of succeeding abbots, William accorded the spiritual and moral authority of the governing structure of Cluny with the legal standing to self-govern. In so doing, the duke ensured that neither pope, king, nor lord could sell the offices at Cluny to reward loyalty or buy allies, nor could any clergy who lived outside of, or wanted to bend, the Rule be installed there. In a world in which church lands and offices were under the authority of feudal lords (e.g., emperors, kings, dukes) the status of Cluny stood as a beacon of reform, which, over the course of the next century, spread to over a thousand monasteries in all corners of Europe and, by the eleventh century, had garnered the support of the papacy itself. Indeed, at the hand of Gregory VII, born Hildebrand (c. 1020–1085), reforms associated with the monastic order at Cluny were unilaterally imposed by papal decree on the Catholic church.

Gregory was not the first pope who was either part of or influenced by the Cluniac reform movement, nor was the movement, at its genesis or as it gained momentum, restricted to the regular clergy. For centuries before and after the founding of Cluny, there had been calls to "raise the levels of religious life by attacking the ecclesiastical power of feudal and local rulers"; power which had been gained, and augmented, by commingling secular interest and church wealth.[35] Freeing the church from worldly influence, however, required convincing temporal authorities, viz., emperors, kings, princes, and dukes, to not only willingly relinquish their interests and rights over the properties they endowed to the church but also to help purge the offices *within* the church

34 "Foundation Charter of Cluny, 910," in *Select Historical Documents of the Middle Ages*, trans. Ernest F. Henderson (London: George Bell and Sons, 1910), 329–33.

35 Berman, *Law and Revolution I*, 90.

from the influence of temporal authorities. To help accomplish the latter, the highest office within the Latin church needed to be wrested from men who appeared to be more interested in political affairs and possessions than the work of God and the care of souls. The papacy, and indeed all offices in the church, needed to be liberated from feudal bonds and temporal influence in the same way as the Abbot of Cluny was, namely by law and legal authority.

Before such reform could be undertaken, however, it was first necessary to break control of the Roman aristocracy over papal elections. This was attempted by Henry III (c.1016–1056), who, after being elected Holy Roman Emperor in 1046, deposed three rival popes before appointing a succession of popes of his own choosing. The most successful of them was Henry's own cousin, Leo IX (born Bruno of Egisheim-Dagsburg), who served as Pope from 1049 to 1054. "In assessing the fate of the papal reform movement in Germany, it must be remembered," Ronald G. Witt reminds us, "that Henry III had created the reform papacy out of the eagerness to eradicate nicolaitism, [viz., concubinage] that is, to impose celibacy on the clergy."[36] At the same time, however, "Henry III would have rejected the papal demand that the emperor abandon his claim to govern the imperial church."[37] Yet, his choice to appoint Leo opened the door to a reform movement that would challenge the very authority the emperor exercised by appointing him.

Leo not only rejected "the concept of the papacy as a bishopric of the emperor," he also asserted the primacy of the papacy, and its independence from within and beyond Henry's empire.[38] To assert his independence, Leo drew on a legal tradition and an abundance of sources that reached back to Pope Gelasius I's (r. 491–496) *Duo sunt*.[39] Completed in 494, Gelasius argued that temporal authority and spiritual authority occupied two distinct spheres concerned with two different, but related, things. The former was concerned with the mundane and corporal world, whereas the latter was concerned with the eternal salvation of souls. If spiritual and secular authorities were not in conflict or making competing demands on their subjects, Gelasius argued, the laws of the worldly rulers and the laws of the church could exist in harmony, and subjects could obey both authorities without complication.

When sacred and secular authorities made conflicting demands on their Christian subjects, however, no subject could obey the laws of one without

---

36 Witt, *The Two Latin Cultures*, 218.

37 Ibid.

38 Berman, *Law and Revolution I*, 94.

39 Gelasius, "Letter of Pope Gelasius to Emperor Anastasius on the superiority of the spiritual over temporal power," in Colman J. Barry, *Readings in Church History, vol. 1: From Pentecost to the Protestant Revolt*. (Westminster, Md: Newman Press, 1960), 147.

breaking the laws of the other. To avoid the corporal punishment of their temporal lord and the spiritual admonishment from their sacred one, a hierarchy of authority had to be established and agreed on among rulers. This was precisely where Gelasius' argument, which was otherwise clear cut, became muddled.[40] At the same time as he argued that spiritual authority was superior to temporal authority (e.g., authority held by Christians under the church's care) because it was universal and concerned the care of souls, he implied that when it came to matters clearly entrenched in the secular domain, priestly authority was inferior to temporal authority.

Rather than presenting a clear line between sacred and secular authorities, Gelasius put forth an argument that was ripe for multiple interpretations by popes and rulers as well as their advisors and administrators. The spiritual rulers could use it to claim dominance over temporal ones, as easily as temporal rulers could use it to assert their power over ecclesiastical ones. In the realm of the church, Gelasius' *Duo sunt* served as a catalyst—one of many—for the systemization of canon law. Indeed, by the eleventh century, a variety of church laws, decrees, and decisions already provided Leo, and subsequent popes, a cache of precedents they could use to make their case for the supremacy of the pope over the Catholic church and to support their claims that the church should be free from the influence of temporal rulers.

This quest to clarify and extend the principles embedded in Gelasius' doctrine—along with the subsequent canon laws that attempted to define authority within the church and its freedom from the secular rulers—led to the expansion of interest in such questions within monastery and cathedral schools, wherein students, as part of their liberal arts education, had started to acquire a distinctly juridical approach for treating them.[41] These students adapted the methods of exegesis and analysis that Bernold of Constance (1054–1100), Ivo of Chartres (1040–1115), Alger of Liège (1055–1131), and Peter Abelard (1079–1142), originally developed to interpret theological texts, in order to explore legal documents and decrees that were becoming increasingly

---

40 Notable, significant attempts to un-muddle the distinction in the fourteenth century include Dante Alighieri's *De Monarchia* (w. 1313–1314), William of Ockham's *Dialogus* (written between 1332 and 1347), and Marsilius of Padua's *Defensor pacis* (1324), which, along with the works of Bartolus and Baldus, helped lay the foundations for sixteenth-century juridical and political thought. For a detailed discussion of their impact see Brian Tierney, The *Idea of Natural Rights: Studies in Natural Rights, Natural Law and Church Law, 1150–1625* (Atlanta, GA: Scholars Press, 1997); Skinner, *Foundations of Modern Political Thought. Volume 1*; and Joseph P. Canning, *Ideas of Power in the Late Middle Ages, 1296–1417* (Cambridge: Cambridge University Press, 2014).

41 Ascheri, *The Laws of Late Medieval Italy*, 53.

important as the eleventh century unfolded. The knowledge and practical expertise that they acquired in doing so not only prepared them to help administer the church as it expanded but also to develop skills that helped popes like Leo to encase arguments for spiritual authority in a latticework of legal precedent.[42] Scholars and scribes who mastered such an education at monastery and cathedrals schools could also marshal these skills to question what they saw as overreach by the pope as well as defend the regalian and customary rights of temporal lords over their subjects and territories. In this respect, the die was cast for a legal confrontation well before Henry appointed Leo in 1049 and the break with the East in 1054.

Pope Leo IX surrounded himself with those, including Hildebrand, who shared his ideas about the supremacy of the papacy over the rest of the church. In addition to calling for the end of clerical marriage and the selling of offices, Leo's supporters called for the freedom of the clergy—all clergy—from political and feudal bonds. Although the 1059 council at Rome declared, for the first time, that the pope would be elected by Roman cardinals, and thus not by kings or emperors, other reforms would have to wait. The papacy was no monastery; it could no sooner be reformed by turning its back on worldly politics than it could disregard its obligation to provide guidance to, and care for, Christians spread across Europe and beyond. Unable to free the church from worldly influence and corruption, Leo and those who followed him set to the task of bringing the world into closer alignment with the church. The manner and means they used to do so had a revolutionary impact on political and legal structures throughout Latin Christendom.

As decisive as putting the selection of the pope in the hands of the cardinals was, if the offices in the church were under the influence and auspices of feudal lords, then the overall aims of the reformers would be stalled. Until bishops and cardinals were chosen by the pope, rather than by emperors and kings, the church would remain unable to fulfill its mission to serve God and the community of the faithful as it was intended. To remedy this, Cluniac reformers continued to push for the hierarchical arrangement of power within the church to reflect the arrangement of authority that tied all Cluniac monasteries together. The structure that developed as the order expanded was well suited to the task of church governance, as far as reformers were concerned, precisely because each monastery was overseen by a single prior, who was, in turn, subject to a single Abbot at Cluny. Moreover, just as the Abbot was elected by those who were part of the order, and thus followed the Rule, so too were the priors. This meant, effectively, that no one who held office could be installed by external

42 Ibid.

agents, and everyone, no matter their status, was subject to the jurisdiction of the same authority.

Unlike Cluny, however, eleventh-century reformers did not have the ability to enact reforms based on a single legal charter, nor did they have ability to build an institution from scratch. As such, they had to find ways to end long-held customs and practices by reclaiming the church on two fronts. Namely, by abolishing simony, viz., the buying and selling of offices practiced by temporal and spiritual lords, and ending clerical marriage and concubinage. If bishops and priests were no longer permitted to marry, they would no longer be distracted by family interests, a change that would free them to serve the church more fully and effectively. If marriage and concubinage were prohibited, then those already entangled by such bonds would be forced out of office. Moreover, if simony were abolished, then the church could be purged—albeit slowly—of those who used it to enhance their wealth, advance their status in the feudal hierarchy, or appease their enemies. Freed from the demands of familial and feudal bonds as well as the pressure of politics, all clergy could serve the will of God and tend to the needs of the poor. Ending simony and marriage would also reduce the problem of absenteeism, a measure which would, in turn, enhance the ability of ordinary Christians across Latin Europe to receive the sacraments and other resources from their local clergy when they needed them.

The problem with each of the changes outlined above was that they could not be put into practice without the help of secular authorities. Without the cooperation of temporal rulers, any attempt to purge the church of worldly corruption and influence was a non-starter, especially those aimed at ending simony. Neither the papacy nor the Cluniac reform movement was strong enough to accomplish their goals without the backing—by arms and by law—of emperors, kings, and princes. Yet, there were few feudal lords who could afford to relinquish their rights over church properties or risk the rebellion of subjects who depended on married priests. As such, reform, if any came at all, was piecemeal until Hildebrand took matters into his own hands when he became Pope Gregory VII (r. 1073–85).

"Although," according to Witt, the new pope initially "showed restraint in his relationship with the German emperor, the radical character of his concept of papal power emerged by 1077/78."[43] With his letters and actions after 1077, Gregory effectively created his own charter by combining the same principles contained within *Duo sunt* with those laid out in William's bequest of Cluny,

43 Witt, *The Two Latin Cultures*, 165. For a broader discussion of Gregory's ambitions see Berman, *Law and Revolution I*, 94.

when he asserted that all spiritual and legal authority stemmed from a single office, viz., the papacy. Discarding all pretended rights and practices, Gregory asserted that the pope alone could appoint and unseat bishops, and only he had the power to depose emperors and kings who interfered, or even questioned, his supremacy over the church. Furthermore, Gregory claimed that, as the highest power in Latin Christendom, he had the authority to release all Christian subjects from their bonds of fealty to any ruler he deposed, along with the power to excommunicate members from the church if they failed to enact or abide by his other reforms.

As extraordinary as all the above was, the fact that Gregory claimed the legal authority to enforce those subjects to his authority to obey him, regardless of the status, customs, or perceived rights of the offender, was revolutionary. So too was the appeal to and use of law by rulers and clergy to dispute his claims.[44] At the same time, Gregory's claims looked backward, in the sense that he was trying to restore the church to what it had been before it was corrupted by temporal bonds, and forward, in the sense that from henceforth the church would be a self-governing and a self-administering institution, with a clearly demarcated hierarchy of authority within it. What connected each was his emphasis on law and legal authority. With these claims, Gregory inverted the Byzantine principle of caesaropapism when he asserted that the pope, not the emperor, sat at the apex of the church and held ultimate authority over all its members regardless of their worldly status (political or otherwise).

After asserting the spiritual and legal supremacy of the papacy, Gregory addressed the problem of simony and marriage in two bold strokes. First, in 1074, he banned lay investiture—only the clergy could install clergy into office—and then, in 1078, he forbade all Christians from accepting sacraments from married priests as well as from those who were living in concubinage. The former made it abundantly clear that any clergy member who accepted an office, and thereby investiture, "from the hand of an emperor or king or of any lay person, male or female," would "lie under excommunication until fitting satisfaction shall have been rendered."[45] The latter required that all priests choose between "their responsibilities to their wives and children and their responsibilities to their parishioners."[46] Change, however, did not come easy. Riots broke out among those who opposed Gregory's boycott of the clergy,

44 See Berman, *Law and Revolution I*, 94–100; and Ascheri, *The Laws of Late Medieval Italy*, 73–75.

45 Gregory issued a decree in 1073 forbidding prelates to receive their churches from lay rulers, but the original was lost. The text quoted here is taken from a reenactment of the same prohibition in the 1078 ban in *Select Historical Documents of the Middle Ages*, 365.

46 Ibid.

missives were penned throughout Christendom questioning Gregory's authority within the church, and feudal lords challenged his legitimacy to exercise power within their territories by appealing to both law and arms. Yet, nothing dissuaded Gregory of his power, nor ended his quest for reform, not even a direct confrontation with some of the most powerful temporal rulers of the age including the Holy Roman Emperor.

Henry IV (1050–1106), who had come out of his minority in 1065, used every means at his disposal to consolidate power over territories subject to the Holy Roman Empire. This meant, effectively, that no matter how sympathetic he may have been to Gregory's reforms in theory, he was in no position to accept them in practice. In fact, acutely aware of his need to quell rival magnates, Henry exercised his regalian rights to invest both Italian and German bishops, as well as to bestow his loyal friends—and to buy off enemies—with high ranking and well-endowed church offices throughout his realm. Knowing, moreover, that a fair number of his bishops opposed Gregory's consolidation of papal power, Henry did not dare to enforce the pope's will or mandates on his subjects. The stakes were simply too high for him to do so. Rather than forfeit or rescind his rights and the monies the church generated for him, or to alienate his nobles or clergy, Henry opted to ignore papal decrees and mandates. Not surprisingly, a showdown between empires—sacred and secular—ensued.

Pope and emperor came into direct conflict over Milan in 1075. As the strategic key to *Regnum Italicum*, Henry made no qualms about installing the Milanese priest Tedald (d. 1085) as Archbishop, thereby directly challenging Gregory's assertion that the pope, and the pope alone, could invest bishops. This affront came after Henry had also declined to compel German bishops and high-ranking clergy to attend Gregory's synod in Rome. By installing Tedald, who also happened to be his personal chaplain, Henry added insult to injury, pushing Gregory to respond directly. By December of 1075, Gregory provided a full account of his powers when he scolded Henry for his actions—and lack thereof—by reminding him that, if he continued to act "contrary to the canonical and apostolic decrees in those things which the religion of the church enjoins as the chief ones," he would have no choice but to excommunicate him. Henry's response to Gregory's assertion that he and the imperial bishops of Rome were subordinate to the pope was simple, if short-sighted. In a letter of January 1076, Henry deposed "Hildebrand, at present not pope but false monk," ordering him to "descend and relinquish the apostolic chair which thou hast usurped" and "to be damned throughout the ages"[47]

47 Henry IV, Letter to Gregory VII, Jan 24, 1076, in *Select Historical Documents of the Middle Ages*, 372–3.

In return, after defending his legal authority and supremacy to Henry's subjects—lay and clerical—in a series of letters and pronouncements, Gregory excommunicated Henry (for the first time) in the spring of 1076. In so doing, the Pope also released all the emperor's subjects from their vassal ties to him, including those who had opposed Henry's election in the first place. Henry was then faced with a choice: either he gained absolution from the pope within one calendar year, or he would be deposed as emperor. His enemies within Germany, galvanized by the possibility of his deposition, set to work preparing for a new imperial election. Political rivalries soon gave way to armed conflict in some regions, pitting Henry's armies against those of his own sons. By 1077 it was clear to Henry that his only chance of remaining Emperor and restoring peace was to seek absolution from Gregory at Canossa. Skeptical of Henry's volte-face, Gregory delayed granting him absolution until he was convinced of his contrition.

The conflict between Gregory and Henry did not end there, nor did Henry's troubles in the empire or Gregory's in the church. In fact, three years later Gregory, after declaring support for Henry's rivals, excommunicated Henry a second time. This time, Henry set out to remove Gregory by arms, rather than beg for his forgiveness. By 1081, Henry installed Guibert of Ravenna (1029–1100) as Pope, though it was not until Palm Sunday 1084 that Henry was able to enthrone Clement III in Rome. Within weeks of the ceremony, Henry and his armies were beat back from Rome at the hands of Gregory's Norman ally, Robert Guiscard (1015–1085). Although Rome was liberated from Henry's forces by Robert's army, Gregory never returned. Under the protection of the Normans, the displaced pope was taken to Salerno, where he died in 1085.

Despite all of Gregory's assertions about the legal and spiritual supremacy of the pope over all Christians and his efforts to bring about reform to the church, he fell at the hands of the very authority he was trying to curtail and, eventually, abolish. Yet, Gregory's failures fueled a political revolution, Berman argued, that gave birth to the Western legal tradition itself. In fact, the struggle for authority that he and other church reformers were engaged in not only prompted legions of scholars—lay and clerical—educated in monastery and cathedral schools, as well as *litterati*, to scour libraries and archives to support competing claims for supremacy, but also gave rise to a new kind of legal reasoning and thinking that went beyond textual exegesis.

Those who agreed with Gregory's claims, as well as those who opposed them, set out to find legal and historical evidence to support their positions. Unable to find precisely what they were looking for, scholars developed methods to interpret and systematically arrange ideas ensconced in customary legal traditions, especially compilations commissioned by rulers when they converted to Christianity, vulgar Roman law, and canon law, as well as in official donations, decrees, testaments, and/or letters of sacred and secular rulers, such as the fabled Donation of Constantine. Put differently, in the absence of charters or constitutions that clearly marked the boundaries between church and empire, scholars, notaries, and eventually lawyers created them from fragments. They then argued that such fragments served as evidence that the subordination—or independence, as the case may be—of temporal and spiritual authorities had existed since antiquity. As the conflict between popes and emperors (as well as the popes and kings) intensified, so did the interest in and demand for experts to find and interpret legal sources to their advantage.

The search for canon law documents, and the interpretation of those documents once found, enabled specialists—secular and sacred—to justify the new with reference to the old. This was to argue, essentially, that what appeared to be novel regarding the organization or governance structure of the church was, in fact, traditional; that the aims of reformers were to restore what was lost, rather than to create something new. The search for precedents in customary and local laws led to a revival of interest in Roman law. Once found, excerpts from the *Code*, the *Institutes*, and other fragments preserved since antiquity could be marshaled to support the emperor and other temporal rulers who, in response to changes in the church, were determined to reassert their regalian rights, rooted in historical custom, over their subjects (including the clergy) who lived within their territorial and dynastic domains.

This search for textual evidence to support political and spiritual claims were not, of course, limited to legal texts, yet they turned up one of the most consequential texts within European legal history, namely the Roman *Digest*.[48] This text, once found, served as the catalyst for the founding of universities in northern Italy. Indeed, "five hundred years after its compilation," as Peter Stein put it, "Justinian's *Digest* came to be used in Western Europe as a source of rules and arguments."[49] Initially of interest to only a handful of scholars, notaries, and advocates, the *Digest* became the centerpiece of legal education by the end of the eleventh century. The University of Bologna was the first—and most important for our purposes—university wherein the formal study of Justinian's *corpus* was organized. Although the university proper was not

48 Gratian's *Decretum* and other compilations of canon law were also significant, yet the emphasis here is on the Roman *Digest* precisely because Budé set out to restore it to its original (or so he claimed) in his 1508 *Annotationes*.

49 Stein, *Roman Law in European History*, 43.

officially founded until 1088, students began to flock to the city of Bologna to hear lectures on the *Code* (absent the *Tres libri*), *Institutes*, and *Digest* as early as the 1070s.

Driven by contemporary concerns (as much as by antiquarian interests) the original texts of the Latin *Digest* were recovered by medieval scholars in three parts over the late-eleventh and early-twelfth centuries. The *Vetus* included Books 1 through 24.2, the *Infortiatum* Books 24.3 through 38, and the *Novum* Books 39 through 50. The name of each section, Stein suggests, likely indicated the order in which the three parts were discovered: first the old, then the new, and finally, the middle.[50] Although all modern editions of the full *Digest,* viz., all three parts bound together in one codex, extend from a twelfth-century copy, fragments of the *Digest* had been scattered throughout libraries and archives since it first arrived in the Italian peninsula with Justinian's invading armies in 533.

Nevertheless, the sheer bulk and cumbersome form of the *Digest*, whether the *Vetus*, *Novum*, or *Infortiatum*, made it as difficult for scholars (both within the bounds of Byzantium and beyond them) to read and understand. Even though the language of the Latin *Digest* was more immediately accessible to scholars in medieval Europe, some of the terms and ideas within it were far enough removed from the world in which they lived that they had to draw on canon, customary, Lombard, and feudal law to try to make sense of its contents. Without access to the original sources of the *Digest*, or the Byzantine legal tradition more generally, the task of understanding how specific passages or excerpts worked together in a book or title, or how the text held together as a whole, was challenging to even the most talented scholars of the age, no matter how great—or urgent—their interest in law. In fact, the study of the *Digest* was an intimidating task even for those who had already acquired an understanding of, or at least benefited from exposure to, the *Institutes* and *Code*, while studying the liberal arts (which, on account of its emphasis on grammar and rhetoric, exposed students to ancient ideas) at monastery and cathedrals schools, through independent study with itinerant scholars and private tutors, or through apprenticeships to become notaries and scribes.

By the last decades of the eleventh century Justinian's *Digest*, and with it the *Institutes*, had garnered enough interest from scholars that the 1080 Italian manuscript, known as *Collecto Britannica* (because it is held at the British Library) included ninety-three extracts from the *Digest*—ninety of which came from the *Vetus*. This collection, moreover, "became the source of all canonist

50 Ibid.

collections made north of the Alps."[51] In addition to such collections, we also know that by the mid-1080s, Pepo (n.d.) was familiar enough with fragments of the *Digest* to make reference to them within his lectures on Justinian's *Code* (the first seven books) and the *Institutes* to audiences gathered in Bologna.[52] Integrating the *Digest* in lectures in this way, he brought it to the attention of the next generation of lawyers and scholars, including his most famous student, Irnerius (1050–1125), whose teaching ultimately led to the official founding—by students from across Latin Europe who gathered there—of the University of Bologna in 1088, and with it the first law school in Latin Christendom dedicated to the study of civil (Roman) law. Where precisely these fragments of the *Digest* collected in the 1080 manuscript, or those cross-referenced by Pepo, originated is unclear. We do know, however, that texts of Roman law could be found within the Benedictine monastery of Monte Cassino. We also know that by 1090s, the French canonist Ivo of Chartres (1040–1115) was drawing on archives in Rome for his own collection of Roman and canon laws, which included excerpts from the *Vetus*.[53]

As for the twelfth-century codex, known since the fifteenth century as the *Littera Florentina*, it originated in Amalfi under the governance of the Exarch of Ravenna (584–751) before it was passed on to Pisa in the twelfth century. The manuscript was divided into two, rather than three parts; the standard division that continues to be used today followed the division within the *Littera Florentina*.[54] This codex remained in Pisa until victorious armies moved it to Florence in 1406, where it remains in the Laurentian library to this day. The fact that the manuscript was accorded such respect and importance, making it a war prize, speaks to its importance as a link to antiquity for rulers, as well as for scholars, by the turn of the fifteenth century. It also speaks to the increasing importance of the study of law, and regard for Roman law, in the *Regnum Italicum*. The codex also provides insight into how unprepared most scholars were to treat the manuscript in its original, or 'as is'. For example, the codex included Greek passages of the *Digest*, which were "neglected by the glossators because, as with other learned men of the time, they knew no Greek."[55] As such, the text that served as the centerpiece and reference point for scholars in the universities, viz., the *littera Bononiensis* or vulgate version of the *Digest*, not

---

51 Ibid, 44.

52 Ascheri, *The Laws of Late Medieval Italy*, 52–3; Berman, *Law and Revolution I*, 123–6; and Stein, *Roman Law in European History*, 46.

53 Stein, *Roman Law in European History*, 44.

54 Ascheri, *The Laws of Late Medieval Italy*, 24.

55 Ibid, 25.

only omitted the Greek but also followed the tripartite division of the *Vetus*, *Infortiatum*, and *Novum*.[56]

Why did fragments of the *Digest*—and eventually the *Digest* as a whole—garner so much interest from scholars within Latin Christendom that it effectively led to the founding of universities in post-Roman Italy, and with it the so-called Western legal tradition? In other words, why didn't other fragments from—or complete editions of—Justinian's *corpus* have the same impact on scholars (secular and sacred) throughout Latin Europe before the late-eleventh century? Beyond the context of notarial formularies, the Investiture controversy, and the practical need for law in growing cities, duchies, and kingdoms across the Italian Peninsula (all of which fueled and expanded interests in advanced education), the rediscovery, and then recovery, of fragments and codex was monumental, according to F.W. Maitland, precisely because

> The *Digest* was the *only* book in which medieval students could obtain a knowledge of Roman law *at its best*. The *Institutes* are a slight textbook. The *Code* is made up of detached ordinance. The *Novels* are not merely detached ordinals but are penned in a pompous, verbose style, likely to do as much harm as good ... but for the *Digest* Roman law could never have reconquered the world ... Men would never have become enthusiastic students of other books ... the man who first teaches the *Digest* is the man who first teaches what the modern world has meant by Roman law ... it was only in the *Digest* that men could get any notion of a keen and exact legal argument, precise definitions, etc.[57]

It was also the *Digest* that appealed to the collective memory and even historical imagination of scholars and students who, despite approaching questions of law and justice by asking different questions and in vastly different circumstances and contexts, nevertheless utilized a common language (Latin) and drew from long-established principles, ideas, and tropes rooted in Classical moral philosophy and Christian theology. Thus, they could explore and interpret a text, even though it was alien to the world in which they lived, for use in augmenting debates about the origins and limits of spiritual and secular authorities and as a model for systematizing, organizing, and reducing customary and canon legal traditions which had, by the eleventh century, become increasingly unwieldy.

---

56 Ibid.

57 Quoted from Stein, *Roman Law in European History*, 44.

Had the copies of the *Digest* preserved within European libraries and archives been written in Greek with Latin fragments, rather than in Latin with some Greek notes, the text would have been far less accessible to the educated elite, and thus may have remained buried rather than expounded in universities, appealed to by rulers, or utilized by lawyers and jurists across Western Christendom. Although Greek was not entirely lost to scholars, the majority of those who benefited from formal and informal instruction by tutors or in monastic and cathedrals schools did so to become literate in Latin letters. Studying the official language of the church and the *lingua franca* of diplomacy within Europe, equipped students with the skills they needed to secure positions within both church and state. Beyond its practical and instrumental aspects, the pursuit of Latin literacy also provided access to the spiritual, intellectual, and cultural inheritance of antiquity.

Not surprisingly, the first generation of scholars who studied and taught the *Digest* approached it as if it was a direct link to the society and culture they had already encountered through their previous studies, rather than as an artifact of sixth-century Byzantium. Indeed, these early scholars took the *Digest* as evidence that "an earlier civilization, the Roman Empire, had survived until their time, in the West as well as in the East," and, in the process of doing so, they assumed that it "had a universal and permanent quality."[58] They took Justinian's law, according to Berman, "as truth—the way they took the Bible as truth and the works of Plato and (later) Aristotle as truth."[59] To access, understand, and teach the 'truth' embodied in the *Digest* "as the true law, the ideal law, and the embodiment of reason," required the mastery and application of the very methods developed, refined, and utilized by scholars, who were educated at an expanding number of monastery and cathedral schools prior to the rediscovery of the *Digest*. Once found, the ability to fold this new body of law into existing legal traditions, and to purge existing traditions of contradictions with this new law, became an increasingly sought-after skill that required an education that was more advanced, beyond that provided in the schools, by apprenticeships, or by private tutors. By the turn of the twelfth century, that need was met by universities, wherein one could pursue a Doctorate in civil and/or canon law after completing their Masters in the liberal arts.

58 Berman, *Law and Revolution I*, 122.

59 Ibid.

4 *Modus docendi*: The Methods of the Schoolmen and the Advent of the *Studia humanitatis*

Before the expansion of education at the turn of the twelfth century, there were three main avenues of learning within post-Roman Europe: to learn from the clergy, to hire a private tutor, or to learn to read and write as part of a trade or apprenticeship.[60] The latter was the most likely route to literacy for merchants, notaries, scribes, and others who needed to read and create documents and letters in Latin as well as in their vernacular. Children of nobles and other wealthy elites were more likely to be educated by the *literati*, viz., itinerant scholars who found a stable living by tutoring a full spectrum of subjects, including Latin letters. The third, and perhaps most common, path to literacy in Latin and one's vernacular was to attend monastery schools scattered throughout the European countryside or cathedral schools in towns and cities.

The curriculum in monastery and cathedral schools focused on the seven liberal arts. The *trivium* included introductory, and advanced instruction in grammar, rhetoric, and logic, whereas the *quadrivium* was often limited to basic knowledge of music, astronomy, arithmetic, and geometry. The standard text used to teach grammar was the *Ars grammatica* (*Art of Grammar*), written by the fourth-century Roman grammarian Aelius Donatus (d. 380). The

60 The general narrative in this section is informed by Ascheri, *The Laws of Late Medieval Italy*; Baldwin, *The Scholastic Culture of the Middle Ages*; Berman, *Law and Revolution I*; Bellomo, *The Common Legal Past of Europe*; Brundage, *The Medieval Origins of the Legal Profession*; Robert Black, "Italian Renaissance Education: Changing Perspectives and Continuing Controversies," *Journal of the History of Ideas* 52, no. 2 (1991): 315–34; Myron Piper Gilmore, *Argument from Roman Law in Political Thought, 1200–1600* (Cambridge, MA: Harvard University Press, 1941); Paul F. Grendler, *The Universities of the Italian Renaissance* (Baltimore, MD: Johns Hopkins University Press, 2002); Paul F. Grendler, *Schooling in Renaissance Italy: Literacy and Learning, 1300–1600* (Baltimore, MD: Johns Hopkins University Press, 1989); Charles Homer Haskins, *The Rise of Universities* (Ithaca, NY: Cornell University Press, 1957); Kristeller, *Renaissance Thought and Its Sources*; Nauert, *Humanism and the Culture of Renaissance Europe*; Peter Stein, "Legal Humanism in Legal Science," *Tijdschrift Voor Rechtsgeschiedenis /Legal History Review* 53, nos. 3–4 (1986): 297–306; Stein, *Roman Law in European History*; Witt, *The Two Latin Cultures*; Francesco Maiolo, *Medieval Sovereignty: Marsilius of Padua and Bartolus of Saxoferrato* (Delft: Eburon Academic Publishers, 2007); Ian MacLean, *Interpretation and Meaning in the Renaissance: The Case of Law* (Cambridge: Cambridge University Press, 1992); James Q. Whitman, "The Lawyers Discover the Fall of Rome," *Law and History Review* 9, no. 2 (1991): 191–220; Thomas Kuehn, "The Renaissance Consilium as Justice," *Renaissance Quarterly* 59, no. 4 (2006): 1058–88. Moreover, this section—and this book as a whole—is indebted to the work of Donald R. Kelley who, along with Guido Kisch and Steven Rowan, has excavated the foundations of legal humanism over a lifetime of research. See Bibliography of this volume.

first half, the *Ars minor*, introduced students to basic parts of speech through a question-and-answer method, whereas the second part, the *Ars major*, focused on the uses of speech including sarcasm, metaphors, and allegory as well as rhetoric devices, such as zeugma and anaphora. Rhetoric was taught, for the most part, by drawing on Priscian's (n.d.) *Institutiones grammaticae* (*Institutes of Grammar*). This multi-volume work, created while he was teaching at Constantinople at the turn of the sixth century, stands as a compilation of passages taken from a variety of authors used to illustrate a variety of rhetorical devices. In addition to serving as examples, these passages also preserved and passed on fragments of the history, philosophy, and culture of antiquity.

Equipped with at least a working knowledge of Latin and exposed to a range of literary forms and styles, students predominantly studied the third subject of the *trivium*, viz., logic, as well as the *quadrivium* through the texts of Boethius (477–524), a sixth-century Roman senator, consul, and philosopher. His *De consolatione philosophiae* (*The Consolation of Philosophy*), written in 523 while he was imprisoned waiting to be tried for treason against Theodoric the Great (454–526), King of the Ostrogoths, served as a significant conduit for the transmission of the Classical Greek tradition preserved and passed down in Latin to students and scholars within medieval Europe. In addition to his *Consolation*, Boethius' textbook on arithmetic and geometry as well as his translations of and commentaries on Aristotle's logic provided students with tangible links to classical antiquity. The liberal arts, as taught in schools and by tutors, effectively created a common core of knowledge, or at least reference, among those who had some kind of formal education that went beyond acquiring the practical skills of reading and writing documents in Latin and the vernacular through apprenticeships.

The principal function of formal instruction in Latin letters and grammar in the schools was to prepare students for quasi-professional and specialist tasks, wherein literacy in Latin would be essential. Some who, after completing their education in the schools, wished to continue their studies in Latin letters might seek additional instruction, often in tandem with others, from scholars, viz., *literati*, who specialized in classical studies. Clusters of students in cities and large towns tended to combine their resources to draw scholars to them, whereas individuals in the countryside or small towns tended to migrate to join existing clusters of students in cities. Still others pursued their interest while they took up positions in sacred (church) and secular (state) administration, taking advantage of libraries and archives, including those at Rome, to advance their knowledge.

Whether gathered in groups or working independently, the increased interest in, availability of, and quest for knowledge among scholars throughout

Europe expanded dramatically in the last decades of the eleventh century and over the course of the twelfth. In addition to sources that turned-up as a consequence of searching for legal precedents to either support or attack claims of papal supremacy and the independence of the church from temporal authority and influence, new texts and methods of instruction were transmitted to Europe as contact increased with Jewish, Muslim, and Christian scholars from Islamic Spain and Byzantium. In each case, texts that were thought to be lost were unexpectedly 'found', and texts that were previously unknown were 'discovered'. The most consequential for the development of the *scholastica methodus*, or the method of the schoolmen, was the new logic of Aristotle, viz., texts that went beyond Boethius' translations and commentaries.

By the end of the twelfth century, nearly all monastery and cathedral schools had tweaked and expanded existing methods of teaching, interpretation, and exegesis, viz., their *modus docendi,* to accommodate and apply the influx of knowledge that had begun in the late-eleventh century. One feature of these methods was the application of syllogism, whereby the validity of an argument depended on the logical relationship, or not, between the claims and the conclusion (If A requires B and B requires C, then A requires C). A second feature was the use of deductive reasoning, whereby a conclusion could be reached by applying general rules in a reductive manner (If all cats are not dogs and a beagle is a dog, then a beagle is not a cat, *and* no cats are beagles). After Aristotle's *Posterior Analytics* was translated in the mid-twelfth century, the use of inductive reasoning, whereby an argument moved from first principles to general conclusions, was folded into the scholastic method (dog A barks, dog B barks, dog C barks, therefore all dogs bark). Unlike syllogistic and deductive reasoning, inductive reasoning led to probable conclusions, based on evidence, rather than to certain truths or valid arguments. As such, it was a method of reasoning and arguments that was as well-suited for law as it was for theology. By the thirteenth century, as more students became proficient in these methods and more of his works were understood, the use of Aristotle's syllogistic methods of argument and analysis, combined with dialectics, viz., the science of deductive and inductive reasoning from plausible premises, increasingly dominated both the *trivium* and *quadrivium*.

There were, of course, monastery and cathedral schools where the scope and manner of teaching and reading these new sources was neither determined nor limited by the new logic. At Chartres, for example, the influx of so many new texts, interpretations, and types of knowledge generated a renewed interest in ancient grammar, rhetoric, moral philosophy, and history. Exposure to new ideas also generated a renewed interest in Stoicism, Epicureanism, Skepticism, and Neoplatonism; ideas that not only questioned aspects of Aristotelian logic but also the universal applicability of it to all forms of knowledge. The *modus docendi* that began to develop at schools like Chartres—adapted and extended by *literati* and scholars in the service of the church, schools, and nobles across Europe—corresponded with the methods of a later movement, viz., the *studia humanitatis*, that began to emerge in the *Regnum Italicum* in the early-fourteenth century.

The sources associated with the *studia humanitatis*, viz., the study of grammar, rhetoric, poetry, moral philosophy, philology, and history, and the comparative and critical methods used to interpret them, were the same kinds of methods that the so-called fathers of legal humanism—Budé, Zasius, and Alciati—brought to bear on the study, interpretation, and teaching of the *Digest*, and indeed the *corpus iuris civilis*, in the early-sixteenth century. Hence, it is worth asking why methods that began to emerge at schools like Chartres as early as the turn of the twelfth century, which were specifically developed to understand and interpret a full range of sources that were newly discovered and recovered, were not readily applied to the formal study and interpretation of Justinian *corpus* within law faculties at universities—one of the most consequential new sources that had been recovered from antiquity—until the early-sixteenth century. The answer boils down to two reasons: 1) the ubiquity of scholastic methods within universities; and 2) the needs of notaries, scribes, and advocates, when the students began to gather in clusters to study the *Digest*.

When the schoolmen, who studied at schools that emphasized logic even in the study of grammar and rhetoric, went to university they took their methods with them, whereas those who completed their studies at schools (and with tutors) that emphasized grammar and rhetoric did not. That is not to say that arts and grammar had no place at the university (for example, a Master of Arts was required before advancing to higher faculties like law), or that scholars who excelled in classical studies and Latin letters did not go to the university, or even that universities had no place for teachers of grammar and rhetoric, but that the *modus docendi* that dominated the universities, especially the higher faculties, were the methods of those who founded them. For example, Aristotle's texts not only permeated the liberal arts at the Masters' level, which included a focus on logic, philosophy, and the natural sciences, but they also dominated the four higher faculties of Theology, Philosophy, Law (Roman and Canon), and Medicine. Moreover, as universities grew—by drawing students from across Europe to acquire expertise and credentials from the experts located there—so too did the emphasis on logic (syllogistic, deductive, and inductive) in pre-university education. While grammar and rhetoric still mattered at schools, universities, and in the world at large, the capacity to argue, debate, and write like a scholastic increasingly took precedence over the ability to think, deliberate, or compose like an orator, political leader, or poet. Not surprisingly, the scholarship that universities produced, suffused with scholastic methods of interpretation and exegesis, became increasingly standardized for and by scholars at large across Europe.

Among the materials produced within the universities were the *commentaria*, or classroom lectures on specific texts, the *questio* and *disputatio*, or university disputations related to either a specific text or problem within a text, and the *summa* and *concordia*, which were essentially textbooks generated by the combination of *commentaria* and *questio*. Professors also produced the *glossae*, which consisted of specific definitions as well as logical explanations and arrangements. Originally devoted to texts such as the Bible or the *Digest*, the *glossae* eventually led to the production of *commentaria* which were, in turn, further enriched by the addition of further layers of explanation and logical reasoning. The latter would provide a nested text, wherein only a few lines of the original text being glossed might appear on a single page. These few lines (and in some cases only a few words) would then be surrounded or followed by yet another layer of text—explanations, questions, and distinctions—to make full use of the margins. The more numerous the notes, annotations, and references dedicated to a particular passage in a text, the more likely it was to generate even more attention and commentary. Among the most distinguishing characteristics of the knowledge produced by universities and transmitted through these nested texts was the use of logic not only to reconcile contradictions but also to fill in omissions in a body of knowledge by means of syllogistic, deductive, and inductive reasoning.

Drawing on logical devices, scholars created an extensive latticework of definitions, distinctions, and apologetics one could use to explain the relation between reason and faith, provide a proof of the existence of God, demonstrate the relationship between theology and metaphysics, and, in the case of legal studies, account for variations between distinct kinds of laws (e.g., eternal, divine, natural, civil). One could also, by means of these scholastic methods, account for variations within a specific body of law (e.g., canon, Roman, customary), and even fashion new laws and interpretation—linked to present conditions—not treated in Roman law. For example, armed with expert knowledge of the principles of Roman law governing property and the ability to use deductive and inductive logic, one could, as in the case of feudal law, work out an entire body of procedures and regulations and treat them as if they were always 'in' the Roman law, which would provide the new laws with historical and moral authority.[61] Such laws, in other words, could be treated as if they were recovered after being lost, or restored after being corrupted, once Justinian's *corpus* became the cornerstone of legal education, and thereby civic jurisprudence.

The problem, for many, was that as the layers of analysis became more extensive and the logical assumptions expanded as a result of university study, it was difficult to determine what was in the original text (*ad fontes*) under examination, as opposed to what the scholastic methods enabled scholars to infer and deduce from them. It was also difficult to determine where the authority of the text ended and the authorities of the interpreters of the text began. Moreover, as texts became increasingly complicated, so too did the methods used to clarify and interpret them. In some instances, interpretations were so convoluted and burdened by exegesis that even scholastic Doctors, viz., those who earned the highest degree at university, lamented how cumbersome they were. Yet, the proclivity to use the same methods to clarify points or streamline arguments in confusing and overburdened texts tended to create more distinctions, definitions, and annotations, rather than to reduce them. The universities, in other words, promoted the creation of texts, which were inaccessible to nearly everyone outside of them.

As a result of the production of such unwieldy scholarship, permeated with confusion and specialized nomenclature, the term *scholastica*, viz., scholastic, came to take on a more negative meaning. Indeed, it was used as a pejorative by those who were critical of the authority and position that the scholastic Doctors had claimed for themselves in the universities as well as of their influence beyond them. Regardless, the term 'scholastic' continued to refer—even as the method itself was undergoing change—to texts produced by those trained in the universities, as nearly everyone associated with them were producing texts (e.g., lectures, notes, disputations, commentaries), wherein logic was the primary method used to establish clarity and definitive understanding.

The application of the scholastic methods to the texts of Roman law had two related but distinguishable aspects: the application of logic to reconcile contradictions and fill in gaps within Roman law and the development of the *glossae*. Although the combination of these methods was also significant in

---

61 See Donald R. Kelley, "De Origine Fuedorum: The Beginnings of a Historical Problem," *Speculum* 39, no. 2 (April 1964): 207–28; Kelley, "The Rise of Legal History in the Renaissance," *History and Theory* 9, no. 2 (1970): 186–90; Skinner, *Foundations of Modern Political Thought. Volume 1*; and Kathleen Davies, *Periodization and Sovereignty: How Ideas of Feudalism and Secularization Govern the Politics of Time* (Philadelphia: University of Pennsylvania Press, 2017).

regard to theology, in terms of Roman law the combination of logic and *glossae* created a new kind of text, by which commentators were able to establish their own authority as experts, equal to the compilers of the *Digest*, even though they lacked the original sources from which it had been created, or an understanding of the Byzantine tradition the compilers thought they were preserving. It was especially the combination of logic and the *glossae* and the continued authority of the commentaries that came to distinguish the application of the scholastic method to law in Italian universities as the *mos italicus*, viz., the Italian manner.[62]

By 1087, when Irnerius (following Pepo) was teaching Roman law at Bologna, an important aspect of his teaching method was the gloss. Before one could teach Roman law to those who wished to apply it, or in accordance with scholastic methods, one had to define and explain the terms therein. After reading part of the *Digest* aloud, Irnerius would then go over the text line by line for the students, sometimes simply offering a definition for an unknown word and other times offering an interpretation of the law, with regard to contemporary cases, practices, and customs.[63] In addition to providing such glosses, scholars also made use of logical distinctions and dialectics to reconcile disparities, contradictions, and gaps within a specific text, legal or otherwise. This was also the method used in the 1140 *Decretum* (*Concordia discordantium canonum*) attributed to a canon lawyer at Bologna named Gratian (d.~1159).[64] In fact, it was the standard method of teaching and interpreting both Roman and canon law until the fourteenth century. By the mid-fourteenth century, however, commentaries written by distinguished professors of civil law became the centerpiece of study and, as a result, the glosses and the original *corpus* increasingly served as points of reference to understand the commentaries rather than the focal point of lectures and disputations.

62 For a comprehensive discussion of the Italian and French manner see Donald R. Kelley, "Civil Science in the Renaissance: Jurisprudence Italian Style," *The Historical Journal* 22, no. 4 (1979): 777–94; Donald R. Kelley, "Civil Science in the Renaissance: Jurisprudence in the French Manner," *History of European Ideas* 2, no. 4 (1981): 261–276; and Kelley, *Foundations of Modern Scholarship*. See also Part 3 of this volume, which focuses on the "father" of the *mos gallicus*, Andrea Alciati.

63 Pepo and others did this despite the provision within Justinian's dedication of the *Digest* that expressively forbade it. See Donald R. Kelley, "*Jurisconsultus Perfectus*: The Lawyer as Renaissance Man," *Journal of the Warburg and Courtauld Institutes* 51 (1988): 84–102; Kenneth Pennington, *The Prince and the Law 1200–1600: Sovereignty and Rights in the Western Legal Tradition* (Berkeley: University of California Press, 1993); and MacLean, *Interpretation and Meaning in the Renaissance*, especially, 50–9.

64 See Winroth, *The Making of Gratian's Decretum*.

The use of distinctions to 'fill in' and harmonize Roman law by combining practical examples and logic methods was necessary for early scholars like Pepo and Irnerius precisely because, upon rediscovery and recovery, Justinian's *corpus* was considered an unchanging and universally applicable body of law, as if it were still very much in effect and never had a period of dormancy or decline. It was in this respect sacrosanct. However, to address contemporary issues in which there were no corresponding sections in the *Digest*, or which did not self-evidently follow from a stated principle in Roman law, as in the case of feudal law and Lombard law, jurists constructed solutions based on the *corpus* to meet present needs and circumstances through abstraction. Over time, the texts developed to do so included the *notabilia* or notable points which gave short summaries of a specific law, the *brocardica* or maxims that stated the principles that underlay the law and could be extracted from it, and the *consilia* or legal opinions that were written by the scholastic Doctors based on the *glossae*, *notabilia*, *brocardica*, and *distinction*, wherein subdivisions and intricacies of legal points and terms could be related to a more general term or principle—much as species is related to a genus—in order to make a case for a specific outcome of a dispute as just or to argue on behalf of the interests of one claimant against another.

Precisely because the *Digest*, like the Bible, was considered by some to be normative, complete, and static, it could not be corrected; it could only be mediated by the interpretation of experts. As such, two contradictory true statements within the text could not be resolved with reference to or by a higher authority beyond the text. Cut off from the original sources that the *Digest* was compiled from, along with an understanding of it as a reduced and thereby incomplete text, Irnerius and those who followed him were limited to using logic, common sense, and experience to reconcile such contradictions. In the process, they became the authorities on the text as well as the source of the text's authority. As the study of Roman law developed and the numbers of jurists and experts expanded, conflicting truths made the study of law increasingly cumbersome, especially for those who were more interested in how they could use it to win a case or sway a judge.

Irnerius' methods of teaching drew scholars and practitioners from all over the peninsula and beyond to Bologna. These students essentially founded the university to ensure that the *Digest* would continue to be taught as Irnerius taught it: in a direct and practical manner. Already by the early decades of the twelfth century, however, the same methods that were changing the study of the arts and all the other higher faculties, including canon law at the university level, were also changing the study of civil law. For example, the number of glosses on the *Digest* and on the interpretations of those glosses exploded as quickly as their marginalia, prompting Azo (1150–1230), an Italian jurist and glossator at Bologna, to begin to synthesize and systematize "detailed case discussions of the previous generations of glossators" so that they could be used more easily by civil lawyers.[65] His collection or *summa* on the *Code* proved indispensable, so much so that it prompted the adage "who does not have Azo, should not go to court."[66] It was, however, his student Accursius (1182–1263) who produced the standard *Gloss* on Justinian's *corpus*, which became a staple in the curriculum of Roman law faculties in universities across Europe.[67]

By the mid-thirteenth century, commentaries, annotations, and glosses on Roman law—crafted by medieval jurists—increasingly became the centerpiece of study. As secondary sources eclipsed primary ones, the study of Ancient Roman law evolved into the study of the interpretations of it by scholastic Doctors teaching at universities within and beyond Italy. The standard gloss from 1250 onwards was that of Accursius (among his more famous students was Dante Alighieri (1265–1361)). After roughly 1330, the standard commentary was that of Bartolus de Saxoferrato (1313–1357), whose authority nearly rivaled the *Digest* in the universities and came to have legal authority in courts beyond them from the mid-fourteenth century. By the sixteenth century, the glosses, and commentaries on the *corpus* of Roman law, combined with the commentaries and glosses on canon law, including the *Decretum*, established the intellectual structure of the *ius commune*, viz., "the amalgam of Roman and canon law that long furnished the starting point for European legal education."[68]

Even though the Italian peninsula was teeming with opportunities for students to study the *corpus* of Roman law, most of the faculty that taught at Perugia, Padua, Pisa, Siena, and Naples, etc., either took their degrees at Bologna or studied under the direction of someone who had. Thus, no matter how far removed one might have been from the city itself, the law faculty continued to serve as the epicenter of scholastic jurisprudence well into the sixteenth century. It should be of no surprise then, that we can trace both the intellectual and methodological inheritance of Bartolus and, by extension, of

65 Stein, *Roman Law in European History*, 48.

66 Ibid.

67 Ascheri, *The Laws of Late Medieval Italy*, 197–201.

68 Richard H. Helmholz, "Christopher St. German and the Law of Custom," *The University of Chicago Law Review* 70, no. 1 (2003): 129–39; 131. For a succinct discussion of the *ius commune*, especially in relation to statute and customary law in Northern Italy see Aldo Mazzacane, "Law and Jurists in the Formation of the Modern State in Italy," *The Journal of Modern History* 67, Supplement: The Origins of the State in Italy, 1300–1600 (1995): S62–73.

his most famous student, Baldus de Ubaldis (1327–1400), as well as the rejection of scholastic methods and jurisprudence by humanist Francisco Petrarch (1304–1374) back to the university at Bologna. Nor should it be much of a surprise, Donald R. Kelley tells us, that "while the study of legal history, which had roots in antiquity and grew up largely in the confines of the legal profession, had another parent: it was equally, if somewhat illegitimately, the offspring of Renaissance humanism. Consequently, it bore the scars of a conflict between the champions of the liberal arts [like Petrarch] and the defenders of the scholastic method."[69]

Forced to begin his legal studies when he was twelve, Petrarch wasted no time quitting after his father (who had insisted he study law in the first place) died, nor did he waste an opportunity to lament the time spent at the university at Montpellier (1316–1320) and at Bologna (1320–1323). Lest one assume that his complaints were the result of his own shortcomings, Petrarch was quick to assert that it was the manner in which the ancient texts were studied that he resented, and not the law itself; indeed, Petrarch "placed the ancient jurisconsults among the founding fathers of the humanities."[70] He denounced scholastic jurists and lawyers precisely because they did not approach the *corpus* as a key to unlock and understand the Roman past, but rather to address and solve contemporary problems and, in the end, to acquire fees for doing so. Of course, not every lawyer or jurist that Petrarch encountered over seven years of study cared more for money than antiquity or justice. At Bologna, for example, Petrarch studied with Cino da Pistoia (1270–1336/37) who, like Petrarch, had started his studies in France before completing them in Northern Italy.[71] After earning his doctorate in 1314, Cino taught at Bologna, Siena, Florence, Naples, and Perugia. Among his most notable students at Perugia was Bartolus who also completed his degree at Bologna after spending several years with Cino. Upon earning his doctorate in 1334, Bartolus took up his first teaching position at Pisa before moving back to Perugia, where among his most promising students was Baldus.

Notable here are not simply the connections—or genealogy—of humanist and scholastic methods that we can trace to a specific university, but also the links to a particular teacher, Cino, who was not only a jurist but also a poet and friend of Dante. As a poet, Cino was among those who wrote in the *dolce stil novo*; as a jurist he was among the few who cited poets and historians as well as

69 Kelley, "The Rise of Legal History in the Renaissance," 176.

70 Kelley, "Jurisconsultus Perfectus," 85.

71 Cino, in turn, had studied under the direction of Dinus de Rossonis (died c. 1298), who was among the first teachers of Roman law to earn a salary from the University.

jurists and orators, in his commentaries.[72] Thus he embodied a link between the sources and methods associated with the *studia humanitatis* and the scholastic study of Roman law in his teaching and interpretations. That is not to say that Cino anticipated humanist jurisprudence, nor that he was himself a legal humanist, but that there was a link (albeit modest) that already existed between the study of law and the *studia humanitatis* as early as the fourteenth century, well before Erasmus of Rotterdam (1466–1536) and others celebrated the novelty of Budé's, Zasius', and Alciati's methods. This link, however, was acrimoniously severed, in large part by the grammarians (*grammatici*) and not, despite humanist claims, by the *Accursians* (the glossators) or the *Bartolisti* (the commentators) by the turn of the sixteenth century. Indeed, as Kelley has brilliantly demonstrated repeatedly, the ground had already been cleared for Budé's scathing attack against scholastic jurisprudence by Dante, Petrarch, Lorenzo Valla (1407–1457) and Agnolo "Poliziano" Ambrogini (1454–1494), who had levied criticisms against the Italian manner of teaching both Roman and canon law, on account of what they deemed as barbarisms in language and accommodations of vulgar (non-Roman) law.

What incensed these early humanists to declaim against the scholastic Doctors so bitterly and frequently? Part of the problem was that Cino was not only committed to the old, but he was also open to the new. For example, he rejected the linguistic and interpretive errors that followed from the canonists attempts to bring church law up to date yet recognized that the ancient *corpus* of Roman law had to be accessible and adaptable to modern conditions. Or, as Kelley put it, Cino's teaching "In juridical and academic terms" invited his students to move "from the specificity of ancient experience, that is, the letter of the civil law, to a more general or equitable meaning which could serve and enhance modern society, in particular the Italian city states."[73] This, in turn, required "modernization through rationalization" and the development of new methods to transform the study of law into a legal science. Law, in other words, came to surpass letters in the teachings of Cino and his students.

Even though these new methods became the core of the *mos italicus*—the Italian manner of interpretation—from the thirteenth century onward, they can be traced back to innovations undertaken by jurists in France, at the University of Orleans, especially Jacques de Révigny (1230–1296). Révigny and

---

72 See Kelley, "Civil Science in the Renaissance: Jurisprudence Italian Style," 780; Bellomo, *The Common Legal Past of Europe*; and Roger T. Simonds, "The Teeth of the Law: Legal Interpretation in the Italian Renaissance," *Explorations in Renaissance Culture* 8 (January 1982): 97–106.

73 Kelley, "Civil Science in the Renaissance: Jurisprudence Italian Style," 781.

others combined Aristotle's four causes with dialectic methods of argumentation, which were originally developed and deployed within the arts faculties across Europe.[74] Adopting such a manner of teaching required Cino to lay out divisions within a law and to provide the facts of a case, engage in comparisons, address objections, and pose and answer questions. Such a systematic approach ultimately meant that facts combined with dialectic would necessarily trump opinion and preference. Although cumbersome, and even meandering, in the hands of those who followed him, the conclusions reached through the application of this method could appear logically sound and even unassailable. What is more, this manner of teaching was attractive because it was practical and pragmatic; everything one needed to know was contained within the examples, which could be cross-referenced with authorities that drew from bodies of knowledge that reached beyond the specific law or principle under examination. As such, over time the authority of the texts and the authorities on the text became equivalent.

Proficiency in Roman law required proficiency in these scholastic—indeed, Italian and French—methods and the nest of references that increasingly cluttered the texts (and littered their margins) that accompanied them. Employed by jurists like Bartolus and Baldus, such methods could be used to profound effect to settle concrete problems and explain complicated relationships, whereas in the hands of lesser minds they tended to be twisted and bent into a tangled mess. Hence, humanist vitriol against the heap of barbarisms, confusions, and vulgarities that permeated university-based jurisprudence tended to be focused, above all, on the glossators—those who came before Bartolus and Baldus—and those who followed them. Recognizing and respecting the interpretations of Bartolus and Baldus did not mean, however, that grammarians like Valla or Poliziano did not criticize their methods or their interpretations as historically inaccurate.

The fact that neither Cino nor Bartolus, nor Baldus, approached the *corpus* as a mere artifact from a distant past effectively enabled them to put it in direct comparison and conversation with fragments from other types and bodies of law, ranging the spectrum from the laws of the church (canon law) to the statutes and laws of the communes (Lombard laws). This in turn, enabled scholastic jurists to use the ancient texts of Roman law to provide gravitas to laws that were not only new but also distinctly un-Roman. The latter was, as James Q. Whitman suggests, what drove Petrarch and others to attack university-based

74 Ibid. The application of Aristotle's four causes was not limited to jurists; see Thomas Aquinas, *Summa theologica*, written between 1265 and 1273.

jurisprudence so vehemently. Precisely because the *mos italicus* was both practical and accommodating, it led to the barbarization of Roman law, whereas if Roman law had been left in the hands of humanist teachers and antiquarians, it could have been protected as a fixed shrine to a glorious past that had been lost due to the Lombard invasions. Instead of venerating Roman law as monument to antiquity, university-based jurists used it to address problems and controversies in their present time—in Northern Italy, these were steeped in conflicts of law, competing claims of *imperium*, and sometimes in bloody conflict.[75] Perhaps the great irony here is that some humanists criticized the scholastics for using the *corpus* beyond academic settings, rather than reserving it for historical study or grammatical exposition, despite the early link between humanism and law—a link that Roberto Weiss even went so far as to claim enabled the "Dawn of Humanism in Italy."[76]

By the sixteenth century, the authority of Bartolus, and Baldus, was so deeply entrenched in university education, and, as a result, in the *ius commune*, viz. interpretations and *consilia* that drew on canon, customary, feudal, vulgar, and Roman law, as well as local jurisprudence, that legal humanists lamented the degree to which Bartolus and Baldus were treated as if they were the source of law, rather than merely interpreters of it. Worse, even though the opinions of Bartolus and Baldus reflected the world they lived in and were shaped directly by political and legal conflicts that dominated the fourteenth century, their interpretations were so thoroughly entrenched within university-based jurisprudence, and so highly regarded and emulated, that they continued to define and shape the Roman law curriculum for centuries after their deaths.

The elevation of the commentaries by Bartolus' and Baldus' above the original texts of Roman law in the universities, and the steadfast devotion to their interpretations by those who earned their credentials by studying them, was especially problematic for humanists like Budé. This was not simply because some of their opinions were antiquated by the sixteenth century, but also because scholastic Doctors were ignoring new sources (many in Greek) that

75 The conflict between Lombard law (feudal and statute) and Roman law was especially relevant to cities across Northern Italy. For an excellent discussion of the implications of how Bartolus and others addressed and tried to resolve conflicts see Magnus Ryan, "Bartolus of Sassoferrato and Free Cities: The Alexander Prize Lecture" *Transactions of the Royal Historical Society* 10 (2000): 65–89; Skinner, *Foundations of Modern Political Thought. Volume 1*, Whitman, "The Lawyers Discover the Fall of Rome"; Constantin Fasolt, *The Limits of History* (Chicago: University of Chicago Press, 2004); and Pennington, *The Prince and the Law.*

76 Roberto Weiss, *The Dawn of Humanism in Italy: An Inaugural Lecture* (London: H. K. Lewis, 1947).

had emerged over the course of the fourteenth and fifteenth centuries, which revealed fundamental errors in previous interpretations of the *Digest* and the *corpus* more generally. Instead of drawing on new translations to expand their knowledge of Roman law as the Romans knew it, scholastic jurists remained locked into methods and interpretations that seemed to bend the law to their purposes. Even so, Budé levied his most damning assessments against Accursius because it was his *Gloss* that set the parameters for later commentaries and interpretations.[77]

Indeed, Budé suspected that those who followed in the footsteps of the Doctors like Accursius, Bartolus, and Baldus did so either because they lacked the critical capacity to do otherwise or, worse, they were camouflaging changes they were making to Roman and customary legal traditions to suit the desires of their patrons, by burying them in quotations and references to glosses and commentaries. Such concerns, voiced by Budé in his 1508 *Annotations,* were not limited to the misinterpretation of Roman legal vocabulary, or the logical sleights of hand employed by those who taught it at universities beyond the Alps. Indeed, Budé feared that if those who mastered the *mos italicus* were entrusted with reforming French laws, they might use their logical sleights of hand, inelegant Latin, and Italian commentaries to undermine ancient rights, customs, and liberties long held by the king and his subjects in France.

77 It is possible that Budé's fixation on the *Gloss* stemmed from the fact that he abandoned his study of law at university almost immediately after he took it up. Had he completed his studies, like his humanist peers, he might have realized that neither Bartolus nor Baldus held that Accursius' *Gloss* was flawless.

CHAPTER 2

Excavating, Restoring, and Redefining *Jus* at the Foundations of Humanist Jurisprudence

1 A Humanist, Not a Lawyer

As a legal humanist, Guillaume Budé was uncommon in that he did not have a legal degree, nor did he teach law in the universities.[1] However, he was influential in introducing the application of humanist philology to the study of law in France and played a substantial role in the founding of the Collège Royale (now the Collège de France). As Royal Secretary, Budé collected copies of rediscovered manuscripts from antiquity as well as new Greek-Latin translations of existing texts. While the creation of Renaissance libraries under the direction of humanist scholars was typical throughout the fifteenth and sixteenth centuries, the collection that Budé started was unique in that it formed the basis of the library at Fontainebleau, which later became the nucleus of the Bibliothèque Nationale in Paris. Budé was also among the first humanist

1 Although Budé studied some Roman civil law at the University of Orléans, he did not earn a university degree in law. In fact, Budé's time at Orléans was remarkable, as noted by scholarship as well as by his contemporaries, for how little time he spent studying Roman law. He hated it because of the scholastic method by which it was taught, and instead spent his time teaching himself classical Latin and Greek. For detailed biographical information on Budé see Domenico Maffei, "Les Débuts de l'activité de Budé, Alciat et Zase ainsi que quelques remarques sur Aymar Du Rivail," in *Pédagogues et Juristes: Congrès Du Centre d'études Supérieures de La Renaissance de Tours: été 1960*, ed. Pierre Mesnard (Paris: J. Vrin, 1963), 23–9; Domenico Maffei, *Gli inizi dell'umanesimo giuridico* (Milano: Giuffrè, 1956); Kelley, *Foundations of Modern Historical Scholarship*; Donald R. Kelley, "Civil Science in the Renaissance: The Problem of Interpretation," in *The Languages of Political Theory in Early-Modern Europe*, ed. Anthony Pagden (Cambridge: Cambridge University Press, 1987), 57–78; Donald R. Kelley, "Vera Philosophia: The Philosophical Significance of Renaissance Jurisprudence," *Journal of the History of Philosophy* 14, no. 3 (1976): 267–79; Donald R. Kelley, "Guillaume Budé and the First Historical School of Law," *The American Historical Review* 72, no. 3 (April 1967): 807–34; Guido Kisch, *Erasmus und die Jurisprudenz seiner Zeit: Studien zum Humanistischen Rechtsdenken* (Basel: Helbing & Lichtenhahn, 1960); Richard J. Schoeck, "Humanism and Jurisprudence," in *Renaissance Humanism: Foundations, Forms, and Legacy*, ed. Albert Rabil (Philadelphia: University of Pennsylvania Press, 1988), 310–26; and Hans Erich Troje, *Humanistische Jurisprudenz, Studien zur Europäischen Rechtswissenschaft unter dem Einfluss des Humanismus*. Internationale Bibliothek der Wissenschaften (Goldbach: Keip Verlag, 1993).

scholars to write extensive treatises and textbooks on the Greek language and to use his mastery of Greek letters and Ciceronian Latin to correct errors within existing Latin translations of ancient texts. Drawing on this expertise and on his own collection of manuscripts, Budé set out to systematically apply philological, comparative, and historical methods to the *corpus* of Roman law in the first decades of the sixteenth century. In so doing, Budé adapted some, not all, of the methods and techniques that had been originally introduced by Lorenzo Valla and Agnolo "Poliziano" Ambrogini to his own project of restoring the language of Roman law and, by extension, civil jurisprudence in France.[2] Although Budé followed the path that Valla and Poliziano had begun to cut through the labyrinth of scholastic mistranslations and misinterpretations, he did not follow directly in their footsteps.

Instead, Budé not only set out to restore Roman law without recourse to legal training, or even an expansive understanding of legal interpretation, but also chose to focus his attention on secular rather than spiritual authority. Indeed, Budé sought to cleanse traditional jurisprudence of what he considered to be anachronisms, misinterpretations, and mistranslations proliferated by scholastic glosses and commentaries—in other words, to restore the *corpus iuris civilis* as the Romans had known it. At the center of his methods was philology, that is, a focus on the structure and historical development of language as well as the grammatical relationships within and between languages over time.[3]

2 For information on Valla and his methods see Lisa Jardine, "Lorenzo Valla and the Intellectual Origins of Humanist Dialectic," *Journal of the History of Philosophy* 15, no. 2 (1977): 143–64; Lodi Nauta, *In Defense of Common Sense: Lorenzo Valla's Humanist Critique of Scholastic Philosophy* (Cambridge, MA: Harvard University Press, 2009). For information on Poliziano's methods and their reception see Anthony Grafton, *Defenders of the Text: The Traditions of Scholarship in an Age of Science, 1450–1800* (Cambridge, MA: Harvard University Press, 1991). For a broader discussion of the place of new humanist philological methods on the interpretation and restoration of texts see Jacob Burckhardt, *The Civilization of the Renaissance in Italy*, trans. S. G. C. Middlemore (2nd ed., 1878; repr. New York: The Modern Library, 1995); Skinner, *Foundations of Modern Political Thought. Volume 1*; Myron Piper Gilmore, *The World of Humanism, 1453–1517* (1952; repr., Westport, CT: Greenwood Press, 1983); Celenza, *The Lost Italian Renaissance*; Witt, *'In the Footsteps of the Ancients'*; Hankins, *Virtue Politics*; and Christopher S. Celenza, *The Italian Renaissance and the Origins of the Modern Humanities: An Intellectual History, 1400–1800* (Cambridge: Cambridge University Press, 2021).

3 Kelley, "Guillaume Budé and the First Historical School of Law," 814: "To Budé as to Erasmus, in short, philology was a real 'science' based upon the *studia humanitatis*. It was a combination of grammar according to the famous definition of Poliziano and rhetoric according to the notorious views of Valla. In other words, philology involved the historical (that is, the literal) interpretation of texts considering the so-called 'encyclopedia' of liberal arts; at the same time, it depended upon eloquence, which 'binds together this cycle of learning ... like a living body', and without which (Budé added in Valla's words) 'learning is blind, especially in civil law'. As a literary ideal, philology stood above history—a possession of all the ages (*dicendi facultas ars sit omnium temporum et locorum*). In the sixteenth century, however,

Concentrating specifically on the basic terms, idioms, and definitions within the *Digest*, Budé attempted to demonstrate the intention, sense, and meaning of words within the texts of Roman law according to their original context and to their original authors. Once established, he then set out to show the mistakes and misunderstandings by the Byzantine compilers of the *Digest*. Finally, and at issue here, he attempted to show how medieval jurists misunderstood and misapplied aspects of Roman law, and ultimately compounded the errors of the compilers in their own glosses and commentaries on the *Digest*. As such, Budé's work had a considerable influence on the development of the interpretation and the historicization of Roman law in the early-sixteenth century, and indeed provided a rich source of historical-comparative linguistic explanations for other legal humanists. It is for this reason that Budé was considered by Erasmus to be among 'le grand triumvirate' of humanist jurisprudence, along with Ulrich Zasius in Southern Germany and Andrea Alciati in Northern Italy.[4]

Budé's place in 'le grand triumvirate' was buttressed as much by his influence within France as by how he positioned himself within broader humanist circles across Europe. As a counselor to Louis XII (r.1498–1515) and to Francis I (r. 1515–1547), and as one of the most famous and influential humanists of his day, Budé was able to convey his understanding and interpretation of law and justice to a broad audience. In addition to having the king's ear in private, he was part of a vast network of humanists across Europe, which included Zasius and Alciati, as well as Erasmus, Thomas More (1478–1535), and Boniface Amerbach (1495–1562).[5] In his letters, Budé shared his excitement about the texts that Zasius and Alciati were composing on Roman law as well as their discoveries. However quick to either praise or criticize the works of his counterparts, Budé

it had become rather a technique for resurrecting the past (*philologia olim ornatrix … hodie instauratrix et interpolatrix*). For Budé, then, philology was both a 'cornucopia' of classical learning and a historical method."

4 For a discussion of Budé's fame as a legal humanist within and beyond France, in addition to the literature in note 1 above, see Louis Delaruelle, *Études sur l'humanisme français: Guillaume Budé, les origines, les débuts, les idées maîtresses* (Paris: H. Champion, 1907); David O. McNeil, *Guillaume Budé and Humanism in the Reign of Francis I* (Geneva: Droz, 1975); Michael Leonard Monheit, "Guillaume Budé, Andrea Alciato, Pierre de l' Estoile: Renaissance Interpreters of Roman Law," *Journal of the History of Ideas* 58, no. 1 (January 1997): 21–40; Jean Plattard, *Guillaume Budé (1468–1540) et les origines de l'humanisme français* (Paris: Les Belles Lettres, 1966); and Kelley, *Foundations of Modern Historical Scholarship*.

5 Guillaume Budé, *Epistolae Gullielmi Budéi, secretarii regii, posteriores* ([Paris]: Iodoco Badio, 1522); *Correspondance de Guillaume Budé: introduction et notes par Guy Lovoie avec la collaboration de Roland Galibois* (Sherbrooke: Centre d'études de la Renaissance Université de Sherbrooke, 1917); Marie Madeliene de la Garancleria, ed., *La correspondance d' Erasmus et de Guillaume Budé* (Paris: J. Vrin, 1967); and Loius Delaruelle, *Repertiore analytique et chronologique de la corespondance de Guillaume Budé* (Toulouse: E. Privat, 1907).

was not receptive to criticism of his own methods, style, and interpretations, especially if the point of critique was legal instead of philological.

Similarly, Budé was not open to a response from scholastic jurists. Their criticisms were unimportant to him because (he claimed) they lacked virtue insofar as their interests lay not in attaining wisdom, and therefore benefiting from correction, but rather in gaining profit and praise by their "snare of words."[6] For Budé, the proper study of law, Roman or otherwise, should have been undertaken as a means to understand justice and right, not to gain power or profit.[7] The only clear path to that end was to read and understand Greek and Roman sources in their original (*ad fontes*). While his emphasis on Roman sources was typical, this insistence on the importance of Greek letters to Roman law was not. He was far more adamant about the necessity of this than his legal humanist contemporaries and, as a result, he focused far more on the language of law—and misinterpretation of it—than on the practice of law in his attack on scholastic jurisprudence.

As a result of this emphasis on the meaning and significance of words, it is perhaps ironic that when it came to practical understandings of law and jurisprudence, Budé did not share the same language of those he attacked, nor of the legal humanist counterparts with whom he wished to identify. Although he wrote his treatises on Roman law in Latin, as a law school drop-out (like

6 Guillaume Budé, *Annotationes Gulielmi Budaei parisiensis secretarii regii in quatuor et viginti pandectarum libros ad Ioannem Deganaium cancellarium Franciae* ([Paris]: Ab Iodoco Badio Ascensio impressae, 1508), fo. V.

7 For nuanced discussions on the relation between rhetoric and wisdom see Jerrold E. Seigel, *Rhetoric and Philosophy in Renaissance Humanism: The Union of Eloquence and Wisdom, Petrarch to Valla* (Princeton, NJ: Princeton University Press, 1968); Eugene F. Rice, Jr., *The Renaissance Idea of Wisdom* (Cambridge, MA: Harvard University Press, 1958); Eugenio Garin, *Italian Humanism*, trans. Peter Munz (New York: Harper and Row, 1965); Witt, *"In the Footsteps of the Ancients"*; and Celenza, *The Italian Renaissance and the Origins of the Modern Humanities*. As for eloquence in particular, Hanna H. Gray's classic statements still hold: "The Renaissance humanists believed that education should equip a man to lead a good life, and that therefore the function of knowledge was not merely to demonstrate the truth of given precepts, but to impel people toward their acceptance and application. They believed also that men could be molded most effectively, and perhaps only, through the art of eloquence, which endowed the precept with life, immediacy, persuasive effect …" (500); and "True eloquence, according to the humanists, could only arise out of the harmonious union between wisdom and style, its aim was to guide men toward virtue and worthwhile goals …" (498). Hanna H. Gray, "Renaissance Humanism: The Pursuit of Eloquence," *Journal of the History of Ideas* 24, no. 4 (October 1963): 497–514. To explore the link between learning, eloquence, and civic action see Gouwens, "Perceiving the Past: Renaissance Humanism after the 'Cognitive Turn'"; James Hankins, *Renaissance Civic Humanism: Reappraisals and Reflections* (Cambridge: Cambridge University Press, 2003); and Hankins, *Virtue Politics*.

Petrarch) he lacked a shared understanding of legal principles that university-trained lawyers across Europe used as common points of reference in their legal interpretations and instruction. Equally important, Budé had an insufficient understanding of how legal principles had come to be applied over time on the ground, beyond the pages of the *Digest*, the *Gloss*, and various commentaries. As a result, he ultimately restored the language of Roman law, underpinned by a theory of universal jurisprudence, which had little connection to legal practice or to the ancient jurists that Byzantine compilers drew definitions and excerpts from in the first place. Notwithstanding this dissonance, Budé launched a systematic and unrelenting attack against professional and university-based jurisprudence with the publication of his *Annotationes* in 1508. It was this attack that helped lay the foundations for the broader project of reinterpreting the relation between justice, right, and law, and thereby the source and extent of legal and political authority, by early-sixteenth-century humanist jurists.

2 The 1508 *Annotationes*: Answering—and Amplifying—the Call for Change

Published in the context of calls for legal reform throughout much of Europe, the purpose of Budé's 1508 *Annotationes* was not to correct scholastic jurisprudence, so much as to eviscerate it. To that end, the text consists of a steady stream of attacks against medieval jurists, wherein Budé relentlessly denounced their interpretations of Roman law. Equally important, he set out to show that their misinterpretations followed directly from faulty methods; methods associated above all with the *mos italicus*, or the Italian manner of interpretation, which although originally developed and taught at the University of Bologna, dominated jurisprudence throughout the continent from the turn of the twelfth century onward.[8]

Paired with the corruption of legal terms and principles underpinning Roman law, Budé also adamantly rejected the legal formalism of those trained in these Italian (viz. scholastic) methods, especially as it applied to French customs, laws, and jurisprudence. Rather than merely focus on legal rules, use

8 For a comprehensive discussion of the Italian manner see Kelley, "Civil Science in the Renaissance: Jurisprudence Italian Style." For a concise discussion of what distinguishes the scholastic methods of argument and interpretation from humanist methods, especially within law faculties, see Berman, *Law and Revolution* 1; Paul Vinogradoff, *Roman Law in Medieval Europe* (Oxford: Clarendon Press, 1929); and Chapters 1 and 5 of this volume.

logic, or engage in semantic wordplay as the scholastic jurists had done, Budé argued that it was imperative for properly-trained lawyers to explore the universal principles that underlie all law, over time, by means of critical and comparative methods; that it was necessary to study law and legal principles by first placing them in linguistic and historical context and, second, by comparing them with other classical sources, rather than merely using logic to determine their meaning.[9] By historicizing Roman law, Budé challenged traditional (and fixed) understandings that characterized the interpretations of those followers of Bartolus "who believe such laws not to have been written or conceived by man, but to have fallen down from heaven."[10]

Only when jurists had come to understand that the meaning and significance of legal terms was both embedded in and encapsulated by the thick context of society, language, and history, rather than by systems of logic, would it be possible for them to comprehend the relation between justice, law, and right in principle and practice. In addition to their defective methods, which prevented them from understanding the true nature of justice, Budé attacked scholastic lawyers and jurists for their attempts to establish themselves as the sole interpreters of law, Roman or otherwise, to elevate their profession—and themselves—to positions of power. He denounced, above all, those who used their expertise in law and logic to advance their patron's interests before justice and, in some cases, to place their own interests above the law and the common good.

Notwithstanding the fact that Budé spent the majority of the *Annotationes* tearing apart—word-by-word—traditional, viz., scholastic, jurisprudence, the text itself was not simply a polemic. In addition to knocking down the edifice that medieval jurists had erected based on their erroneous interpretations of key terms within Roman law, Budé effectively set out to offer a new basis for understanding the *Digest*, and thereby jurisprudence. As part of his extensive philological explanations, drawing upon and intermingling a variety of Greek and Roman sources in order to return to the language of Roman law and the principles it embodied, Budé also set out to restore older methods to interpret it. Indeed, the methods he set out to restore were essentially the very methods, he argued, that had been corrupted by medieval jurists in the first place.

Although Budé claimed that his project was to merely restore Roman law, he expected his work to revolutionize aspects of legal interpretation, at least

9 For an account of the history and development of these methods as applied to Roman and canon law see Chapter 1 of this volume.

10 Budé, *Annotationes*, fo. VIII, 'Verum hoc istis bartholistis persuaderi non potest: qui leges istas non ab homine scriptas ac conceptas: sed de coelo ruisse credunt …'.

among humanist jurists. This was especially the case in his restoration/reinterpretation of *ius* as the art of what is good and what is fair, conjoined, and *ius* as an inherent quality or characteristic of man *qua* man.[11] As such, Budé attempted to offer his humanist contemporaries a direct alternative to the explanations found in the *Gloss* of Accursius, the standard *Gloss* used to teach and interpret Roman law in universities since the thirteenth century. Furthermore, Budé sharply criticized the methods and interpretations of those who he thought—albeit mistakenly—simply followed Accursius' interpretations, most notably Bartolus and his student Baldus, whose commentaries (especially Bartolus') were so authoritative that, by the time Budé wrote, they had long held legal authority in courts.[12]

However, Budé pitted his harshest criticisms against the scholastic jurists of his own time, whom he referred to simply as the "sect of Accursians," who "just as a bailiff [stinks of] garlic," continue to "stink of barbarity, everywhere and always," because they had access to texts, methods, and knowledge—linked to the new influx of Greek texts as well as corrected Greek-Latin translations that distinguished the period—which Accursius, Bartolus, and Baldus did not.[13] In light of new knowledge and new texts, they should have set out to reform the errors that stemmed from the glossators, commentators, and commentaries long before the early-sixteenth century. Had they adapted, for example, the critical methods of Valla and Poliziano to the study and interpretation of civil law, it is possible that Budé would not have found his time studying law at Orléans so repellent and, perhaps, might have completed his legal studies in the first place.

Given that the primary focus of the *Annotationes* was the proper translation and interpretation of the meaning and significance of Roman legal vocabularies and idioms, it is important to note that Budé's emphasis on the literal

11 This was especially the case in relation to his understanding and discussion of *ius* as equity. See Kisch, *Studien zur Humanistischen Jurisprudenz* (Berlin: de Gruyter, 1972); Kisch, *Erasmus und die Jurisprudenz seiner Zeit*; and Kisch, "Humanistic Jurisprudence." For a good discussion of the link between equity, good faith, and legal interpretation among Renaissance jurists, scholastic, and humanist, see MacLean, *Interpretation and Meaning in the Renaissance.*

12 For a discussion of Bartolus' and Baldus' legal and political thought see Berman, *Law and Revolution I*; Maiolo, *Medieval Sovereignty*; Guido Kisch, *Bartolus und Basel, Basler Studien zur Rechtswissenschaft* (Basel: Helbing and Lichtenhahn, 1960); Fasolt, *The Limits of History*; Gilmore, *Argument from Roman Law*; and Joseph P. Canning, *The Political Thought of Baldus De Ubaldis* (Cambridge: Cambridge University Press, 1987).

13 Budé, *Annotationes*, fo. III, 'Qui nisi ut villicus allium: ita ipsi barbariem ubique ac semper obolverint: decorum illud Accursianae sectae servare se non credunt.'

and historical interpretation of words effectively meant that he was a realist. A realist, to be clear, in the sense that he held that knowledge, and its universal and inherent nature, was expressed through and by language in context and in time; words were, in fact, literal representations of the reality and ideas they described. In this respect, Budé revealed his debt and connection to his predecessors in France, who, under Charlemagne (r.768–814), "assumed that grammar, by means of its methodologies—that is, analogy, allegory, and etymology—provided the tools for discovering all truth available to human reason. That assumption was nourished by the more basic assumption that knowledge of the origins of words and the structure of language revealed the structure of being."[14] This realist aspect to his thought helps to illuminate why understanding terms within the *Digest* properly was so central to him, why the use of language seemed to matter above all else in his interpretations, and why Budé was so critical of those in the legal profession whom he characterized as using the "sly interpretation of words" to gain reputation, power, profit, and applause.[15] For Budé, one would only be able to understand Roman law properly if they tended to the language of it in textual and historical context. Indeed, it was the power of words, and therefore the necessity of understanding what was meant by a term in context, as well as the ability to correctly convey its proper sense and meaning, that drew Budé to restore the *Digest* in the first place.

We know this because well into the first title within his *Annotationes, Ex lege prima de iustitia et iure*, Budé told us so. Directly after noting some definitions and differences in word use that he learned from reading Valla's *Elegantiae linguae Latinae* (*Elegances of the Latin Language*), he explained that reading this work had encouraged him to re-read the *Digest* and the glosses and commentaries concerning it.[16] Aside from having had the opportunity to see—though not read—the recovered text of the *Digest* up close while visiting Florence and having access to Poliziano's notes on it, Budé (like everyone else) also read the *Digest* through Accursius' *Gloss*.[17] However, returning to Accursius after reading Valla inspired Budé to see the *Gloss* differently:

14 Witt, *The Two Latin Cultures*, 27–8.

15 Budé, *Annotationes*, fo. IX.

16 Ibid, fo. VIII, 'Hoc tamen Laurentii elogium me impulit ut diligentius digestorum libros legerem.'

17 The recovered text was originally called the Pisan manuscript until it was moved to Florence around 1406 or 1411. The Florentine text was likely a copy of the *Digest* made about a century after it was originally compiled by Tribonian and other jurists but was thought to be the original. It was held under lock and key in the ducal palace in Florence, and only a select number of scholars were granted access to it. Budé was able to look at

> In the course of this reading, not only did I discover that in many places the volumes themselves had been, in part damaged, in part erroneous, but also, in fact, that which I judge to be the far more shameful thing—many words, not of trivial, but of ancient and proven coinage, through the ignorance of the times, I discovered, have been translated into a different meaning. Greatly disturbed by this indignity, I dared, at a proper time, to boast among my friends, rather rashly, that one day I would bring it about that the Pandects [*Digest*] would be read more correctly and more intelligently.[18]

After three years of working on this project, however, he was near the point of abandoning it altogether. During that period, he had become "thoroughly disgusted with this undertaking," not only with working with the corruptions introduced by medieval jurists but also with having to constantly appeal to others for help, especially from those who had formal legal training and practical legal experience.

Frustrated and exhausted, he explained, "I gladly convinced myself that I was, at last, going to be freed from this annoyance," or so he initially thought:

> But lo, when my friends were calling me careless of my task, and charging me, as it were, with a debt put off, and harping at me constantly with a reminder of my voluntary promise, then I perceived that I had been ferociously dragged from the point from which shame forbids me to retreat (just as the fellow says), and that straightway I had to either undertake the task to which I was in no way equal to, or I would soon, when I had been exposed for my rashness, and had admitted it, become a laughing-stock to everyone.[19]

---

it through a grating; he was not permitted to study it up close. Poliziano's copy of the *Digest*, with an elaborate philological and grammatical commentary, is preserved in the Laurentian library at Florence.

18 Budé, *Annotationes*, fo. VIII, 'qua in lectione cum multis in locis volumina ipsa partim mutilata partim mendosa deprehendi: tum vero (quod flagitiosius esse multo arbitratus sum) verba multa non trivialis sed antiquae ac probae monetae: in alienum usum ignorantia temporum translata esse animadverti: ea indignitate per motus ausus sum pridem inconsultius iactare inter amicos me aliquando facturum ut pandectae emendatius atque intelligentius legerentur.'

19 Ibid, 'Ecce autem huius negocii securum appellantibus amicis. & tanquam procrastinati debiti arcessentibus: ultrone aeque pollicitationis admonitu itentidem vellicantibus: eo tum me sensi ferocule evectum unde pedem referre pudor vetet (ut inquit ille) continuoque aut rem suscipiendam mihi cui par omnino non essem: aut temeritatis manifestum ac confessum ludibrio mox omnibus me futurum.'

He was only able to persevere as a result of the constant encouragement of his sponsor and friend, a man (whom he did not identify by name) with "remarkable knowledge of the law" and "one of a small number of men who do not seem to have betaken themselves to the study of the civil law unprepared."[20] Inspired by Valla and yet daunted by such an enormous task, Budé included this anecdote, perhaps to justify his choice of sources cited, the methods employed, and the conclusions drawn in the text. The brief account served as a defense of his efforts, as within it he acknowledged that once the text was completed and published, it very well may not live up to the expectations that his contemporaries, namely humanist jurists engaged in similar projects, had set for it.

Despite the extended time Budé spent on the 1508 *Annotationes*, and the concession that it was not what he had hoped it would be, he announced in his dedication letter to the newly appointed Chancellor Jean De Ganay (1455–1512) that "about seven months ago and a little after you had taken up that office for the king, I had begun to write certain annotations on the Pandects."[21] Claiming that his *Annotationes* was completed far more quickly than he recounted in the text itself, he imparted it with a renewed sense of urgency and, possibly, a more direct defense of its form. Budé admitted in the same dedication letter that his book would likely undergo a sustained and critical attack by lawyers and jurists. As such, he thought that his "little" commentaries "were going to be insufficiently believable coming from me as the author," and thus should have attached to them "some great and august name when they went out to the public."[22] Linked to the authority of the Chancellor's office, name, and reputation, Budé hoped his *Annotationes* "might better withstand the judgement of critics."[23] Though not an uncommon humanist dedication letter, Budé's choice to publish his text under the auspices of the Chancellor,

20 Ibid fo. IX, '… iam primum praeter singularem iuris peritiam: doctrina est etiam illa miscellanea ac politico homini aut necessaria aut utili perpolitus: iudicio non mediocri ac saepe nobis probato praeditus: cui etaim de me plus quam meo propemodum tribuo. unus est denique ex paucorum numero qui non illotis pedibus ad studium iuris civilis contulisse se videntur.'

21 Budé, "Praefatio," in *Annotationes*, fo. a.ii–a.iii, 'Quae res mihi imprimis exoptanda fuit: vir illustrissime Ioannes Deganai: ea mihi hoc tempore forte (ut spero) fortuna evenit. Nam cum abhinc septem plusminus menses: paulo postquam tum ad principem istum magistratum assumptus es: annotationes quasdam in pandectas scribere coepissem:' fo. a. ii.

22 Ibid, a. ii, 'iam inde in mentem mihi venit faciendum omnino mihi esse: ut hic nostri commentarioli parum ab auctore me futuri plausibiles: amplum aliquod nomem augustumque praeferrent exeuntes in publicum: cuius velut auspiciis freti …'.

23 Ibid, '… ancipitem iudiciorum aleam secure experirentur.'

the officer responsible for overseeing the judicial administration of the French realm, rather than fold it into the more narrow project of reforming university-based jurisprudence by dedicating it to his humanist peers, is significant. This is the case because attacking scholastic jurisprudence within the *Annotationes*, despite only holding a Master of Arts, meant that Budé was also attacking those jurists who made up France's *parlements* (that is, the regional supreme courts, especially the one in Paris that sat above all others and thus served as the ultimate appellate court), who were trained in the Italian methods.

For Budé, the problem with the *parlements* was their ability—as a consequence of being armed with faulty interpretations and scholastic methods—to block edicts that attempted to limit their authority. Worse, some could engage in a kind of judicial activism, whereby they could create new laws as well as reinterpret or even abolish older ones in their opinions and decisions. As such, they could exercise a power of making and abrogating laws that was reserved for the king. Within and beyond the *parlements*, jurists and lawyers could also use the law, and their position as its interpreters, to promote their own self-interests or, just as dangerous, sell their expertise for profit or applause, for patronage and glory, to those who wished to use the law to expand their power and influence. Although not all lawyers, judges, and jurists used the law to promote power over justice, private good over public good, or profit over security, for Budé, the bad methods of teaching and interpreting the law in the universities seemed to encourage it. Indeed, as far as Budé was concerned, it was the faulty understanding and bad interpretations within the universities that had fostered the misapplication and corruption of the law and jurisprudence in nearly every legal and juridical context and institution throughout France.

Since the text was both a critique of university-based jurisprudence and of practicing lawyers and sitting jurists and judges, it made sense for Budé to dedicate his corrected version of the *Digest* to a French magistrate rather than to his humanist peers beyond France. Moreover, given the continual process in France (especially after King Louis XII issued his Ordinances of Blois of March 1499) of the transformation of unwritten and customary law into written form and codes, and legal reform more generally, it was paramount that the newly appointed Chancellor had, above all, a text that could explain the underlying principles of Roman law—principles such as justice and right—that also underlie French customary and written law properly; that the Chancellors have a text at hand to help foster and confirm just customs, practices, and laws rather than repeat and augment corrupted and unjust ones.[24]

24 For discussions of this process and of the changes in politics, law, and French society that were part and parcel of it see Frederic Baumgartner, *France in the Sixteenth Century*

Dedicating the text to the Chancellor also speaks to Budé's sense that the methods and interpretations of scholastic jurisprudence at play in legal interpretation throughout France, particularly when linked to the relationship between lawyers and the Holy Roman Emperor or the Pope, represented—especially in the context of the Italian Wars—a threat to the integrity and supremacy of the ancient customs and written laws practiced by the French people and approved by the French monarch.[25] Thus, for Budé, nothing less than French dominion, majesty, and *imperium* was at stake when it came to legal reform. It was therefore imperative that he brought his work, which had been delayed for too long, directly to the attention of De Ganay by dedicating it to him.

The aggressive, and sometimes belligerent, tone that permeates the *Annotationes* also enabled Budé to make an argument—in what he deemed a plain and direct manner, even if his readers found it convoluted—as to why it was urgent to restore the sense and meaning of terms within the Roman *Digest* to their original and, by extension, to reform the teaching and interpretation of it in universities across Europe. In the process of making his case, he spared no criticisms. However, these criticisms, albeit harsh, were as constructive as they were destructive. By laying bare the problems that underpinned traditional jurisprudence as he saw them, and with it the corruption of basic legal terms and idioms by those trained in Italian methods, Budé set forward a critique in which he attempted to offer an alternative means of interpreting and understanding the foundational and underpinning principles of all law, across the boundaries of time and space. In so doing, he reinterpreted the Roman term *ius* as an objective signifier of justice, viz., the right order of things, and an inherent quality of man (what we might call subjective right, although Budé

(New York: St. Martin's Press, 1995); Robert Descimon, "The Birth of the Nobility of the Robe: Dignity Versus Privilege in the Parlement of Paris, 1500–1700," in *Changing Identities in Early Modern France*, ed. Michael Wolfe (Durham, NC: Duke University Press, 1996), 95–123; Janine Garrisson, *A History of Sixteenth-Century France, 1483–1598* (New York: St. Martin's Press, 1995); Franco Simone, *Culture et politique en France á l'époque de l'humanisme et de la renaissance* (Turin: Accademia Delle Scienze, 1974). For an account and commentary on these changes by Budé, in addition to the *Annotationes*, see *De asse et partibus eius libri quinque* ([Paris]: Venundantur in edibus Ascensianis, 1514). Although this work is primarily concerned with ancient measures and moneys, it also provided—in a series of digressions and additional annotations—a history of France with political commentary, focused on the regimes of Louis XII and Francis I, the last two parts of which were concerned with the regime change between the two kings.

25 Although French claims in Italy, which ignited the Italian Wars, informed Budé's perceptions of traditional jurisprudence, the wars themselves more directly affected Alciati's career. See Part 3 of this volume.

never rendered it as such), in such a way that it ultimately stood at the foundations of and served as a limit to legal (and political) authority.[26]

That he did so in the early sixteenth century, and indeed was inspired to complete the text as quickly as possible after a new Chancellor was appointed, reminds us that Budé's work, and humanist jurisprudence more generally, was not a mere semantic, esoteric, or scholarly endeavor—nor a mere series of insults and complaints. The conflict between the proper interpretation and application of law—historical and formal—at the center of humanist critiques of traditional jurisprudence and scholastic methods was at base a conflict about imposing order in the face of disorder, legitimizing new forms of governance, and mediating the relations between and among disparate authorities and offices within kingdoms, city-states, and empires, both religious and secular.[27] In the early sixteenth-century and in the context of early

26 For a succinct survey of the meaning subjective right (as well as objective right) see John Witte, Jr., "A Short History of Western Rights," in *God's Joust, God's Justice: Law and Religion in the Western Tradition*, ed. John Witte, Jr. (Grand Rapids, MI: Wm. B. Eerdmans Publishing Company, 2006), 31–48. For a far more in-depth discussion of the relation between objective and subjective right in the languages of political and legal theory reaching back to William of Ockham see especially Michel Villey, "*La genèse du droit subjectif chez Guillaume d'Occam*," *Archives de philosophie du droit* 9 (1964): 97–127.; and Jonathan Robinson, "Ockham, the Sanctity of Rights, and the Canonists," *Bulletin of Medieval Canon Law* 31, no. 1 (2014): 147–204. For a broader discussion of subjective right, spanning the medieval and early modern eras, see Michel Villey, "Les origines da la nation de droit subjectif," *Archives de philosophie du droit* 2 (1953–4): 163–87; Villey, *Le droit et les droits de l'homme* (Paris: Presses universitaires de France, 1983); Tierney, *The Idea of Natural Rights*; Richard Tuck, *Natural Rights Theories: Their Origin and Development* (Cambridge: Cambridge University Press, 1979); Annabel S. Brett, *Liberty, Right, and Nature: Individual Rights in Later Scholastic Thought* (Cambridge: Cambridge University Press, 1997); Annabel S. Brett, *Changes of State: Nature and the Limits of the City in Early Modern Natural Law* (Princeton, NJ: Princeton University Press, 2011); Francis Oakley, *Natural Law, Laws of Nature, Natural Rights: Continuity and Discontinuity in the History of Ideas* (New York: Continuum, 2005); John M. Finnis, *Natural Law and Natural Rights* (Oxford: Clarendon Press, 1980); John M. Finnis, "Grounding Human Rights in Natural Law," *The American Journal of Jurisprudence* (Notre Dame) 60, no. 2 (December 2016): 199–225; and Petar Popovic, "The Concept of «Right» and the Focal Point of Juridicity in Debate between Villey, Tierney, Finnis and Hervada," *Persona y Derecho* 78, no. 1 (January 2018): 65–103. Finally, for a detailed discussion on why the distinction between subjective and objective right can be problematic see Thomas Mautner, "How Rights Became 'Subjective'," *Ratio Juris: An International Journal of Jurisprudence and the Philosophy of Law* 26, no. 1 (2013): 111–32.

27 For a good discussion of the urgency that underlay calls for legal reform in teaching and practice see Bouwsma, "Lawyers and Early Modern Culture"; Constantin Fasolt, "Visions of Order in the Canonists and Civilians," in *Handbook of European History, 1400–1600*, eds. Thomas A. Brady Jr., Heiko Augustinus Oberman and James D. Tracy (Grand Rapids,

modern state and empire-state formation, the humanist rejection of scholastic jurisprudence and their reinterpretation of *ius* as the art of what is good and what is fair conjoined as well as a distinguishing characteristic of man *qua* man had significant and far-reaching implications for their own time (and for ours). This is evident in their interpretation of the relation between *ius naturale* (natural law), *ius gentium* (law of nations), and *ius civile* (civil law), wherein the moral authority of *ius* as a higher criterion of justice was not only central to reforming unjust laws but also to grounding the universal rights and obligations of man which transcended the confines and constructs embedded in the *ius commune*.[28]

3 Hidden in Plain View: Radical Departure, Traditional Scholarship

In the first book of the *Annotationes*, following the structure of the *Digest* precisely, Budé set forth a detailed explanation of the essence and relation between *ius* (right), *lex* (law), and *iustitia* (justice) as well as natural law, *ius gentium* (law of nations), and civil law. Within this explanation, he presented a root and branch critique of traditional jurisprudence and effectively redefined *ius* as both a criterion of justice and an attribute of man. Despite this, historians who focus specifically on the development of modern political thought as well as on the natural law and natural rights tradition have assumed that humanists, like Budé, were neither interested in nor had much patience for these fundamental categories of law and politics.[29] Moreover, historians who study the history and development of Western/European legal traditions tend to underemphasize—and, in some cases, even ignore—the advent of legal

MI: Wm. B. Eerdmans Publishing Company, 1984), 31–60; and Brundage, *The Medieval Origins of the Legal Profession*.

28 For a discussion of this in humanist jurisprudence see Susan Longfield Karr, "'The Law of Nations Is Common to All Mankind' *Jus Gentium* in Humanist Jurisprudence," in *Morality and Responsibility of Rulers: European and Chinese Origins of a Rule of Law as Justice for World Order*, eds. Janne Nijman and Anthony Carty (Oxford: Oxford University Press, 2018), 73–92. For a discussion of this within scholastic jurisprudence see Herzog, "From *ius gentium* to Natural Law: Making European Law Universal I," in *A Short History of European Law*.

29 See especially Skinner, *The Foundations of Modern Political Thought. Volume 1*; Skinner, *The Foundations of Modern Political Thought. Volume 2:* (Cambridge: Cambridge University Press, 1978); Tuck, *Natural Rights Theories*; Tierney, *The Idea of Natural Rights*; Brett, *Liberty, Right, and Nature*; Brett, *Changes of State*; Witte, *The Reformation of Rights*; and James Tully, *Public Philosophy in a New Key*, 2 vols. (Cambridge: Cambridge University Press, 2008).

humanism and its influence on legal interpretation and education throughout Europe, even as they acknowledge a fundamental shift in method aimed at scrutinizing texts in historical context rather than interpreting them through the lens of logic and, with it, a fundamental shift in understanding of aspects of juridical and political thought in the first decades of the sixteenth century.[30]

Thus we might well wonder why, on the one hand, Budé began his text with these basic definitions (just as his legal humanists counterparts did), and, on the other, why historians and political theorists have overlooked the fact that he (and his counterparts) directly engaged with and put forward theories about the relationship between justice and right that fall well within the parameters of the history and development of modern political and legal thought as well as the history and development of rights (natural, civic, and human) and international law. The answer to the first question is rather straightforward: Budé began his *Annotationes* with the categories of justice and right, natural law and *ius gentium*, because the *Digest*, which he set out to restore to its original condition before the schoolmen glossed it, began with these same categories. Given, however, that his reinterpretation of *ius* as a signifier of justice (the right order of things) and a fundamental attribute of man *qua* man, and indeed a marker of man's dignity and rights (inherent *ius*) as well as his obligations, the answer to the latter question is more complex and even perplexing.

Budé's discussion may have escaped the attention of some scholars of political and legal thought because he engaged primarily with fundamental categories like *ius*, natural law, and *ius gentium*, to restore them to what he deemed was their original meaning to the Ancients rather than to use them to buffer or ground existing religious or political norms. In other words, it may appear that Budé's interest was a matter of mere semantics or exercises in philological inquiry rather than attention to ideas and problems of immediate concern to him. Still, those aware of his discussions may have deemed his work irrelevant on account of the fact that Budé neither explicitly focused on reconciling different types of law into a grand normative system, as his scholastic predecessors and counterparts had done, nor did he seek (directly or indirectly) to add to their discussions of natural law, *ius commune*, or civil jurisprudence

30 See Kelley, *Foundations of Modern Scholarship*; Kelley, "Civil Science in the Renaissance: The Problem of Interpretation"; Donald R. Kelley, "Law," In *The Cambridge History of Political Thought, 1450–1700*, ed. J. H. Burns and Marke Goldie (Cambridge: Cambridge University Press, 1991), 66–94; Kisch, *Erasmus und die Jurisprudenz seiner Zeit*; Maffei, *Gli inizi dell'umanesimo giuridico*; Douglas J. Osler, "Images of Legal Humanism," *Surfaces* (Montréal) 9 (2001): 101–6; Schoeck, "Humanism and Jurisprudence,"; and Troje, *Humanistische Jurisprudenz.*

more generally.[31] Indeed, the fact that Budé set out to provide an alternative to traditional jurisprudence and, in so doing, abandon the scholastic modes of interpretation and arguments altogether may help explain why his work tends to stand beyond the parameters of investigation by modern scholars who focus on the history and development of legal thought and interpretation—especially those scholars who tend to explore the tradition through the lens of scholastic jurisprudence, civil and/or canon, in order to illuminate the history and development of the *ius commune* or the reception (and rejection) of Roman law across Europe.[32]

It is just as likely, on account of the form and methods of his arguments, that Budé's discussion, especially the key term of *ius*, escaped the notice of those who focus on the history and development of rights because Budé offered his understanding by pulling ideas and definitions together, mostly from Aristotle and Cicero, thereby emphasizing, above all, man's capacity to pursue justice rather than his propensity to violate it. For example, Budé grounded his definition and interpretation of *ius* in man's dignity rather than man's depravity; his foundational definition of *ius* was not dependent on, embedded in, or related to violence (self-preservation/punishment/war) but man's inclination to pursue a common good in tandem with others. Thus, Budé did not focus on *ius* as an inherent right to meet force with force or self-preservation, instead he focused on *ius* as a marker of dignity and criterion of justice. Given that legitimate and illegitimate violence—whether as a means to explain conflict within a particular community or between communities, as in the context of punishment and just war theory—has tended to set the parameters for and has limited the scope of natural law and natural rights scholarship in recent decades (and by extension the history of political and legal thought), it's not difficult to imagine that had Budé put forward an understanding of *ius* within the context of a broader discussion of violence, punishment, and/or war, then his work would have drawn more attention. That he did not do so has meant, effectively, that his ideas have remained, for many, hidden in plain view.

31 See Tuck, *Natural Rights Theories*; Tierney, *The Idea of Natural Rights*; Brett, *Liberty, Right, and Nature;* Tully, *Public Philosophy in a New Key*, vol. 1; and Herzog, *A Short History of European Law*.

32 See Lorenzo Manoscalco, "Interpretatio ex aquo et bono: The Emergence of Equitable Interpretation in European Legal Scholarship," in *Networks and Connections in Legal History*, eds. Michael Lobban and Ian Williams (Cambridge: Cambridge University Press, 2017), 233–61; Berman, *Law and Revolution I*; Kelley, "Law"; Harold J. Berman, *Law and Revolution II: The Impact of the Protestant Reformation on the Western Legal Tradition* (London: Belknap, 2004); Bellomo, *The Common Legal Past of Europe*; and Herzog, *A Short History of European Law*.

Moreover, had Budé emphasized man's passions over his dignity more generally, scholars who trace the origins of so-called modern conceptions of natural rights, as well as republican and neo-liberal interpretations of them, might well have taken his definition of *ius* more seriously.[33] Likewise, the fact that Budé offered a discussion of *ius* in relation to man's natural state rather than the so-called state of nature helps to account for why his discussion of *ius* has been, for the most part, overlooked or ignored by historians of political thought whose main intent is to place Thomas Hobbes' innovation into a broader intellectual context in order to show, first, how Hobbes broke from what came before, and, second, the extent to which Hobbes influenced political and legal thought since the seventeenth century.[34] Concerned with different issues, and responding to different problems, Budé's ideas no sooner fit into the paradigms that shape current scholarship than they did in his own

---

33 See Skinner, *Foundations of Modern Political Thought. Volume 1*; Phillip Pettit, *Republicanism: A Theory of Freedom and Government* (Oxford: Oxford University Press, 1997); Quentin Skinner, *Liberty before Liberalism* (Cambridge: Cambridge University Press, 1998); Quentin Skinner and Martin van Gelderen, eds., *Republicanism: A Shared European Heritage*, 2 vols. (Cambridge: Cambridge University Press, 2002); J. G. A. Pocock, *The Machiavellian Moment: Florentine Political Thought and the Atlantic Republican Tradition* (Princeton, NJ: Princeton University Press, 2003); Quentin Skinner and van Gelderen, eds., *Freedom and the Construction of Europe*, 2 vols. (Cambridge: Cambridge University Press, 2013).

34 In addition to the works above see Annabel S. Brett, James Tully, and Holly Hamilton-Bleakley, eds., *Rethinking the Foundations of Modern Political Thought* (Cambridge: Cambridge University Press, 2006); Quentin Skinner, *Visions of Politics*, 3 vols. (Cambridge: Cambridge University Press, 2012); Tuck, *Natural Rights Theories*; Tuck, *Philosophy and Government*; Tierney, *The Idea of Natural Rights*; Richard Tuck, *The Rights of War and Peace: Political Thought and the International Order from Grotius to Kant* (Oxford: Oxford University Press, 1999); Phillip Pettit, *Made with Words: Hobbes on Language, Mind, and Politics* (Princeton, NJ: Princeton University Press, 2008); and Quentin Skinner, *From Humanism to Hobbes: Studies in Rhetoric and Politics* (Cambridge: Cambridge University Press, 2018). For critiques of these approaches (and progressive/linear narratives more generally) see Witte, *The Reformation of Rights*; John M. Headley, *The Europeanization of the World: On the Origins of Human Rights and Democracy* (Princeton, NJ: Princeton University Press, 2008); Paul J. du Plessis and John W Cairns, eds., *Reassessing Legal Humanism and its Claims: Petere Fontes?* (Edinburgh: University of Edinburgh Press, 2015); Nijman and Carty, eds., *Morality and the Responsibility of Rulers*; David Gress, *From Plato to NATO: The Idea of the West and Its Opponents* (New York: The Free Press, 1998); Carol Pateman, *The Sexual Contract*. 2nd ed. (Stanford, CA: Stanford University Press, 2018); Charles W. Mills, *The Racial Contract* (Ithaca, NY: Cornell University Press, 1997); and Bruce P. Frohen and Kenneth L. Grasso, eds., *Rethinking Rights: Historical, Political, and Philosophical Perspectives* (Columbia, MO: University of Missouri Press, 2009).

time—even as they helped to fundamentally transform the latter and can help us test, and even readjust, the former.

However, breaking free of the limitations set by the dominant scholarship, and thereby treating Budé's ideas and innovations in their own time and context, is no easy task, especially when compared to the more systematic texts and treatises that followed on the heels of humanist jurisprudence. Indeed, it's fair to suggest that because his work falls outside the bounds of what came before, in terms of traditional, viz., scholastic, natural law theory and what comes after, viz., modern, natural rights theory, Budé's innovations have effectively remained obscured by the form in which he presented them. For many, the sprawling and disjointed nature of his *Annotationes* may well appear, at first sight, to be merely a collection of tangents, loosely connected by excerpts from Roman law, interspersed with extensive quotations and references of Greek and Roman sources, which are, in turn, interrupted by *ad hominem* attacks on Accursius and those who followed him. This structure of the text—or seeming lack thereof—likely stemmed from the difficulty of Budé's project to break new ground and, in so doing, to leave traditional methods and interpretations behind. It also, no doubt, extended from Budé's haste to complete it as well as the sheer contempt he held for university-trained lawyers and jurists, thus imitating the tone that Petrarch and Valla used in their own attacks on scholastic doctors and lawyers, albeit without the expertise that both brought to their own scathing critiques of scholastic methods of interpretation.

The form of the text also likely stems from Budé's attempt to establish the authority of his interpretations with reference to Greek and Roman sources, often substituting the words of Aristotle and Cicero for his own. Indeed, Budé's tendency to use the *Annotationes* to showcase his own classical learning and his adherence to Stoic moral philosophy led him to render the definitions in the *Digest* even more obscure, despite his claim of illuminating them. Hence, taken as a whole, Budé's *Annotations* offered little more than extensive quotes taken from a wide range of ancient authors (and *ad hominem* attacks on scholastic jurists) and interspersed with references to definitions and excerpts from the *Digest* itself. Leaving it up to his readers to make sense of the text (and each annotation within it), Budé ultimately failed to produce what he had promised. However, that did mean that those who followed him, namely Zasius and Alciati, did not find certain aspects of it useful. Therefore, when accessing and exploring his discussions, we—just as his contemporaries—must tend to the details in the text, even when it seems like they are buried in tangents or are convoluted and meandering. Only in doing so can we begin to grasp the full implications of Budé's desire to restore the fundamental terms of Roman law. We must begin, in other words, not only by tending carefully to Budé's treatment of Book One, Title One of the Roman *Digest*, *De iustitia et iure* (*On Justice and Right*), but also by being mindful of the ways in which he used this treatment to restore/redefine *ius* as both a measure of universal justice and a universal attribute of man. At the same time, however, we must recognize that when dealing with a rambling and convoluted text like the *Annotationes*, the question as to whether Budé understood university-based jurisprudence is secondary precisely because—regardless of his references to Aristotle, Plato, Pliny, Cicero, St. Augustine, Livy, and Vergil, etc. when discussing *ius*, natural law, and *ius gentium*—he scarcely mentioned scholastic jurisprudence (canon or civil) outside of his opening salvo against Accursius and those who followed him.

4 Splitting Good from Fair: Accursius' Error and Budé's Entanglement

To launch his attack against traditional jurisprudence—and to clear the way for his own interpretations—Budé began his assault by highlighting significant incongruities in the first definition set out within the first book of the *Digest* and the treatment of it in Accursius' *Gloss*. While his readers would likely have had the precise words of the *Gloss* and the *Digest* in mind or at hand when reading the *Annotationes*, some definitions and interpretations are reproduced here to enable modern readers to see the basis of, and thus more fully understand, Budé's objections to the *Gloss*.

From the start, Budé contrasted the following definition of *ius* from D.1.1.1.:

> Ulpian, *Institutes*, Book 1: A law student at the outset of his studies ought first to know the derivation of the word *ius*. Its derivation is from *iustitia*. For, in terms of Celsus' elegant definition, *ius* is the art of goodness and fairness.[35]

with Accursius' interpretation of it:

> For there is the good and useful part of it [*ius*], and note that the good is one thing, equity another; for there is a certain thing both good, and equitable; and there is something good, and not equitable: like usurpation

35 D.1.1.1. Budé's discussion was also informed by D.1.1.11: Paul, Sabinus, book 14: The term *ius* is used in several senses: in one sense, when *ius* is used as meaning what is always far and good, it is natural law (*ius naturale*); in the other, as meaning what is in the interest of everyone, or a majority in each civitas, it is civil law (*ius civile*).

> [viz., the acquisition of property by use or prescription]; there is a third thing equitable and not good.[36]

Drawing attention to the disparity between the two, Budé railed against traditional jurisprudence by calling Accursius' definition—and thereby his entire understanding of Roman law—into question. Indeed, considering the difference between the *Digest* and the *Gloss* above, Budé asserted that: "*Jus* is the art of what is good and what is equitable. In relating this passage, Accursius judges the good to be one thing, and the equitable to be another: he does not explain this enough."[37] Determined to correct and not simply to point out Accursius' error, Budé set the Roman *Digest* aside for the moment and turned instead to Greek and Roman sources.

Focusing on the comparison between the Latin term and its Greek equivalent (*epieíkeia*), Budé explained that Aristotle understood *ius* as something higher than law (*lex*), which was an expression of both goodness and fairness (equity).[38] In essence, he explained that for Aristotle goodness and fairness were crucially linked as attributes of justice. After drawing out the gap between Aristotle's understanding of the relation between law and justice and that of Accursius', Budé then accused the latter of fundamentally misunderstanding, and thereby misrepresenting, *ius* when he "separated equity

---

36 Accursius, 'JUS EST ARS. hoc potest inteligi tribus modis. Primo, ut dicas difinitum ius in genere, & sic est ars, id est, scientia finita, quae arctat infinita. nam ars est de infinitis finita doctrina, secundum Porphyrium. Secundo dic describi quamlibet speciem iuris, ut praetprium, vel cive, vel naturae, vel gentium: & tunc ponetur pro praecepto coarctante. Sed hoc non placet, cum istae partes iuris non sint artes, sed artis partes. Vel tertio, ars, id est artificium. nam auror iuris est homo, iustitae deus, & quod subiicit, boni & aequi, id est eius quod est aequum & utile. & non quod aliud est bonum. & aliud est aequum: ut hic, est enim quoddam bonum, & aequum.' Quoted from *Digestum vetus sive pandectarum iuris civilis totus primus ex pandectis Florentinis, quae olim Pisanae dicebantur, quod eius fieri potiut, repraesenatus. Commentariis Accursi, & multorum insuper aliorum tam veterum quam neotericorum iurisconsultorum scholiis atque observationibus illustratus* (Paris: 1566), fo. II.

37 Budé, *Annotationes*, fo.I, 'Ius est ars boni & aequi. Accursius hunc locum enarrans aliud bonum esse censet: aliud aequum: nec satis hoc explicat.'

38 See Aristotle, *Nicomachean Ethics*, Book V, X; for a discussion of how jurists interpreted and integrated Aristotle's discussion of equity in the Renaissance, especially among humanists, see Kisch, *Erasmus und die Jurisprudenz seiner Zeit*; Kisch, *Studien zur Humanistischen Jurisprudenz*; and Kisch, "Humanistic Jurisprudence." For an interpretation that challenges the latter, as well as arguments (by Tierney et al.) that suggest that an understanding of natural rights originated in—or at least not before—the late- sixteenth century see Merio Scattola, *Das Naturrecht vor dem Naturrecht: Zur Geschichte des >ius naturale< im 16. Jahrhundert* (Tübingen: Max Niemeyer Verlag, 1999).

and good in an improper and ignorant fashion."[39] By doing so, Accursius clearly demonstrated to Budé that he failed to understand a crucial aspect of universal jurisprudence. However, Budé merely assumed that Accursius' error stemmed from his misunderstanding of Aristotle, which also helped to account for his misunderstanding of Ulpian; Budé provided no evidence to that effect.[40]

Even so, attacking Accursius as part of his restoration of the definition of *ius* as the art of equity and good conjoined (as explained by Ulpian and Aristotle) was essential to Budé precisely because he thought that *ius* could be used to hold the law—as well as those who created, interpreted, and administered it—to a higher standard of justice (*iustitia*). To explain this, Budé relied, once again, on Aristotle who, in *Book V* of the *Ethics*, "eloquently discusses justice and law: he specifies these as two different [things]: [but] they are not of different sorts: *ius* is both good and equitable,"[41] adding that "although good and equity is something of the law: *ius* is more excellent or better: not however as a different genus: it [*ius*] is superior to law [*iure*]."[42] If Aristotle was understood correctly, Budé continued, then judges ought to judge "either according to law, or according to customs" by making use of *ius*, that is, equity and good conjoined "just as artisans and builders of stone masonry are making use of the Lesbian norm"—in other words, a building tool that Aristotle used metaphorically to indicate flexibility—insofar as "they apply the norm to the natural structure, not the structure to the norm."[43] In this way, "the highest courts

39 Budé, *Annotationes*, fo. I, 'Proinde Aristoteles uno verbo epiices appellat: quod nostri aequum & bonum dicunt: & interdum aequitatem: ut Aristoteles epiician: Male igitur & inscite Accursius aequum & bonum distinxit.'

40 The literature that explores the impact of the recovery and translation of Aristotle's works on European scholars is far too extensive to adequately reference here. For a brief account of how the rediscovery of Aristotle's texts shifted methods of interpretation and teaching within the schools see "*Modus Docendi*: The Methods of the Schoolmen and the *Studia Humanitatis*" (and the corresponding notes within) in Chapter 1 of this volume.

41 Budé, *Annotationes*, fo.I, 'Aristoteles libro quinto ethicorum de iustitia & iure copiose disputans: duo haec tanquam differentia ponit: non tanquam genere diversa: ius & aequum bonumque.'

42 Ibid, 'Bonum & aequum (inquit) cum sit cuiusdam iuris: ius est praestantius vel melius: non autem ut genus aliud aequum & bonum: iure praestantius est.'

43 Ibid, 'Quibus verbis (si quidem recte vertimus) Aristoteles significat eos iudices quibus ex bono & aequo iudicare: aut legibus: aut moribus licet (cuiusmodi sunt suprima tribunalia quae proscripto iuris usque quaque non astricta sunt: idem quae interdum pro re nata liberam causarum disceptationem habent) aequo & bono ita uti debere ut caementarii fabri & structores lesbia norma utuntur. Cum enim caeteri fabri soleant structuras suas ad normam exigere: lesbii soli plumbeam normam habentes pro arbitratu suo flexibilem & subinde immutabilem: ita ad normam structuram suam exigunt: ut interdum

sometimes do not direct according to a rule of law" but in accordance with justice when they take into account the inflexible things (the natural structure) and, "with the scales of equity and good," they judge matters with regard to the "conditions of the times, peoples, places, and other qualities."[44]

However, following Accursius' split of equity from good, Budé assumed that jurists and lawyers had departed from Aristotle, Ulpian, and the methods of ancient judges. Taking full advantage of Accursius' error, Budé held that lawyers and jurists have been able to transform *ius* from a universal standard of what is good and fair into something that essentially equated with law (*lex*) itself and that *ius* was merely an expression of law rather than a criterion of justice. As a result, scholastic jurists were able to abandon the Lesbian norm altogether—rather than being obligated to conform the law to justice (to conform the structure to the stone), they were free to conform justice to the law (to conform the stone to the structure). In this scenario, law determined what was just, rather than what was just determining the law. When law determines what is just, the letter of the law—and its intent—becomes fertile grounds for semantic exercises, which, in turn, increase the demand for and value of those trained in the scholastic methods of argument. The problem for Budé was that syllogistic logic rather than justice increasingly determined the outcome of legal questions and disputes, thus further enabling lawyers and judges to quibble over the letter of the law instead of carefully exploring its meaning, intent, or consequence. In other words, narrowly focusing on the literal and strict interpretation or wording of a specific law (*summum ius*) made it possible for some jurists and lawyers to altogether bypass consideration of justice and right.

Budé vehemently attacked these tactics and those who employed them throughout his *Annotationes*. In so doing, he relied on the authority of Aristotle to support and advance his understanding of *ius* as fairness and goodness conjoined, and also on the authority of Cicero to set forth an interpretation of justice in relation to objective and inherent/moral right. Using both authorities in tandem served two fundamental purposes.

First, it enabled him to move his critique to a broader level, for all the problems attendant on Accursius' error in interpreting *ius*, the fact that he had

si lapidis natura non facile ad structuram aequabilis pervicerit: normam ad structuram inflectant: & structurae normam non normae structuram accommodent: quo scilicet opus suum consummari possit.'

44 Ibid, 'Sic & suprema tribunalia iterdum non modo iuris praescriptum: sed ne suarum quidem sententiarum praeiudicia non sequuntur: praegravante aequi bonique lance in perpendendis temporum: personarum: locorum & aliis qualitatibus.'

neither knowledge of nor access to the extensive range of sources that were available to scholars by the sixteenth century helped to account for his errors. Similar limitations also applied to Bartolus and Baldus. However, based on the influx of sources and on the advances in learning made by the early sixteenth century (including contributions made by Budé), the fact that the jurists were still interpreting *ius*—and its relation to law and justice—in accordance with the *Gloss* and the commentaries made their efforts more damnable for Budé. After all, by the early sixteenth century, Aristotle's *Ethics* had been fully recovered and available in new humanist translations.[45] Despite having tools at hand that would have enabled them to do otherwise, the fact that his scholastic contemporaries continued to misinterpret principles, which underlay and structured universal jurisprudence, served as ample evidence for Budé that they were doing so on purpose.

Second, quoting from Cicero gave Budé's attack added gravitas. As brilliant as a scholar as he thought himself to be, Budé lacked the credentials necessary for his critiques to be taken seriously by his scholastic contemporaries, especially lawyers and jurists. Here, it is useful to recall that he effectively failed out of law school, having neglected his legal studies while at Orléans. Lacking credentials, Budé used Cicero to argue his case for him. Rather than simply complain that the scholastic jurists have corrupted the law through their methods, he integrated extensive quotes from Cicero to admonish those who twisted and bent the letter of the law to advance their own interests—and in the process were able to violate justice despite appearances that they were promoting it. Indeed, Budé's specific reliance on Cicero's *Oration on Behalf of Caecina* to launch an attack against his contemporaries in his *Annotationes* provides a particularly apt example of this. He frequently turned to Cicero's argument in this case because therein he "seems to have described these things [the problems] in a few words."[46]

Cicero delivered this oration in 69 BCE. The case involved Sextus Aebutius who made a claim against Caecina regarding a farm that had come into his possession after the death of his wife, Caesinnia. Aebutius argued that even though he was an agent of Caesinnia at the time of the original purchase, the purchase was for him—not her—and it was his property. As she never owned

45 See C. B. Schmitt, *Aristotle and the Renaissance* (Cambridge, MA: Harvard University Press, 1983); Maniscalco, "Interpretatio ex aquo et bono"; and David A. Lines, *Aristotle's Ethics in the Italian Renaissance (1300–1650)* (Leiden: Brill, 2002).

46 Budé, *Annotationes*, fo. 1, 'Utrumque autem horum Cicero in oratione pro Cecinna eleganter descripsisse paucis verbis videtur.'

it, Caesinnia could not have bequeathed the farm to Caecina. When Caecina tried to enter the property, Aebutius met him with a band of armed slaves, something expressly forbidden by Roman law. Faced with the threat of violence, Caecina fled from the property and sought an interdict. When the case was argued, Aebutius stated that the farm was never the property of Caecina and, even if it had been, Caecina had fled and thus forfeited any claim he may have had in the first place.[47]

In arguing the case on behalf of Caecina, Cicero made two central points. First, that Aebutius was in the wrong not only in claiming the property as his own but also in meeting Caecina with armed slaves. Second, the point that Budé emphasized above all others, that Aebutius and those who argued on his behalf incriminated themselves with their lies and trickery of words. If they were allowed to make these fallacious arguments, then the entire foundation of property and law would come under threat. For example, in response to Aebutius' argument for why he did nothing wrong, namely "I did not drive you out, I opposed your entrance,"[48] Cicero asked,

> What law, what resolution of the senate, what edict of the magistrate, what treaty, or covenant, (to return to man's private affairs), what will, what judicial decision, what bond, what formula of bargain or agreement cannot be invalidated and torn to pieces, if we choose to bend facts to words, and leave out the question of the intention, and design, and authority of [those] who wrote them. In truth, even our familiar and daily discourse will cease to have any coherence, if we are to spend all our time in word catching.[49]

And further, "words have been invented, not to hinder people's intentions, but to point them out."[50]

Extensively quoting the above passage, Budé used it to assault his contemporaries for engaging in the same kind of specious reasoning,

47 For more background on this case and its implications see Vladimir Zorić, "Banished with No Force: Exile and Metonymy in Cicero's Pro Caecina Oratio," *Diacritics* 40, no. 4 (2012): 72–103.

48 See Marcus Tullius Cicero, "Pro Caecina," in *The speeches: pro lege Manilia, pro Caecina, pro Cluentio, pro Rabirio perduellionis*, trans. Humfrey Grose-Hodge (London: W. Heinemann, Ltd., 1927), §.11; and Budé, *Annotationes*, fo. 1.

49 Cicero, "Pro Caecina," §. 18.

50 Ibid.

> And with these words the sophistries of the more recent lawyers can be most appropriately refuted, who believe they draw out exceptionally strong arguments by this sort of quibbling of words for establishing certain new doctrines of their own; as if each syllable of the law, both civil and pontifical, had a certain fixed power of its own.[51]

Rather than allow the lawyers to play with the language of the law in this way, Budé argued that, "The specific word used to designate something of the law ought to be drawn together from the jurists and a few others."[52] When Budé referred to jurists in a positive fashion, he was speaking predominantly of Cicero and those whose words made up the *Digest*, not the *Gloss*, the commentaries, or his contemporaries. Budé's concern did not cease there.

Budé pushed this discussion to its limits when he argued that jurists were not the only ones who needed to gain an understanding of why law must be based on universal principles of justice and right. Indeed, rulers who approved customs and determined civil law for their people were also in need of a more comprehensive—and correct—understanding of *ius* as the art of both what is good and what is equitable. Expanding his explanation beyond Cicero and the lawyers, Budé turned to G. Suetonius Tranquillus' (c. 29–112) *De vita Caesarum* (*The Lives of the Caesars*), and specifically to his treatment of Claudius (10 BCE–45 CE), to provide an example of a case when the letter of the law and justice had suffered because of the arbitrary sentiments of the ruler. In scenarios such as this, it would have been advantageous to surround said rulers with properly-trained jurists and councilors (or, by implication, Chancellors) who had a proper understanding of law and justice.

As told by Suetonius, Claudius did not always rule in accordance with the letter and spirit of the law, but often ruled according to his own idea of what was just or fair. In some cases, Claudius would even grant someone a second hearing of their case. Lest this appear to be a sign of undue leniency and benevolence, a harsher penalty followed for those who still lost. Furthermore, "with regard to such as were convicted of any great delinquency, Claudius even exceeded the punishment appointed by law, and condemned them to be exposed to wild beasts."[53] Thus, it was not always the case that those rulers who

---

51 Budé, *Annotationes*, fo. I–II, 'Quibus verbis appositissime refelli possunt iurisconsultorum recentiorum cavillamenta qui huiusmodi verborum aucupiis argumenta validissima elicere se credunt ad nova quaedam sua dogmata constituenda: quasi unaquaeque syllaba iuris & civilis & pontificii vim suam quandam certamque obtineat.'

52 Ibid, fo. II, 'Stricti autem iuris vocabulum peculiare est iurisconsultorum ut & alia pauca.'

53 Ibid, 'Nec semper praescripta legum secutus duritiam lenitatemque mulctarum ex bono & aequo perinde ut afficeretur moderatus est. Nam & iis qui apud privatos iudices plus

overruled the letter of the law or even followed its strict wording (*summum ius*) in the name of the common good did so with regard to a higher notion of justice. Rather, it could also be the case that they were more radically violating the principles of justice and *ius*, out of sheer passion or as an attempt to demonstrate their power.

Budé held that it was imperative that rulers be surrounded by learned and virtuous men; men who would not spend their days in word-catching or use their expertise to interpret the law to further the will of the ruler. Nor should the administration of the law simply be in the hands of the king alone, especially if he was of such a temperament to disregard *ius* and act only in accordance with his interests. Even in this brief discussion of Claudius, advisors and jurists steeped in moral philosophy and right action remained the main focus of Budé's attention, as the only viable means to ensure that a ruler oversaw his realm justly was to surround him with men of good letters, viz., humanists, who had a proper understanding of *ius* and justice.[54] Moreover, administering justice rather than merely applying the law not only necessitated a nuanced understanding of the principles that underlie the law and the application of it but also proper training in the methods that underpinned and organized the law in the first place.

Before turning to the precise methods needed, Budé once again offered a cutting critique of his contemporaries, especially in relation to whether they were more inclined to follow justice and equity or the strict letter of law and, even—through the play of words—use the law and its study to satisfy their own egos and those whom they served. In the latter case, Budé argued that disputes about law were in the interest of the lawyers and judges because they provided them with ample opportunities to exercise their expertise in the courts as well as in texts, gaining fees, glory, and patronage.

For example, referring primarily to the books that jurists produced, relied on, and turned to—the *consilia* as well as the commentaries—that made the jurists "seem no more expert in law than in justice,"[55] he argued,

---

petendo formula excidissent: restituit actiones: & in maiore fraude convictos legitimam poenam supergressus: ad bestias condemnavit.'

54 See, for example, Budé, *De l'institution du prince* ([Paris], 1547); Budé, *De asse*; Ehsan Ahmed, "Wisdom and Absolute Power on Guillaume Budé's Institution du prince," *Romantic Review* 96, no. 2 (2005): 173–85; and John M. Headley, "The Problem of Counsel Revisited Once More: Budé's *De asse* (1515) and *Utopia I* (1516) in Defining a Political Moment," in *Humanism and Creativity in the Renaissance*, ed. Christopher S. Celenza and Kenneth Gouwens, (Leiden: Brill, 2006), 141–70.

55 Budé, *Annotationes*, fo. 11, '... nec magis se iuris quam iustitiae consultos videri ...'

> By the heaping up of books of this kind, superfluous when taken in good part, that ancient and genuine majesty of jurisprudence was obscured, first around the period of Alexander the emperor, and afterward [that which] was tried to be restored and made new under the auspices of Justinian and the leadership and toil of Tribunian [sic] and renewed in a more correct fashion. Now, in fact, it has even been wiped out through the madness of the [commentators] and the conspiracy of those who follow them—as is normal when, composing their own writings, they are not content to obtain the position of interpreters, but wish themselves now to be cited and (if I may use the term of law) to be praised as though they were the legislators.[56]

With regard to the authors and those who studied these scholastic interpretations, he argued, "let them believe that they are speeding through weeded (if I may put it thus) and leveled [passages] with no effort, thinking those laughable and unfortunate who struggle through the uneven and thorny part of the law wretchedly, especially for no [financial] gain."[57] Through their studies and their arguments concerning the law, lawyers had been able to use the law for their own profit and to rejoice in doing so—much like a farmer who celebrates a hearty harvest—whereas those who toiled with the study of law as the study of justice were forced to contend with weeds and thorns.[58] Justice is hard; law is easy.

More contemptible, their scholastic methods, advantageous interpretations, and their play with words, enabled lawyers—in no small part thanks to Accursius' errors in splitting good from fair to define *ius*—to add to and even change law, and thereby interfere with justice,

---

56 Ibid, 'Huiusmodi librorum bona ex parte supervacaneorum congerie: prisca illa germanaque maiestas iuris prudentiae obruta est: primum circa tempora Alexandri principis: subindeque Iustiniani auspiciis & Tribuniani ductu atque opera restitui instaurarique tentata verius quam instaurata. Nunc vero in sania scripturientium eorumque sequacium conspiratione etiam deleta: utpote cum scribentes sua scripta enarrationum vicem obtinere non contenti: citari se iam & (ut verbo iuris utar) laudari pro legislatoribus velint.'

57 Ibid, fo. II–III, 'Eorum vero sectatores labori suo bellissime consulentes: per illa interpretationum velut latifundia fructum se iuris studii percipere gaudeant: in quibus spinosa salebrosaque iuris loca: runcata (ut ita loquar) complanataque nullo negocio percurrere se credant: ridiculos eos infelicesque putantes qui per confragosa iuris senticosaque loca nullo praesertim quaestu misere conflictentur: id quod ne accideret: ne Iustinianus quidem ipse vno & altero edicto quamlibet imperiosis praestare posteritati potuit.'

58 Ibid.

> Add advice and even (if it pleases the gods) sureties, as they themselves call them—that is to say, pure displays of cleverness and sly anglings for words, repeatedly tricking popular simplicity and civic probity, providing to advocates an opportunity for slandering, sometimes impossible to be disentangled by the judges, [and] very often disadvantageous to the law—which those sorts of men, nevertheless, think to be prize worthy for themselves.[59]

Just in case Budé's readers mistook his position regarding the lawyers, he announced: "I consider to proclaim war: and as soon as I come, I throw (as I make use of the words of Plautus) a javelin of blame."[60]

For this direct attack, Budé introduced two Greek terms, *misocalos* and *philodicos*, to distinguish those who interpreted the *Digest* from those whose words were compiled within in—especially Ulpian and Gaius. The use of these two Greek terms, and the distinction that they entailed, were two of the sharpest javelins in Budé's arsenal. With them, he was able to fully express his contempt for his scholastic contemporaries, including those in the *parlements*:

> Which (lest someone think that I have been speaking about men learned in the law in general) I wish to be understood [to be speaking about] those whom Minerva, goddess of wisdom, declined to bless with her gifts at birth, those whom the Greeks call *misocalos* as if [they are] haters of all literary refinement and effort of learning, shrinking from all the more civilized forms of learning: rustics: charmless men: men without refinement: men who smell like goats.[61]

Those men who hold law as the highest discipline, that is, those who teach in the universities, he prefers to call *philodicos*, viz., men "rejoicing in the racket of quarreling," viz., lawsuits.[62] Yet, even though the *misocalos* and *philodicos*

---

59 Ibid, fol. III, 'Adde consilia atque etiam (si diis placet) cautelas ut ipsi vocant. id est vafritias meras & commentitia verborum aucupia: simplicitati vulgari & probitati civili saepe numero imponentia: advocatis ansam calumniandi praebentia: iudicibus interdum inextricabilia: optimo iuri per saepe captiosa. Quae tamen isti sibi palmaria esse putant.'

60 Ibid, '... bellum indicere mediter: continuoque adveniens (ut Plauti verbis utar) pilum reprehensionis iniiciam.'

61 Ibid, 'Quod (ne quis putet de iurisperitis in universum me dixisse) de illis intelligi volo sinistra Minerva natis: quos graeci misocalos vocant quasi omnem literarum elegantiam: nitoremque dicendi perosos: ab omnibus doctrinis humanioribus abhorrentes: rusticos: invenustos: illepidos: hircosos.'

62 Ibid, 'Ego vero philodicos potius vocitandos censuerim id est litium strepitum gaudentes.'

were detestable, the study of law itself should not be abandoned. For Budé, what should have been abandoned was the notion that studying the letter of law and the techniques of arguing it, rather than the study of justice, was a higher form of knowledge than moral philosophy, history, or philology. He was, in short, disgusted by the idea that there was something honorable in the selling of one's voice in court, and that the quarreling of words and trickery, which characterized the teaching and practice of law, was deemed a legitimate skill. All of this served to overshadow the necessity for those studying and practicing law to acquire an understanding of the universal principles of justice and right.

Yet, bearing in mind the nature of his project, it was not enough for Budé to state that the jurists in the universities and beyond them were wrong when it came to their methods and understanding of the law, and thereby justice. Instead, he had to demonstrate why improper training in law was dangerous, no matter the capacity served by those who received a scholastic education, or whether they were teaching the law in universities, interpreting it in courts, or advising rulers in private. Demonstrating the latter via his own critique helped infuse his call for the reform of legal education with urgency. For example, his discussion thus far—based on his reliance on authorities like Aristotle and Cicero, and rejection of Accursius—enabled him to claim that he, unlike the *philodicos* (the scholastic professors of canon and civil law teaching in the universities), was explaining the *Digest* correctly, in accordance with the true definition, meaning, and sense of *ius* as the art of what is good and what is fair conjoined. This was no small claim, given that the majority of those who occupied positions of legal authority had received scholastic training either directly in universities or indirectly by studying the glosses and commentaries on their own. Nevertheless, instead of attacking his contemporaries more directly, Budé simply asserted that he had corrected Accursius' error and had restored *ius* to its proper meaning and place within Roman law by showing "that goodness and equity are absolutes: & that justice is the marrow and sister (so to speak) of *ius*."[63]

Therefore, Budé announced he would not follow the opinions of just anyone experienced in the law. The implication, of course, was that Chancellor De Ganay and others should not follow the opinions either. Experience in the law and the knowledge of justice were two very different things. Indeed, over time experience in the law, which Budé did not have, had corrupted the knowledge

63 Ibid, 'Proinde (ut eo revertamur) unde digressisumus cum aequum & bonum dicimus: absolutam bonitatem aequitatemque significamus: & iuris (ut ita dicam) medullam germanamque iustitiam: quam censendo asse qui non cuiusuis est iurisperiti.'

of justice, as demonstrated by Accursius' misunderstanding of *ius* as well as those who followed him. By not following the *Gloss* and the scholastic jurists, Budé claimed to be providing a correct explanation to his readers. Ignoring or being perhaps unaware that his attacks and criticisms in the *Annotationes* up to this point had overshadowed a substantive discussion of *ius*, he simply concluded this initial treatment of it by stating, "According to what we said above (as I believe) those words of Ulpian have been explained enough. *Jus* is the art of equity & good: & the things that follow them."[64]

5 The Proper Method for Studying and Interpreting the Law

With *ius* restored to its original meaning and explained with reference to Greek and Roman sources, Budé began setting out alternative methods to those used in the universities. He did so by invoking the words and methods of Cicero, whom he and other humanists exalted as a man able to practice law with virtue, to pursue the common good, to dedicate himself to the service of justice, and one who could not be swayed to use the law for his own interests or to play with the language of the law to gain advantages for others. Furthermore, the proper methods of studying law and acquiring an understanding of justice that Budé advocated in his text were Cicero's methods as presented through the words of Lucius Crassus in Book One of *De oratore* (*On the Orator*). If jurists emulated Cicero's character and methods, proper law could be renewed, justice restored, and virtue achieved. Thus, just as Budé wanted to return to the original language of law and justice of the Ancients, he also wanted to return to their exemplary methods of interpretation; the very techniques that had gone awry in the hands of the scholastic Doctors within the universities and of the lawyers and jurists who argued and interpreted the laws beyond them.

For Budé, much of this corruption was the result of the lawyers' lack of classical learning and their willingness to use the law not only to gain money and glory but also—and this is worth special emphasis—to undermine and usurp authority for themselves or their patrons. The corruption of legal education and interpretation made it possible for jurists to treat Roman law as a static and unchanging embodiment of norms, rather than a dynamic historical-legal artifact. Historicizing Roman law would enable Budé and his humanist counterparts to demonstrate how and to what extent Roman law—and indeed

64 Ibid, 'Ex iis quae diximus (ut arbitror) satis illa verba Ulpiani explicatasunt. Ius est ars boni & aequi: & quae sequuntur. Circa hoc enim philosophari (ut verbo eius utar) hoc est omni animi intentione incumbere: proprium est iurisconsultorum institutum.'

all law—reflected man's actions and interests over time, for good and for ill. Moreover, attention to how law changed over time, especially in the hands of jurists, would make it possible for all to see the extent to which jurists and lawyers were using their expertise to undermine the common good, rather than to serve it. In this respect Budé was exemplary, not exceptional, and thus can serve as an apt example of how early sixteenth-century legal humanists launched an attack on the scholastic tradition on two fronts.

First, they attempted to restore the meaning and significance of terms according to their original context through philological methods; second, they showed the historicity of law with recourse to examples from ancient texts and historical examples; they used law as a lens to explore the past and they used the past to explore the law. Rejecting the position that Roman law was static and instead approaching it as record of man's actions and customs, which changed over time, enabled Budé—in theory—and his humanist jurist contemporaries—in practice—to explore why specific laws varied according to conditions, needs, and circumstances as well as how and to what extent the principles that underlie the law (customary, Roman, French, and otherwise) remained constant. In the early-sixteenth century, this method of study was, even after the innovations of Valla and Poliziano, a radical departure from traditional and university-based jurisprudence. Even today, this method of study is more often found outside of law schools rather than within them, especially in law and society or legal studies programs (drawing on the disciplines of history, philosophy, linguistics, and anthropology) because such methods often offer a fundamental critique of the dominant modes and paradigms of professional legal education and training, which remain, in many ways, embroiled in legal formalism and scholastic methods of debate.

Linking philology and history, allowed Budé: (1) to show the corruption of terms and laws; (2) to restore a term, concept, or idea to what he thought it had meant at its origin; and (3) to argue—with reference to discrete moments in time—that even though laws changed, a universal understanding of *ius* and justice remained constant precisely because *ius* was, in its objective aspect, justice itself. The latter aspect then allowed Budé to argue that he, the Greeks, and the Romans—despite the distance in time and difference in context—were in unison since they shared a common understanding insofar as they defined, explained, and discussed universal principles such as *ius* as justice and as right. Further, it allowed him to argue that they were all advocating the same critical and historical methods to study law and to pursue the common good. Finally, it enabled him to argue that those who claimed to be drawing on the same traditions—even as those traditions changed and with them so too the meaning of the terms—did so without warrant because they had corrupted the law so thoroughly by their wordplay.

What is more, not only had the language of the law been degraded in the hands of scholastic jurists, so too had the dispensation of justice (or the lack thereof) been moved from the domain of moral philosophy—the pursuit of wisdom, virtue, and justice—to the domain of the lawyers, who, in turn, had put it up for sale,

> the study of the law now has thoroughly degenerated from that old and correct [study], unless, indeed, we judge that philosophy, that is, the pursuit of wisdom, was once done for profit, and ancient philosophers (the sort that lawyers wish themselves to be) set down monetary gain as the sole goal for their labor—that which men learned in the law of our time do: who, casting aside all sense of shame, are accustomed to pursue profit and praise, as if it were something to be applauded.[65]

For Budé, those who exchanged their voice and knowledge for money and glory should not have been counted among jurists, but among sophists. Indeed, referring to Ulpian's assertion that:

> Anyone may properly call us [jurists] the priests of this art [of knowing what is good and what is fair], for we cultivate justice and profess to know what is good and equitable, dividing right from wrong, and distinguishing what is lawful from what is unlawful; desiring to make men good through fear of punishment, but also by the encouragement of reward; aiming (if I am not mistaken) at a true, and not a pretended philosophy.[66]

Budé held that knowledge of the law was not only "the most holy civic wisdom, but a profession which ought not to be valued monetarily."[67] He further held, in line with what we'd expect from a humanist critique, that those "men

65 Budé, *Annotationes*, fo.111, 'Ex quo colligere possumus id quod ante dicebamus: studium nunc iuris prorsus ab antiquo illo veroque degenerasse: nisi vero arbitrabimur philosophiam id est studium sapientiae quae stuariam olim fuisse: nummariumque praemium: unicum laboris sui finem philosophos antiquos (quales se iurisconsulti esse volunt) sibi proposuisse: id quod nostri temporis iurisperiti faciunt: qui cum frontem perfricuere etiam ut plaudendum profiteri ac gloriari solent:'

66 This follows directly after the explanation of *ius* drawn from Ulpian in D.1.1.1.

67 Budé, *Annotationes*, fo. 111, '... est nam res quaedam sanctissima civilis sapientia: sed quae precio nummario non sit aestimanda.'

learned in the law of our time" were prostituting themselves for money. In contrast, true jurists, viz., Ulpian, Gaius, Cicero, etc., did not study law as a means for a reward but rather understood their work as a reward in and of itself. It allowed them to understand, administer, and live by justice and right, thereby pursuing peace, security, and the common good in tandem.

Not only the texts of Roman law—and thereby the principles that underpinned them—need to be restored, so too the methods of organizing, studying, interpreting, and applying them. To explain the proper and correct methods, Budé asserted, "I prefer to respond in the words of Cicero rather than with mine." He then followed this statement by offering his reader an extensive quote from Lucius Crassus, whereby Cicero explained that to learn the law, one need only look to its sources and aims.[68]

Just as Budé used Cicero's words to advance his argument against the lawyers' methods, so too did Cicero use Crassus' to advance his argument about the significance of law, and thereby the study of it: "The explanation is that all of its material lies right before our eyes, it is part of the practice of daily life, of people meeting each other, of the activity in the forum, and it can be found entirely in writings and books that are neither massive nor numerous."[69] For those determined to resort to these volumes as part of their study, they will find that "the same material was published by several people; moreover, it was written down again and again, with only slight changes in formulation, even by the same authors."[70]

In either case, one who attempts to understand the law, whether in the forum or in the library, must better understand the context in which laws were made and interpreted, and thereby familiarize themself with history and politics. Following Cicero, word for word, Budé continued:

> For, if anyone enjoys the studies made so popular by Aelius, then all areas of the civil law, as well as the books of the priests and the Twelve

68 Budé, *Annotationes*, fo. III–IIII, 'Verumenimvero quid de iuris studio censeam (quandoquidem id etiam ad hoc nostrum institutum pertinet) malo Ciceronis verbis quam meis respondere: qui in dialogis de oratore in persona Lucii Crassi magni illius oratoris ac iurisperitissimi de facilitate perdiscendi iuris civilis in hunc modum loquitur.' Given that Budé included extensive (and verbatim) portions of Cicero's *De Oratore*, Book One, §. 184 thru §197 in what follows, the location of the Latin in Budé's work is cited, but is it not reproduced in the footnotes. The English translations of Cicero, in this discussion, are from Marcus Tullius Cicero, *On the Ideal Orator* (*De Oratore*), translated by James M. May and Jakob Wisse, (Oxford: Oxford University Press, 2016). Hereafter: *De Oratore*.

69 Budé, *Annotationes*, fo. IIII; Cicero, *De Oratore*, Book I.§. 192.

70 Budé, *Annotationes*, fo. IIII; Cicero, *De Oratore*, Book I.§. 192.

> Tables offer him a rich picture of the past. One can learn about ancient, archaic words there, and also, certain types of legal formulas reveal our ancestors' customs and their way of life. Or if anyone likes the discipline of politics (which Scaevola thinks is not the province of the orator but rather of someone at home in another kind of expertise), he will find that this is entirely contained in the Twelve Tables, because all useful institutions and the whole organization of the community and the State are described there.[71]

By studying how the laws were arranged in the Twelve Tables, one finds "what is honorable is especially to be pursued, since virtue and hard work, performed with justice and rectitude, are adorned with high offices, rewards, and glory." At the same time, one discovers that "vices and offences are punished by fines, degradation, fetters, flogging, banishment, and death."[72] This was the case because, "We are also taught, not by endless, over polemical discussions, but by the authoritative nod of the laws, to subdue our lusts, to hold in check all our desires, and to protect our own property, while keeping our thoughts, our eyes, and our hands off what belongs to others."[73]

Employing these words of Cicero, Budé launched an attack against those who had managed to corrupt the study and practice of law to advance their own reputations, fame, and interests. In so doing, Budé emphasized that, despite their claims of expertise and necessity, it was the laws—not the lawyers nor those who trained them in the universities—that taught one to live in mutual company, to manage one's desires, and to pursue virtue and the common good. Thus, the laws themselves—before they were turned, twisted, debated, and bent by lawyers—reflected the universal principles of justice, not the lawyers' arguments about or their interpretations of them.

If one wished to understand justice, then they should set aside the vast accumulation of interpretation and arguments produced by lawyers and advocates and turn instead to the Twelve Tables. They should do so, Budé continued to quote Crassus, because "the Twelve Tables alone is weightier in authority and richer in usefulness than the libraries of all the philosophers."[74] Moreover, to understand how these original sources of the law should be arranged and interpreted, one need only look, once again, to Cicero,

71 Budé, *Annotationes*, fo. IIII; Cicero, *De Oratore*, Book I.§. 193.
72 Budé, *Annotationes*, fo. IIII; Cicero, *De Oratore*, Book I.§. 194.
73 Ibid.
74 Budé, *Annotationes*, fo. IIII; Cicero, *De Oratore*, Book I.§. 195.

> Thus, the civil law may be said to have the following purpose: the preservation of equality of rights, founded on statute and custom, in the concerns and judicial disputes of our citizens. Next, we must identify the various classes of cases, reducing them to a definite number, which should be as small as possible. Now a class is that which includes two or more species that are similar to one another because they have certain things in common, but are different by virtue of their appearance. Species, in turn, are those categories that are logically subordinated to the classes from which they derive. And as to all the names of both the classes and the species, the meaning of each must be described by definitions. A definition is, of course, some short, concisely expressed statement of those features that are proper to the object we wish to define.[75]

After establishing the general type and species and the relation between them, one should then follow the divisions and principles of the law and, as Cicero explained in his *Topica* (*Topics*), "pursue the analysis until you produce its own distinctive quality which can be transferred to no other thing."[76] This deserves emphasis, as this was not only at the heart of Budé's discussion of *De iustitia et iure* in his 1508 *Annotationes*, but it was also the method that permeated it. Indeed, paring down *ius* to its essential properties by removing the scholastic interpretations and definitions of it was precisely what Budé had done, thus emphasizing its original definition in the *Digest*, namely a particular property that cannot be transferred to anything else. In relation to law, that property was justice (*iustitia*); in relation to man *qua* man, as shown below, it was *ius*.

Starting with an essential term like *ius*, Budé followed the methods prescribed by Cicero: first, he offered a general definition, and second, he explained it in relation to other concepts and examples—invoking Aristotle to do so—until he could take the definition no further. Although it must be noted that at this point in the text Budé was only able to illuminate—not further define—*ius* beyond the definition provided by Ulpian; he had nonetheless restored it to its original meaning in the objective sense, that is, as a criterion of justice. In this respect, Budé had accomplished his task of excavating the original meaning, to clear the way for the words of the ancients, particularly those of Cicero. Even so, Budé pushed this definition further in the next section of

75 Budé, *Annotationes*, fo. IIII; Cicero, *De Oratore*, Book I.§. 188–9.

76 Budé, *Annotationes*, fo. IIII–V; English translation from Marcus Tullius Cicero, *De inventione: de optimo genere oratorum, topica*, trans. H. M. Hubbell (Cambridge, MA: Harvard University Press, 2014), *Topica*, §.29.

the *Annotationes* by following the method of exploring the general types of law in the *Digest* (natural law, *ius gentium*, and civil law). He compared "two or more species that are similar to one another because they have certain things in common, but are different by virtue of their appearance," so as to arrive at a definition of *ius* that could meet the criterion of being a "distinctive quality which can be transferred to no other thing." Before proceeding with this, however, Budé concluded his discussion as to how the categories and precepts of law, and by extension the study of them, should be ordered, and why. Not surprisingly, he once again chastised traditional and university-based jurisprudence in doing so.

The best method of ordering and interpreting the law, Budé continued, was the method that "Cicero, after he had accepted it from Aristotle," handed down and "translated into beautiful Latin in a lengthy paraphrase [of the Greek] for his friend Trebatius."[77] It was also the same method employed by the Roman jurist Quintus Scaevola (d. 82 BCE), "who first set up the civil law by types by collecting it in 18 books."[78] Moreover, it was the very method that Budé assumed was used by the compilers to create the *Digest* in the first place. Yet, as exemplified by the extensive production of commentaries, opinions, and *consilia*, the method had gone terribly wrong in the hands of medieval jurists. Rather than treat the law in an orderly fashion as they should have, scholastic jurists—interested in using Roman law to support their self-interest and that of their patrons, rather than understanding the Roman law as it was—had managed to throw the law itself into disarray. After about three centuries, the task of cleaning up the mess left behind by the jurists in the universities and by the lawyers beyond them amounted to clearing out the Augean stables for Budé. Even so, at times Budé's rhetoric lent more to burning down the edifice altogether to make way for a new one, instead of preserving it by removing the waste.

According to Budé, the use and abuse of law was so great by the early-sixteenth century that there were no limits placed on scholastic readings and lawsuits. Indeed, the disputes by the Doctors and lawyers since the eleventh-century rediscovery of the *Digest* and the founding of the first Roman law faculty in Italy (at Bologna) had become more frequent and numerous,

---

77 Budé, *Annotationes*, fo. v, 'Reliqua de genere & forma, id est, specie: de differentia partitionis & divisionis & alia eodem pertinentia: Cicero ab Aristotele accepta: Trebatio amico suo tradidit: compendiosa paraphrasi in latinum sermonem venustissime traducta.'

78 Ibid, 'Hoc Illud est autem quod Pomponius infra de origine iuris de Quintio Scaevola dixit: qui ius civile generatim primus constituit in libros decem & octo redigendo.'

> Certainly, they would in no way at all have left behind those vast and manifold volumes of commentaries on the law—material and kindling for setting legal disputes ablaze: with which now Gaul burns in every direction with the comments of advocates, which, like torches blazing to the greatest degree, gain strength day by day, through the indulgence of judges, who are not very hostile to litigious persons …[79]

This could have been avoided, Budé argued, if—following Justinian's edict—"the volumes of our law should have become inviolate."[80]

Those who wrote about the laws should have been limited to adding indexes or simple headings. Instead, they were allowed to change and add to the law.[81] As a result, Budé acknowledged that he "seems to cut the quick" when he argued that only after the fourteenth century—roughly two centuries after Accursius' *Gloss* was completed—was it no longer permitted to change or add to the *Digest*.[82] It was only after the commentaries of Italian jurists such as Bartolus and Baldus had acquired an authoritative standing in universities and in courts throughout Latin Christendom that an "agreement [among] our

---

79 Ibid, fo. II, '… profecto immensa illa & numerosa commentariorum iuris volumina haud quaquam reliquissent: materiam & fomitem accendendarum litium: quibus nunc gallia passim flagrat: incendo quidem vix unquam deflagraturo: quippe causi dicorum commentis quasi facibus ardentissimis indies invalescentibus: iudicumque indulgentia litigiosis haud magnopere infensorum.'

80 Ibid, fo. VI, 'Maxime igitur oportuit post edictum illud Iustiniani quod extat titulo de veteri iure enucleando (vulgo nunc ut video neglecto: sed tamen non spernendo si emendate legatur) volumina iuris nostri tribunitiam potestatem accepisse.' Budé was referring to the following from the *Composition of the Digest, The Emperor Caesar Flavius Justinianus, Pious, Fortunate, Renowned, Conqueror and Triumpher, Ever Augustus, Greets Tribonian His Quaestor.*, §. 12, 'We command that our complete work, which is to be composed by you with God's approval, is to bear the name of the *Digest* or *Encyclopedia*. No skilled lawyers are to presume in the future to supply commentaries thereon and confuse with their own verbosity the brevity of the aforesaid work, in the way that was done in former times, when by the conflicting opinions of expositors, the whole law was virtually thrown into confusion. Let it suffice to make some reminders by indexes alone and simple headings, in such a way that no offense arises through interpretation.'

81 Budé, *Annotationes*, fo. VI, '… ut omni prorsus scribenti nihil in ea licuisset: nisi hactenus ut indices rerum tantummodo & titulorum argumenta quaedam ascriberent: quae paratitla (ut ipse inquit) dicuntur quod titulis apposita: sin ad viuum resecare videor: post Bartholum certe & Baldum ut ne attingere ea cuique licuisset. ut certa fix atque aliquin iurisconsultorx dogmata essent: nostratibusque cum transalpinis de iuris tandem apicibus conveniret.'

82 Ibid.

people together with those across the Alps on the fine points of the laws" was possible.[83]

By the sixteenth century, the works of Bartolus and Baldus on Roman law—rather than the texts of Roman law—dominated university study in Western Europe. This amounted to French jurists depending on scholastic, and especially Italian, authorities. It also meant that jurists were confined to playing with the language of the law, quibbling over points to gain reputation and fame, rather than exploring more important questions of justice. In this respect, fixing the letter and interpretation of Roman law as well as studying it in scholastic manner, viz., *mos italicus*, left professors, lawyers, and jurists with little opportunity to advance their name and careers. They tended instead to use their expertise in semantic debate and word catching to promote their own reputations and/or the interest of their patrons:

> Those who write to increase their own fame (as is the nature of human character) resolve to disprove the words of greater men: to alter the written texts of the pandects and constitutions: to distort: to twist: to destroy: to do violence to the text: a quibbling of words: the little snares of word catchers: to devise traps of letters [of the law]: in short to undertake everything for the sake of illuminating their own name. For what did very many of the more recent [jurists] accomplish and do which is different than to misrepresent the civil law: and to get the better in an argument of the words of the law?[84]

Meanwhile, those who held Bartolus and Baldus in high esteem elevated them into a position vis-à-vis the law that had been hitherto reserved for lawgivers—kings, emperors, senates, or councils—rather than for those who interpreted it. This, in turn, undermined the authority of the law itself insofar as jurists—not laws—were celebrated. This became the norm for Accursius, Bartolus, and Baldus as well as for those who followed them. This veneration extended beyond university lectures and scholastic exercises in dispute and recitation,

83 Ibid.

84 Ibid, fo. v, 'cum scribentes aucupandae famae gratia (ut est humani ingenii natura) dicta maiorum refellere: pandectarum ac constitutionum scripta invertere: distorquere: contorquere: corrumpere: vim textui afferre: verborum aucupia: syllabarum tendiculas: literarum decipulas comminisci: nihil denique non incoeptare in animum induxerint illustrandi nominis sui gratia. Nam quod adhuc fecerunt faciuntque per multi recentiorum quid est aliud quam ius civile calumniari: verbaque legum captare?'

to the practice of law. This was especially the case when there was a contradiction in the law, notably when passages in the *Digest*, customary laws, and in the unwritten laws of specific people were at odds, or when canon and civil laws were in conflict.[85] Then, emperors, kings, princes, and councils looked to professors, lawyers, and jurists for definitive interpretations for settling disputes among and between them as well as between those subject to their jurisdictions. In the latter case, appellate courts throughout France and the supreme *parlement* in Paris became especially important, and thus had the potential to become as dangerous—depending on the nature of the dispute or the conflict of law they were called to settle—to the authority of the king and his ministers as the ecclesiastical courts might be.

In short, being tasked to interpret the law and being exalted for their ability to do so enabled secular and sacred jurists to consider themselves—and to be considered by others—to be above the law and even to be regarded as the source of law. Thus, jurists in the universities and lawyers, judges, and advisers beyond them, armed with their specialized methods and their pursuit of wealth and glory, could overstep their bounds. Jurists acting in accordance with their own self-interests could therefore use their expertise to change and even make new laws, a power reserved for the lawgivers alone. On the other hand, as specialists, jurists could also place themselves above the law, something even a ruler was unable to do without being accused of tyranny.

As a result of the laws being prone to the desires of the jurists, everyone in the profession seemed to be corrupting the law at the expense of security and stability, including the basic relationships of property, possession, and inheritance,

> Add on the specious pretexts of the ambitious, disreputable, unfair, that is, hostile judges, who after the authority of any interpreter you like has been thrown in the way—however more plausible, he is unheard of by the public (for this is accustomed to happen)—will watch over the most corrupt opinions more tenaciously. Moreover, how dangerous this is can

85 For discussions by and of Bartolus in particular, see: Bartolus, *On the Conflict of Laws*, trans. Joseph Henry (Cambridge, MA: Harvard University Press, 1914); Canning, *The Political Thought of Baldus*; Antony Black, *Political Thought in Europe, 1250–1450* (Cambridge: Cambridge University Press, 1992); Fasolt, *The Limits of History*, Maiolo, *Medieval Sovereignty*; Ryan, "Bartolus of Sassoferrato and Free Cities"; Nikitas Emmanuel Hatzimihail, "Bartolus and the Conflict of Laws," *Revue Hellenique de Droit International* 60 (November 2007): 12–79; and Cecil N. Sidney Woolf, *Bartolus of Sassoferrato: His Position in the History of Medieval Political Thought* (Cambridge: Cambridge University Press, 1913).

> be understood from the words of Cicero: Oh, admirable principle, (he says [in *Pro Caecina*]) and worthy of being maintained by you on this account, O judges! For, indeed, what is the civil law? A thing which can neither be bent by influence, nor broken down by power, nor adulterated by corruption, which, if it be, I will not say overwhelmed, but even neglected or carelessly upheld, there will then be no ground for any one feeling sure either that he possesses anything, or that he shall leave anything to his children.[86]

Indeed, the fundamental argument that Budé emphasized throughout his discussion of the first title of the *Digest* was that the guardians and ministers of the law, viz., the professors, the lawyers, and the jurists, who employed scholastic methods and modes of arguments, had corrupted the law itself. They studied, they taught, they practiced law, and they judged without an eye to the intentions or spirit of the lawgivers, to universal principles within law, to *ius*, and to the right order of things, but by looking to the legal profession as means to further their reputations and interests. Consequently, those teaching law in the universities allowed the law to be bent by influence, shattered by power, and corrupted by wealth, while directly contributing to such corruption.

The need for reform by Budé and others, including Louis XII, was immediate. This crisis existed because professors, lawyers, and judges had undermined order, created uncertainly, and stirred up discord and disputes, rather than use their expertise in law to establish order, to protect the security of persons and possessions, or to seek a common good. Continuing to let Cicero argue his case for him, Budé paired his lament in *Pro Caecina* directly to Ulpian's definition of *ius*,

> For there is nothing in a political community that must be maintained so diligently as the civil law. In truth, if this is taken away, there is no possibility of anyone feeling certain what is his own property or what belongs

86 Budé, *Annotationes*, fo. v, 'Adde speciosos praetextus ambitiosorum: sordidorum: iniquorum, id est, infensorum iudicum: qui corruptissimas sententias cuiuslibet enarratoris auctoritate obiecta quo magis vulgo inauditi: eo plausibilioris (Sic enim assolet) pertinacissime tuebuntur. Hoc autem quam sit perniciosum ex verbis Ciceronis intelligi potest: O rem praeclaram (inquit) vobisque retinendam iudices: quod enim est ius civile: quod neque inflecti gratia neque perfringi potentia: neque adulterari pecunia possit? Quod si non modo oppressum sed etiam desertum aut negligentius asservatum erit nihil est quod quisque se habere certum aut a patre accepturum aut relicturum liberis arbitretur.'; Cf. Cicero, "Pro Caecina," §.26.

> to another; there is nothing which can be equal to all men, or is the same in every case. Hence, *ius* is the art of what is good and fair.[87]

For humanists like Budé, the reason why law had been eroded in such an extreme way was rooted in the misunderstanding of *ius*, that is, the splitting of what is good from what is fair by Accursius and by those who followed his distinction. This split produced a contradiction insofar as it made it possible to argue that even if something was not good, it could be deemed as fair and vice-versa. Without a proper understanding of *ius* as good and fair conjoined nothing was stable, nothing was secure; there could be no justice or right, only legal interpretation.

The need to restore *ius* to its original meaning was also urgent because *ius* itself had a far more significant place in Budé's universal jurisprudence than it had for Accursius or for the Romans (Ancient and Byzantine).[88] Though not yet defined in the *Annotationes* as "its own distinctive quality which can be transferred to no other thing," it nevertheless stood as the common grammatical antecedent—or even the essence—that bound the categories (and corresponding idioms) of *ius naturale* (natural law), *ius gentium* (law of nations), and *ius civile* (civil law) to one another.[89] *Jus,* as explained by Ulpian and as restored by Budé was a measure of what is good and fair, and stood linguistically, morally, and historically at the core of justice, viz., *ius* is the stem of *iustitia*.[90] Moreover, for Budé it was as a distinguishing characteristic of man *qua* man, that is, it was an attribute of man's universal and inherent dignity, across time and space, which could not be divided and should not be destroyed. To arrive at the latter distinction, Budé had to first return to his treatment of the opening definition of the *Digest* since, up to this point, his preoccupation with attacking jurists and showing off his knowledge of Cicero had hindered

---

87 Budé, *Annotationes*, fo. v, 'Nihil est enim in civitate tam diligenter quam ius civile retinendum. Et enim hoc sublato nihil est quare exploratum cuiquam possit esse quid suum: quid alienum sit: nihil est quod aequabile inter omnes atque unum aut omnibus esse possit. Proinde Ius est ars boni & aequi: inquit Ulpianus: cuius merito quis nos sacerdotes appellat.' Here again, Budé reproduced Cicero's words verbatim, before adding a definition of *ius*, which he took from Ulpian. Cf. Cicero, "Pro Caecina," §.71 and D.1.1.1. respectively.

88 For a detailed discussion of equity within humanist discourse that reaches far beyond the scope of this case study of Budé's annotations on the first title of the *Digest* see Kisch, *Erasmus und die Jurisprudenz seiner Zeit*; and Kisch, *Studien zur Humanistischen Jurisprudenz*.

89 Budé, *Annotationes*, fo. IIII–V.

90 In D.1.1.1., Ulpian defines the relationship thus: "The law obtains its name from justice; for (as Celsus elegantly says), law is the art of knowing what is good and just."

him from advancing beyond Ulpian's definition of *ius* and his description of jurisprudence as a true philosophy. To illuminate it further, Budé turned attention, once again, to D.1.1.1.

6 *Jus* as a Defining Characteristic of Justice and Man *qua* Man

Pushing this discussion beyond the first lines of the *Digest* and bypassing the confusions and complications introduced by traditional interpretations and understandings, secular and religious, Budé artfully ignored Accursius and those who followed him when he turned to natural law, *ius gentium*, and civil law. Instead, he used this section of the *Annotationes* to further articulate *ius* as both a criterion of justice and as an inherent attribute of man. This required him, above all, to pinpoint the fundamental difference—in essence, action, and scope—between the laws of nature (instinct) and natural law (morality). Distinguishing between the two required a grasp of how and why natural law (shared by animals and man alike) and *ius gentium* (common only among mankind) diverged. Only by distinguishing these two types of law would it be possible to identify the fundamental and essential quality or attribute that humans possessed and animals lacked; the aim was to reach an understanding of justice and right based in and encapsulated by moral philosophy and human virtue.[91]

Judging by his opening discussion of the *Digest*, it should be no surprise that Budé's unlocking of the distinction between natural law (inherent instinct) and *ius gentium* (observed action) to arrive at a better understanding of the relation between law and justice, ultimately rested on a proper understanding of *ius*. In the context of distinguishing two types of law, however, a single aspect or definition of *ius* could only take the discussion so far. Delving deeper not only required an understanding of *ius* as the art of what is good and fair but

91 Although systematically comparing definitions of Roman law to arrive at the essence of natural law, *ius*, and *ius gentium* was commonplace, the fact that Budé chose to set jurisprudence aside to explore this relationship is telling. It is yet another instance in which his lack of legal training, and his sheer disregard for jurists more generally, effectively made his *Annotationes* irrelevant for the very audiences he proclaimed to be writing for. It also, ironically, betrays his disregard for (legal) history. For a broad overview of the relation between the different categories of law, in addition to *ius gentium*, found in the opening pages of the *Digest* by jurists and theologians see Dante Fedele, "*Ius gentium*: The Metamorphoses of a Legal Concept (Ancient Rome to Early Modern Europe)," in *Empire and Legal Thought: Ideas and Institutions from Antiquity to Modernity*, ed. Edward Cavanagh (Leiden-Boston: Brill Nijhoff, 2020), 213–50; and Scattola, *Das Naturrecht vor dem Naturrecht*.

also necessitated an understanding of *ius* as a distinguishing property or quality of man *qua* man. To explain *ius* as a quality or characteristic of man that could not be divided or diminished, Budé tested the veracity of Ulpian's distinction between natural law and *ius gentium* rather than to attempt to restore or rely on it.[92]

After defining *ius* and its relation to justice, Budé cited Ulpian's distinction between public and private law. In turn, Ulpian's definitions of the three main categories of Roman law were preserved in D.1.1.1. as well:

> (2) Private law is threefold in its nature, for it is derived either from natural precepts, from those of nations, or from those of the Civil Law. (3) *Jus naturale* is that which nature has taught to all animals; for it is not a law specific to mankind but is common to all animals—land animals, sea animals, and the birds as well. Out of this comes the union of man and woman, which we call marriage, and the procreation of children, and their rearing. So we can see that other animals, wild beasts included, are rightly understood to be acquainted with this law. (4) *Jus gentium*, the law of nations, is that which all human peoples observe. That it is not coextensive with natural law can be grasped easily, since this latter is common to animals whereas *ius gentium* is common only to human beings among themselves.[93]

While Budé agreed, in principle, with Ulpian's assertion that all animals, including man, shared natural law, whereas *ius gentium* was only common among mankind, he did not agree that it was so easy to distinguish the laws from one another or that behavior was the property by which the distinction between these types of law could be made, especially as it might appear that man and animals shared certain behaviors in common—beyond union, procreation, and the care and nurturing of offspring.[94] As such, observation

92 For a nuanced discussion of the Ulpian's understanding of the tripartite division both beyond and within the passages compiled in the *Digest*, especially in relation to Gaius' and Paul's definitions of *ius gentium*, see Scattola, *Das Naturrecht vor dem Naturrecht*, 116–24.

93 D.1.1.3.

94 Although Scattola asserted that Budé interpreted the clause D.1.1.3. as attributing moral or moral-like actions to animals, he nevertheless argued that Budé lacked an understating of right or law that would enable him to significantly depart from Ulpian's emphasis on what man and animals shared. Indeed, lacking the ability to reach beyond medieval understanding of this passage, according to Scattola, Budé interpreted it by drawing on his understanding of divine law (*lex divine*) and his distinctly stoic moral philosophy

would unlikely reveal a "particular property ... which cannot be transferred to anything else" that could be used to clearly distinguish natural law from *ius gentium*.[95] If, however, one were to shift the focus from conduct driven by instinct to voluntary action, then it would be possible to ascertain the criterion necessary to distinguish natural law from *ius gentium*, insofar as *ius gentium* reflected man's ability to act deliberately, whereas natural law—as the excerpt from Ulpian defined it—did not.

Furthermore, not only were appearances deceiving, but intentions could not be observed—they could only be found out. In the case of human behavior, an action may appear to be driven by intention, yet it may well be the result of instinct. In this instance, why someone acts the way they do can only be determined by inquiry, not supposition. Likewise, although animals might appear to be choosing their actions, upon closer examination it becomes clear that they are acting either because of instinct or because of training. The same goes for restraint: inaction may be an instinct for man as much as it may result from training for animals. Finally, in the case of man, action and inaction might be a matter of sheer whim as much as it might be the result of deliberative choice. Thus, the fundamental question for Budé was not whether the actions of mankind and animals differed, but how one determined whether an observed action was in fact the result of choice, instinct, or habituation.

Unlike his critique of Accursius' definition of *ius*, Budé could not simply state that Ulpian's distinction was inadequate; he had to show why it fell short. To make his case, Budé used examples from the natural world. In the first instance, Budé turned to the conduct of storks. Like most animals, storks are compelled by nature to nourish and care for their young in infancy. However, unlike most animals, when storks are no longer capable of caring for themselves, their offspring are compelled by nature to return to the nest and nourish them. While some humans may be inclined to this same kind of behavior, they are driven to it for different reasons than storks are. Whereas storks are acting on instinct, humans care for their aging parents on account of love, duty, necessity, or even civil compulsion.

---

acquired through his understanding of Cicero. Even so, Scattola overlooked Budé's immediate shift to Gaius in his *Annotationes*, wherein he not only took Ulpian to task but also utilized the kind of thinking that Scattola argued was rare before the late-sixteenth and early-seventeenth centuries to arrive at a more refined understanding of *ius* as an inherent quality of man *qua* man and its relation to *ius gentium*, not simply natural law. See Scattola, *Das Naturrecht vor dem Naturrecht*, 116–24 and 162–5.

95 Budé, *Annotationes*, fo. IIII–V.

Even if one were to assume that this behavior was instinctual, given how common tending to one's parents appears to be in any given society, the fact that it is not shared across all societies and all times served as evidence for Budé that it was a customary behavior, and thus not a matter of mere instinct. One cannot, in other words, deduce a general principle from individual actions; the fact that A, B, and C appear to share an impulse to care for their elderly parents does not mean that there is a universal instinct shared among all mankind to do so. Moreover, if this behavior were instinctual, Budé suggested, then the creation of the so-called Roman Stork laws—modeled after the natural behavior of storks and adapted from *ius gentium*—would have been unnecessary. Invoking this legal (and historical) evidence did not change the fact that, from the point of view of the observer, storks and humans engaged in the same behavior. It did, however, draw out one fundamental problem with Ulpian's distinction; to distinguish the two types of law based on observed behavior alone, one would have to assume that either man was following natural law or that the storks were following *ius gentium*. That neither was true, but the behaviors of both were the same, suggested that another criterion to differentiate these laws was needed.

Budé drew out this same problem in a second example, but from the inverse perspective. Turning from birds to mammals, thereby inverting the order in Ulpian's definition of natural law, this second case involved the attribution of human behaviors and virtues to animals. Budé made his argument by turning to Gaius Plinius', viz., Pliny the Elder (23–79 CE), *Historia naturalis* (*Natural History*). According to Pliny, "certain brute animals had been reported to be of a certain intelligence, therefore [they] were agreed to be a source of admiration for us above the remaining animals."[96] What is more, some even went so far as to credit elephants with a sense of what is good and what is fair:

> The largest land animal is the elephant, and it is the nearest to man in intelligence: it understands the language of its country and obeys orders, remembers duties that it has been taught, is pleased by affection and by marks of honour, nay more it possesses virtues rare even in man, honesty, wisdom, and justice.[97]

---

96 Budé, *Annotationes*, fo. x, 'Animalia igitur quaedam bruta naturali quadam intelligentia prodita: propterea censentur, id est, admirationi nobis sunt pro caeteris.' Here, Budé was referring to Gaius Plinius Secundus. See Pliny the Elder, *Natural History*, trans. H. Rackham (Cambridge, MA: Harvard University Press, 1962), Book VIII, 1.

97 Budé, *Annotationes*, fo. x: Pliny, *Natural History*, Book VIII, 1.

Pulling Pliny into the *Annotationes*, and thus engaging with a common motif in ancient and early modern texts of anthropomorphizing elephants, illuminates just how dangerous Budé considered merely resting the distinction between natural law and *ius gentium* on behavior to be. If elephants were accorded moral sensibility, a quality—along with reason and will—that distinguished man *qua* man, then this would not only accord elephants the capacity to exercise virtue but it would also effectively accord them with *ius*, a distinguishing characteristic of justice—inviting one to question man's place in the great chain of being.

Bracketing the latter for the moment, this second example led to precisely the same place as the previous one: to distinguish the two types of law based on observed behavior alone, one would have to assume that either man lived solely in accordance with natural law or that elephants followed *ius gentium*. Likewise, to make the distinction, it would be necessary to turn one's attention away from observed conduct and ask, instead, why actions were taken (or not) in the first place. Just as in the case of the storks, Budé held that elephants had no choice in their actions since instinct and habituation compelled them. Humans, on the other hand, had the capacity to choose their actions, even if it meant acting contrary to both instincts and education. That man had the capacity to choose his actions not only made some actions moral but also helped to account for why, in some cases, his lack of action amounted to neglecting his duty, whereas elephants and storks appeared to always fulfill theirs.

Budé once again drew from Pliny's *Natural History* to emphasize the distinction between acts stemming from volition and act triggered by instinct:

> But the very same animal [an elephant], if he meets with the traces of a man, before he meets the man himself, trembles in every limb, for fear of an ambush ... No doubt, it is Nature's law and shows her power, that the fiercest and largest wild beasts may have never seen a thing that they ought to fear and yet understand immediately when they have to fear it.[98]

Therefore, Budé asserted that "we are able to say that all animals owe respect to man according to natural law."[99] The inverse, however, was not the case. Invoking the great chain of being, Budé followed this point with a brief, but significant, reference to the Bible, specifically the account in Genesis wherein

98 Ibid, Book VIII, 5.§.10.

99 Budé, *Annotationes*, fo. X, 'Ex his Plinii verbis dicere possumus reverentiam iure naturali animalia omnia homini debere ...'

God gave man dominium over all the animals in the air, in the sea, and on land.[100] Of course, Budé's point was that God infused animals with an instinct to fear man and gave man the ability to choose his own actions—even to act in such a way as to put himself or others into harm's way. And it was this ability to choose his actions that elevated man above mere beasts who, barring abnormality, could only act because of their instinct or their training. Pairing Pliny and Genesis, Budé was able to reassert man's place in the great chain of being as well as refocus the argument at hand; choice stood as the distinctive property that could not be distinguished, divided, or transferred to anything else when determining if actions were moral or not. Choice, not behavior, characterized the difference between man and animals and, by extension, the difference between natural laws shared among both, and *ius gentium* known only to and practiced by man.

Using these examples, Budé rejected wholesale Ulpian's grounds for the distinction between natural law and *ius gentium*. However, the fact that the distinction between the two categories of law could not be made based on observed behavior could not serve as an explanation as to how natural law and *ius gentium* were related. Something more substantive and systematic was needed. To provide the latter, Budé turned to Gaius' definition of *ius gentium* as set out in D.1.1.9. Budé did so because, rather than juxtaposing natural law with *ius gentium* as Ulpian did, Gaius defined *ius gentium* in contradistinction to civil law. The latter enabled Gaius to define *ius gentium* with reference to natural reason, something that man possessed but animals, despite appearances, did not. According to Gaius,

> All nations who are ruled by law and customs make use partly of their own law, and partly of that which is common to all men. For whatever law any people has established for itself is peculiar to that State, and is called the Civil Law, as being the particular law of that State. But whatever natural reason has established among all men is equally observed by all mankind, and is called the Law of Nations [*ius gentium*] because it is the law which all nations employ.[101]

Jus gentium, as a form of natural law known only by natural reason, was distinguishable from the natural law that man and animals shared because animals lacked reason. By showing why Ulpian's definition was inadequate and

100 Ibid, 'ut sit illud Geneseos primo: Dominamini piscibus maris & volatilibus coeli & universis animantibus quae moventur super terram.'

101 D.1.1.9.

turning to Gaius instead, Budé arrived at the fundamental distinction that underpinned his understanding as to how it was possible that natural law and *ius gentium* could share the same antecedent—*ius*—at the same time as he held that *ius* was a fundamental characteristic of man *qua* man. This was possible because natural law, shared among animals and man, illuminated the right order of things as in objective *ius*, whereas attention to *ius gentium* as customs in common shared among all mankind—and only mankind because of man's reason—illuminated *ius* as an inherent attribute of man and a marker of man's inherent dignity.[102]

To further flesh this out, Budé turned once again to Cicero. In this case, he used the latter's *De legibus* (*On the Laws*), *De natura deorum* (*On the Nature of the Gods*), and *De finibus bonorum et malorum* (*On the Ends of Good and Evil*) to convey to his readers that natural law was not only "innate in all" but it also included an innate knowledge of its author in man.[103] This enabled Budé to emphasize the moral authority of *ius gentium* as well as denote its universality; he did this to show that *ius gentium* was not simply a category of Roman law, but was, instead, an attribute of universal jurisprudence that extended across time and space. Strategically using Cicero to emphasize the distinction made by Gaius, along with illustrating the connection between natural reason and a supreme legislator in such a way that it echoed Genesis, also enabled Budé to move rather quickly through the remaining definitions of *ius gentium* in the *Digest* by selecting only aspects of them that supported his interpretation and by ignoring those that did not.

---

102 It is worth emphasizing that Budé chose to do all of this without referring explicitly to scholars steeped in university-based jurisprudence, civil or canon, or theology, Thomistic or otherwise. The only texts he drew on were texts that predated or were contemporary to the excerpts included in the *Digest*. It is also worth highlighting again that despite Scatolla's argument, in *Das Naturrecht vor dem Naturrecht*, that prior to the late 16th and early 17th centuries few had explored Ulpian's understanding of natural law by juxtaposing it to Gaius', Budé did just that in his *Annotationes*. What's more, Zasius and Alciati did so as well in their own interpretations and lectures that sought to explain the relationship between justice and right for their students. That the legal humanists, all Catholic, did so prior to the Reformation does not call the innovations of Protestant jurists like Grotius into question, so much as it invites us to ponder how and why shifts already underway by the first decades of sixteenth century—steeped in reforms underway prior to the onset of religious reformations and European exploration—are so readily identified by historians of political and legal thought as wholly original, and even revolutionary, in the wake of religious wars and European expansion at the turn of seventeenth century.

103 Budé, *Annotationes*. fo. XI, 'Omnibus enim innatum est & in animo quasi insculptum esse deos, quales sint varium est: et nemo negat.' For a more nuanced discussion of Cicero and *ius gentium*, see Max Kaser, *Ius gentium* (Köln: Böhlau Verlag, 1993).

To do so, however, required Budé to explain how a category of law that was grounded in Rome's specific culture and historical context could be interpreted to reach beyond it. Rather than turn to sources beyond the *Digest*, Budé began simply enough by invoking a definition within it, namely one provided by Pomponius, who explained *ius gentium* as the type of law that concerned "religious duties toward god."[104] Budé used this definition as evidence that *ius gentium* encompassed innate and universal ideas of the divine and moral duties to one's God, one's father, and one's community. Taking this one step further, Budé infused *ius gentium* with moral authority by extensively quoting the explanation provided by Caius Vellius, as extracted from Cicero's *On the Nature of the Gods*, as to why man's knowledge of God, and thereby his religious duties toward him, were innate and universal:

> For since this belief [in the divine] of ours is not based on any prescription, custom, or law, but it abides as the strong, unanimous conviction of the whole world. We must therefore come to the realization that gods must exist because we have an implanted, or rather an innate, awareness of them.[105]

In essence, for Budé, *ius gentium* included religious duties toward God, not as a matter of mere human convention and customs but as a gift from God to man, like man's ability to exercise his free will and capacity of reason.

Although one might well expect Budé to have followed this assertion with a discussion of specific religious doctrines and practices, he did not; indeed, to this point in the *Annotationes* he remained firmly focused on universal aspects of moral philosophy and the actions of man, rather than on the particularities of specific theological debates or doctrines. This was the case when he seemed to pair Paul's understanding of *ius* in D.1.1.11, namely, "when *ius* is used as meaning what is always fair and good, it is natural law" with Ulpian's assertion that "*ius* as the art of what is good and fair" in D.1.1.1., Budé signaled that he, unlike his scholastic peers and predecessors (sacred and secular), was not interested in debating the veracity of Ulpian's statement that natural law was shared among man and animals and what that might mean in relation to man's place in the great chain of being, so much as discovering what distinguished natural

104 D.1.1.2. "Pomponius, Manual, sole book: For instance, reverence towards god, and the obedience we owe to parents and country."

105 In this part of the *Annotationes*, Budé's returned to having Cicero speak for him, and thus argue his case. Cf. Budé, *Annotationes*, fo. XI.; and Marcus Tullius Cicero, *The Nature of the Gods*, ed. Peter G. Walsh (Oxford: Oxford World's Classics, 2016), Book 1.§.44.

law from *ius gentium*.[106] Indeed, rather than try to explore Ulpian's definition with reference to Thomistic or scholastic thought, Budé's focus remained thoroughly fixed on the Ancients.

After establishing the fundamental distinction between man and animals as threefold, namely the capacity to will, the attribute of natural reason, and the innate knowledge of God, Budé turned his attention to exploring how *ius*, natural law, and *ius gentium*, propel man to seek peace and pursue justice in mutual company. This account was short and to the point, providing an opportunity for Budé to explain in full the inherent nature of *ius* by linking it to man's dignity in clear and unveiled terms.

7 *Jus* Has Been Given to All Mankind

Invoking the words—and authority—of Cicero's discussion of justice as a universal virtue, Budé integrated an extensive quote from *On the Ends of Good and Evil* to offer his readers a brief account of human society from its origins:

> But in the whole moral sphere of which we are speaking there is nothing more glorious nor of wider range than the solidarity of mankind, that species of alliance and partnership of interests and that actual affection which exists between man and man, which, coming into existence immediately upon our birth, owing to the fact that children are loved by their parents and the family as a whole is bound together by the ties of marriage and parenthood.[107]

Continuing with Cicero's words, Budé presented a description of the development and spread of human society, of man's interactions with families, communities, and even disparate peoples across the globe and over time:

> For it gradually spreads its influence beyond the home, first by blood relationships, then by connections through marriage, later by friendships, afterwards by the bonds of neighbourhood, then to fellow-citizens and political allies and friends, and lastly by embracing the whole of the human race. This sentiment, assigning each his own and maintaining

---

106 D.1.1.11. For a discussion of how Paul's understanding of *ius* (D.1.1.11.) corresponded with Ulpian's see Scattola, *Das Naturrecht vor dem Naturrecht*, 116–8.

107 Budé, *Annotationes*, fo. XI; Marcus Tullius Cicero, *De finibus bonorum et malorum*, Book V.23.§.65.

> with generosity and equity that human solidarity and alliance of which I speak, is termed Justice; connected with it are dutiful affection, kindness, liberality, good-will, courtesy and the other graces of the same kind. And while these belong peculiarly to Justice, they are also factors shared by the remaining virtues. For human nature is so constituted at birth as to possess an innate element of civic and national feeling, termed in Greek *politikon*; consequently, all the actions of every virtue will be in harmony with the human affection and solidarity I have described.[108]

The former description laid out the domain of natural law and the origins of the family, whereas the latter presented the domain of *ius gentium* and the history of society. All men possessed the attributes of reproduction and association, no matter the varied conditions in time, circumstance, or place. Precisely because men were inclined to join in mutual company and pursue the common good in civil society, this served as evidence that all men possessed the innate virtues of justice and the inherent inclination of sociability.

The importance of the principles of human association from its origins and through its history was further underscored by Budé when he turned once again to providing a definition of *ius* as a link between natural law and *ius gentium*, and thus as a universal attribute shared among all mankind. To explain this link, Budé turned to Cicero's *On the Laws*, specifically to his emphasis on natural equality. For example, in response to Atticus' observation that he was "certainly going a long way back in your search for the basis of justice," Marcus responded,

> Of all human affairs circulating in the arguments of the learned nothing is so excellent as that it is plainly understood that we are born for justice. For it will be obvious that *ius* has been established, not by opinion, but by nature, if you examine the society and relationship of men among themselves. For no one thing is so similar to another, so very equal, as we are all among ourselves. If corrupt habits and foolish opinions did not twist and turn aside our feeble minds from their original paths, no individual would be more like himself than everyone would be like everyone else. Thus, however one defines man, the same definition applies to us all. This is a sufficient proof that there is no essential difference within mankind.[109]

108 Budé, *Annotationes*, fo. XI; Marcus Tullius Cicero, *The Republic and The Laws*, edited by N. Rudd and J. G. F. Powell (Oxford: Oxford University Press, 2016), Book 1.§. 28. Hereafter: *The Laws*.

109 Budé, *Annotationes*, fo. XI; Cicero, *The Laws*, Book 1.§. 28–9.

Precisely because *ius* was both a universal attribute of man *qua* man and a fundamental characteristic of justice, Budé effectively did three crucial things by integrating this passage from *On the Laws* with those drawn from *The Nature of the Gods* and *On the Ends of Good and Evil.* First, by solely appealing to the ideas expressed in these texts (and indeed allowing Cicero to make his case for him) and ignoring texts that we might expect in this discussion, like those of Aquinas or those produced by scholastic jurists—sacred and secular—more generally, Budé signaled to his readers just how unimportant he considered definitions of justice and right in such texts to be to the endeavor of interpreting the fundamental terms and ideas that underlay the *Digest* and, by extension, universal jurisprudence. In so doing, he not only showed his contempt for traditional jurisprudence but also his own lack of legal training. For Budé, legal reform started with mastering classical studies, not scholastic jurisprudence.

Second, he used Cicero to assert, in no uncertain terms, the equality of man *qua* man; all of humankind had an innate sense of justice, the ability to choose to pursue virtue and the common good, and an inherent distinctive quality, viz., dignity. Third, he reinforced the idea that man strove to live in accordance with justice precisely because man had an inherent sense of justice within him. This, in turn, set up his overall argument that *ius* was a fundamental attribute of justice, natural law, and *ius gentium*, and also of man *qua* man. In essence, Budé offered his readers a definition of *ius* that encompassed universal justice, man's inherent dignity, and the equality of all mankind. To further stress that *ius* was an inherent attribute of man, directly linked to man's capacity to reason and to an objective standard of justice, he once again let Cicero make the argument for him:

> Reason in fact—the one thing in which we are superior to the beasts, which enables us to make valid deductions, to argue, refute our opponents, debate, solve problems, draw conclusions—that certainly is common to us all. While it may vary in what it teaches, it is constant in its ability to learn.[110]

The emphasis on the faculty of reason as common to all is paramount because it simultaneously elevates man above beasts and equalizes all mankind. As an innate quality in man, reason distinguished man from animals from his origins as well as before the law. Thus, reason—like dignity—was an inherent distinctive quality of man *qua* man. It was, for Budé, also inseparable from *ius*. If all humankind possessed the inherent quality of reason (and

110 Budé, *Annotationes*, fo. XI; Cicero, *The Laws*, Book 1.§. 29.

dignity), then *ius* was common to all mankind as well. All mankind, regardless of place or time, likewise had the capacity to think, to understand, to form judgments, and to share customs in common, viz., *ius gentium*, as well as to structure and moderate mutual company. Everyone, without distinction, had the capacity to pursue peace, justice, and the common good. And everyone, precisely because these characteristics were universal among humankind and shared with God, had the capacity—and obligation—to live in accordance with justice, viz., what was good and what was fair conjoined. The latter is especially important to bear in mind given that Budé so painstakingly framed his discussion of *ius* by first restoring Ulpian's meaning before trying to use it to differentiate between natural law and *ius gentium*. Lest his readers mistake his meaning, Budé underscored all the above by, once again, letting Cicero argue for him,

> What is there, I will not say in man, but in the whole of heaven and earth, more divine than reason (a faculty which, when it has developed and become complete, is rightly called wisdom)? Since, then, there is nothing better than reason, and reason is present in both man and God, there is a primordial partnership in reason between man and God. But those who share reason also share right reason; and since that is law, we men must also be thought of as partners with the gods in law.[111]

In effect, Budé used Cicero to link his humanist moral philosophy, which focused on the centrality and dignity of man, to the underlying principles of law and justice through his reference to God. He did so before concluding his discussion of *ius* by accentuating the link between law, *ius*, and justice, by combining two passages from *On the Laws* into one,

> Moreover, those who share law [*lex*] share *ius*. Furthermore, all those who share these things are common, ought to be regarded as belonging to the same commonwealth [civitas] ... For those who have been endowed by nature with reason have also been endowed with right reason, and hence with *lex*, which is right reason in commanding and forbidding; If *lex*, so too *ius*: to all reason has been given. Therefore, *ius* has been given to all.[112]

111 Budé, *Annotationes*, fo. XI; Cicero, *The Laws*, Book 1.§. 22.

112 Budé, *Annotationes*, fo. XI; Cicero, *The Laws*, Book 1.§. 22. and 33, respectively.

Having used Cicero to make a resounding closing argument, the only question that remained was how all of this squared with definitions and discussions of *ius gentium* within traditional jurispudence that appeared to suggest that slavery and servitude, and the inequality each entailed, were seemingly natural and even just conditions. Budé had to address slavery for two reasons. First, because Ulpain linked it to *ius gentium* in D.1.1.4 (reproduced below), and, second, just as justice, *ius*, reason, and dignity distinguished man from animals, so too did slavery. Furthermore, if all mankind—without distinction—were essentially equal in their capacity of reason and inherent quality of dignity, then why was a shared practice—across time and space—premised on, and indeed legitimated by, a custom that was not good and not fair? The answer was singular for Budé: slavery existed as a result of man's actions; it was an artificial, rather than a natural condition. Departing from Aristotle on this point without comment, Budé referred, in rapid succession to Gaius, St. Augustine, Vergil, and Livy, yet in doing so did not add much to his initial point because, as far as Budé was concerned, slavery and all that accompanied it—no matter if a product of war or a condition of peace—was not good and fair, and thus violated *ius*. No sleight of hand could make it into something else, nor could it diminish the fact that it was manumission, and not slavery, that bridged the gap between *ius,* natural law, and *ius gentium* in D.1.1.4., that is, in Ulpian's definition of manumission:

> Manumissions also belong to *ius gentium*. Manumission means sending out of one's hand, that is, granting of freedom. For whereas one who is in slavery is subjected to the hand (*manus*) and power of another; on being sent out of hand he is freed of that power. all of which originated from *ius gentium*. since, of course, everyone would be born free by the natural law, and manumission would not be known when slavery was unknown. But after slavery came in by *ius gentium*, there followed the boon (*beneficium*) of manumission. And thenceforth, we all being called by one natural name "men," in the *ius gentium* there came to be three classes: free men, and set against those slaves and the third class, freedmen, that is, those who had stopped being slaves.[113]

The fact that slavery, as Ulpian explained it above, was neither a natural condition nor a permeant one was perfectly in line with Budé's overall argument and emphasis on *ius* as a marker of dignity and equality in the first title of his 1508 *Annotationes*.

113 D.1.1.4.

Indeed, understanding *ius* as what is good and fair conjoined, and thereby justice as well as a signifier of man's inherent dignity, meant that Accursius' error in dividing *ius* in the *Gloss* stood as nothing short of an affront to human dignity for Budé. This was in no small part because such a division could be used to assert that slavery, although not good, was fair insofar as it preserved one's enemies (rather than killing them). Likewise, conditions of servitude—even those that essentially placed one under the unrestrained power of another—could also be deemed as fair, even when they were not good. Highlighting slavery and servitude and thinking about how each violate *ius*—in both its objective and subjective/inherent aspects—helps to illuminate why Budé's call to restore the meaning of *ius* to its original, as what is good and what is fair conjoined, was so urgent. If we keep in mind how essential getting *ius* and everything related to it right was for Budé, it is not surprising that his attacks were so bitter and, at times, relentless. By corrupting *ius*, in his estimation, scholastic jurists and lawyers not only corrupted law and abandoned justice but they also created the legal apparatus to affront man's dignity in exchange for profit, glory, fame, and applause.

Thus, Budé's understanding of *ius*, and all that it entailed, not only illuminates why his attacks against traditional jurists were so acerbic but also helps to shed light on why other legal humanists found his work useful. Not only did Budé restore the definition of *ius* as justice, the art of what is good and what is fair conjoined, he also defined *ius* as an innate attribute that all mankind possessed without distinction of time or place. In so doing, he linked *ius* directly to man's faculties of reason and will, both of which stood as fundamental attributes of man's dignity, which, in turn, stood at the very foundations of Budé's conception of universal jurisprudence.

Moreover, through the words of Cicero, Budé also provided an account of man's common origins, wherein he explained that all men shared inborn ideas of the divine, along with justice, charity, and virtue. Recounting the spread of human association from its origins, Budé emphasized man's impulse to join mutual company, to pursue the common good, and to seek justice in common, all of which were conjoined by *ius*, understood as a universal justice and as an inherent attribute of man. Finally, in his attempt to restore Roman law, Budé fundamentally reinterpreted *ius gentium* not simply as a kind of law, but as a form of natural law that was universally known to all mankind on account of natural reason. In essence, *ius gentium* was infused with moral authority by Budé—in a way that it was not accorded by Roman jurists, Byzantine compilers, or scholastic jurists—precisely because of its relation to *ius*, as both the art of equity and good conjoined and as an inherent attribute of man *qua* man.

8 Significance of Budé's Re-interpretation of *Jus* and *Jus Gentium*

Attention to Budé's treatment of *De iustitia et iure* in his *Annotationes* enables us to see why Budé offered a crucial distinction that helped advance the work of his peers. It also helps to illuminate how *ius gentium*—a relatively insignificant category of law for Roman and medieval jurists—became central to theories of universal jurisprudence among legal humanists in the first decade of the sixteenth century, nearly four decades before it acquired increasing importance among early-modern political theorists, jurists, and theologians, such as Francisco de Vitoria and Bartolomé de las Casas (c.1484–1566), who utilized the category of *ius gentium* to respond to problems associated with European expansion, conquest, colonization, and religious conflict within and beyond Europe.[114]

Attention to Budé's treatment of fundamental categories within Roman law also invites us to think more critically about how and why, as early as 1508, humanists like Budé (and those who followed him) began to understand *ius* as

114 That is not to say that *ius gentium* was not important before the sixteenth century, but rather to emphasize that in the context of calls for legal reform *ius gentium* was increasingly marshaled by the Renaissance jurists, humanist, and scholastic alike to do a different kind of work than it was utilized to do in the recent (and distant) past. There is a rich and growing literature, which is too expansive to list in detail here, that is dedicated to re-thinking the history and development of *ius gentium* from the ancient to the modern era. This turn to rethinking *ius gentium* extends from the turn to international and global intellectual history over the last three decades. Yet, even considering this renewed interest in the dynamic character of *ius gentium*, humanist jurisprudence remains outside of this history. See David Armitage, *Foundations of Modern International Thought* (Cambridge: Cambridge University Press, 2013); Armitage, ed., *Theories of Empire, 1450–1800* (Aldershot: Ashgate, 1998); Benno Teschke, *The Myth of 1648: Class, Geopolitics and the Making of Modern International Relations* (London: Verso, 2003); Antony Anghie, *Imperialism, Sovereignty and the Making of International Law* (Cambridge: Cambridge University Press, 2005); Hent Kalmo and Quentin Skinner, eds. *Sovereignty in Fragments: The Past, Present and Future of a Contested Concept* (Cambridge: Cambridge University Press, 2010); Benedict Kingsbury and Benjamin Straumann, eds. *The Roman Foundations of the Law of Nations: Alberico Gentili and the Justice of Empire* (Oxford: Oxford University Press, 2010); Martti Koskenniemi, "'International Community' from Dante to Vattel," in *Vattel's International Law from a XXIst Century Perspective / Le Droit International de Vattel vu Du XXIe Siècle*, eds. Vincent Chetail and Peter Haggenmacher (Leiden: Brill, 2011), 49–75; Martti Koskenniemi, "Vitoria and Us." *Rechtsgeschichte/Legal History* 22 (2014): 119–38; Austin Sarat, Lawrence Douglas, and Martha Merrill Umphrey, eds. *Law without Nations* (Stanford, CA: Stanford University Press, 2011); William Bain, *Medieval Foundations of International Relations* (London: Routledge, 2017); Edward Cavanagh, ed, *Empire and Legal Thought: Ideas and Institutions from Antiquity to* Modernity (Leiden-Boston: Brill Nijhoff, 2020); and Nijman and Carty, eds., *Morality and the Responsibility of Rulers.*

something that could transcend the limits and confines attendant on, and reified by, the *ius commune*. Further, it invites us to ask why they didn't trust that the law common to all of Europe—thanks to university-based jurisprudence (civil and canon)—could address the issues that they found most pressing. Further, it raises the question as to why the Roman category of *ius gentium*, infused with moral and historical authority by humanist jurists, served as a more useful, and even more pliable, tool for critique and reform than the European *ius commune* did, especially given that it was *ius commune*, not *ius gentium*, that embodied the common legal past of post-Roman Latin Christendom.[115]

Although Budé's main aim was to restore *ius* to its original—and in the process demonstrate how much Accursius had corrupted it—he ultimately reinterpreted it. He did not, however, include a systematic discussion of *ius gentium* that pushed his understanding of *ius* beyond an inherent characteristic shared by all mankind, without distinction, across time and space. Given his task to cleanse the *Digest* of errors, which often served as an excuse to launch into acerbic attacks against lawyers, it is not surprising that Budé did not work out a full-fledged theory of *ius gentium*, despite its importance to his understanding of *ius*. As such, to explore the implications of Budé's choice to restore *ius* and then link it directly to *ius gentium* as he did, we need to turn our attention from France to Germany—from Budé's advice to the French Chancellor to the lectures and juridical works of Ulrich Zasius, the preeminent legal humanist within the Germanies. Doing so is useful because Budé's interpretation was limited by his own context as subject to a single ruler within a single political entity (or, *civitas*), whereas Zasius' treatment of *ius gentium* reflected the complexity of a disparate, often contested, patchwork of political and legal authorities that were bound together—in principle more so than in fact—by the legal vocabularies and apparatus, which often pitted territorial and imperial claims against one another within the Holy Roman Empire.

115 Cf. Peter Stein, "The *Ius Commune* and its Demise," *The Journal of Legal History*, vol. 25, no. 2 (August 2004): 161–167. According to Stein: 'The decline of the *ius commune* may be attributed to two opposing forces, one universal and the other particular. The first was the rise of natural law, which marked a switch in emphasis from *ius civile* to *ius gentium* and the second was the replacement of the Vernacular' (165). However, Stein places this switch from the *ius civile* to *ius gentium* with the Spanish Dominican Scholastics at the School of Salamanca, under the tutelage of Vitoria, when was elected as Chair of Theology in 1524. That is, sixteen years after Budé published his *Annotationes*; eighteen years after Zasius was appointed a Professor of Jurisprudence; six years after he had published his *Lucubrationes* with the 1518 preface (see Part 2 of this volume); and nine years after Alciati published his *Annotations on the Last Three Books of Justinian's Code*; six years after he took up his first teaching position in Avignon, and thus after Alciati's methods became synonymous with the *mos gallicus*.

PART 2

Ulrich Zasius: Jus, Jus Gentium, *and Rights*

CHAPTER 3

Re-defining *Jus* to Restore *Justitia*

Ulrich Zasius' Methods in Word and in Action

1 Humanist First, a Lawyer Second

As obscure as the name might be in our own time, Ulrich Zasius was considered by his contemporaries to be one of the greatest German jurists of his age and one of the most brilliant humanists of the early-sixteenth century. While his immediate influence was on the city and university of Freiburg, his works helped transform legal thought and legal education throughout Germany and Europe in the early modern period. Zasius was appointed as a Lecturer of Rhetoric and Poetry in 1500, and then, in 1506 (at the age of 40), became an Ordinary Professor of Civil Law.[1] While serving as a professor, Zasius continued to practice law, acted as a legal councilor for the city of Freiburg, and, in 1508, became an imperial councilor to Maximilian I (1459–1519). In addition to his teaching and service, Zasius was also well known throughout Germany for his work on the vernacular 1520 Freiburg *Code*, which became a model for many other sixteenth-century cities and principalities engaged in rationalizing and transforming their own local law from customary, piecemeal, and unwritten legal traditions to systematic written ones.[2] Beyond the Empire, he was known for his positions on controversial legal, political, and moral issues as well as his orations, his lectures, and his published treatises on Roman law—the latter

1 Unlike many professors of law who took degrees in both canon and civil law, Zasius only held an advanced degree in Roman civil law. See Rowan, *Ulrich Zasius*.

2 Ulrich Zasius, *Neue Stadtrechte und Statuten der Stadt Freiburg im Breisgau* [1520] (Aalen: Scientia Verlag, 1968), and Theodor von Liebenau, *Der Humanist Ulrich Zasius als Stadtschreiber von Baden im Aargau* (Lucerne: Kath. SchweizBll, 1898). For a detailed discussion of this and a more in-depth biographical information on Zasius see Hans Jürgen Knoche, *Ulrich Zasius und das Freiburger Stadtrecht von 1520* (Karlsruhe: C. F. Müller, 1957); Leo Alexander Ricker, *Freiburg: Aus der Geschichte einer Stadt* (Reprint. Freiburg, 1982); Rowan, *Ulrich Zasius*; Johann August Roderich von Stintzing, *Ulrich Zasius: Ein Beitrag zur Geschichte der Rechtswissenschaft im Zeitalter der Reformation* (Basel: Schweighauser, 1857); and Hans Thieme, *Kaiser Maximilian I im Leben und in den Werken von Ulrich Zasius* (Publication du centre Européen d'Études Burgondo-Médianes, 1963). For a discussion of works by Zasius that are not explored in this chapter see Paul Gerhard Schmidt, *Humanismus im Deutschen Südwesten: Biographische Profile*. 2nd ed (Stuttgart: Thorbecke, 2000).

 | DOI:10.1163/9789004528451_005

of which were part of the 'canon' of political and legal thought well into the seventeenth and eighteenth centuries.[3]

In short, Zasius' presence distinguished the city and the university of Freiburg in the first third of the sixteenth century as a home for the 'new humanist jurisprudence'. Germans who wished to study law in accordance with the new *modus docendi*, or *studia humanitatis*, in the teaching and interpretation of law no longer had to travel to Italy or France to do so. Upon receiving their education under the direction of Zasius, many became counselors to cities, counts, dukes, and princes, and played a central role in legal reforms across the Germanies, whereas others became professors at universities—new and old—across the Empire.[4]

As influential as he was, however, Zasius was at no loss for detractors among his peers, colleagues, and even students. Steven Rowan tells us, for example, that Erasmus, after having the chance to meet Zasius in person during an early trip to Freiburg, found him to be so crass and overbearing that he went out of his way to avoid him during subsequent stays. Among his colleagues at the university, many found Zasius to be so intolerable that they attempted to exclude him from faculty meetings. In addition, some students, including Johannes Eck (1486–1543), left Freiburg rather than continue to matriculate in a legal faculty that included Zasius, and spared no energy disparaging Zasius' name across Europe in the process.[5]

Nevertheless, even those who did not admire Zasius as a man respected his ability as a jurist. Their respect was premised on the combination of humanist methods and legal expertise that he employed to invite students—as well as his scholastic and humanist peers—to think about law in new ways: not as written reason or logical artifice, but as a record of the customs and actions of man over time. To think about the law historically rather than logically, Zasius

3 See Zasius' *Questiones de parvulis Iudaeorum baptisandis* (Strassbourg: Grüninger, 1508), and *Apologetica defensio contra Ioanne[m] Eckium theologum, super eo quod olim tractauerat, quo loco fides non esset hosti feruanda. Videbis lector Eckium iura ciuilia non perspecte intellexisse. Defensa magni Erasmi assertio, quam in elegantiss. Scholijs super septimo Matthei capite docuit. Experiere lector, quàm omnino periculi plenum sit, in alienam excurrere professionem* (Basel: Ioannem Frobenium, 1519).

4 For a discussion of Zasius' students see Hans Winterberg, *Die Schüler von Ulrich Zasius* (Stuttgart: W. Kohlhammer Verlag, 1966); Kelley, "Law"; Kisch, *Studien zur Humanistischen Jurisprudenz*; and Rowan, *Ulrich Zasius*. For a thorough discussion of Zasius' influence in Germany, Italy, and France see Hans Thieme, "Les leçons de Zasius" and "L'oeuvre juridique de Zasius," both in *Pédagogues et juristes: Congrès Du Centre d'études Supérieures de La Renaissance de Tours: été 1960*, ed. Pierre Mesnard (Paris: J. Vrin 1963): 31–8, 39–48.

5 Rowan, *Ulrich Zasius*.

demanded that his students put aside the traditional practices of reading law solely through the perspectives of scholastic jurisprudence and legal authorities, and, instead, challenged them to read, study, and understand legal texts in their original (*ad fontes*). That is, rather than only reading authorities on the Roman *Digest,* Zasius invited students to read the *Digest* itself, which required them, in turn, to challenge traditional authorities by asking new questions. Zasius' goal then was not to disregard traditional jurisprudence, but rather, as Guido Kisch put it, to "reach, with the help of Bartolus and Baldus, beyond Bartolus and Baldus."[6]

To understand the significance and meaning of laws within the *Digest,* Zasius also expected his students to study its sources, including those rooted in moral philosophy, grammar, rhetoric, and history. This was no small task for students who had joined the law faculty at Freiburg before Zasius took up his position, as it required trading scholastic methods and texts for humanist ones; for some, it might even have meant starting their studies all over again. Those who took up the challenge were also expected to develop and exercise their imagination to study law in historical perspective. Only by using one's historical imagination to consider the origins of law and the first principles within it, as well as by asking critical questions as to why and how laws responded to problems in particular contexts at specific moments, would it be possible to understand why and to what end laws, legal remedies, and legal interpretations came to be in the first place. Moreover, combining critical and historical modes of inquiry, investigation, and imagination would allow students, lawyers, and jurists alike to see that law changed over time, for ill and for good, because it was a reflection and the embodiment not simply of reason, but also of the interests and needs of those who created and administered it.

Given that Zasius called on his students to approach the study of Roman law differently, and in so doing set out his methods through his orations, preliminary remarks, and lectures, a modern reader is well served to engage Zasius' ideas and interpretations in a similar manner. By first encountering Zasius through his orations, we get a sense of why and how he convinced students to depart from traditional jurisprudence, and to take up instead the study of law with him.[7] Next, by following those who were persuaded by Zasius to attend his lectures, we can engage with the structure and substance of his

6 Kisch, "Humanistic Jurisprudence," 79.

7 Although called orations in his *Opera omnia*, these speeches are exemplary of humanist *declamatio*. See Marc van der Poel, "Oratory and Declamation," in *A Guide to Neo-Latin Literature*, ed. Victoria Moul (Cambridge: Cambridge University Press, 2017), 272–88.

interpretations of justice and right, and thus gain a better grasp of why he held that legal reform was not only necessary but also urgent.[8]

Although a select cadre of his students who shared his house, dinner table, and private library would have had the opportunity to discuss his ideas with him beyond the lectern, we—like most others, including his humanist peers across Europe—must turn instead to his published *Lucubrationes*, or 'night musings', to find his additional insights on law, including his conception of the relation between natural law, *ius*, and *ius gentium*.[9] Unlike his contemporaries, we also have access to his voice and ideas through texts that were 'lost' as the sixteenth century unfolded. These were texts that Zasius edited (and even removed) from his bound collections as political and religious tensions of the 1520s and 1530s intensified throughout the Holy Roman Empire. Whether on their own or in combination, attention to texts from each of the genres that Zasius utilized to convey his understanding of Roman law and the universal principles that underlie it enables us to observe his methods of interpretation, understanding, and argument in action.

Within his *De iustitia et iure* lecture, Zasius not only offered his students an entirely different understanding of the relation between *ius* and *iustitia* from his scholastic predecessors and contemporaries (explored in this chapter), he also departed from traditional jurisprudence when it came to exploring the categories of natural law and *ius gentium* as well as their correlation and interconnection via *ius* as criterion of justice and a marker of inherent and inviolable rights (explored in the next chapter). As important, even while he adopted Budé's definition of *ius* as the art of what is good and fair conjoined and shared his understanding of *ius* as an attribute of man *qua* man, and thus a marker of human dignity, Zasius pushed this definition further, especially in terms of its interconnection to *ius gentium*, viz., customs shared among all mankind. In the process, he departed from Budé and contemporary scholastic jurists as well as from the Romans when he argued, first, that *ius gentium* was a form of natural law, and second, that *ius gentium*, on account of its relation to *ius*, could be used to hold civil laws and civil authorities to a higher criterion of justice. The latter was possible precisely because *ius gentium* was the source of obligations and of rights shared by all humankind, regardless of time and place.

8 Although students had access to his lectures via a depository maintained by his students in Freiburg, we will access those lectures through his *Opera omnia*.

9 In Zasius' estimation, he was not only overworked, but also underpaid. Beyond complaining about his pay and constantly trying to get more money from the university, Zasius also rented rooms in his house to select students in order to supplement his income.

2 Combining Methods: Historicizing Law to Observe Justice

Trained as a lawyer, Zasius' project of reforming civil jurisprudence was steeped in legal knowledge and practice more so than grammar and rhetoric. Thus, unlike his humanist counterpart Budé, Zasius did not reject traditional jurisprudence—or its methods—wholesale. Though he agreed that faulty interpretations and misunderstandings of basic terms of Roman law needed to be corrected, he nevertheless combined aspects of the scholastic and humanist methods of interpretation in his own attempts to restore Roman law to its original.

One of the most notable aspects of the scholastic methods of interpretation that Zasius accommodated was the practice of reconciling different species of law (e.g., natural, civil, *ius gentium*) into a comprehensive system. However, unlike his scholastic peers and predecessors, Zasius, as a humanist, employed understandings of moral philosophy and history, not logic or theology, to explain how and why these categories of law, often appearing to be entirely divergent from one another, were related and, in some cases, even co-original. Moreover, rather than look to abstract principles (*ab initio*) or logic to account for the source of the law, he looked instead to texts (*ad fontes*), in time and in context, to observe how man's actions—and the laws that attempted to direct and order them—had changed over time.[10]

In effect, through a close reading of Roman law and its sources Zasius set out to discover the universal principles that all types of law shared, namely justice and right (*iustitia* and *ius*). Once identified, he then historicized these universal principles by seeking their discrete origins in the actions and customs of man. Next, he attempted to show that although these first principles were universal, the laws themselves, as a creation of man, changed over time—reflecting less

10 In their discussions of the relation between justice and right, Budé, Zasius, and Alciati tended to emphasize moral philosophy (how man ordered the world in which he lived) rather than moral theology (how the world was ordered by a single divine entity). Therefore, in their discussions on the first title of the *Digest*, they left nuanced debates and understandings that were at the center of Thomism aside, and instead focused their attention almost exclusively on more secular—or worldly—manifestations of just and unjust actions. This was especially the case for Zasius and Alciati, who, unlike Budé, were training future jurists and lawyers who would be tasked to effect civic reform, within and beyond the Germanies and Northern Italy. For a discussion of the impact of Thomism on political and juridical thought see especially Tierney, *The Idea of Natural Rights* and Brett, *Liberty, Right, and Nature*. For a more recent discussion and interpretation of the importance of Thomism for the broader history and development of *ius gentium* see Martti Koskenniemi, *To the Uttermost Parts of the Earth: Legal Imagination and International Power 1300–1870* (Oxford: Oxford University Press, 2021).

or more justice. Only by understanding the origins of these principles as well as how and why laws embodied and expressed them throughout history would it be possible to, first, identify corruptions in the law and, second, enact legal reforms whereby justice and right could be restored.

This combination of scholastic and humanist methods, at work in how he tried to reconcile different categories of law in accordance with history and the fundamental principles of moral philosophy, is the same that he used to draw students to the study of law and, once they were convinced, to help them undertake it through his lectures. As such, the oration *In Praise of the Law* (*In laudem legum oratio*), delivered as early as 1508, offers modern readers a direct and succinct example of Zasius' methods in word and in action.[11] The defense of law and legal education within this oration also indicates that Zasius had a far more expansive audience in mind than prospective and current students: his scholastic colleagues and his humanist peers in and beyond Freiburg.

3 In Praise of the Law: A True and Useful Science

Speaking to both a local and a distant audience, Zasius began this piece by admonishing those who—like Accursius and the Doctors who followed him—adhered too strictly to traditional scholastic methods as well as those who placed far too much emphasis on certain aspects of the *studia humanitatis* in the study of law—such as Budé and those who followed him. To prepare his audience for attacks on each, Zasius first narrowed his attention to two

11 Zasius composed and delivered several orations in praise of the law, which he included in his 1518 *Lucubrationes* and which were also bound in his 1550 *Opera omnia*, such as: *Oratio habita in legum praeconia, post ferias aestivas*; *Quarta legalis oratio*; *Oratio legalis post caniculi ferias Friburgi habita*; *In laudem legum oratio, cum post ferias aestiuas lectiones ordinarias auspicaretur, Friburgi frequentissimo eius auditorio habita*; *Mixto genere oratio Friburgi post vacationes an ordinariis lectionibus habita: in qua & sui purgationem adversus locutuleios quosdam adducit, & legum eminentiam praedicat*; and *Oratio de laudibus legum, Friburgi agno auditorum coetu dicta*; *In laudem legum oratio, nouissime Friburgi habita*. These orations lack notation signifying the precise year in which they were written or delivered. However, they are arranged in the same order in the 1550 *Opera omnia* as they are within the 1518 *Lucubrationes*, and the oration under direct examination in this chapter falls between the *Oratio legalis post caniculi ferias Friburgi habita* and *In laudem legum oratio, cum post ferias aestiuas lectiones ordinarias auspicaretur, Friburgi frequentissimo eius auditorio habita*, in both the 1518 *Lucubrationes* and the *Opera omnia*. The oration *In Praise of the Laws* is the center of attention here because with it, unlike the other orations, Zasius offered an explicit critique of the methods of the scholastic jurists and aspects of the *studia humanitatis* to recruit students to take up their studies with him.

contending methods of argument, one represented by logicians and the other represented by rhetoricians. The trouble with philosophers (those who too narrowly focused on logic) and orators (those who are too narrowly focused on rhetoric) was that each, for different reasons, had given the law a bad name and, by extension, each had undermined legal education and practice more generally.

The former had done so because legal arguments by philosophers, bound up with the rules of logic, appeared to be entirely disconnected from questions of justice and right; the latter because orators, concerned more with how they argued than what they argued, appeared to lack an understanding of the law and legal interpretation. As a result of their focus on form rather than content, neither had given the study or practice of law the respect and attention it deserved as a true and useful science. This tarnished the reputation of law as the noblest faculty within the university and the greatest of all human pursuits beyond it.[12] Having set up two straw man arguments to get his audience's attention, Zasius spent the remainder of his oration knocking each one down.

Distinguishing his own methods from those of a logician, Zasius explained that he knew "from a good many sources" that the philosophers, including the scholastic jurists and theologians who fashioned their methods after Aristotle's *Politics*, had "claimed to have shown that their method of reasoning surpasses all other disciplines" because they brought together and reconciled opposites.[13] That's not all; they also held themselves above all others because they believed that, on account of their logical reasoning, they were able to decipher true principles from false, and therefore were able to reach true knowledge. While Zasius conceded that "[h]aving acquired that same method, I cannot deny it was useful and agreeable," he nevertheless argued that in comparison "to that method, I had preferred by a great distance the knowledge of our law."[14] Not surprisingly, acquiring a true knowledge and understanding of the

12 Zasius, "In laudem legum oratio," in 1518 *Lucubrationes*, 112, 'Si qui sint, nobiles & spectati viri auditores integerrimi, qui legalem nostram scientiam caeteris praestare humanis disciplinis negaverint (quorum nonnullos idipsum controvertentes audivimus) ii mihi haud quamque ex veritate sentire videntur.'

13 Ibid, 'Scio ex literatis plerosque, & in primis Politianum, qui Dialecticen supra caeteras sese disciplinas explicuisse afferant: quae (testa Plotino) praestet, ut de quocunque ratione dici queat, & per quam facultas sit probandi nostra, convellendi obiecta, argumentorumque acumine in utramque differendi partem, & omnino veri & falsi cognitione praebita, quod scientiae sit, discernendi ab eo quod sit erroris: nec facile fieri posse, si Stoicis credamus, ut actus ingeniosusve, aut sapiens in dicendo vir, quispiam evadat, in quo Dialectice desyderetur.'

14 Ibid, 'Ego auditores utilem & me hercule iucundam esse cognitu eam artem non nego. Sed cui Iuris nostri scientiam magno spatio praetulerim.'

law required one to study 'what the law is' and 'what the law concerns', the very concepts that dialectical methods tended to obscure.

Using a metaphor of deception, namely Penelope at her loom, Zasius explained to his audience those lawyers trained only in logic tended to weave arguments in which they simultaneously asserted and denied, and thus, often said nothing. Worse, those who excelled in the art of dialectics even managed to argue one position while appearing to argue another.[15] In each case, these lawyers performed sleights of hand to serve their own self-interest—and/or the interests of their patrons—rather than justice. However, not all scholastic lawyers and jurists were guilty of deception. Rather, many errors within scholastic jurisprudence resulted from misinterpretations and faulty methods rather than from the malice of those trained in accordance with them. Despite conceding that flawed interpretations followed from these defective and misapplied methods, Zasius did not argue for abandoning dialectics altogether. Instead, he explained why traditional methods of teaching and legal interpretation needed to be corrected through the adoption of new ones.

Zasius explained that although dialectics could "furnish us the tools of arguing more cautiously in the other areas of knowledge,"[16] when it came to jurisprudence, it was the study of law in the humanist manner that ultimately "clears up uncertain things."[17] This was the case because while the careful study of various aspects of law "explains intricate things, [such study] also depends on stable proofs,"[18] namely, the letter and language of the law itself as encapsulated in the laws created by man over time. Given that law appeared to be constantly undergoing change when explored historically, he invited

15 Zasius, "In laudem legum oratio," 112, 'Nos quiddam amplius, veritatem enim sequi, declinare a falsis docemus: illi telam, Penelopes exemplo, nunc texunt, modo retexuut, argutiarumque strophis usi, quae certa fuere, saepe incertant.' This is a refence to Homer's *Odyssey*, Book XIX, 137–56. This use of Penelope's loom by Zasius is significant for two reasons. First, it referenced the logicians' cleverness (much like Penelope's) to employ a method by which they were able to delay a conclusion. Their use of seemingly endless distinctions, in other words, allowed them to argue every point, even if such points were not relevant to the task at hand. Second, it referred to the logicians' ability (like Penelope's) to deceive their observers. That is, through their methods the logicians had the ability to make it 'seem' as if they are doing one thing, while they may indeed have been doing another. As with Penelope, only by close observation could such deceptions be found out.

16 Zasius, "In laudem legum oratio," 112, 'Quod si suam dialectice utilitatem inoffensam reliquerimus, hactenus tamen progreditur, ut instrumenta dumtaxat suppeditet in caeteris doctrinis cautius diversandi.'

17 Ibid, 'Lex longe aliter. Nam dubia serenat: involuta evoluit: stabilibus quoque nititur documentis.'

18 Ibid.

the questioning of how—and to what end—something that varied over time could reveal stable proofs.

To address these questions, Zasius turned to a comparison of the study of law and other faculties in the university, especially those concerned with astronomy and medicine.[19] If the systematic study of astronomy and medicine, each of which depended on empirical observation in combination with theory and speculation, could reveal stable proofs (natural law and the laws of nature) by tracking change over time, then it stood to reason that the same could hold true for the study of law. Yet, as much as these empirical studies might share with legal study, according to Zasius, the discipline of law was far more important, necessary, and practical than these other forms of knowledge.

We might dismiss Zasius' assessment as sheer hyperbole, as an example of the kind of exaggerated position expected in an oration designed to call students to the study of law rather than the other faculties. Yet in doing so, we risk overlooking the importance of legal training and lawyers in the early modern era. While there is no question that emerging sciences and technologies were changing the European's landscape, horizons, and practical lives—especially in relation to agriculture, commerce, communication, navigation, and warfare—during the Renaissance, the development of the modern rule of law—and the expanding cadre of university-educated clerks, notaries, lawyers, and jurists tasked with administering and enforcing it—was transforming political structures, local economies, and civil institutions of governance at a much faster pace, and in more immediate ways. This was the case because changes in the law and legal procedures, ranging from private contracts to criminal punishment, affected people at all levels of society and across all boundaries—public and private, secular and sacred, local and national—and not just the highest echelons of political, commercial, and learned society.

Moreover, the ability to interpret and apply the law was the most useful and practical expertise that students could acquire since law was central to the administration of all aspects of civil society, and the relation between these societies in times of war and peace. The knowledge of the law had far greater stakes than other disciplines precisely because of its tangible and concrete impact on society:

> We [lawyers] direct more noble things, even mankind itself; we direct the motion of man, we know the same precepts by which man is able

---

19 Although typical within an inaugural address, or declamations, delivered at the start of the academic year, such a tack typically occurred after the speaker praised the liberal arts and moral philosophy, and not before. See Poel, "Oratory and Declamation," 277–80.

> not [merely] to guess the uncertain location of the stars, but through our methods, man is able to rule those very same stars, he is able to subject the stars to himself. Indeed, we are not fatigued by lines, forms, surfaces, and calculations, but the immeasurable actions of man which neither the geometer is able to measure, nor the calculator is able to count, we collect [them] by means of both settled laws and precepts: and we harmonize each in the same manner.[20]

This momentous task of studying and administering the law demanded that students learn how to gather and examine both precepts and settled laws and to "treat as equal a multitude of things ... of so many peoples concerning a variety of conditions, affairs, causes, and times" in order to observe the underlying principles shared among all laws that order the law itself.[21] Only by systematically researching and studying the law in this manner would it be possible for properly-trained lawyers and jurists to acquire a true knowledge of the law and to use that knowledge to secure, protect, and promote justice and the common good.

For those who may have missed the sheer magnitude of law's importance to every aspect of social life, Zasius emphasized it once again by comparing the study of law to the study of the natural sciences, that is, the study of the laws of nature (*physica*), asserting that:

> if someone had counted the investigation of those hidden and more profound causes, workings, and effects of nature among the noble areas of knowledge, he might have remembered that we also examine natural reasons in our laws, and that possibly we do so in a more excellent manner.[22]

---

20 Zasius, "In laudem legum oratio," 112, 'Nos multo nobiliora, hominem enim ipsum, eiusque motus regulamus, eas profitemur praeceptiones, quibus homo, non incertas astrorum domos divinare, sed astris vel ipsissimis dominari, astra sibi subiicere possit. Denique non circa liniamenta, formas, superficies & calculos fatigamur, sed innumerabiles hominum actus, quos nec Geometres permetiri, nec calculator dinumerare posset, certis & legibus & praescriptis colligimus: utramque lancem concordamus ...'

21 Ibid, '... ponderaque rerum ita coequamus ut admirabile sit in tam immensa tot personarum, conditionum, negotiorum, causarum, temporum varietate, tantam eventuum molem in una velut consepta, & ea praefinita conclusisse.'

22 Ibid, 'Quod si quis occultas & profundiores illas naturae causas, operationes, effectus investigari, inter insignes doctrinas collocarit: is meminerit & nos quoque in legibus nostris naturales scrutari rationes, & idipsum forte excellentius.'

This was the case because those investigating the secrets of nature, just as astronomers, geometers, and mathematicians, were "collecting nothing in accordance with virtue."[23] They were gathering and presenting data merely to describe the world, whereas "we [lawyers] use such natural reasons, on which the law depends, in order to bring human beings into agreement with justice, integrity, and rectitude."[24] The lawyer's task, then, was not simply a matter of observing nature—in this case human nature—but to direct, moderate, and, when necessary, to try to change it. In this respect, the importance of the study of law, as a practical study that concerned the condition of man, outweighed even the study of medicine. Whereas medicine had the capacity to remedy the body, it was the law—and the law alone, for Zasius—that "remedies the soul."[25] Indeed, he even went so far as to argue that while medicine had the ability to improve man's physical condition, the law alone provided "integrity to all aspects of human life."[26]

Having promoted the Faculty of Law above both the Faculty of Arts—which included the study of grammar, logic, rhetoric, arithmetic, geometry, music, and astronomy—and the Faculty of Medicine, one might expect Zasius to have offered his audience some remarks about the relation between the study of law and the Faculty of Theology, especially given the centrality of theology in interpretations of civil and canon law. Instead, Zasius posed a rhetorical question: "For what do we [lawyers] reflect upon more than what is moral? What leads to a virtuous and beautiful life?"[27] Putting forward the question so bluntly and omitting moral theology in doing so, Zasius made it clear that the key to regulating man's moral condition in society, as well as to remedying the maladies of man's soul, was not to be found in the Faculty of Theology but rather in the Faculty of Law. Moreover, he argued that the study of law surpassed all other studies because the law embodied the most excellent and

23 Ibid, 'Illi enim in caeteris rebus nihil ad virtutem conferentibus occupantur.'

24 Ibid, 'Nos ex naturalibus istis rationibus, quibus lex nititur, mortales ad iustitiam, ad integritatem, ad rectitudinem componimus.'

25 Ibid, 'Sed nihil hoc ad legis nobilitatem: illi enim deteriorem, lex meliore hominis portionem curat. Siquidem illi corpori medentur, nos animae.'

26 Ibid, 'Neque enim obscurum est huiusmodi artem ab eius factionis professoribus mirum in modum celebrari, in primisque monstrabilem praedicari, humanae quippe conditioni, sicuti sanitatem sola praestet, ita perpetui quodam modo aevi propagatricem videri. Sed nihil hoc ad legis nobilitatem: illi enim deteriorem, lex meliore hominis portione curat.'; and 'Lex omnimodam vitae synceritatem suppeditat.'

27 Ibid, 113, 'Verum enimvero ea celebratione legum professio ingenti splendoris accessione illustratur: quid enim aliud versamus quamque quod morale sit? quod virtutibus pulchrisque vitae institutis conducat?'

noble habits of life, viz., the principles and precepts of moral philosophy, more so than any other discipline. In essence, law was moral philosophy in action for Zasius, and, as such, the moral authority of law did not rely on how it was communicated—whether through dialectics or rhetoric—but rather on the moral principles embodied within the law itself.[28]

Shifting away from the other university faculties to focus on why the study of law was the most important thing one could dedicate their mind and time to, the problem of rhetoric reemerged rather quickly in the oration. This was the case because, for humanists like Zasius, it was the result of eloquence that man came to understand and live in accordance with principles of moral philosophy—such as justice and right, in the first place—and it was through instruction that the discipline of law and the principles of jurisprudence were communicated, understood, interpreted, and applied.[29] Zasius' oration served as a case in point for all of the above, insofar as he was calling students to study with him so that they might gain a proper understanding of law, which they could use to help to direct man to live in accordance with justice and right within society. Given that law embodied moral philosophy (and moral philosophy taught man how to pursue virtue and avoid vice), there could be no question that law and eloquence were inextricably linked, even if how they were linked was contested. For example, while Zasius acknowledged that moral philosophy "was the first to teach the virtues, which directs everything including royal power, communities, households, and families and which directs each to its optimum," he nevertheless held that it was the *law*—not rhetoric or eloquence—that first taught man to pursue justice, security, and the common good in tandem.[30] As such, he held that how law was communicated and how it was taught should never be held in higher esteem than, or mistaken for, the content of the law itself.[31]

Knowledge of the law—natural, customary, and civil—as a whole (as opposed to specific laws) and the understanding of it as the embodiment of

28 Ibid, 'Hi [humanae literae] namque eloquentiam, & caeteris disciplinis & omnino iuris civilis scientiae anteponunt. Eam non solum humanae civilitatis autorem, sed omnium etiam ingenuarum artium parentem praedicantes.'

29 Although Zasius was as influenced by—and in agreement with—Cicero as Budé was, Zasius used Cicero's work to amplify and underscore his points, rather than let Cicero speak for him.

30 Zasius, "In laudem legum oratio," 113, 'Moralem praeterae Philosophiam summis esse exornandam laudibus evidentia docet, quae prima virtutes docuit, quae regna, civitates, domos, familias, hominem ad optima quaeque dirigit.'

31 Ibid, 'Sed age auditores: maius mihi certamen moveri video ab eloquentiae studiosis, ab his qui humanas literas tanquam filiolam omnium pulcherrimam osculantur.'

justice and right, superseded both logic and rhetoric because dialectical and discursive methods were equally susceptible to error; indeed, over time, the improper exercise of each had led to the corruption of civil law and civic jurisprudence. Nevertheless, Zasius appeared to concede that the duplicitous use of rhetoric by humanists was more problematic than the use—and misuse—of logic by scholastic jurists. Without a solid understanding of civil law and the ways lawyers and jurists have interpreted it over time, those humanists, like Budé, who tended to use rhetoric as part of their broader project to eviscerate scholastic, viz., traditional, jurisprudence had the potential to be even more dangerous than those who, on account of their training, were susceptible to reproducing its errors.

The problem of privileging form over substance, viz., eloquence over stable proofs, among those humanists who made too much of the role of rhetoric in the study and practice of law, extended, for many, from how they interpreted Cicero's *De inventione* (*On Rhetoric*), wherein he explained that the establishment of the commonwealth, and with it the civil law, was made possible by the power of speech.[32] In a short, but significant passage, Cicero recounted an imagined history or conjectural account of how man was persuaded to give up living in his isolated and rude state by a wise man, who, through an oration on the benefits of living in civil society, convinced his auditors to join in mutual company in order to pursue justice, security, and the common good. In essence, by appealing to man's reason and imagination through eloquent speech, this sage called man from the wilderness—akin to what later becomes known as the 'state of nature'—and taught him the benefits of living in accordance with civil laws.[33] However, for Zasius, even if this (imagined) founding

32 Cicero, *De inventione*, Book I, 1. §. 2–3.

33 The emphasis on man's original, or natural, state, that is, the state or condition in which he lived before he entered in a civil society administered by civil laws, serves as one of the most important ideas that underpins the development of the modern rule of law precisely because it depicts man—for worse and for better—as equally devoid of justice and as equally incapable of achieving security outside of society—both secular (the state) and spiritual (the church). As such, it not only rejects Aristotle's argument in the *Politics* that the state itself was natural, but also rejects Aristotle's claim that the inequality of man within and before the law was likewise natural. In contradistinction to Aristotle, Roman jurists like Cicero—and those who followed him in their reasoning—argued that the inequality that existed within civil society was a matter of human volition. That man's choice to become part of the state, and thereby subject to law, was the result of a transaction or contract in which one exchanged their original condition (natural) for a civil one (artificial) to secure the benefits of stability and security. Voluntary associations, like the state or the church, because they were created by man's choice to pursue individual and mutual benefits in tandem, were infused with moral authority by these thinkers precisely

moment was seminal to the adoption of the rule of law, it was the content of the speech, not simply its form or the wise man's eloquence, that ultimately persuaded man to exchange his natural state in order to live in society structured and administered by law.[34]

Yet, even considering the role of reason—the appeal to one's sense of justice, fairness, and a common good—in drawing men together in Cicero's account, some humanists (*optimas humanas literas*) still held that it was eloquence, not law, which stood at the origins of society. They regarded eloquence as the mistress of instruction because from it "all good conduct has sprung up as if from seeds," and indeed, some even went so far as to proclaim that "by the splendor of oratory ... [that] refuge is offered to enemies, peace is encouraged, [and] wars [are] averted."[35] It is therefore no surprise that they also held that those destined to serve and administer civil society—in their capacity as princes and patricians, councilors and lawyers—should study and master the art of rhetoric, above all, since eloquence "perfects the reason and the power of understanding, directs [men] towards things sublime, and renders them apt to any kind of study, including even the most difficult ones."[36]

Once again reinforcing the straw man argument before dismantling it, Zasius explained that many learned men held eloquence to be so central that, "if it is lacking, not only are the remaining disciplines cast aside, as if they have been rolled about in the mud, but even most especially our civil knowledge becomes dirty, disregarded, and disdained."[37] Taking this one step further, he revealed that some even held that law itself becomes rigid and fierce "unless it

---

because the aim of each was to provide man a means to pursue peace and secure justice in tandem.

34 This emphasis on what was said by the wise orator, rather than merely how he said it, was a main point of emphasis that Alciati shared with Zasius when he too set out to distinguish himself from Budé. See Part 3 of this volume.

35 Zasius, "In laudem legum oratio," 113, '... in communem quippe societatem, in conventum civilem agrestes olim homines sola eloquentiae autoritate coiuisse, atque inde velut seminario omnes artes bonas prodiisse: denique eam [eloquentiam] omnis eruditionis dominam videri, quod nulla re quam nitidi sermonis elegantia, ad optimas literas inviteris: orationis splendore res secundas ornari, adversis praeberi perfugium, pacem foveri, amoliri bella, omnem quoque reipublicae salutem in ea residere: eloquentia, aiunt, rationis, intelligendique vim perpoliri, in sublima erigi, & ad quaecunque vel difficillima studia fieri expeditos.'

36 Ibid.

37 Ibid, '... quae [eloquentia] si desit, non solum caeteras doctrinas iacere & velut luto involui, sed vel maxime civilem nostram scientiam sordescere, fastidiri, contemni, rem alioqui austeram & implacidam, nisi orationis luce fulgeat, dicendique nitore subleuetur: haec & his similima adducentes caeteris doctrinis a loco deturbatis, primas eloquentiae sedes praerogaverunt.'

glistens with the light of the power of eloquence and is raised up by the splendor of speech."[38]

Having lured his audience by means of elegant speech, Zasius then forcefully rejected this position and, in fact, flipped it on its head, when he proclaimed that, "eloquence is imperfect and useless unless it is supported by knowledge of the civil law."[39] Indeed, he asserted that he "will establish by strong arguments [that] the knowledge of the civil laws surpasses the knowledge of eloquence by a great distance and is nobler by many a degree."[40] It was necessary to do so because, "Eloquence itself possesses nothing illustrious or important, unless supported—as if by a pillar—by the assistance of the other sciences and especially by the civil law."[41]

To distance himself from those who held eloquence in higher esteem than the study of the law, Zasius posed a simple but telling question. He asked his auditors and readers: "How will the orator maneuver in the courts without practical knowledge of the law?"[42] While such an orator is unlikely to be effective in legal venues and may even make a mockery of himself and his patrons, the greatest danger of one who speaks on behalf of the law without a proper understanding of it occurs in the realm of politics. In other words, in front of an audience steeped in law, their influence would be limited because it would become very clear, very fast, that they were speaking nonsense. In the realm of politics, however, their ignorance might be harder to detect.

Moreover, if such orators were able to acquire positions of political power and influence, then what would keep them from using their ability to persuade and dissuade rulers and subjects alike from gaining the power to wage and direct wars?[43] What check would there be against their influence, if it was garnered and expanded on account of their eloquent speech rather than their

---

38 Ibid.

39 Ibid, 'Ediverso manifestum est eloquentiam, nisi iuris civilis cognitione adiuuetur, mancam esse & sterilem.'

40 Ibid, 'Sed si vacarit, veritatemque placidi admiseritis, luculenter ostendam, quamque a vero aberraverint illi verbositatis artifices: & quando ea res huius mei sermonis praecipua fuit occasio, argumentis validis convincam iuris civilis scientiam eloquentiae longo antestare intervallo, plurimoque gradu esse nobiliorem: quo breviter percuso, finem faciam.' Note that Zasius also said he preferred the true knowledge of the law over the scholastic method in similar terms, viz., at a great distance.

41 Ibid, 114, '... usque adeo nihil habet eloquentia vel illustre vel amplum, nisi caeterarum doctrinarum, & potissime iuris civilis auxilio velut tibicine fulciantur.' Note that the page number is misprinted in Zasius' *Opera omnia*. This page is misprinted as 144 instead of 114.

42 Ibid, 113, '... quomodo in iudiciis sine iuris peritia Orator versabitur?'

43 Ibid, 114 (144), 'Suadeat sane Orator, dissuadeat, laudet, vituperet (quae extra forum, potissima ipsius sunt officia), quis arma administrabit? An solis continebitur eloquentiae finibus?'

expertise, knowledge, or even virtue? Though the latter question might appear far more speculative (and exaggerated) than the former one, Zasius used it to invite his audience to think more carefully and critically about how crucial a proper knowledge of law was for those who held influence beyond the confines of the legal profession, especially for those who served as councilors, and thus expected to draw on their legal education to advise cities, princes, popes, and emperors in times of war and peace.

Furthermore, if these orators were able to persuade the audience of their positions by grounding them with authorities, that is, by linking their arguments and claims to ancient philosophy, or history, or to principles of Roman or canon law, then they were more likely to convince their audiences that they were experts on whatever they were arguing—even if these orators were, in fact, charlatans. If these imposters, on account of their eloquence and their use (and misuse) of the methods and sources of the *studia humanitatis* in their speeches, were accepted by their audiences as authorities themselves, then subjects and rulers alike might be unwittingly convinced or manipulated by them.[44] As dangerous as this could be when they spoke broadly about matters related to war and peace, it paled in comparison to the danger that orators who possessed no formal legal training or proper knowledge of the law posed when they used the language of justice and right to buffer those claims.

Indeed, if such orators were able to persuade, knowingly and eloquently, their audiences of the fact that they were speaking the truth—even when they were not—or that they were speaking for justice and the common good when, in fact, they were undermining it to promote their own advantage and interest, they were far more dangerous than those who erred on account of traditional jurisprudence and scholastic methods of argument.[45] The latter at least had knowledge of the law and thus were cognizant of the limits of how and to what ends it could be manipulated and used to manipulate, whereas those

44 Ibid, 'Non censeo, sed vel a Philosophis, vel ab Historiis, iureve publico, vel ab illis ipsis Legalibus institutis, dictionis suae corpus commodabit, paucis ex suo adiectis, quibus comere, ornare, ordine disponere possit, quod ab aliis erat mutuatus. Quod si qui vel linguae volubilitate, vocisve, aut nudae artis confidentia concitati, in publicum eruperint, necessario eveniet, vel fractum nescio quid, vel enerve inculctantes, aut fluant marcidi, aut dubitabundi vacillent, aut vagentur ignari, aut temerarii praecipitentur.'

45 Zasius made this point through contrast in the oration, Ibid, 115, 'Iurisconsultus qui iusto sine leges consectatur, formulis causidicorum non fatigatur, vocem non venditat, iudiciorum basilicas, turbida fora non inquietat, nisi vel respublica urgeat, vel efflagitent amici: cuius officium est de iure respondere, ambigua dissolvere, publiceque & privatim suis prodesse consiliis.'

armed only with eloquence and elegance were subject to exaggeration without limit.[46] As such, those orators who did not know the laws, could not be trusted.

It should not be surprising that Zasius, as a humanist, launched his most bitter attack in this oration against those who applied the methods of the *studia humanitatis* to the law without credentials. After all, Zasius was—as he himself reminded us—trained as a jurist in accordance with scholastic methods. Thus, drawing on his scholastic expertise in the law, Zasius attacked his humanist counterparts outside the universities, like Budé, because they lacked a proper understanding of legal principles as presented in the *corpus* of Roman law and, equally important, they lacked an understanding of legal interpretation and practice as it had developed over time. Holding merely a Master of Arts and not a Doctor of Law, they lacked an awareness of how and why jurists emphasized and applied some aspects of the *corpus*, while ignoring others; they also failed to fully understand the very errors that they were trying to correct and how, in their attempts to correct them, they often committed new ones. Drawing on his humanist expertise, Zasius also distanced himself from his scholastic counterparts in the universities by arguing that his interpretation and understanding of the law was superior to theirs because he was able to avoid errors that stemmed from their traditional (dialectical) methods and the faulty interpretations that underpinned them. He was able to surpass each because the combination of his humanist studies beyond the law and his scholastic training in the law enabled him to understand 'what the law is' and 'what the law concerns' in a more direct, clear, and substantive manner.

It also enabled him to come at the study and teaching of law from a different perspective, given that his studies and training had taught him that the law was of complete force and effectiveness because it was the law; that its integrity relied on the principles on which it was based (justice and *ius*) and

46 Zasius, "In laudem legum oratio," 114 (144), 'Omitto non modicam in ista arte, in eius artificibus, verborum ne dicam mentiendi licentiam: commendationis enim finem, si faveant, sin vero oderint, vituperationis modum facere non possunt: adeo a rei & negocii veritate vel augendo excedunt, vel premendo deficiunt, fallacique verborum modillatione, & rasis (ut ille ait) anthitetis velut quodam laruarum praetentu, aures liniunt, mentesque praesentium ludificantur, Taceo quod parum habent constantiae. Nam quod ante pulchre laudarunt, hoc modica post arrepta occasione, mox foede dilacerant, possem eius rei, in magno illo nostro Cicerone, possem in aliis argumenta praebere, nisi me quaedam, ut ita dixerim, veneratio tantorum virorum sevocaret. Sed quid quod neuuli isti, ne dicam vitia, honestioribus vocabulis inumbrantur: mendacia enim, hyperbolim ex cessumque Rethoricum, laudasse quod vituperaris, temporaria epitheta nominant, neque esse tam laborandum, ut res vera sit, quamque ut verisimilis videant: proinde amplificari, extendi digredi, fingi (vellem adderent mentiri), oportere, quod totum, ut verba Pici usurpem, quod aliud est quamque mera impostura, merum praestigium?'

the end to which it was created (to preserve the peace and to promote the common good), rather than on how it was explained or the purposes for which it was argued.[47] And it was their knowledge of the law, in terms of what the law—natural, customary, and civil—was and what it did, not their mastery of rhetoric or logic, that would allow his students to become properly trained lawyers and jurists as well. In turn, they could direct man to curb his desires, and thereby his actions, in civil society in order to pursue a common good:

> By how much are you adorned by a greater skill? You impose a burden for no one, but you refute deceit: the declaration of your words illuminates, it does not dull ... you deal in clear, true, unveiled, stable words, you teach man to have tamed desires, to keep [his] hands, eyes, and thoughts from one another, and you teach him both what is his and of another, and you apportion to each what is his with the highest equity.[48]

Moreover, the law and those who administer it drew power, force, and moral authority not from logic, nor from rhetoric, but from the foundational principles of justice, which was demonstrated by what the law concerned for Zasius:

> For only law alone suffices, whether about [social] orders, dignities, duties, public offices, or whether about penalties or entirely about the public punishments of man, or of marriage, of children, of consanguinity of the father's side, of wills, of freedom, of slaves, of creditors, of contracts, of rulers, of commonwealths, of land, of water, and to say it in one word, of any public and private matters, and even if the lights of heaven and hell are at stake. The law, I say, is such a signpost, so satisfactory in all respects, that no other aids need to be used.[49]

---

47 Ibid, 'At lex ipsa perfecta est, absoluti roboris est, quae prodire in publicum, nullo subeunte bacillo non vereatur, iustum & aequum in omni re lex per se ipsam tractat.'

48 Ibid, 114 (144)–5, 'Quanto maiori dexteritate decoraris? Tu nemini imponis, sed dolos repellis: tuorum sermonum declaratio illuminat, non perstringit. Mendacia, fraudes, technae, simulationes, procul absunto, quoniam principium verborum tuorum veritas, tota pulchra, tota candida es, sub cuius labiis, ore, lingua, mella distillant, tuoque odore vel ipsa aromata superantur, quae nihil aulei scenici, nihil Trageodiarum nunc ad gratiam, iam ad invidiam commoves: sed lucidis, veris, apertis, stabilibus verbis virtutes tractas, domitas doces habere cupiditates, manus, oculos, mentem ab alieno abstinere, & quod cuiusque est, cuique summa aequabilitate distribuis.'

49 Ibid, 114 (144), 'Si enim de ordinibus, de dignitatibus, si de honoribus, denique si de poenis, & omnino de capite hominis res sit, si porro nuptiarum, si liberorum, si agnationum, si testamentorum, si libertatum, si mancipiorum, si nexorum, si contractuum, si regnorum,

The law was the most important thing in human affairs because it was the "standard of equity, the measure of justice, the unity of people, the assignor of duties, the parent of virtues, the destruction of vices, and as Solomon said, the light of morals, the way of life."[50] The law was "a gift from God."[51] It, and it alone, enabled man to pursue justice and achieve security in mutual company within discrete societies as well as beyond them.

After having declared why the knowledge of the law was the noblest discipline—because 'what the law concerns' is the actions of man—and how methods within the law itself—the methods of a properly trained lawyer—surpassed those of the logicians and orators, Zasius turned his attention to what students should expect if they heeded his call to take up the study of law with him. Up to this point, Zasius had only demonstrated his methods by critiquing the methods of others. Thus, one might expect him to close the oration by providing a detailed account or summary of his own *modus docendi*. He did not. Rather, in these final remarks he provided only a glimpse as to what the students should expect if they studied Roman law with him.

Here, it is important to recall why Zasius, a German jurist and councilor, was teaching Roman law and why his students, who would not practice *de facto* Roman law in their capacity as lawyers, advisors, or councilors, would be studying it in the first place.[52] Given that upon earning their degrees students would be tasked to carry out and reform local laws and customs throughout the Germanies (and even the Empire), studying Roman civil law would help prepare them to do so because local laws and customs shared the same tenets as Roman law—in terms of universal principles and historical development and influence. Studying with a humanist like Zasius, and thus drawing on methods associated with the *studia humanitatis*, would enable them to better grasp that all law—local, customary, Roman, and otherwise—was rooted in

---

si civitatum, si terrae, si aquae, & ut uno verbo loquar, quarumcunque vel publicarum, vel privatarum rerum, quinetiam si coeli, si inferni iura versentur, sola lex sufficit: lex inquam illa directionis virga, adeo in omnibus satisfacit, ut nullius aliunde suffragationis ei sint opes implorandae: quod praeclare attigisse.'

50 Ibid, 115, '... qua in rebus humanis (ut quidam inquit) eminentius nihil inveniri poterit, quae & dei sit donum, aequitatis forma, regula iustitiae, unio populi, officiorum distributrix, parens virtutis, ruina vitiorum, & ut cum Salomone loquar, lux mortalium, via vitae.' In framing this part of his oration, Zasius posited Cicero's speeches against Marcus Antonius, but did not indicate for his audience which speech he was referring to.

51 Ibid.

52 See Neff, *Udalricus Zasius: Ein Beitrag Zur Geschichte Des Humanismus Am Oberrhein*; and Neff, *Ulrich Zasius: Ein Freiburger Humanist.*

and structured by the same fundamental principles, even as it varied over time and place.[53]

Apprehending the universality of these fundamental principles, such as justice and right, was paramount to properly administering the law and aptly advising cities, rulers, popes, princes, and emperors; acquiring mastery of the Roman civil law, and by extension the universal principles that underpinned and organized it, would enable his students to serve as checks against corruption upon completion of their studies. Moreover, the Roman *corpus* was so detailed and comprehensive that it provided a wealth of practical examples, procedures, and principles that students could draw from to reform and expand local laws. Thus, although his students would not practice Roman law per se, they would gain substantial benefits and knowledge from studying the *Digest* and the *Institutes*; they could then use this knowledge to transform customary and common legal traditions into written ones.[54]

For his own part, Zasius argued there "is nothing more useful, nothing more powerful, and nothing more conducive to security, than the knowledge of the law."[55] For all of these reasons "the knowledge of the law is accompanied by much glory, honor, favor, and dignity," yet it was an extraordinarily difficult knowledge to obtain.[56] Contrary to those who studied Roman law with his scholastic peers in the universities or his humanist peers beyond them, those who choose to study law with him, "with concise attention and unyielding

53 See Chapter 1, especially *Modus Docendi: The Methods of the Schoolmen and the Studia humanitatis* in this volume.

54 For a discussion of the reception—or lack thereof—of Roman law in Germany see Paul Koschaker, *Europa und das römische Recht* (Munich: C. H. Beck, 1953); Wolfgang Kunkel, "The Reception of Roman Law in Germany: An Interpretation," in *Pre-Reformation Germany*, ed. Gerald Strauss (New York: Harper & Row, 1972), 263–81; Georg Dahm, "On the Reception of Roman Law and Italian Law in Germany," in *Pre-Reformation Germany*, 282–315; Franz Wieacker, *A History of Private Law in Europe with Particular Reference to Germany* (Oxford: Oxford University Press, 1995); Marie Theresa Fögen, "Learned Law and The Desire of Politics," in *Law and Learning in the Middle Ages: Proceeding of the Second Carlsberg Academy Conference on Medieval Legal History 2005*, eds. Helle Voft and Mia Münster-Swendsen (Copenhagen: DJØF Publishing, 2006), 29–40; and Antonio Padoa-Schioppa, *A History of Law in Europe: From the Early Middle Ages to the Twentieth Century*, trans. Caterina Fitzgerald (Cambridge: Cambridge University Press, 2017).

55 Zasius, "In laudem legum oratio," 115, 'Quae cum ita sint, auditores integerrimi, & iam plane sit factum perspicuum iuris nostri scientiam, primori eminentia praefulgere, sit porro vobis perquam saepe & superioribus annis, & praesenti anno demonstratum, nihil esse lege utilius, nihil potentius, nihilque ad omnem securitatem salubrius, atque itaque nullum insumi laborem fructuosius, quam qui in nostris studiis esudatur ...'

56 Ibid, '... tantaque gloria, tantus honor, tantus favor, tanta dignitas iuris studiosos comitetur.'

vigor," would learn how to practice law properly.[57] He then closed the oration by assuring prospective students that he would present the law in "a clear, plain, and open manner."[58] However, they would have to attend his lectures for insight on the exact methods he would use to do so.

4 Theory Meets Practice: Zasius Explains His Methods

As an Ordinary Professor of Civil Law, Zasius presented lectures on the *corpus iuris civilis*, which served as the centerpiece of the academic day.[59] Although Zasius' preliminary remarks or prefaces to his lectures on the *Digest* likely would be delivered in one morning session, the length of the lectures themselves, as well as the time of day delivered, varied according to the title under examination; they might be read over several sessions or, less frequently, over several weeks and even months. Other lectures—those that integrated extensive sources beyond the *corpus*—most often occurred in the afternoons and, depending on the topic, were likely spread out over a considerable span of time. For example, Zasius gave a comprehensive lecture *On Obligations* (*De obligatione*), in bits and pieces, over the course of several years. These were interrupted by his ordinary lectures and, as the 1520s progressed, the religious upheaval of the Reformation and the Peasant Wars in Freiburg.

It is important to keep the type of lecture and the span of time over which it was delivered in mind, as Zasius and his legal humanist counterparts declared that on account of their methods—returning to original sources to peel away the layers of commentary, confusion, and disputes of the scholastic jurists—they would be able to teach the whole of Roman law to their students. They did not achieve this lofty goal and perhaps did not intend to do so. Indeed, it would have been near impossible to teach all fifty books of the *Digest* as well as the *Institutes*, the *Code*, and the *Novellas* to students, who, if only pursuing a degree in civil law, were expected to complete their studies within three to four years.[60] Even if Zasius wished to teach the entire *corpus* to each cohort

---

57 Ibid, '... praestabo, ut nisi me vires, labor, vox, lingua deserant, ea quae difficilia profundave vobis putabunter, clara, plana, & aperta me redditurum confidam.'

58 Ibid.

59 Rowan, *Ulrich Zasius,* 85. These lectures drew students from across the university faculties; indeed, many students who attended his daily lectures were seeking their degrees outside of law.

60 Even those pursuing degrees in both laws (*in utroque iure*) were expected to spend no more than three to four years attending lectures on civil law, after which—and, in some cases, at the same time as—they were expected to attend lectures on canon law.

of students through traditional methods, leaving humanist ones aside, there simply would not have been enough time to do so. Nor would much of the *corpus* be applicable to those who hoped to help administer the affairs of cities, princes, and emperors in sixteenth-century Germany.

Over the course of his appointment at Freiburg, Zasius spent most of his time delivering lectures focused specifically on the titles that dealt with testaments, good faith, obligations, procedures for legal actions, the rights of creditors and debtors, usufruct, public authority, and specific problems and rights related to property. Hence, instead of trying to cover it all, Zasius focused on the essential titles and topics that his students would need after completing their studies. Significantly, and in addition to this focus on practical matters, Zasius also concentrated on the essence and basic definitions of law, its fundamental principles, and its origins.[61] By narrowing his focus, he was able to combine scholastic and humanist methods and to engage with both theory and practice. Zasius laid out for his students and readers how and to what end he intended to do so in his *Praefatio: in primam digestorum, sive pandectarum partem paratitla* (*Preface: Notes About the First Part of the Digest, or Pandects*).[62]

Zasius began these remarks by announcing: "Having been persuaded by your request [to teach the law], I promise to accomplish this, and I hope to prevail, as long as, you will listen eagerly to what I am faithfully gathering, and you will not be seized by an impulse toward novelty."[63] Over the course of study, we will "proceed in accordance with the summary of the ancient *Digest*," which they "shall neither render uncertain," and "in such tempo that we neither long tarry nor cast ourselves headlong in hasty diversions."[64] Studying Roman law this way required them to begin with the *Digest* itself, rather than the scholastic glosses, interpretations, and commentaries that developed after its 'rediscovery'.

The turn to original sources (*ad fontes*), both to acquire a better understanding of the subject at hand and to show the errors of interpretation, was a typical feature of the *studia humanitatis* and a common tactic employed by humanists

61 Many of these are bound within various editions of his *Opera omnia* and his *Lucubrationes*.

62 Zasius, "Praefatio. Dn. Udalrici Zazii iureconsulti clarriss. In primam digestorum, sive pandectarum partem paratitla. 1550," in *Opera omnia*, vol. 1, cols. 13–4. Hereafter "Praefatio, In primam digestorum."

63 Zasius, "Praefatio, In primam digestorum," col. 13.§.1, 'Hoc, precibus vestris adductus, facturum me polliceor, & praestiturum spero, dum quae fideliter colligo, auidem excipiatis, & non impetu quodam novitatis capti, faciles incipiatis, facilius desinentes.'

64 Ibid, col. 13.§.2, 'Nos in hac Digesti veteris Summula colligenda (haec enim vobis accepimus) eo passu procedemus, ut nec gradum suspendamus, nec temerario excursu praecipitemus.'

to set themselves apart from scholastics. However, unlike his legal humanist counterpart Budé, Zasius did not believe that scholastic jurists were wrong on every point of interpretation, even though some of their interpretations had led to fundamental errors in jurisprudence. Nevertheless, he did not discount their work wholesale; they were to be read in conjunction with the *Digest*. In fact, Zasius often conceded scholastic conclusions on points of law, although he arrived at these same conclusions through different methods.

The quintessential difference between how Zasius and the scholastic Doctors approached the *Digest* stemmed from the questions they asked of—and about—the *corpus* of Roman law.[65] For example, many scholastic jurists attempted to show how the texts of Roman law followed from their understanding of abstract first principles (*ab initio*), such as the universality and immutability of justice. If an aspect of Roman law appeared to deviate from these first principles, dialectics could be employed to show how and why, despite any such initial impressions, it did not. Moreover, logic could be used to reconcile contradictions between various precepts of Roman law if each could be shown to be just, or at least to have a glimmer of justice within them, thus transforming contradictions into minor deviations. In this respect, the questions jurists asked were very much prescribed by the first principles and the understanding of them that they initially brought to the texts.

In contradistinction to the scholastic focus on harmonizing justice and law, Zasius focused on realigning justice and right. That is, Zasius approached the study of the *Digest* from the opposite perspective and thus asked different questions. Instead of superimposing preconceived ideas (*ab initio*) onto Roman law, and forcing it to align with them, he studied the texts and sources of Roman law (*ad fontes*) to arrive at an understanding of its first principles. Examining the *corpus* in this way, from the bottom up (inductively) instead of the top down (deductively), required tending to its inconsistencies and variations to discover how and why the laws within it changed over time. This, in turn, enabled him to observe what all law shared, even if only in the breach, namely the universal principles of justice and right.

65 The questions they asked, and why they asked them, likewise accounts for the fundamental differences between the "fathers of legal humanism"—Budé, Zasius, and Alciati—and those who followed them. Precisely because Zasius asked foundational and theoretical questions throughout his lecture, he left us a much richer discussion of his ideas about and interpretations of *ius*, *iustitia*, and the relation between natural law, *ius gentium*, and civil law than Budé or Alciati. Indeed, Zasius offered his students/readers a full-fledged theory of jurisprudence in his lecture on the first title of the *Digest*.

Once discovered and understood, these universal principles (or stable proofs) could then be used as fundamental criteria to determine the justness of any civil law, Roman or otherwise, and of any civic institution. If, against these criteria, laws and institutions were found to have deviated from justice and right, they needed immediate reform. The fundamental task of a properly trained jurist, then, was not to reconcile contradictions and variations between aspects or precepts of laws, but rather to show why and how the laws deviated from justice. Only by demonstrating how law and justice had fallen out of joint would it be possible to bring them back into agreement. In short, contrary to scholastic methods, which tended to conceal disparities in law or to reconcile conflicts, Zasius' methods served to illuminate them.

Discovering and analyzing these disparities, however, was no easy task since it required studying continuity and change in Roman law as well as paying attention to continuity and change within scholastic jurisprudence. The proper study of law and jurisprudence demanded, as Zasius put it, tireless effort on account of its immense importance and its extensive nature:

> I am often wont to say, dear audience, [that] nothing in civic life is more beneficial than knowledge of the law inasmuch as through it one acquires virtue and is united with others in readiness for justice. Indeed no one could ignore how truly difficult gaining such knowledge can be, without the mastery of a huge body of legal texts, to say nothing of the infinite tangled mess of commentaries.[66]

Only by avoiding the haphazard approach that led to these heaps of commentaries would it be possible to engage with and master Roman law and its sources in "a clear, plain, and open manner."[67]

Therefore, after the order of the *Digest* had been "rendered short and brief,"[68] which he did in the preliminary remarks (prefaces) that accompanied each lecture, specific titles would then be treated "either with regard to the

66 Zasius, "Praefatio, In primam digestorum," col. 13.§.1, 'Saepe soleo dicere, Auditores acceptissimi, Nihil in vita civili, legis cognitione esse salubrius: utpote per quam in sese homo virtute, ad alios dexteritate & iustitia componitur. At vero difficilem esse ad legem consequendam aditum, ignorare nemo potest, nisi cui librorum legalium immodica moles non sit comperta, si infinita commentariorum congeries interim taceatur.'

67 Zasius, "In laudem legem oratio," 115.

68 Zasius, "Praefatio, In primam digestorum," col. 13.§.2, 'Ordo dabitur titulis pulcher & brevis.'

texts" of Roman law or "with regard to select glosses."[69] If (and when) these select glosses drawn predominantly from the *Gloss* of Accursius had departed from the original meaning or sense of a specific term or law in the *Digest*, Zasius would reference select commentaries to help clear up confusion. However, these commentaries would not be studied in full, but rather treated "according to a point, especially the texts of Bartolus and Baldus, and of other Doctors, whenever necessity may require it, [because] they should not be passed over."

Attention to the works of Bartolus and Baldus was crucial for Zasius, precisely because if they were ignored (as Budé for the most part did), then one might assume that Bartolus and Baldus blindly followed Accursius and offered no notable interpretations of their own. Using scholastic commentaries in this way not only allowed students to engage with and critically evaluate problems that emerged from mistranslations, non sequiturs, and faulty arguments in the *Gloss*, it also allowed them to explore the extent to which Accursius' errors were either corrected or reproduced by later jurists. Only by studying the law in this manner would it be possible to acquire a proper understanding of the history of Roman law and scholastic jurisprudence in tandem. Anything less, as Zasius warned in his oration, would not clear up uncertainties in the law so much as further compound them.

Anticipating, perhaps, that some students, especially those who had already begun their studies in accordance with scholastic methods and sources, might be hesitant to undertake new ones, Zasius explained:

> It should not trouble you that a part of our effort goes over ground that has already been covered in years past: for many things will be renewed and will be treated either more briefly or in a more useful manner, and indeed, if you will persevere, the future utility for you will be significant.[70]

Indeed, regardless of their prior exposure to Roman law, by studying it in the humanist manner they would expand and refine their knowledge of 'what the

---

69 Ibid, col. 13.§.2. 'Porro & quae vel in textibus vel glossae selecta putavero, velut ad puncta congeram, Bartoli potissimum & Baldi, & aliorum doctrinis, si quando necessitas exigat, non praetereundis.'

70 Ibid, col. 13.§.2, 'Nec vos angat, quod laboris nostri partem, anni etiam superiores excepe-runt: novabuntur enim multa, & vel brevius vel politius tractabuntur, & erit mehercule, si perseueraveritis, non modica vobis futura utilitas.'

law is' and 'what the law concerns' in its original context and in the contexts to which it was adapted.[71]

Here it is essential to remember that, for Zasius, understanding the conditions under which aspects of Roman law were utilized and interpreted by the scholastics was as important as knowing why, and to what end, the precepts of Roman law were written in the first place. As significant as each were on their own terms, studying them together rendered the historical-linguistic context of legal interpretation clear and revealed how the practical application of law changed over time. Placing the law in historical perspective and studying the development of jurisprudence over time, however, did not equate to simply studying legal history. Given that law was an expression of moral philosophy in action, a kind of knowledge that was permeated and structured by first principles such as justice and right, Zasius drew from Aristotle's epistemology in developing and presenting his own theory as to why the proper study of law was crucial.

The commonplace integration of Aristotle's four causes within Zasius' explanation of his own methods may have served as yet another reminder to anxious students that he was not rejecting traditional learning and ideas, even as he was introducing new perspectives and methods to them. Indeed, using the language of Aristotle, Zasius explained that the *Digest* was the efficient cause of their studies, whereas their discussions of specific titles informed by the glosses and commentaries constituted the formal cause. Zasius then divided the material cause into two parts, namely 'what the law is' and 'what the law concerns'; the former focused on the ordering principles of justice, right, and equity (*Justitia, Jus, & Æquitas*), and the latter on the actions of man. The final cause, echoing Cicero, was the common good, or that which ensured tranquility in civil matters.[72]

The question remained, however, as to how all of this amounted to practical knowledge; after all, the students were taking up the study of law to become lawyers, jurists, councilors, legislators, and advisors, not simply theorists. Even those who hoped to teach law in the universities would need to know how all of this translated into action. Zasius acknowledged the link between theory and practice by once again invoking Aristotle and Cicero. Once mastered,

71 Ibid, col. 13.§.2, 'Nam & in casibus quibuscunque obuiis, ad praesentem certe necessitatem, doctrina, eruditione, consilio, magnis apti, expetiti, prompti reddemini, & ad subtilia legalium arcanorum, via vobis commodior exhibebitur.'

72 Ibid, col. 13.§.5, 'Causam finalem nostrae scientiae, Cicero commune bonum nominat, cum honestate vitae, seu concordem in re civili tranquillitatem.'

knowledge of civil law taught one how to pursue virtue (*Ethics*), how to govern the family (*Economics*), and how to govern the commonwealth (*Politics*). Moreover, all of the above—in accordance with Cicero—amounted to the final and practical end of jurisprudence: to promote justice, peace, security, and the common good.

Zasius' emphasis on first principles and practical application when setting out his methods and announcing how and why the students would proceed through the *Digest* under his direction should be no surprise. After all, he asserted that the Roman jurists have taught us to declare our true philosophy by setting out the three types of law before all else in the *Institutes*.[73] In essence, any jurist who lacked an understanding of first principles (what the law is) and how they were applied to and helped to direct the actions of man (what the law concerns) not only lacked an understanding of the law, but also lacked an understanding of justice. Both were required for a properly trained jurist to track errors, reform jurisprudence, and administer and practice local laws and customs in a 'more excellent manner' than those trained in traditional methods and jurisprudence—and especially those who had little or no formal training at all.

To explore why Zasius held this to be the case, a close reading of his full *De iustitia et iure* lecture is as important for modern readers as it would have been for his students and contemporaries. In no small part, of course, because this first title of the *Digest* begins at the beginning insofar as it included basic definitions of law, explanations of justice and *ius*, and theories as to how various categories of law, such as natural law, *ius gentium*, and civil law, were related to or departed from one another. Given the emphasis that Zasius and his legal humanist contemporaries placed on original sources, it should be no surprise that how they interpreted this first title of the *Digest* bore significant weight in their works overall. So much so, in Zasius' case, that he specifically referred his students and readers alike back to his prefatory remarks and lecture on this title. He did so because without exposure to his discussion of the foundational and fundamental terms in this first title of the *Digest*, they might not grasp just how innovative his interpretations were or, more importantly, just how urgent and necessary he thought legal reform was.[74]

---

73 Ibid, col. 14.§.5, 'Tria haec civilis scientia complectitur, ut non mirum sit, quod Iurisconsultus in Instit.I.i.i. nos veram profiteri philosophiam tradiderit.'

74 Zasius, "Praefatio, In primam digestorum," cols. 13–4.

5 Ordinary Lecture, Exceptional Interpretation

Just as in the case of Budé's treatment of the first title of the *Digest*, at the heart of Zasius' *De iustitia et iure* preface and lecture lies his claim that there was a fundamental error in Accursius' *Gloss*, namely a misinterpretation of the term *ius* as something related to but separate from justice; an error which had been reproduced and compounded in scholastic jurisprudence for centuries. Rejecting Accursius' explanation of *ius* in the *Gloss* and, by extension, his explanation of the relation between justice, law, and right, Zasius spent much of this lecture (and the *paratitla* for it) focusing on defining and explaining *ius*. In so doing, he did not simply reproduce Budé's definition, nor did he entirely abandon it. As a jurist, not just as a humanist, Zasius was more acutely focused on *ius* as a criterion, and not merely a signifier, of justice in the objective sense. At the same time, he also emphasized *ius* as an inherent characteristic of man *qua* man and as a universal right shared by all mankind. Moreover, Zasius' discussion of justice, *ius*, and law in this lecture and in the preface that introduced it stands as an example of his rejection of certain aspects of the scholastic and humanist methods as well as an example of his own methods in action.

In reading the first title of the *Digest* with his students, Zasius first identified the errors of the scholastic Doctors. Then, he turned to an exploration of the essence and origins of justice, *ius*, and law to demonstrate how they misinterpreted it. To make his points, he drew on ancient sources, particularly those of Aristotle, historical examples, and imagined scenarios. He did not leave it at that; he also tried to account for the development of—and variations within—law over time. In other words, as the lecture unfolded, Zasius historicized justice and *ius* in imagined and concrete terms to illustrate the importance and necessity of doing so for jurists and lawyers. He emphasized the latter, no doubt, to help his own students grasp how fundamentally important it was for them to have a proper understanding of law, justice, and right in order to practice, interpret, and reform law once they completed their studies.

6 'What Is Justice; What Is *Jus*?'

There are three major questions that structure Zasius' preface and lecture: "What is justice; what is *ius*? In what manner is justice divided? And, what follows from law?"[75] To address the first question, Zasius directed his students'

75 Zasius, "Paratitla, De justitia et iure," in *Opera omnia*, vol. 1: cols. 14–7 (Lyon: Sebastianum Gryphium, 1550); col. 14.§.0, 'Supra diximus Legem civilem versari circa iustitiam & ius,

attention to the *Gloss*, wherein Accursius treated Ulpian's statement: "the law obtains its name from justice."[76] To explain Ulpian's statement, Accursius used the analogy: "justice is the mother, *ius* is the daughter."[77] Based on this analogy, Accursius then argued that one could discern justice through the image of law (*iure*) just as one could discern the likeness of a mother through the image of the daughter. However, even if each premise was true, Zasius held that neither was sufficient—alone or together—to arrive at the conclusion that one could discern justice through *ius* or, by extension, justice through law, in this manner. Furthermore, Zasius explained, Accursius' analogy did not clarify Ulpian's meaning. Asserting that A is to B as B is to A left open the question as to what A and B were. Indeed, the analogy veiled the fact that Accursius neither defined justice, law, or *ius* nor added anything to Ulpian's original statement in D.1.1.1. As such, it amounted to little more than a fallacious argument, viz. begging the question, affirming the consequent, and presenting a faulty analogy.

Moreover, this analogy was not just mistaken on account of its logic but was also dangerous on account of its implications. Embedded in this analogy was an argument that law did not simply get its name from justice, but rather descended from it. This was problematic on several levels, not least because Accursius used the term *ius*, not law (*lex*), when he stated *"iustitiam esse matrem, ius vero filiam"* in the context of explaining the relation between law and justice.[78] The problem stems from the fact that the term *ius* has no single meaning in Latin; sometimes *ius* means law and in others it means right (as in the right order of things). The precise meaning of the term is usually revealed by the context in which it is used or by the additional commentary provided by those who use it. In the context of Accursius' discussion, it is not clear whether he meant right (objective), law, or both. As such, the analogy suggested that both *ius* and law descended from justice.

Whether Accursius meant law or right (objective, legal, or inherent) may seem like an esoteric distinction, yet tending to the logic shows why it is not. If law descends from justice, just as a daughter descends from a mother or, to further the analogy, one can discern the image of justice through the image of law, then—by implication—all laws are just or have at least a glimmer of justice within them. Yet given that not all laws are just, whatever one might think

tanquam suam materiam, unde cognitio eius praemittitur. Tria sunt videnda. Primo, quid sit Iustitia, quid Ius. Secundo, qualiter dividatur. Tertio, quid ex iure quoquo prodierit.'

76 D 1.1.1., 'Est autem ius à iustitia appellatum.'

77 Zasius, "Paratitla, De justitia et iure," col. 14.§.2, 'Et dixit gloss, iustitiam esse matrem, ius vero filiam: quod tu per umbram similitudinis, non autem proprie intelligas.'

78 Ibid.

they can discern by studying any given law, might well be something other than justice. If Accursius meant that *ius* is something distinct from yet still related to law and descended from justice, then a different chain of reasoning would ultimately lead to the same problem. For example, if *ius* descended from justice, and *ius* and law are related, then—following Accursius' analogy—one could discern justice through law. What if, however, a specific law was unjust?

The *Gloss* followed with a second analogy designed, perhaps, to help shore up the weakness of the first one. This time, Accursius avoided the question of resemblance altogether by stating, "justice is the mother of *ius*, just as obligation is the mother of action."[79] Once again, he neither specified what he meant by justice or *ius* nor did he differentiate whether he meant right (objective) or law. Despite the lack of detail and the fact that this was yet another faulty analogy, Zasius conceded that the understanding of justice, as expressed through the obligation/action connection, corresponded with the definition of justice in the *Institutes*—namely, "Justice is the constant and perpetual will, to give to each his right (*ius*)."[80] Nevertheless, this second analogy did not make the first one any less fallacious, nor did it do much to render the definitions of justice, *ius*, or law in "a clear, plain, and open manner."[81]

Thus, the discussion of *ius* in the *Gloss* that was meant to clarify the relation between justice and *ius* had only introduced confusion into the *Gloss*, and, by extension, Zasius' explanation of it. By not being specific enough and by using faulty analogies, Accursius left too many questions unanswered and made too many assumptions. Each analogy implied, by different means, that *ius* and law were related, but neither clarified how. This lack of clarity in Accursius' discussion, in turn, invited the quandary of whether *ius* and law were equivalents or the same thing. If they were neither equivalents nor the same thing, then what distinguished one from the other? This same question could be asked about the relation between justice and *ius*. If the difference merely comes down to sequence, then how can one discern whether *ius* descended from justice or that justice descended from *ius*?[82] By extension, returning to the problem introduced by the first analogy: if one could discern justice through *ius*, and *ius*

79 Zasius, "De iustitia et iure (lecture)," in *Opera omnia*, vol. 1: cols. 241–69; col. 243.§.4, '… iustitia secundum glossum est mater iuris, sicut obligatio actionis. Nec obstat Inst.I.i. eodem ubi dicitur: Iustitia est constans & perpetua voluntas, ius summ &c.'

80 Ibid.

81 Zasius, "In laudem legem oratio," 115.

82 Zasius, "De iustitia et iure," col. 243.§.6, 'Nunc videamus veritatem. Suntne ista quae iam diximus, recepta? Estne ius proles iustitiae, vel quomodo differunt? An iustitia prior fuerit iure, vel econtra? Audite quid ego sentiam.'

and law were equivalent, then what would happen if a law was unjust? Would that mean that *ius* was unjust? If *ius* referred to justice, or—as Budé and Zasius suggested—an inherent attribute in man, then was it even possible for it to be unjust? And if *ius* could be unjust, then what could justice be or mean?

All of the above questions stemmed from the inadequacy of the *Gloss* in defining justice and *ius* as well as the relation between them. It should then be of no surprise that Zasius rejected Accursius' interpretation entirely. In fact, he advised his students—after rehearsing these analogies for them—that if they attempted to perceive justice as the *Gloss* suggested, they would neither acquire a true understanding of justice nor be able to interpret, apply, or practice law properly.[83] Indeed, if they understood justice and *ius* (he used the term *ius*, not law) to be two different but related things, they would fail to see that "justice and *ius* are one."[84]

With this single bold assertion, Zasius reinterpreted the relation between justice and *ius* as well as called into question the *Gloss's* understanding of how the link between justice and *ius* was reflected in and by law itself. Opening this gap, in turn, he invited his students to think about how and why variations in law existed in the first place, in kind (natural, civil, and *ius gentium*), and in terms of content, that is, why some laws seemed to contain less or more justice than others. Apprehending this single point—that justice and *ius* were one—would help them to understand how *ius* and law were different, why some laws missed the mark of justice, and why and how *ius* could be used as a fundamental and foundational criterion to reform unjust laws.

Saying that *ius* and justice were one and the same was easy; explaining why this was the case proved to be more challenging, as it required defining justice before defining *ius*. Drawing from Aristotle, Zasius set out to do just that by instructing his students to:

> Listen to what I think. I say that justice is virtue distributing to each his own. This virtue is a certain habit, just like any virtue, which was unformed, confused, and uncertain. The virtue of justice was innate in man so far as its origins are concerned, but it is illustrated through actions.[85]

83 Ibid, col. 243.§.1, 'Principium huius legis tres partes habet. Prima, quis aditus iuris cognoscendi sit docet. Secunda, quid sit ius, legali diffinitione. Tertia ponit effectus & consequentias, quid sit consequens professorem iuris. Summa: Intraturo campum iuris, scire conveniet, ius esse artem aequi & boni: quam cognitionem multa sequuntur commoda.'

84 Ibid, col. 243.§.4, 'ergo iustitia & ius sunt unum.'

85 Ibid, col. 243.§.6–7. 'Audite quid ego sentiam. Ego dico iustitiam virtutem distributoriam cuique quod suum est. Ista virtus est habitus quidam, sicut quaelibet virtus, qui fuit

Expanding on this, and in the process signaling his clear departure from traditional jurisprudence, he argued:

> It is not true what the *Gloss* says, that *ius* is the offspring of justice, although the Doctors think thus: but *ius* is the rule of justice, since justice is virtue in habit. The rule, the precept, the pronouncement, the light of justice, is *ius* itself, or law, which is the same thing.[86]

However, as the lecture unfolded, Zasius clarified that *ius* and law (*lex*) could only be understood as equivalents, when and if law (*lex*) was just. Indeed, even in the definition of justice above Zasius did not use the terms of *ius* and *lex* as synonyms, nor even interchangeably, as did Accursius. Instead, he linked them to one another through the rule of justice, which, in turn, invited his students to begin to think about how and why justice and *ius* came to be expressed in the law in the first place.

To apprehend justice properly required one to reflect on the conduct of man as recorded in law and in history (real and imagined). Attention to man's conduct over time is necessary because these actions reflect the pursuit of virtue for individuals and members of society. Studying man's actions in relation to virtue is useful because justice was virtue in its abstract form, whereas "*ius* is the accomplishment of this virtue" in practice.[87] Though one might hold the ideal of justice as virtue to be the greatest good and the most noble of human pursuits, it was *ius* in practice and in action that "comes closer to regulating the activities of men."[88] As important as the ideal of justice was for Zasius, unless it had been habituated into action, it would have remained a matter of metaphysics rather than ethics. In line with Aristotle, Zasius held that action transformed the abstract idea of virtue into virtuous conduct because, although initially formless, justice was given its material form through man's actions: "just as shoe is always in leather, form is always in the substance, thus

---

informis, confusus, incertus. Virtus iustitiae fuit innata homini quo ad seminaria, licet per actus illustrata.'

86 Ibid, col. 243–4.§.9, 'Non est ergo verum quod hic gloss dicit, ius esse prolem iustitiae, licet Doctores ita sentiant: sed ius est regula iustitiae, cum iustitia sit virtus in habitu. Regula, praescriptum, pronunciatio, lumen iustitiae, est ipsum ius, vel lex, quod idem est.'

87 Zasius, "Paratitla, De justitia et iure," col. 15.§.4, '[Nota] Iustitiam esse virtutem, ius autem eius virtutis executium'; and 'Paratitla, De Justitia et iure,' col. 14.§.1, 'Et dicimus, Virtutis habitum: quia licet actu non sit iustitia, sufficit tamen quod in habitu ad rectitudinem respiciat …'

88 Ibid, col. 14.§.2, 'Vnde iustitia in rectitudine mentis consistit, ius propius ad facta hominum regulanda procedit.'

ius was always in justice according to this condition."[89] Expressed in timeless and universal terms, justice is *ius* in abstract form, whereas *ius* is justice in concrete form and in action.[90]

On the level of theory, to truly apprehend that *ius* was justice in action, viz., justice in concrete form, would allow a properly trained jurist to understand the extent to which laws and customs ultimately serve as a record of man's ability or inability to pursue justice, peace, and the common good over time. This, in turn, would prompt them to think about how civil laws and civic institutions could be reformed and refined in order to direct man's actions towards virtue in civil society. On the level of practice, applying this knowledge to the study of how the actions of man have been ordered by—and reflected in—the laws over time, would make it possible for lawyers and jurists to determine whether a specific law was just and how to reform it if it was not. It would also permit them to study why particular laws were created in the first place and, by the same token, why particular laws had fallen out of use. This ability to trace and track changes in laws over time, to study law historically, and to apply their understanding of *ius* and justice to decipher what those changes revealed would also allow them to observe man's progress in understanding and living in accordance with justice, for worse and for better.[91]

To achieve all of the above, however, they would have to develop their own historical imagination, as only in doing so could they then place law and jurists into historical perspective. Indeed, Zasius' focus on the origins and relation between justice and *ius* required an engagement with the origins and development of law on a more substantive and intensive level than either the *Digest* or the glosses and commentaries offered.[92] Again, Zasius deferred to the works

89 Zasius, "De iustitia et iure," col. 243.§.8–9, 'calceus semper est in corio, forma semper in materia, ita ius semper fuit in iustitia, quo ad habitum '; The full example, from col. 243–4.§.7–9 is as follows.: "That, while it [justice] was shapeless, was just like shapeless wood (bark), to which a shape has not yet been added. Whence the lawmaker, when he was making dispositions about the law, now has given a shape to justice, now, justice has been illustrated, now justice can be practiced, now the record which is properly his can be distributed to each person, which distributive virtue previously hid in the condition of justice, and thus *ius* was always virtually in justice. Just as shoe is always in leather, form is always in the substance, thus *ius* was always in justice according to this condition."

90 Zasius, "Paratitla, De justitia et iure," col. 14.§.2, 'Iustitia est recti habitudo in abstracto: Ius rectitudo actuum in concreto.'

91 Compare with Hugo Grotius, "Prolegomena," in *The Rights of War and Peace*, ed. with intro. by Richard Tuck, from the edition by Jean Barbeyrac, 3 vols. (Indianapolis, IN: Liberty Fund, 2005).

92 For a discussion of how Zasius (and the *Gloss*) treated the second title of the *Digest* provides a historical account of Roman law see the works of Guido Kisch and Donald R. Kelley (spanning their careers).

of Aristotle and Cicero to account for the origins, the purpose, and the history of law itself, and not merely a type of law within and among peoples and persons. He also employed additional historical examples and sources, and, when he encountered the limits of each, he drew on his imagination through memory, myth, and hypothetical scenarios, viz., historical fictions and conjectural histories.

However, when Zasius reached beyond recorded history to an imagined one, the historical account he offered to explain the relation between justice, *ius*, and law as well as the relation between various categories of law from their origins, was not presented as a simple teleology or tautology. He did not fall into a cyclical history or present a circular argument. Instead, he presented the history of law and society as an organic one, in which change, continuity, and contingency were equally important. Furthermore, he did not use the past to legitimize the *status quo*. Rather, he turned to history, especially to the customs, laws, and jurisprudence of those who came before, to understand his present and, when necessary, to try to change it.

Unlike Budé's emphasis on man's moral development (invoking Cicero's words), Zasius' focused as much on man's decline as he did on man's progress.[93] He concentrated on both because man's understanding of justice as well as his ability to live in accordance with it was reflected in the laws that he created and the methods used to interpret and apply them over time, viz., throughout history. Attention to the history of law and society revealed that some laws were just, and some were not; some bodies of law, on account of reform, had also become more just over time, whereas others, on account of corruption, had fallen away from justice altogether. Moreover, attention to contradictions in and conflicts of law within a single *corpus*—or among several—revealed that no matter how perfect justice might be, man most certainly was not. Even the most just society, in other words, had been subject to unjust laws. This was the case because, from their origins, justice and law have been out of joint and in need of reform. To grasp why this was so required an understanding as to how and why law was promulgated in the first place. Here, attention to original lawgivers and those who interpreted the laws they gave was as important as attention to the laws themselves.

Following Aristotle, Zasius believed that law stood in need of reform because it was imperfect from its origins:

93 He did not see his own time as a period of progress but, like many humanists, he saw the world as in decline, at least in the sense that serious and sustained reform was necessary in all areas to stem the tide of corruption.

> The legislator is the maker of the law, justice is the material from which [it is made], but the act/deed of men is the material it concerns. Now because at the beginning all things are imperfect, the *ius* or *lex* that was made first was imperfect: for it is characteristic of *ius* or *lex* to provide for the universal, not to provide for the particular. The lawgiver must consider what is useful in general, not what is useful to me, or to you, or Titius or Sempronius. The legislator is obligated to take heed of the universal: and thus, not all particulars had [originally] been able to be encompassed by the law.[94]

Although the business of lawyers was to interpret (just) laws on a case-by-case and point-by-point basis, the practical application of law required jurists and judges to interpret them more broadly. That is, tasked with the responsibility to apply a rule of law (universal), not simply the rules of law (particular), jurists were expected to settle disputes and offer advice in such a way that their words would promote stability and the common good, even as the law itself was in flux. In essence, law changed over time because lawyers and judges changed it. Roman law was neither fixed nor universal, no matter how those who began to "rediscover" it in the late eleventh approached it.[95] If lawyers and jurists had not changed it, then they would not have been able to address a multitude of problems that the original legislators could not have anticipated, let alone imagined, when a law was first commissioned and promulgated. As a result of simply being put in practice and adapted to new situations, all law—including Roman law—had constantly undergone alteration, even when it appeared settled and static. As commonplace as this may seem to us today, approaching law historically rather than normatively had the potential of revealing a sleight of hand at work behind legal remedies, as well as the instability of civil society rather than its stability.

It is possible for the law to appear fixed and stable, even when it was undergoing revision, because in applying the law and adapting it, jurists grounded their decisions and their judicial authority by appealing to the will of the original legislator(s). At the same time, they rooted their interpretations, and with it their moral authority, in the universal principles of justice and *ius*. If they

94 Zasius, "De iustitia et iure,", col. 244.§.10–1, 'Legislator est artifex iuris, Iustitia materia ex qua, sed actus humani materia circa quam. Nunc quia omnia a principio sunt imperfecta, ius vel lex quod principaliter conditum est, imperfectum fuit: nam iuris vel legis proprium est, quod ad universa, non ad particularia respiciat. Legislator considerare debet quid in universum utile sit, non quod mihi, vel tibi, vel Titio, vel Sempronio utile sit. Necessarium habet ad universa respicere: & sic non potuerunt omnia particularia iure complecti.'

95 See Chapter 1, especially the section entitled *Rediscovery and Recovery* in this volume.

failed to do the former, then they risked losing the confidence of the legislator; if they failed to do the latter, then they could not apply the law justly. Tending to both by grounding their authority in the will of a legislator/ruler—either past or present—and in the universal virtue of justice, thus allowed jurists to change the law in the name of restoring it. Changes to law could then be justified if they asserted that they were merely bringing a specific law in line with the legislator's original intent, thereby bringing it back into accordance with justice. This was effectively what Maximilian I called jurists to do when, at the Diet of Worms in 1495, he called for a comprehensive reform of the administration of law across the Holy Roman Empire.

As such the ability to administer and reform the law in the service of legislators—while at the same time applying the law in accordance with justice—was the greatest challenge that Zasius' students would face as lawyers, judges, advisors, and as councilors to princes, cities, electors, and even emperors. Explaining why the laws and justice might be out of joint and providing them with the tools they could draw on to address conflicts of law, enabled Zasius to prepare students to meet this challenge in a careful and nuanced manner. Part of providing them with those tools was to ensure that they understood that justice could not be divided, even though the *Gloss* and the Doctors had argued that it could be. If they understood all of this, then they could, just as those who had preceded them, effect legal reform justly.

7 The Historical Necessity for and the Moral Authority of Lawyers and Jurists

Over time, all bodies of law, no matter how imperfect and incomplete they were at their origins, would come to embody more justice by being applied, interpreted, and modified by properly trained jurists. This was possible because such jurists had understood that *ius* and justice were one. To provide evidence to support his claim, Zasius called on history—though not on historical sources. Many ancient laws, he explained, were unjust because they addressed very specific needs without considerations of equity. However, when the 'first jurists' arrived (where they came from, he did not specify), they were able to reform these harsh and unjust laws because they understood *ius*. These first jurists not only understood *ius* as justice, but they also understood it as an expression of "what is good" and "what is fair."[96] They knew that their

96 Zasius, "De iustitia et iure," col. 243.§.1, 'Summa: Intraturo campum iuris scire convenient, ius esse artem aequi & boni: quam cognitionem multa sequnntur commoda.' See also Budé's discussion of *ius* as the art of equity of good in Chapter 2 of this volume.

understanding of *ius*—as a manifestation of justice as fairness, justice as virtue, and justice in action—would help them identify and then reform unjust laws, practices, and institutions.

Focusing on these 'first jurists' Zasius did three things. First, he grounded their moral authority in a proper understanding of *ius* and, by extension, the moral authority of all jurists who shared that understanding. In so doing, he called into question, by implication, the moral authority of those who, like Accursius and those who followed him, misunderstood the relation between justice and *ius*. Second, he affirmed the historical necessity of properly trained jurists; had it not been for their existence, harsh laws would not have been reformed. Reaffirming the importance of those who take up the study of the law in the first place, along with the importance and necessity that, in doing so, they come to understand *ius* properly, Zasius hinted at the historical role that his students would play as well. Finally, he introduced his students to another aspect of *ius*, namely that it was an expression of "what is good" and "what is fair." This definition followed from the *Annotationes* of Budé, who had developed it from the first definition in the *Digest*, wherein Ulpian stated: "for *ius* is the art of knowing what is good and what is fair." Zasius turned, just as Budé had, to Book Five of Aristotle's *Ethics* in order to explain why this was the case.[97]

Invoking Aristotle, Zasius asserted that justice "requires a proportionate mixture of equity and good. For equity and goodness ... corrects the rigor of the law, it moderates the law," and "unless you keep the mean [a proportionate mixture of equity and goodness] dependent on *ius* itself, in the opinion of Terentius, injustice will become very great. Therefore, the Jurists said [that] *ius* is goodness and equity, conjoined."[98] *Jus*, as justice in action and the expression of equity and good, conjoined, is the standard by which a specific law could be deemed as just or unjust. However, to determine the justice of a particular law, jurists must understand the relationship between *ius* and justice properly, an exercise which included apprehending that for a law to be deemed as just, it had to embody *ius*, and thereby meet the criteria of being good and fair, conjoined. They had to understand, in other words, that *ius* was justice in action.

97 See Kisch, *Erasmus und die Jurisprudenz seiner Zeit*; Kisch, *Studien zur Humanistischen Jurisprudenz*; and Kisch, "Humanistic Jurisprudence."

98 Zasius, "Paratitla, De justitia et iure," col. 15.§.5–6, '... unde temperamento aequi & boni ius indiget. Aequum enim & bonum, teste philosopho, V. Ethicorum, legis rigorem emendat, moderatur, & velut Lesbiam normam iuri scripto accommodat. Hanc usus nominat Temperamentum, Graeci [epieikeia] secundum Budaeum. Quod Temperamentum nisi serves ex summa iure aptem, sententia Terentii, summo fiet iniustitia. Proinde non otiose dixit Iureconsultus in D.I.i. in principium: Ius est artem aequi &boni, iuncta.'

Yet, when treating Ulpian's definition in the *Gloss*, Accursius interpreted *ius* as the art of knowing either what was good or what was fair, and not both. One can imagine Zasius' sheer frustration (like Budé before him) that Accursius, despite having other definitions in the first title to help clarify aspects of Ulpian's, managed to make two fundamental errors when treating the very first lines of the very first book of the *Digest*, and that these errors were repeated and compounded for centuries. Hence, Zasius urged his students (in no uncertain terms) not to follow Accursius and the Doctors on this point, given that when they split fairness from good in their definition, they essentially divided justice rather than explaining it.[99]

For a law to be just by definition, according to Zasius (and Budé), it must meet the criteria of being both good and fair.[100] To believe otherwise is an example of the kind of errors that result from an overreliance on scholastic methods, especially dialectics. If fairness and goodness are not understood as co-extensive, but are seen as two discrete but related categories, then it would not be difficult to argue that a particular law that was not good could indeed be considered fair, and vice versa. Moreover, if *ius* were understood as descending from justice, this would allow reconciliation between laws that appear to be in contradiction with one another because they each would have at least a glimmer of *ius*—and therefore justice—within them. Whether by dialectics or through resemblance, these laws could be folded or reconciled into a normative system in the same way as a species fits within a genus, or a premise fits within a syllogism.

This approach would enable the creation of a science of law in which each of the component parts fit into a hierarchical order that essentially governs the "right order of things." Even if aspects of this order, viz., some civil laws, were corrupt, the order could still be deemed as just. This would be possible because, by definition, if law descended from justice, then it would have to

99 Zasius, "De iustitia et iure," col. 243–4.§.23, 'An aequum & bonum separari possint, ut alterum sine altero in lege inveniatur? Accursius hic tenet posse: dat exempla ut in glossa. Tu tene intrepide contrarium. Nam quod Graeci [epieikeia] dicunt, hoc nos aequum & bonum interpretamur, ut ita sint connexa, sicut dictio graeca una est: & usque adeo apud autores latinos ista duo verba, aequum & bonuum, prout hic sumuntur, connexa sunt, ut sine coniunctione dicere soliti sint, aequum bonum, vice unius verbi. Cicero in Bruto: Aequum bonum testatoris sententias & voluntates tutatus est. Sic vulgo dicimus, aequi boni facio. Vel, aequi boni, id est, temperate, parabiliter, cum moderatione: quia teste Budaeo, cum aequitatem solam nominant autores, aequum & bonuum intelligunt. Igitur a via declinant Accursius & Doctores omnes (quod praefatus veniam dixerim) qui putant inveniri legem bonam, quae non sit aequa.'

100 Ibid, col. 244.§.32, '[colligitur] iustitiam colere, nihil aliud est, quam aequum & bonum profiteri.'

have at least a glimmer of justice within it. If all laws have a glimmer of justice in them, then that glimmer might allow one to argue that a law that is only good or only fair is just. By splitting fair from good in this way, for Zasius as well as Budé, scholastic jurists did nothing less than violate justice, and thereby, the rule of law. Scholastic jurists did so by arguing that a law or practice, even if it was good for some though not fair to all (e.g., the acquisition of property by use or prescription in Roman law; adverse possession of property), could still be deemed as just within a specific society, and that a customary practice, although not good in and of itself (e.g., enslaving war captives), could still be viewed as just because it equally applied to enemies, and thus was fair to all.

Justifying this split of equity from good—in addition to splitting justice and *ius*—using dialectical methods, paired with applying faulty definitions and misinterpretations, allowed scholastic jurists to weave together all laws—the good but not fair, the fair but not good, and the good and fair—into a composite whole and to provide moral authority and legitimacy to any law they liked, even if that law missed the mark of justice. That is not all. These methods and definitions made it possible for lawyers, judges, and advisors, who lacked proper training in the law, and thereby a proper understanding of *ius*, to manipulate the laws to serve their own interests and those of their patrons, rather than justice. These fundamental errors in the opening definition of the *Digest* informed their remaining interpretations of that same title (*De iustitia et iure*), which dealt with nothing less than the first principles that structured Roman law and indeed all law, including the distinctions between public and private law, the relation between natural law, *ius gentium*, and civil law, and questions of right.

For Zasius, those who attempted to amend and expand Accursius' faulty definitions, fallacious arguments, and sleights of hand had produced a labyrinth of jurisprudence that concealed additional mistranslations, misinterpretations, and manipulations of justice and *ius* by dialectical methods, thus creating a body of knowledge that only they could understand. Having woven such a complex web, scholastic jurists and lawyers considered themselves the only ones capable of deciphering, interpreting, or unraveling it. When Zasius and his legal humanist contemporaries set out to clean jurisprudence of confusions, mistranslations, and sleights of hand, they hoped to replace what had essentially become a rule of lawyers based on specialized knowledge with a rule of law based on justice and right.

Thus, when he set out to restore Roman law to its original, Zasius did so with the intent of using it to reform traditional jurisprudence and the whole of legal education, interpretation, and practice. However, in his attempts to restore Roman law as the Romans had known it, he fundamentally reinterpreted it—just as his scholastic predecessors had done—through the lens of his own time and context. This is especially apparent in the remaining parts of the lecture, when he addressed the fundamental questions: 'In what manner is justice divided' (explored below) and 'What follows from *ius*' (explored in the next chapter). It is with these central discussions that Zasius invited his students to place divisions within law into historical perspective and to exercise their historical imaginations to think about the origins of society and the laws that structure it, including the universal rights and obligations shared by all humankind that existed prior to the advent of both.

8 'In What Manner Is Justice Divided?'

In exploring this question, Zasius acknowledged from the outset that it was common among lawyers and jurists to divide justice in the same way that law had been divided in the *Digest* and the *Institutes*. Although not as straightforward as the division between private and public law, the distinction between private and public justice was rooted in the assertion that "public laws are of public advantage, [whereas] private laws are of private advantage: and between those two is the law of nature."[101] Bracketing the category of natural law for the moment, he put pressure on these distinctions when he asked: "is not private utility a part of public utility" and vice versa?[102] Furthermore, Zasius proposed that if public and private utility are interlinked, then "it appears that public law is not separate from private law."[103] With these brief comments, he drew his students' attention to the fact that the line between private and public law and, by extension, public and private justice was anything but clear-cut.

To answer the question of how justice was divided, Zasius set aside the *Gloss* to consider, first, when public and private justice—and with it public and private utility—first came to be distinguished from one another; and second,

101 Zasius, "De iustitia et iure," col. 247.§.1, 'Summa: Publica iura sunt publicae utilitatis, privata sunt privatorum: inter quae est ius naturale, quod natura omnia animalia docuit.' Here, Zasius was referring to the distinction by Ulpian as rendered in the D.1.1.1: "(2) Of this subject there are two divisions, public and private law. Public law is that which has reference to the administration of the Roman government; private law is that which concerns the interests of individuals; for there are some things which are useful to the public, and others which are of benefit to private persons."

102 Ibid, col. 247.§.4, 'Nota, quoddam ius esse publicum, & aliud esse privatam. Publicum, quod principaliter ad publicam utilitatem pertinet: privatum, quod principaliter ad privatos. Sed oppono: Nonne publico in est privatum?'

103 Ibid, col. 247.§.5, 'Et sic videtur publicum a privato non secerni.'

what followed from that distinction. He proceeded by invoking an imagined, yet plausible, case. Suppose, Zasius instructed his students, that he had manipulated a river that ran across his property to help irrigate his neighbors' meadows.[104] Although diverting a bit of water from the river as it crossed his land might increase its utility for those who had previously lacked access to it, others would likely be harmed by these changes. For example, damming the river might cause floods upstream or siphoning off water by creating a canal might cause shortages and even droughts downstream. No matter the benefit or harm that followed from his actions, if Zasius decided to change the river's flow on his own property it might appear, from the distinction in Roman law as set out above, that doing so would be a matter of private utility and thus would fall under private law.[105]

Following this line of reasoning, it might also appear that any problems or conflicts that stemmed from his actions would be the concern of private persons who could either agree to settle their disputes peacefully on their own or seek redress through law.[106] Given that any disputes that might arise from Zasius' actions would be between him and his neighbors, one might also assume that village, municipal, city-state, or imperial authorities would only get involved in order to serve as mediator, and thus they would not be a party to, or have an invested interest in, the flow of the river on private lands. His students might assume, in other words, that any disputes over his actions would be resolved by private law. However, all of these assumptions would have neglected the fact that when and if private actions affect—and disturb—enough members within a community, any contests, conflicts, and disputes that arise from those actions falls under the domain of public law.

104 The example that Zasius put forward in his lecture invited his students to explore a practical case by drawing on a recognizable and common problem. This section of the lecture is short but illuminating, especially in terms of drawing his students' attention to the origins of specific practices by appealing to their speculative and historical imaginations.

105 Zasius, "De iustitia et iure," col. 247.§.6, 'Sume exemplum naturale: Duco aquam ex fundo tuo in meum: ista est servitus: si ista aqua rivulos faciat, & prata aliorum vicinorum irrigarit, hoc non attenditur, non nascetur servitus. Sic senties de privato: quia non habetur ratio si ex consequentia utilitas publica promoveatur, ita Baldus hic elegantur, qui applicat ad statutum, quod cavet turbatores civitatum puniendos esse. Certe si quis vicinos suos turbaret, vel privatas personas, & ex hoc oriretur inquietudo civitatis, iste non incideret in statutum: nisi statutum ita diceret, Quisquis faciat aliquid ex quo quies populi turbetur: quia tunc incideret.'

106 Questions dealing specifically with the damming of rivers and changing their course are taken up in D.43.13*: That Nothing Should Be Done in a Public River Which Might Cause the Water to Flow Otherwise Than It did Last Summer.*

Yet, this was not always the case, in no small part because public law, as a branch of civil law within discrete societies, was created over time to address and solve problems that stemmed from living in society. While, initially, the flow of rivers—and how to use them—likely only concerned immediate neighbors, as primordial communities expanded, those who were affected by changes to waterways also expanded. With this imagined scenario, Zasius not only suggested why public laws came into existence, he also suggested that tensions between public and private utility emerged from the development and expansion of society itself. As civil societies developed and expanded, public law statutes were created to manage conflict between private interests and the public good. Consequently, no categories of law were as fixed or as disparate as they appeared to be. Extrapolating from this analogy, Zasius explained that in addition to rivers, laws concerning streams and coastal areas as well as those that concerned the use and upkeep of spaces such as palaces, temples, and other common buildings and monuments, had also been moved from the category of private law to public law, and thereby from private utility to public good, as societies developed in sophistication and size.[107] Notable exceptions to this, however, were woodlands and forests, which, Zasius held, concerned private utility and thus should remain a matter of private interests, law, and justice.[108] Teaching and writing in southwest Germany, where conflicts over the use of forests helped to add fuel to the fires of the peasants' revolts and wars in the early 1520s, Zasius' assertion that the forest was private property—and thus not part of the commons—is telling. It demonstrates that the ideas underpinning his theory of universal jurisprudence were, in this case, distinctly local.

Even so, the example of changing a river's flow highlighted the importance of recognizing—despite the assumptions Zasius attributed to traditional/scholastic jurisprudence—that no body of law was fixed or inflexible; that law changed over time to reflect, first, the progress of life among men, and later,

107 Zasius, "De iustitia et iure," col. 247.§.8, 'Circa ius publicum colligare & ut sequentia melius intelligas adverte. Publicum dicitur variis modis. Primo quo ad usum. Quod est in usu publico, dicitur quodammodo esse iuris publici: ut sunt littora maris, sicut est via regia, quae non potest mutari alluuione.'

108 Ibid, col. 248.§.8, 'Secundo, publica dicuntur quae sunt in usu territorii, civitatem, castrorum, non autem cuiuslibet de populo: ut sylvae caeduae, & alia nemora. Sic & limites sunt iuris publici, palatia, publicae domus, choreae, forum, pandochium. Tertio dicuntur publica, quia sunt in usu cuiuslibet de populo civitatis, territorii: ut pascua, & sylvia pascuae, ista impertinenter dicuntur publica, quia principaliter respiciunt utilitatem privatam.'

among societies. Furthermore, this imagined case not only explained why something that hitherto fell under the purview of private law was moved to the domain of public law, but it also invited his students to consider when these kinds of changes took place and, by implication, to contemplate how public statutes created to address specific problems in particular contexts and in discrete moments in time could serve as precedents to address more general issues. Moreover, by shifting his students' attention from how public and private were divided to when they were divided, he prepared his students for his theory as to how natural law, *ius,* and *ius gentium* were related and when they came into conflict with civil law and civil authorities.

While placing law into historical perspective (while exercising historical imaginations and collective memory in the process) may seem rather commonplace to us today, it is important to remember that this was still an innovative approach to law within universities in the early-sixteenth century.[109] This reminds us that humanists, like Zasius, effectively helped to create a new kind of jurisprudence—or at least a legal imagination—that was historical and comparative rather than analytical or religious, which broke from the traditional methods and interpretations that dominated university-based jurisprudence—sacred and secular—since the rediscovery of Roman law in the eleventh century. To emphasize how and why the appeal to history and historical imagination enabled his students to think about law differently, a change which in turn helped them to correct errors within, it is worth pausing to consider the ways in which Zasius' lecture itself served as a manifestation of his historical and comparative methods in action.

9 Methods in Action: *Ex fontibus ad initium*

Focusing on the misinterpretation of *ius* in the *Gloss*, which informed—and even structured—traditional jurisprudence for nearly three centuries, it was relatively easy for Zasius to transport his students back to the origins of the errors and, in the process, to connect them to the thirteenth century through Accursius' interpretations as well as to the sixth century through the *Digest*. Using this compilation of Roman law, Zasius was then able to take his students' back to antiquity by exploring the original definitions of the foundational and fundamental categories of law by ancient jurists such as Ulpian and Gaius, and

109 See section entitled "*Modus Docendi: The Methods of the Schoolmen and the studia humanitatis*" in Chapter 1 of this volume.

by interpreting them by drawing—implicitly and explicitly—on the ideas of Cicero and Aristotle.

After placing an emphasis on the original meaning and significance of terms, such as justice, *ius*, and *lex* in Roman law—and with reference to both the timeless principles of moral philosophy as well as the various definitions by jurists—Zasius invited his students to exercise their mind's eye to consider a practical case that existed outside of the texts under exploration. Indeed, using an imagined scenario to illuminate the historical antecedents—or at least the conditions—of private and public law, Zasius conjured up an imagined world that existed before the laws that would later become the *corpus* of Roman law. Yet, this imagined world was neither so remote as to seem alien nor so idealized as to seem improbable. Instead, Zasius' examples were set in a world in which conflicts of interests among neighbors prompted the creation of new laws and statutes on a case-by-case basis in order to settle disputes—a world that was not unlike the world that he and his students lived in.

Although this patchwork of remedies and precedents would later become codified and rationalized in the hands of professional jurists throughout Roman history as well as in the hands of Byzantine compilers, it is significant that Zasius purposefully transported his students to a time when this process had not yet fully taken shape. He set the practical case of changing the river's flow at a time in which the basic divisions of property, viz., 'mine and thine' and public and private, already underpinned norms of social life, even if the rules and procedures that regulated and protected them had yet to be compressed into a single overarching body of civil jurisprudence. By doing so, he ultimately provided his students with a context that was comparable to their own. Beyond thinking about the implications of changing the river's flow, his offering of an imagined scenario in which the division of property was deemed as matter of fact, while distinctions between public and private utility were under dispute, enabled his students and readers to think about why and how this basic division between 'mine and thine' came to be deemed as reasonable and just in the first place.

Reflecting on this practical case through the lens of the first part of this lecture ('what is justice; what is *ius*'), it stands to reason that only the changes to the river—by private or public actors—that met the criterion of *ius*, viz., good and fair conjoined, could be deemed as just. Here, Zasius' counterexample of forests is instructive: the woodlands served private interests above all, and thus fell under the domain of private utility and interest; therefore, any claim that attempted to shift real property (immovable) to the public domain had to be accompanied by arguments that doing so would not only promote the utility of all—including those whose interests were at stake—but would also be fair to all—even to those who would lose their possession. Put another way, necessity could not simply trump justice. If it could, then there would be no way to ensure that either the state (no matter its political structure) or those who administered and governed it could not simply use arguments framed by necessity to annex forests and woodlands (or any form of real property including grasslands, meadows, and mines) or place restrictions on their use, at will, by creating new laws that promoted either their own private interests or that of their patrons.

Applicable to local contexts as well as global ones, the implications of this practical case for understanding the relation and limits of public and private law, utility, and justice are clear. If there were no limits on the jurisdiction and power of public law and authority, then there would be nothing gained from agreeing to live in accordance with it. Whereas if there were no mechanisms to protect shared spaces, such as temples and palaces, and shared resources, such as rivers and waterways, then there would be no ability to resolve conflict and to ensure peace, within and among communities. The boundaries, borders, and balance between all of the above was increasingly disputed in the early-sixteenth century, especially in relation to the limits to—and expansions of—public and private jurisdictions over forests, woodlands, and common areas for grazing as well as over water resources; indeed, appeals to natural law and customary practices (falling under *ius gentium*) to infuse new laws with authority as well as to question and resist those that attempted to change existing practices had become increasingly prevalent and contested. In a world undergoing rapid change in nearly every realm of political, economic, religious, and social life, the ability to summon a distant past to ensure that such rights and obligations were not diminished or demolished by new laws was crucial. So too was the ability to use the immediate past to restore rights reduced by conventions and practices that missed the mark of justice.

Moreover, amid these conflicts and contests, the fact that Zasius' account of the transformation of private property into a public resource occurred on a different level, or rather at an entirely different juncture than it did in traditional jurisprudence as well as in so-called modern natural law and natural rights theories is key. Rather than asking his students to imagine a time when all property was held in common in order to explain why and how private property—the distinction between mine and thine—was introduced, he focused their attention on how customs and conventions already in use had become ensconced in and transformed by civil laws, both public and private, as society developed. That Zasius transported his students' historical imaginations to a time when unwritten customs were giving way to the creation of new legal codes—and legal reform, more generally—is significant for at least two reasons.

First, the process of transforming an unwritten tradition into a written one was precisely what many of his students would be expected to take part in after they completed their studies. As such, the imagined case linked theory with practice, providing his students with scenarios that they were likely to confront as advisers, lawyers, and jurists, and encouraging them to think about the benefits as well as the limits of public law and utility. Second, grounding the law in the quotidian practices and customs of communities, rather than in the extraordinary privilege of sacred and secular rulers at a time when temporal and religious authorities were attempting to shore up and augment their power, could serve as a mechanism for properly trained jurists and lawyers to limit their patron's reach and even question a ruler's prerogative to make new laws or to abrogate older ones. The latter becomes especially apparent when Zasius turned to the third organizing question of his lecture, namely "What follows from *ius*?" This question serves as the main focal point of the next chapter.

CHAPTER 4

Breaking with Tradition

Jus Gentium *as a Source of Universal Rights and Obligations*

1 Disentangling *Jus Gentium*, Defining Natural Law

The first part of Zasius' lecture carefully explained the relation between justice and *ius* in order to restore *ius* to what he and Budé deemed to be its original meaning, viz., what is good and fair conjoined, in the *Digest*. Also, the lecture provided students with a scenario that they could adapt to any number of instances to explain how and why public and private law, utility, and justice were different expressions of the same thing. In the second part of his lecture, Zasius set out to explore "what followed from *ius?*" To address this third question, he offered his students an innovative interpretation of the division of the laws, viz., natural, *ius gentium*, and civil, as set out in the opening pages of the *Digest* and the *Institutes*. In the process, he departed in no uncertain terms from Budé, while simultaneously and unwittingly laying the groundwork for Alciati's departure from him.

Among the most striking aspects of Zasius' interpretation of the Roman division was the sheer weight that *ius gentium* carried with it. Even Zasius' investigation of the relation between natural law and civil law was permeated by allusions to the source, content, and function of *ius gentium*. Indeed, over the course of the final third of his lecture, Zasius declared that *ius gentium*—as a repository of customs in common among all mankind—was not only natural law in action but also the substance from which just civil laws were made. More importantly, he claimed that *ius gentium* was a cache of universal rights and obligations that could be invoked to reform unjust civil laws as well as to place limits on political and legal authority more generally. Yet, despite the centrality of *ius gentium* to his understanding of justice and right, explaining all of the above in a clear and open manner for his students and readers was no easy task.

Before Zasius could fully articulate his interpretation of *ius gentium* as the historical and practical link between man's impulse to pursue justice in mutual company and his ability—or lack thereof—to do so, he had to disentangle *ius gentium* from a mass of misunderstandings and errors committed at the hands of scholastic jurists. If *ius gentium* remained disconnected from time and buried within a logical argument that enabled secular and religious jurists

 | DOI:10.1163/9789004528451_006

to explain how—even when it appeared to violate natural law and justice—it fit within God's eternal plan of the universe, then Zasius could not treat the category of *ius gentium*, and all that it entailed, in historical and comparative perspective. The latter meant, essentially, that he not only had to teach students who were not equipped to study the law in accordance with humanist sources and methods how to do so but he also had to explain—or at least summarize—traditional understandings of *ius gentium* before he could offer them a novel understanding of its relation to natural and civil law.

Only by restoring *ius gentium* to its original meaning among ancient jurists, viz., as a common law shared among all mankind, would it be possible to study it as an artifact of the past and as a record of the present rather than a link in the great chain of being or an expression of God's will.[1] Although, as Joseph P. Canning has argued, *ius gentium* was effectively the *ius commune* for the Romans, by the sixteenth century the European *ius commune* consisted of an amalgamation of civil, canon, customary, and statute laws, along with the jurisprudence that legitimated them, which, although it included *ius gentium*, was nevertheless quite distinct from it. Hence, for Zasius, restoring *ius gentium* meant extracting it from the European *ius commune* and returning it to what it once was. He had to do this before explaining why it existed in the first place and what it entailed.[2] It also meant decoupling Budé's conflation of Gaius' definition of *ius gentium* and Cicero's understanding of right reason, dignity, and the common good—a paring which ultimately served to reinforce, rather than disrupt, assumptions underpinning traditional jurisprudence, especially among those who tried to fold Roman law into a grand normative system, viz., God's eternal plan.[3] To see how Zasius effected his extraction of *ius gentium*

1 For the transformation of ius and *ius gentium* within canon law and theology, from Gratian through the sixteenth century, see Fedele, "*Ius gentium*: The Metamorphoses of a Legal Concept"; Kenneth Pennington, "Lex Naturalis and Jus Naturale," *The Jurist* 68 (2008): 569–91; Bart Wauters, "Aquinas, *ius gentium*, and the Decretists," *Journal of the History of Ideas* 81, no. 4 (October 2020): 509–29; and Tierney, *The Idea of Natural Rights*.

2 See Canning, "The Medieval Roman Law and Canon Law Origins of International Law"; and Canning, "Ideas of Empire in the Thought of the Late Medieval Roman Law Jurists," in *Empire and Legal Thought: Ideas and Institutions from Antiquity to Modernity*, ed. Edward Cavanagh (Leiden-Boston: Brill Nijhoff, 2020), 280–99.

3 See Chapter 2 of this volume, specifically *Ius as a Defining Characteristic of Justice and Man qua Man*, which explored Budé's use of Cicero to explain how and why all mankind shared *ius* and *ius gentium*, and, indeed, that *ius* connected mankind with God via reason, thus serving as marker of human dignity for Budé. For comparison, see also Scatolla's *Das Naturrecht vor dem Naturrecht*, 160–5, wherein he argued (presumably in opposition to Donald R. Kelley) that it wasn't until the late-sixteenth century that Gaius' definition of *ius gentium* became a focal point of interpretation and debate, thereby discounting the discussions of *ius gentium*

from the entanglement of scholastic jurisprudence, while simultaneously departing from Budé's understanding of *ius gentium*, it is necessary to view his discussion through multiple lenses. Alternating between zooming in to magnify various aspects of his argument and zooming out in order to see the broader outlines and scope of his overall theory of jurisprudence will enable us to see why something that may have initially appeared to be at the margins of his lecture—or only in fuzzy contrast in his 1518 *Preface*—ultimately turned out to be the central focus of Zasius' theory when placed into its proper perspective.

2 Defining Natural Law and *Jus Gentium*

Taking up the question "what followed from *ius*," Zasius swapped one imagined scenario, viz., changing a river's flow, for another, viz., the origins and development of society, by returning to the original Roman tripartite, wherein private law was defined as that which "is collected and inferred from the precepts of nature [natural law], nations [*ius gentium*], and civil society [civil law]."[4] In so doing, he once again departed from scholastic civil jurisprudence and returned to the original interpretations of these categories by Roman jurists. By initially bypassing the definitions and discussions of the term in the *Gloss* and the commentaries altogether, he drew instead on the first definition of natural law as preserved by the compilers in the *Digest*, namely:

> *Ulpian, Institutes, book 1:3. Jus naturale* is that which nature has taught to all animals; for it is not a law specific to mankind but is common to all animals—land animals, sea animals, and the birds as well. Out of this comes the union of man and woman which we call marriage, and the procreation of children, and their rearing. So, we can see that other

by early legal humanists like Budé. Scatolla appears to have rejected the later, at least in part, because unlike Protestant thinkers and jurists, Budé drew on his understanding of eternal law and, by implication, Thomism, in his explanation of *ius gentium*. That Budé did so, however, is not surprising; indeed, it would be rather shocking if he had not, given that the *Annotationes* were published in 1508.

4 Zasius, "De iustitia et iure," col. 249.§.19, 'Nunc de iure privato colligamus. Ius privatum ideo dicitur tripartitum, quia ex naturalibus, gentium & civilibus praeceptis colligitur: de quo tamen mox plura. Quod autem gloss in verbo, tripartitum, colligit ius publicum etiam habere tres partes, naturale, gentium, & civile, potest verum esse, sed exempla male quadrant, quod tamen non prosequor.'

animals, wild beasts included, are rightly understood to be acquainted with this law.[5]

Zasius' problem with this definition boiled down to the fact that, although Ulpian provided examples of behaviors shared by man and animals, the definition itself lacked any discussion beyond those shared behaviors. As such, it could not be used to explain that natural law extended beyond mere instinct, and therefore it could not account for how man's moral impulses and obligations were linked by, and even grounded in, natural law. Thus, Zasius, just as Budé had done, turned to a second definition, which was also in the first book of the *Digest*.

> *Gaius, Institutes, Book I.* All peoples who are governed under laws and customs observe in part their own special law and in part a law common to all men. Now that law which each nation has set up as a law unto itself is special to that particular *civitas* and is called *ius civile*, civil law, as being that which is proper to the particular civil society (*civitas*). By contrast, that law which natural reason has established among all human beings is among all observed in equal measure and is called *ius gentium*, as being the law, which all nations observe.[6]

Unlike Budé, Zasius did not reject Ulpian's definition of *ius naturale* in favor of Gaius' *ius gentium*, so much as he used both definitions to show how natural law could be demonstrated by instinct (Ulpian) and found out by reason (Gaius), a fact which ultimately showed that *ius gentium* was an expression—or quality—of natural law itself. Indeed, for Zasius, *ius gentium* was natural law in action in much the same way as *ius* was justice in action.

First, he instructed his students that "the law of nature is that which depends upon the inclination of nature: we call this the *ius naturale*," and, second, that "such an inclination, if it is according to sense, is common to all animals; if it is known by reason, it extends only to humans."[7] Next, Zasius dealt with why and

5 D.1.1.3.

6 D.1.1.9.

7 Zasius, "Praefatio, de origine legibus," in *Lucubrationes* (Basel: Ioannem Frobenium, 1518), 1–4; 1, 'Lex autem naturalis ea est, quae inclinationi naturae nititur: nos ius naturale nominamus. Quae inclinatio, si secundum sensum fiat, omnibus est animalibus communis: si ratione constet, ad humanam duntaxat creaturam pertinet.'; and "De iustitia et iure," col. 249.§.19–20, 'Colligitur ius naturale esse commune omnibus animalibus: quod cum salis mica percipies, ut supra declaravi.' Hereafter: 1518 Preface [*Lucubrationes*]."

how these two aspects of natural law—instinct and reason—were conjoined. To accomplish this, he shifted his students' focus from the consequences of an action, viz., the creation of private and public laws, toward a consideration of the first principles, viz., precepts that infuse law with its moral authority. This shift in perspective was necessary because the "law of nature rests in the practical and operative reason, whether by precept or by command, proceeding from the first, and common, known principles concerning what ought to be done and what ought to be avoided."[8] It is important to note that when making such a distinction, Zasius referred, just as Budé had, to Pliny the Elder's discussion of elephants in order to set up his discussion of both natural law and *ius gentium*.

That he began his exploration by tending to first principles shared among both man and animals was to be expected, as this was the fundamental starting point for most discussions among jurists (secular and sacred) on the necessity of natural law as a set of moral precepts that guided man to direct and govern his actions in accordance with reason rather than with passion or desire. Nevertheless, while explaining how these principles were practiced by all humankind across time and space in his *De Iustitia et iure* lecture, Zasius offered a methodical and detailed interpretation of the relation between natural law, *ius gentium*, and *ius*, reimagining the substance of and connection between these categories in new and unexpected ways. Indeed, what followed from Zasius' treatment of natural law, *ius gentium*, and civil law fits more comfortably within the genre of so-called modern natural law and laws of nations treatises that dominated the seventeenth and eighteenth centuries rather than in an ordinary lecture on Roman law delivered in the early-sixteenth century.

3 The First Three Qualities of Natural Law: Instruction, Sociability, and Preservation

At the outset, Zasius' understanding of natural law was perfectly in accordance with traditional secular and religious jurisprudence and the definitions preserved in the *corpus* by Byzantine jurists. Not only did he concede that all living creatures were driven by the first concerns of natural law, viz., reproduction, preservation, and the rearing of offspring but he also agreed that these concerns were tended to differently among men than among animals. Whereas all

8 Zasius, "1518 Preface [*Lucubrationes*]," 1, 'Haec naturae lex (nam de ea nobis sermo est) in rationis practicae & operariae, seu praescripto seu dictamine conquiescit, ex primis & communibus principiis circa agenda & fugienda cognitis procedens.'

creatures were imparted with an instinct towards these actions, all agreed that man alone was morally obligated to live in accordance with them. This meant that man was not simply charged with caring for his offspring, but he was also required to teach them how to live morally, that is, how to pursue virtue and avoid vice—a task which demanded instruction as to how to use their reason to restrain their passions.[9]

Considering Zasius' training in and dedication to the *studia humanitatis*, it should be of no surprise that he emphasized the exercise of right reason in his theory of universal jurisprudence, particularly one's ability to put their innate knowledge of first principles into moral action. By focusing on lessons from moral philosophy, those subject to a proper humanist education would be able to develop a comprehensive understanding of justice and right that they could use to shape their own actions as well as those of others through deliberate acts and speech (oration).[10] Students exposed to this relatively novel emphasis on placing human virtue and actions into historical perspective while studying Roman law could understand that they shared this pursuit of virtue—and thereby justice—with all mankind, across time and space, on account of a set of immutable qualities and precepts of natural law written in the hearts and minds of all humankind—even if not always evidenced by or found in human actions. Reflecting on the qualities of natural law, which Zasius explained through examples and precepts, would not only help his students discern their own inclinations, duties, and experiences, it would also help them to better understand the history and development of society as well as man's moral progress (and lack thereof) in pursuing justice in common, more generally. All the above, in turn, would inspire them to better serve society and to promote the common good in their capacity as advisers, lawyers, clerks, diplomats, and jurists.

Attention to the first quality of natural law—the care and protection of offspring, which directly followed from reproduction—provided insight as to why the moral obligations of man and animals differed and illuminated the division of labor between the sexes in relation to childrearing, a factor which would illuminate the division of duties within human society. For instance, as Zasius explained, the role of all mothers—on land, in the sea, and in the air—was to nourish and protect their children in the first years of life, whereas

9 Zasius, "1518 Preface [*Lucubrationes*]," 1; "De iustia et iure," col. 249–50.§. 25–8.

10 For a detailed discussion on the links between virtue and politics that questions the place of law see Hankins, *Renaissance Civic Humanism*; and Hankins, *Virtue Politics*. For a discussion that centers the relation between political and legal thought, see Tully, *Public Philosophy in a New Key* I & II.

the role of the father—only among humans—was more specific: the father was required to educate them.[11] If a mother neglected her children, it was deemed unnatural. If a father ignored his offspring, it was not a direct offense against nature, as such, but rather a violation of moral norms (natural law) and customs in common (*ius gentium*) shared among all mankind. By fulfilling their duty to educate, fathers met the moral—and often a legal—obligation to prepare their children for meeting the conventions of mutual company, and later, civil society, something which required the triumph of one's reason over one's passions and desires.[12]

This instruction was essential because it served as the mechanism, or catalyst, by which one's internal inclination to pursue virtue rather than vice as well as to live in accordance with reason rather than passion became fused with one's moral obligation to live in concert with others and to seek the common good of all. Combined, the obligation to nurture (mothers) and to educate (fathers) reinforced the links between inclination and obligation and instinct and reason, which stood at the foundations of human society—primordial, civil, and international. At the same time, however, it underpinned the role of choice, responsibility, and even culpability, reflecting the twofold nature of man: his inclination to satisfy his corporeal desires, passions, and selfish interests versus his inclination to use his reason to temper his desires and to pursue his interests in concert with others.

According to Zasius, the second quality of natural law—to be sociable—directly followed from the first and was revealed to man through his inherent reason.[13] Instructed by reason to love one another, to have empathy, and to show it through acts of compassion and expressions of joy reinforced the pleasure and benefits of mutual association in families. These precepts, in turn, engendered trust and compassion in society. It also presumed that humans, unlike animals, did not live in common on account of bare instinct but rather because of their sociability. Understanding and living in accordance with this second quality of natural law, and its corresponding precepts, was essential

11 Zasius, "De iustitia et iure," col. 249.§.23, 'Nota ex textu, [referring back to the definition in the *Digest*] filiorum educationem esse ex iure naturali: verum est, quantum instinctus naturae impellit, [following Baldus], sed necessitas educandi, quod pater cogitur educare.'

12 Compare with Samuel Pufendorf, *On the Duty of Man and Citizen According to Natural law*, ed. James Tully; trans. Michael Silverthorne (Cambridge: Cambridge University Press, 1991), especially *Book II, Section III: The Duty of Parents and Children*. 124–8.

13 Zasius, "De iustitia et iure," col. 250.§.28, 'Et hoc ius naturale producitur ex iustitia per instinctum naturae moderatum ratione: quo genere sunt educare liberos, amare benefacientes, adversis tristari, laetari properis, & si quae sunt alia quae sensualitati subsunt: quod ius naturale non aliter a priore iure naturali distinguitur quam ratione.'

because "as soon as we depend on such inherent characteristics contrary to [our] reason, we are called beasts."[14] In laying out this second quality, Zasius not only further venerated the human capacity to reason and celebrated empathy, but he also emphasized human dignity. Man was worthy of respect and veneration because he chose to curtail his passions and desires to be part of something greater than himself—to live in mutual company and to pursue a common good. In so doing, he transcended his own selfish interests in pursuit of what was good and fair for all by living in accordance with the first and second qualities of natural law. Having an innate sense of these precepts, however, was not the same as understanding them. The latter was made possible by the third quality of natural law.

Just as the first and second, the third quality of natural law—to keep one's promises and to seek peace—was revealed by reason. In following the implications of Zasius' discussion, this third quality needed to be confirmed and reinforced by experience and observation.[15] The precepts that followed from this third quality concerned such things as a parent's love for their children and promise-keeping among neighbors.[16] The actions of demonstrating love for children and practicing good faith were manifestations of an inherent inclination to seek peace, security, and the common good in mutual company, whereas obligations (discussed below) that flowed from this third quality included duties to one's father, *patria*, and God. The third quality of natural law also included teaching man that "he ought not plot against another, injure another, or to steal from another."[17] All the above is known to man through his inherent reason and is also reinforced by observation. These qualities of natural law are also taught to man through the Ten Commandments and the Gospel. Although the second and third qualities of natural law might appear to govern the same behaviors, the former primarily concerned one's internal inclinations whereas the latter one's external actions.

The following example, which is based on but not included in Zasius' lecture, helps to illuminate this distinction. Although one knows inherently—by

14 Zasius, "De iustitia et iure," col. 250.§.28, 'In utriusque sunt motus naturae pares, & simulatque contra rationem nitimur in huiusmodi naturalibus, bestiae dicimur.'

15 Ibid, §.29, 'Tertia qualitas iuris naturalis est, quod producitur ex ratione communibus principiis, simpliciter & sine discursu apprehensis & receptis;' and 'hoc enim est commune principium apprehensum per rationem naturalem sine aliquo discursu …'

16 Ibid, §.30, 'Hoc iure procedit amor patriae, parentum, obligatio ad antidora, id est, esse gratum homini grato.'

17 Ibid, 'hominem homini non insidiari, non furari, & si qua sunt alia precepta Decalogi: & hoc ius naturale dicitur divinum.' And 'Et praecepta Evangelica eius sunt naturae, ut sine aliquo discursu sint recepta & probabilia visa.'

reason and by inclination—that one should not break promises, developing an understanding of the importance of pacts and contracts to a stable and secure society nevertheless required pairing one's experience and observation with one's instincts and inclinations. Linking the idea of promise-keeping with the observation of its practice enabled one to comprehend the effect of both failing to honor agreements and keeping them in real terms. Given the central place of good faith in both law and society, it is worth pausing to consider the implications and suppositions associated with the third quality of natural law.

Putting aside intent for the moment, we might consider the feelings that accompany instances in which one either fails to honor their word or is subject to a broken promise made by another. In each case, an injustice is felt by at least one party. Someone is subject to what they deem as an injury, which is accompanied by a sense of vulnerability and insecurity. If the promise, compact, or agreement was entered into in bad faith by one party, then the extent of the injury, and the corresponding instability and insecurity, is likely to be amplified. Indeed, depending on the severity of the injury, the broken promise, pact, or contract may even lead to an instinctual or impassioned reaction from the one who was harmed by the breach. Bad faith and broken promises could lead to injury and revenge among the parties affected, a development which could create disorder and insecurity within and among families and groups within society.

As promise-keeping stands as a universal and timeless moral principle ensconced in natural law and common among all mankind, even if there is no adequate language to convey the indignity of the offense that follows from its breach or a rational explanation as to why a broken promise is experienced innately, one's instinctual response or feeling is that the wrong should be corrected. This may be true in theory. In practice, however, justice is served by reestablishing security and stability by addressing the transgression through either restorative or retributive actions. Within societies, this is the product of due process—formal or informal—resulting in compensation or punishment (depending on the severity of the offense and the substance of the promise); between societies, it is affected by diplomatic actions or by wars.

Pairing instinctual responses with the ways in which injuries are redressed through one's own experience and the observation of others enables one to understand why and how the pursuit of a common good in tandem—and all that this entails—is not possible without the third quality of natural law, especially its precept that promises must be kept—or, as Zasius emphasized in his lecture on *Obligations* by invoking the well-worn proverb, "ropes bind the horns of bulls, words bind the actions of man."[18] Yet, the importance of promise-keeping is not only observed in its breach but also confirmed by its practice. When promises, compacts, and contracts are fulfilled, one experiences an innate sense—because justice is an innate virtue—that something good, which adds to the stability and security of society overall, has been affected. This, in turn, reaffirms the precepts that follow from the second quality of natural law as well. Amity, empathy, and compassion, and thereby sociability, thrive when promises are made in good faith and are kept in practice, whereas they are disrupted and corrupted when promises are neither made in good faith nor kept.[19] In essence, peace and security in and between societies depend on the third and second qualities of natural law, whereas society itself depends on the first one.

Even with the above example, which was meant to draw out the implications of Zasius' distinctions, his discussion of the first three qualities of natural law in the lecture were not particularly innovative, even though his handling of its qualities and precepts, as covered thus far, was more substantive and systematic than we may have expected based on his exclusion from historiography focused on the history and development of natural law theory.[20] It is also worth noting (once again) that the dominant narrative among modern scholars holds that humanist jurists, like Zasius, were not particularly interested in, nor were they concerned with, natural law or, by extension, natural rights.[21]

18 Zasius, "De actionibus & obligationibus," in *Opera omnia*, "Verba ligant homines, tuarorum cornua funes."

19 In the realm of legal interpretation, Ian MacLean reminds us that *bona fides* was a near synonym of equity in the sense that Aristotle, and later Budé and Zasius, had used it. For a discussion of equity and its near synonyms see MacLean, *Interpretation and Meaning in the Renaissance*, 175–8.

20 See Chapter 2, especially *Hidden in Plain View* in this volume; and, for a more in-depth discussion of the dominant historiography on this point, see Longfield Karr, "'Often We Are Deceived, and We Suffer Glaucoma': Rethinking Legal Humanism in the History of the Western Rights Tradition."

21 See Skinner, *The Foundations of Modern Political Thought. Volume 1*; Tierney, *The Idea of Natural Rights;* Tuck, *The Rights of War and Peace*; Tuck, *Philosophy and Government*; and Tuck, *Natural Rights Theories*; and Tully, *Public Philosophy in a New Key 1*. Early-sixteenth century legal humanism is also absent from Koskenniemi's most recent book, which focuses on *ius gentium* from 1300 to 1870. Although Koskenniemi purposely avoided crafting a linear history of an idea and opted instead to explore legal imagination, the absence of humanist jurisprudence is noteworthy given that there is nearly a two-century gap between his discussion of Thomas Aquinas' (1225–1274) *Summa* at the end of Chapter 1 and his discussion of Francisco de Vitoria's *De Indis* (1483–1546) at the start of Chapter 2. It's also noteworthy given the importance of legal imagination for the 'fathers' of humanist jurisprudence, Budé, Zasius, and Alciati.

Yet, by dividing natural law into qualities and by fleshing each out—pairing them with specific obligations and actions—Zasius not only expanded on some well-worn definitions, precepts, and interpretations of natural law but he also added to them in terms of what he deemed to be the fourth quality of natural law, which he linked to inherent, and thereby natural, rights and obligations.[22]

4 *Jus Gentium* as the Fourth Quality of Natural Law

The fourth quality of natural law for Zasius was *ius gentium*. However, it was not that simple:

> Indeed, through a certain discourse, and it proceeds from accepted customs of peoples: and such operative or practical reasoning produces the *ius gentium*, which is not distinct from *iure naturali* in its very substance, but in the manner, it is derived.[23]

Unlike the first three qualities and their corresponding precepts, which were fixed, this fourth quality of natural law had a history. *Jus gentium*, as a collection of customs and conventions practiced among all mankind, reflected—for worse and for better—man's ability (in accordance with the first three qualities) to transform inherent and practical reason into just and right actions. The fourth quality stood, in essence, as a manifestation of man's inclination, intention, and integrity to keep or break promises, oaths, contracts, and agreements as well as to restrain his passions to pursue peace, security, and the common good in tandem. As a result, the customs that fell under and were associated with *ius gentium* could serve, for Zasius, as a record of man's ability to order everyday life in mutual company from his origins and as a record of the progress of life—from man's transition to living in primordial societies moderated by customary norms and practices to man's living in civil societies, governed by civil, legal, and political authorities.

22 Zasius, "De iustitia et iure," col. 251.§.35, 'Istae sunt quatuor qualitates iuris naturalis. Primam producit instinctus naturae, ut diximus. Secundum instinctus naturae ratione moderatus. Tertiam ratio ipsa naturalis … Quartam ratio discurrens per communia principia absolute recepta, vel per suppositionem, ut iam declaravimus.'

23 Zasius, "De iustitia et iure," col. 250.§.31, 'Quarta qualitas iuris naturalis, quando ratio ex communibus principiis, sed non simpliciter, im[m]o per discursum aliquem, & ex moribus populi apprehensis procedit: & ista operaria vel practica ratio producit ius gentium non distinctum a iure naturali in ista substantia, sed in modis producendi.'

Attention to this fourth quality of natural law, especially when studied historically, sheds light on the customs in common within specific communities, as well as on the principles of justice and right underpinning them across time and space. For a properly trained jurist, it served as an archive that spanned back to the origins of a specific community, thus illuminating why and when some practices were adopted as well as when and why some fell out of use. This was the case, as Zasius explained in his 1518 *Preface* to his 'night musings', because customs and uses "vary according to the progress of life."[24] Moreover, when placed in comparative perspective, *ius gentium* also revealed customs and practices shared between communities across time and space. In essence, *ius gentium* reflected the first three qualities of natural law in action, and it was the material from which civil laws and civil institutions within communities—as well as treaties and agreements between communities—were made.

As original and innovative as Zasius' understanding of *ius gentium* was in comparison to his humanist peers and scholastic predecessors, it nevertheless paled in comparison to his explanation of why and how it was a form of natural law at its origins and why and how it continued to be an expression of natural law, even when it appeared to be in direct conflict with it as societies developed. Explaining the latter was no easy task since, for more than three centuries, secular and religious scholars held that natural law and *ius gentium* were two different—albeit related—categories of law precisely because their content appeared to be in conflict. Indeed, Accursius and those who followed him had no difficulty reconciling this division between natural law and *ius gentium* with Ulpian's assertion that *ius gentium* and natural law were not co-extensive. Such a separation of natural law and *ius gentium* in Roman law was especially useful for supporting arguments that these two categories had two entirely different origins, viz., natural law extended from the will of God, whereas *ius gentium* extended from the depravity of man.

As one might expect, and in light of his critique of other binary divisions in the *Digest* and the *Gloss*, Zasius took direct issue with the division between natural law and *ius gentium*.[25] Not only did he hold Ulpian's account as fundamentally mistaken but he also argued that the division was put to ill effect and exaggerated by later jurists in such a way as to augment Accursius' initial error of splitting good and fair, and thus informed all of the problems that

24 Zasius, "1518 Preface [*Lucubrationes*]," 2. 'Nam ius gentium unum est, quod a iure naturali hominum non separatur, produntur tamen qualitate diversa, ut iam declaravimus, secundum quod mores & usus hominium, processu vitae variarunt.'

25 Zasius, "De iustitia et iure," col. 251.§.36. 'Errant ergo qui ius gentium & ius naturale distinguunt specie, cum sint substantia & origine unum, sed in modo producendi variant.'

followed from it. Zasius' critique, however, went far beyond Ulpian's account of the division of natural law and *ius gentium* and Accursius' rationalizations of such a division in the *Gloss*. In fact, his rejection of the separation of these two types of Roman law—at their origins and in terms of their extent—challenged a fundamental premise underpinning universal jurisprudence (sacred and secular) that permeated legal, religious, and political thought throughout Latin Christendom.

Zasius' challenge to the division between natural law and *ius gentium* did not equate to rejecting the religious doctrine that underpinned traditional jurisprudence. However, it did suggest that universal jurisprudence—to be truly universal, and thus not confined solely to Latin Christendom—had to be able to reach far beyond it in time and in space. Moreover, if universal jurisprudence was truly universal, then its fundamental components could be neither in opposition nor unrelated to one another. This, in turn, bolstered his insistence that *ius gentium* was the fourth quality of natural law; that it not only underpinned and infused everything from civil laws and institutions within communities but also reached across and beyond boundaries between communities regardless of time or space.

This was not an esoteric, half-hearted, or ambiguous claim. Nor was it hidden, buried, or obscured in such a way that only his most astute students might grasp it. On the contrary, he stated outright his objection to the traditional understanding of *ius gentium* in his lecture by asserting that all those who did not recognize "the common origin and substance of natural law and *ius gentium* are in error."[26] He also announced—albeit in less dismissive terms—his position to readers across Europe in the 1518 *Preface* to his *Lucubrationes*, wherein he asserted that "just as customary practice is not distinguished from various customs and uses, then the law of nature, which is *ius gentium*, should not be distinguished [either]."[27] After restoring *ius gentium* to the status he deemed to be the way that the Romans understood it, he proceeded to explore what followed from it. In so doing, in both the preface to his *Lucubrationes* and his lecture on the first title of the *Digest*, Zasius set out a theory of rights and obligations held in common among all mankind, to which properly trained jurists could appeal to reform civil laws, institutions, and authorities that missed the mark of justice.

---

26 Ibid.

27 Zasius, "1518 Preface [*Lucubrationes*]," 2, 'est quasi lex naturae, quod & Baldus teniut … certe sicut ex variatis moribus & usibus consuetudo non scinditur, ita nec lex naturae, quae est gentium, debebit.'

5 Before and Beyond the Lectern: Pairing Zasius' Lecture and *Lucubrationes*

The corresponding context of his interpretation in the *De iustitia et iure* lecture and in the 1518 *Preface* to his *Lucubrationes* is instructive. Keeping in mind the fact that they were written for two different audiences enables us to use them to explore his argument through two separate, yet complementary, lenses. The lecture, of course, was written for his students, who could ask Zasius questions about the underpinning assumptions of his overall theory in person, whereas the preface was written for his peers across Europe, who, if they wished for more clarification, would have had to wait for further explanation—if he was inclined to offer it—in later editions of the *Lucubrationes* or to look to his other publications. Consequently, the lecture provides us with a glimpse of what Zasius thought was most important for those learning the basic features and definitions of Roman law in their preparation to serve as jurists, lawyers, and advisors throughout southern Germany, whereas the preface provides us with a glimpse of what he thought those trained in accordance with traditional jurisprudence needed to rethink and reexamine, especially considering the repeated calls for legal reform.

Notwithstanding all of the above, it is essential to bear in mind that Zasius omitted this preface from later editions of his *Lucubrationes*. Its absence after 1518 likely stemmed, at least in part, from its clarity; within it, Zasius rejected the validity of unrestrained and absolute power by directly calling Bartolus and Baldus' interpretations of slavery—a condition that extended from *ius gentium*—into question. Zasius' criticism of Bartolus and Baldus on this point (even though Zasius took their ideas out of context) could have been read as a blunt and scathing critique of the claims made by both the secular and the religious authorities engaged in centralizing and expanding their political authority and legal jurisdictions within and beyond Europe. This activity was indeed part and parcel of territorial-state and empire-state formation manifested in and accelerated by, among other things, the advent of the Italian Wars which drew much of southern Europe into conflict, including the Holy Roman Empire from 1494 onward. The preface could also have been read as a criticism of the expansion of economic serfdom within the Germanies, as well as an indirect critique of the development and expansion of chattel slavery at the hands of Europeans in the Atlantic.

Moreover, placed within the early decades of the sixteenth century—and with it the stirrings of religious reformations—and paired with the broader context of legal reform in which Zasius developed his overall theory of jurisprudence, this preface went far beyond clarifying aspects of Roman law and, as such, had the potential to become an increasingly precarious document amid the conflicts of authority that permeated the Holy Roman Empire. Zasius did not, however, expunge the ideas or arguments expressed in the preface from his lectures or from his *Responsa singularia* and *Commentaria*, published in the 1520s and 1530s. Therefore, the 1518 *Preface* to the *Lucubrationes* stands as a portal through which we can see why Zasius' reinterpretation of *ius gentium* was groundbreaking.

Reading the preface and the lecture together helps us to better understand aspects of Zasius' argument that we might not otherwise have access to. For example, given that his students already understood the Catholic trinity of eternal law, divine law, and canon law when they matriculated at Freiburg, Zasius was free to focus almost exclusively on the Roman tripartite of natural law, civil law, and *ius gentium* in his *De iustitia et iure* lecture, even though the other categories of law underpinned and helped to structure his overall theory of universal jurisprudence. However, in his 1518 Pr*eface* he followed the well-established practice of discussing how the principles that organized Roman law were in concord with those that underpinned Latin Christendom. He also adhered to the convention of bringing together all six categories of law—eternal, divine, natural, canon, civil, and *ius gentium*—into a single system or 'order of the laws' as part of his comprehensive theory of universal jurisprudence. Without reference to the order of laws in the lecture, we modern readers might assume that Zasius' discussion was entirely secular, whereas without reference to the 1518 *Preface*, we might miss how original—even if pragmatic—his interpretation of the order of the laws and the place of *ius gentium* within it was.

6 Elevating *Jus Gentium*

Zasius began his 1518 *Preface* by explaining eternal law as "the reason for all actions and of all movements, a director toward a determined end, as a plan of directing affairs in accordance with God."[28] To demonstrate that eternal law extended far beyond Universal Latin Christendom, and therefore was timeless and boundless, he supplemented this definition by appealing to Cicero. According to Zasius, Cicero understood eternal law as that which "directs the

28 Zasius, "1518 Preface [*Lucubrationes*]," 1, 'Lex aeterna est omnium actionum motuumue ratio, ad debitum finem directrix, ut sic ratio gubernationis rerum in deo.'

entire universe," as the "intention of the supreme being" that rules "by commanding and by forbidding," even though he did not call it eternal law, or *lex aeterna*, as understood in the Christian tradition.[29] Next, turning his readers' attention from a Roman jurist to a Greek philosopher, Zasius further demonstrated the boundlessness of eternal law and its importance to civil society by claiming that even Plato, in *Book X* of his *Laws*, "accused those of impiety who did not consider all things to be ruled and conducted by god."[30]

Staying well within the bounds of Catholic theology and traditional jurisprudence, Zasius then explained that eternal law was twofold; it was revealed to man over time, in part through divine law and in part through natural law. Corresponding to the dual aspect of eternal law, divine law and natural law were also twofold. Divine law was revealed to man directly by God in the old and new testaments; natural law, if it was "perceived by sense, is common to all animals," whereas "if it is known only by reason, extends only to humans."[31] The latter premise—that man had access to aspects of natural law that animals did not—not only broke with Ulpian's understanding of natural law in the *Digest* but it also reinforced man's place in the great chain of being. Distinct from animals on account of their inherent reason, all of mankind occupied a special place and fulfilled a special role in God's eternal plan, even if divine law was not revealed directly to them. Or, as Zasius put it: "brute creatures who are driven by desire alone, participate in the eternal law to the extent that the divine order had imparted motion and impulse to them," whereas "the kind of natural law that applies to humans participates more truly in the eternal law, namely by intellect and reason."[32]

To this point, Zasius' account in the preface was commonplace; indeed, he followed and cited Thomas Aquinas in his explanation. If he had continued to treat the order of the laws in a conventional manner—in terms of a hierarchy of laws imposed by God rather than in terms of an unfolding development over human history—his next task would have been to explain how canon law and civil law were in accordance with and confirmed principles of divine

29 Ibid, 1, 'legem aeternam referat: quam Cicero noster libro II De legibus non tacuit. Aeternum quiddam esse ait legem, quod universum mundum regat, imperandi prohibendique scientia, quam & mentem dei omnia ratione cogentis vel vetantis nominat.'

30 Ibid, 'Et Plato libro X De legibus, impietatis eos arguit, qui non omnia a deo & agi & gubernari putent.'

31 Ibid, (see note 27 above).

32 Ibid, 'Utraque autem a lege procedit aeterna. Animalia enim bruta, quae solo feruntur appetitu naturali, legum aeternam eatenus participant, quatenus motum & impulsum in eis ordinavit divina series: quae improprie, & pro similitudine, ut Thomas voluit, lex est.'

and natural law. Instead, he turned his attention from explaining the relation between eternal and natural law to an exploration of to how natural law and *ius gentium* were related. In so doing, he thus elevated *ius gentium* in such a way that broke from his scholastic predecessors and contemporaries insofar as "the kind of natural law that applies to humans" was, in fact, *ius gentium*.[33]

For those readers who only had access to the preface, the degree to which he departed from scholastic jurisprudence by elevating *ius gentium* in his account of the order of the laws must have been as striking as his departure from traditional understandings of Roman jurisprudence would have been to those who only had access to his lecture. Nevertheless, in each, Zasius—like his fellow legal humanist Budé before him—preferred Gaius' understanding of the correspondence between natural law and *ius gentium*, viz., "whatever natural reason has established among all men is equally observed by all mankind and is called *ius gentium* because it is the law which all peoples (*gens*) employ," rather than accept Ulpian's interpretation of *ius gentium* and natural law as not being co-extensive[34]

Yet, Budé and Zasius used this definition for different ends. Budé used it to support his broader argument that natural law and *ius gentium* were linked to another via man's inherent reason, and thereby to *ius* in both its objective sense, as an expression of what is good and fair, conjoined, and in its inherent sense, as the distinguishing characteristic of man *qua* man. For Budé, all of the above served as evidence of man's dignity, which had to be respected and protected above all else within civil society and beyond by properly trained jurists. Building on some of Budé's ideas, while simultaneously rejecting others, Zasius used Gaius' definition to support his argument that *ius gentium* was natural law—and thus all its qualities—in action. As such, *ius gentium* was not only an expression of justice and right in theory but also evidence of man's ability—for worse and for better—to pursue justice and right in practice. Zasius also used Gaius' understanding of the relation between natural law and *ius gentium* to argue that *ius*, in its inherent sense and in addition to being the distinguishing characteristic of man *qua* man signifying his dignity, also referred to universal rights and obligations shared among all that could not be diminished by civil laws or civil authorities without violating justice. If civil authorities and civil laws attempted to reduce, nullify, or rescind such rights, or even attempted to

33 Ibid, 'At vero lex naturalis, quae ad hominem pertinet, legem aeternam verius participat, intellectu scilicet & ratione.'

34 D.1.1.9.

interfere with such obligations, such actions and laws would be unjust, and thus stand in need of reform.

By linking *ius gentium* directly to natural law after explaining the relation between natural law and eternal law in the preface, Zasius effectively infused *ius gentium* with a moral authority that it had lacked in the *Digest*. At the same time, linking natural law and *ius gentium* in his lecture gave Zasius' interpretations of *ius gentium* as an expression of natural law a kind of historical authority missing in scholastic jurisprudence. Asserting the relation between natural law and *ius gentium* in terms of moral content and origins, however, was one thing; explaining how, contrary to conventional wisdom, it was possible that natural law and *ius gentium* were two different expressions of the same thing rather than two entirely different types of law was another, given that *ius gentium*—just as eternal law (divine and natural), divine law (old and new), natural law (instinct and reason), and civil law (public and private)—was twofold (primary and secondary). In the case of *ius gentium*, this dual aspect followed from man's twofold nature, insofar as the customs and conventions that extended from primary *ius gentium* reflected man's propensity to live in accordance with natural law, whereas those that fell under the rubric of secondary *ius gentium* demonstrated man's proclivity to depart from it. Primary *ius gentium* (*ius gentium primaevum*), in other words, reflected man's better nature, whereas secondary *ius gentium* (*ius gentium secundarium*) reflected man's baser one. Together, they provided a historical record of the progress of life within and beyond local communities.

It was no small feat to argue that *ius gentium* was the fourth quality of natural law, and thereby embodied customs that aligned with natural law (primary), while at the same time concede that some of practices that fell under it appeared to violate natural law (secondary) without descending into absurdity and confusion. Indeed, accounting for how and why the myriad of customs and practices that fell under the category of *ius gentium*—ranging from punishment to slavery—were related to justice and right, despite being grounded in necessity and utility, helps to explain why Accursius and others had split equity and good, justice and *ius*, public and private justice, and natural law and *ius gentium* into binary opposition in the first place. It also helps to explain why, from the opening lines of his lecture and preface, Zasius' primary task had been to show his students and readers why splitting and separating these categories of law created more confusion than clarity and, consequently, more injustice than justice, which had in turn corrupted the study and practice of law for centuries.

A case in point in traditional jurisprudence, for example, was the fact that the moral authority to punish or to wage war could not simply–or directly—be justified by natural law, given that its precepts taught man not to harm one another, yet could be justified by *ius gentium* if the latter was separated—at its origins—from the former. Once separated, *ius gentium* could be cited as evidence of man's depravity and the consequences of it, which then could be used to justify any number of regressive laws, punishments, and institutions in society as well as provide justifications for offensive and defensive wars and the ways in which they were waged. At the same time, *ius gentium* could also be used to infuse customs like private property (e.g., forests) or shared resources (e.g., waterways) with at least some semblance of moral content to legitimize their existence as "natural." Armed with dialectical and theological reasoning, jurist would be able to eliminate the contradiction in holding that the conventions of *ius gentium* (e.g., slavery) stemmed from man's passions, whereas the conventions of natural law (e.g., property, including ownership of slaves) stemmed from man's reason. In essence, by employing logic and by drawing on doctrine, the division between *ius gentium* and natural law in terms of their origins, as well as their extent, could remain intact. The principles and precepts of natural law and the practices of *ius gentium* could also be brought into alignment in relation to their ends in order to justify the practices of man as part of God's eternal plan for the universe.

Zasius was trained in dialectics and indoctrinated in Catholic theology, and thus could have drawn on each to reconcile the contradictions that arose from his reinterpretation of natural law and *ius gentium*. Yet, he did not. Indeed, given his methods and the interpretations that followed from them, he could not treat the tensions that stemmed from man's twofold nature—as reflected by the double-aspect of *ius gentium*—by following in the footsteps of his scholastic predecessors and contemporaries. Instead, he had to address these contradictions by placing them in historical and comparative contexts rather than by solving them with logic or doctrine. To do so, Zasius had to adopt—and adapt—the well-worn distinction in traditional jurisprudence noted above, namely the distinction between primary and secondary *ius gentium*, despite the fact that he did not agree with how the distinction was drawn by Bartolus and others who held that natural law and *ius gentium* were two different things, instead of referring to two different times (before and after the great flood, for Zasius).[35] Nevertheless, he was steadfast in his position that

35 Zasius, "De iustitia et iure," col. 252.§.33, 'Et ista duo iura gentium a dicuntur Bartolo & sequacibus nominantur primarium & secundarium: quod non improbo, gratia melioris eruditionis: quia fatemur mores populi a principio non fuisse ita corruptos ante diluvium sicut postea, praesertim quo ad bella: quia ante diluvium non legitur fuisse bellum, & sic eo iure non fuerat servitus.'

ius gentium was the fourth quality of natural law and effectively reinterpreted these two aspects of it as two different expressions of the same thing. Once again, pairing his lecture and preface is useful, especially as the latter draws on but does not repeat the former. Taken together, they enable us to see the extent to which the distinction between these two kinds of *ius gentium* stood at the very core of Zasius' theory of universal jurisprudence because it stood at the very core of social life. Indeed, both kinds of *ius gentium* could be used to reform civil laws and institutions that departed from—or violated—justice and right on account of their moral connection and historical proximity to natural law.

In Zasius' theory, this was the case because some laws, institutions, and agreements that extended from primary *ius gentium* were in perfect agreement with natural law, and thereby justice and right, even as others that fell under the rubric of secondary *ius gentium* were not. That some customs and practices that man adopted as part of living in and managing mutual company over time departed from natural law did not mean, however, that they violated justice and right wholesale. Instead, they demonstrated that man's experiences with living in—and his ability to order his actions in—mutual company were mixed. Given that customs, practices, and institutions were accepted on the basis of being either good or fair, and with an eye to achieving security, stability, and the common good, they were not entirely separated from primary *ius gentium* or natural law, even if they were different expressions of the same thing and appeared to be so. The problem, which Zasius explored in relation to slavery (below), was that some civil laws created to advance the interest of some at the cost of the security of others could make the institutions and customs inherited from *ius gentium* more severe, and thus less and less just. The latter was possible because of the split between natural law and *ius gentium* within traditional jurisprudence and because of the errors that followed from it, including what Zasius viewed as too stark of a separation between primary and secondary *ius gentium*.

No matter how closely these different expressions of *ius gentium* were aligned in Zasius' interpretation, they were not equivalent to one another. Primary *ius gentium*, as natural law in action, was always morally superior to secondary *ius gentium*. It guided man's actions toward the pursuit of a universal common good (universal justice), whereas secondary *ius gentium*, as a reflection of self-interests, demonstrated the propensity of humans to pursue their own good at the cost of others. As absolutely good, customs extending from primary *ius gentium* included those "that are not inherently bad, such as the sanctity of ambassadors, so that legates may be sacred [inviolate], the protections of guests, contracts, commerce, obligations, property, what is 'mine and thine.'"[36] It was also historically prior to secondary *ius gentium*, in the sense that primary *ius gentium* moderated and structured interactions within and between primordial communities before the advent of a civil society governed by civil laws and institutions, whereas secondary *ius gentium* moderated and structured interactions between communities under different bodies of civil law after the advent of civil society.

Neither absolutely good nor absolutely bad, the customs that fell under secondary *ius gentium* emerged over time and included boundaries, territories, and kingship as well as war, captivity, and slavery.[37] Here it is imperative to emphasize that Zasius was referring, above all, to slavery as a product of war, whereby the enslaved did not lose all of their rights, but rather could reclaim them once they were no longer captive to their enemy—as a consequence of escape, another war, or ransom. While the condition of slavery that followed from war might appear to be a direct violation of natural law, Zasius—in agreement with traditional understandings of Roman and scholastic jurisprudence—held that it was not. It was, rather, a lesser evil in the sense that "slavery is not good absolutely, but slavery was invented so that captives would not be killed."[38] Although Zasius worked out the latter distinction in some detail as his lecture and preface unfolded, it is important to note at the outset that although the kind of slavery that followed from war did not meet the criteria of *ius*, viz., good and fair conjoined, it nevertheless did not depart from justice altogether. As important, unlike chattel slavery, the form of slavery that followed from war was not a civil relationship in which one party had absolute and total control over the life and the body of another; it was, instead, a convention and custom that extended from *ius gentium* that limited violence. As a custom that extended from war and secondary *ius gentium*, it was deemed as fair for all combatants, given that each were subject to the same outcome if they were captured, even if the institution of slavery itself was not seen as moral in and of itself.

---

36 Ibid, col. 250–1.§.32, 'Producitur autem hoc ius gentium, quod & naturale dicitur, dupliciter. Uno modo absolute, ex moribus sui natura non malis: ut est legatorum sanctio, ut sancti sint legati, hospitum tutela, contractus, commercia, obligationes, dominia, meum & tuum.'

37 Ibid, col.251.§.32–3, 'Alio modo ratio discurrit, apprehendit per communia principia mores supposititie, non absolute, id est, supposita prava hominum voluntate, quae ab initio cum homine crevit, sicut bene testatur Cain, ut plenius capite 6. Genio. Hinc oriuntur bella, captivitates, servitutes: nam bella non sunt recepta ut bona absolute, sed quia aliter pravis voluntatibus humanis satisfieri non poterat.'

38 Ibid, col.251.§.33, 'Servitus absolute non est bona, sed ne capti necarentur, inventa est servitus.'

What is more, all of the customs of primary and secondary *ius gentium* were linked together at their origins. For Zasius, they shared the same history in the sense that they were all expressions of mankind's ability—or lack thereof—to pursue justice and right in mutual company, and thus extended from natural law and reflected the twofold nature of mankind over time. Furthermore, nearly all of the practices of secondary *ius gentium* had stemmed—in a multiplicity of ways—from the distinction between 'mine and thine': ranging from the demarcation of dominion over property and resources to the establishment of boundaries and borders between communities, states, and empires.[39] The distinction between 'mine and thine' was grounded in and by natural law as much as it was in necessity and utility embedded within *ius gentium*, insofar as it provided security and stability, both of which fostered the common good. It was this distinction that underpinned conflicts such as the flow of waterways and other resources within mutual company, and which became the basis of both private and public laws within societies as well as treaties and wars between societies.

All the distinctions and categories above were at the heart of Zasius' engagement with civil jurisprudence because they all followed historically from primary and secondary *ius gentium* and were expressions of natural law. They also followed logically insofar as slavery extended from war; war extended from borders and boundaries; borders and boundaries extended from *ius gentium*; and *ius gentium* extended from natural law. Moreover, the customs and practices of *ius gentium* were not only the basis for the founding of civil society—as well as the founding of kingdoms—they each served as the material from which civil laws and institutions were made. As such, civil laws, and civil institutions, just as primary and secondary *ius gentium*, reflected the principles of natural law directly and indirectly. Although secondary *ius gentium*, even as it appeared to depart from justice altogether, did not—on account of its connection to primary *ius gentium*—violate natural law, some civil laws and institutions often did. However, if the common customs and principles embedded in *ius gentium* were ensconced in civil laws and institutions, then how and on what basis did it come to pass that some civil laws and institutions violated both justice and right? As important, how could such unjust laws and institutions be reformed? For Zasius, the latter could be accomplished by appealing to the original customs of *ius gentium*—as a form of natural law—to hold such civil laws and institutions to a higher criterion of justice.

39 Zasius, "1518 Preface [*Lucubrationes*]," 2.

7 Distinct, but Not Divided: The Double-Aspect of *Jus Gentium*

After providing a concise account of the relation between eternal and natural law, Zasius' next task in the 1518 *Preface* was to offer a succinct and direct account as to how natural law and *ius gentium*—although connected—were communicated to man in different ways. Likewise, after engaging with his systematic account as to the first three qualities of natural law and with the assertion in his *De iustitia et iure* lecture that the fourth quality was *ius gentium*, the next step was to clarify how precisely man came to accept some customs and conventions of *ius gentium*, even though they appeared to depart from natural law, as muted expressions of justice and right in action. The key to advancing his argument in each text lay in his explanation as to why the principles of natural law were known to man through inherent reason, whereas it was only through one's practical reason and interactions with others, viz., social life, that one came to understand the 'original and common principles' of natural law and, by extension, *ius gentium*.[40] To explain this, Zasius had to return, once again, to the definitions of natural law and *ius gentium* within the *Digest*.

Although Zasius shared Ulpian's understanding of *ius* as the art of what was good and fair conjoined, his assertions that justice and *ius* were fundamentally joined and that man and animals followed some of the same aspects of natural law, viz., self-preservation, procreation, and the protection of offspring, he did not agree with Ulpian that natural law was only known through instinct.[41] Rejecting Ulpian on this point, Zasius also rejected what followed from it, namely that natural law and *ius gentium* were not co-extensive in terms of their extent, their origins, or their ends. His problem with Ulpian's definition was that it did not account for—or even implicitly recognize—the precepts and principles of natural law communicated to man through his inherent reason, which was a gift from God as well as a mark of man's dignity and place in the great chain of being. In the context of the third century, Ulpian's interpretation is not surprising, nor was it particularly important that Ulpian had defined natural law and *ius gentium* as he did since his focus appeared to be

40 Zasius, "1518 Preface [*Lucubrationes*]," 1.

41 D.1.1.1. § 3. '*Jus naturale* is that which nature has taught to all animals; for it is not a law specific to mankind but is common to all animals—land animals, sea animals, and the birds as well. Out of this comes the union of man and woman which we call marriage, and the procreation of children, and their rearing. So, we can see the other animals, wild beasts included, are rightly understood to be acquainted with this law.'

on civil jurisprudence above all else.[42] When read through the lens of Latin Christendom, however, Ulpian's definition of natural law and *ius gentium*, and the ways in which he divided them, took on a new significance.

A basic and recurring criticism of traditional jurisprudence embedded in the works of humanist jurists like Zasius stemmed from the significance Ulpian's definition was accorded by Accursius, especially given the fundamental contradiction and corresponding problems introduced by doing so. First, Accursius' acceptance of Ulpian's assertion that natural law was known by all creatures—without distinction—stood in contradiction to the normative premise that man, on account of his inherent reason, had access to natural laws—as a set of moral precepts—that animal did not. Second, it appeared that for Accursius and those who followed him, the assertion that *ius gentium* was known only to man through reason, and not to animals, was secondary to the claim that natural law and *ius gentium* were not coextensive. Rather than understand Ulpian's definition as denoting that *ius gentium* had a moral content that natural law did not, the inverse seemed to prevail, namely that natural law was superior to *ius gentium*. For Zasius, this inversion was both an absurd and a grievous error.

Not only did Accursius ignore that *ius gentium* was a form of natural law, but he also managed to separate—almost entirely—the two categories in terms of their origins and their significance, even as Gaius' definition—included in the same title by the Byzantine compilers—emphasized their connection. Thus, if Accursius had placed Ulpian's definition into context with Gaius', he might well have understood that,

> … the *natural lex*, or natural *ius*, which is common to all men, is not different in kind from *ius gentium*, but only by a certain adventitious condition. For both *ius gentium* and natural law originate in the first common principles of operative reason, save only that the law of nature proceeds simply and absolutely, but *ius gentium* has come forth through the assistance of discourse and customs.[43]

42 For a discussion of the confusing and fragmented nature of Roman law before the Byzantine compilations see Kaser, *Ius gentium*.

43 Zasius, "1518 Preface [*Lucubrationes*]," 2. 'Ex quibus inferimus, legem naturalem, sive ius naturale, quod hominum commune est, a iure gentium specie non distingui, sed qualitate quadam adventicia. Ambo enim ex communibus primis principiis rationis operariae oriuntur, nisi quod lex naturalis absolute & simpliciter, ius vero gentium discursu & moribus adminiculantibus prodiit.'

"But not simply," Zasius continued, but

> ... through a certain discourse, and it proceeds from accepted customs of peoples: and such operative or practical reasoning produces *ius gentium*, which is not distinct from natural law in its very substance, but in the manner, it is produced ... for this law [*ius gentium*] is produced with a certain kind of discourse, and with a discourse concerning custom [mores] concerning those things that happen commonly.[44]

In each case, the link between natural law and *ius gentium*—and the importance of discourse and communication in explaining it—emphasized man's ability to access moral principles through his inherent reason and his practical reason combined. Moreover, this link also underscores the co-extension of precepts and prohibitions within natural law that, over time, became manifested in *ius gentium* as a result of man's experience—for worse and for better—living in mutual company.

Take, for example, Zasius' interpretation of the third quality of natural law, which focused on man's overall inclination towards sociability, amity, and empathy, by reaffirming the importance of loving one's children as well as keeping one's promises. Unlike the first two qualities of natural law that only focused on what man ought to do, this third quality addressed man's inclination towards antipathy, enmity, and hostility, by including prohibitions on behavior teaching man "he ought not plot against another, injure another, or to steal from another."[45] Permissive and proscriptive, the third quality of natural law addressed the twofold nature of man, viz., the tension between his selfish and his selfless interests, by highlighting that even though man inherently knows the precepts of natural law, there is no guarantee that he will live in accordance with them.

The extent to which man does and does not follow the precepts of natural law as well as the consequences—bad and good—that followed from his actions had been recorded, over time, in customs and conventions as much as

44 Zasius, "De iustitia et iure," col. 250.§.31, 'Quarta qualitas iuris naturalis, quando ratio ex communibus principiis, sed non simpliciter, im[m]o per discursum aliquem, & ex moribus populi apprehensis procedit: & ista operaria vel practica ratio producit ius gentium non distinctum a iure naturali in ista substantia, sed in modis producendi. Aliter producitur & simplicius ius de quo ante diximus, aliter hoc ius: quia cum aliquo discursu, & habito discursu ad mores, ad ea quae vulgo fiunt.'

45 Ibid, col. 250.§.30.

in law and constitutions. As such the careful study of *ius gentium* by properly trained jurists had the potential of placing man's ability to live in accordance with the common and universal principles of justice and right into historical and comparative perspective. Regardless of whether these customs suited man's better nature (primary *ius gentium*) or his baser one (secondary *ius gentium*), they were the material from which civil laws and civic institutions were made. Indeed, precisely because civil laws extended from both kinds of *ius gentium*, one could study the history and development of man's progress of life by tracing variations in—and between—civil laws over time, in addition to investigating man's ability (or lack thereof) to administer and govern civil society in accordance with the common and universal principles of *ius gentium*, and therefore natural law, justice, and right in action.[46]

Approaching the relation between natural law, *ius gentium*, and civil law as a historical one cast the variability of some customs and conventions (secondary *ius gentium*)—within and between communities—into sharp relief, just as it highlighted a set of universal, timeless, and immutable ones (primary *ius gentium*). On the level of civil jurisprudence (e.g., Roman law), this comparison of civil laws over time and within a specific community revealed the set of common principles, viz., justice and right, that underpinned them; principles that could be traced back through *ius gentium* to natural law. It also illuminated what specific communities valued and, over time, the extent to which the civil laws and institutions served to safeguard these values, especially those in relation to the division of property, the protection of public resources, and the necessity to ensure overall stability and security.

On the level of universal jurisprudence, the comparison of civil laws across communities (e.g., Roman civil laws with the laws of Freiburg and the multiplicity of laws throughout the Holy Roman Empire) revealed the ubiquity of some of these values among all mankind as well as the safeguards and institutions created to protect and regulate them. This confluence of civil and universal jurisprudence existed because all peoples (*gens*) observed *ius gentium*—as an expression of natural law and as an accepted practice—across time and space. Moreover, because civil jurisprudence and universal jurisprudence were conjoined by *ius gentium*—as an expression of natural law and customs in common among all mankind—attention to it enabled jurists to identify and reform laws and institutions that split equity from good in order to promote the interests of some at the cost of the many.

46 Zasius, "1518 Preface [*Lucubrationes*]," 2.

Conceptualizing the relation between natural law, *ius gentium*, and civil law in this manner—in terms of historical or linear (though not always progressive) development rather than hierarchical stratagem—ultimately showed why and how *ius gentium* could serve as a base criterion for reforming civil laws that missed the mark of justice because "positive law, through defect and likewise through borrowing, declines from natural law and *ius gentium*."[47] Indeed, precisely because *ius gentium* reflected both the universal moral principles that all men shared and the customs that had come into common practice among and between them since time immemorial, studying the history and development of *ius gentium* as part of the broader history and development of civil jurisprudence laid bare those civil laws and institutions that violated justice and right rather than confirming them,

> We conclude, by summary, that natural law is brought forward by certain steps. The first is shapeless; the second takes on some form, the third is better formed because of common principles which have been understood and enjoined without discourse [inborn]: the fourth is still directed in its shape, since discourse of various sorts is applied. And if you should add a fifth, it is the most formed, namely, civil law, which is the precise and perfected form of justice.[48]

Equally significant, this also demonstrated that not all laws stood in need of revision. The latter was especially important given that new laws, as well as changes to older ones made under the pretext of legal reform, were as susceptible to violating justice and the common good as they were to promoting it. Therefore, any changes made to civil laws and institutions, either to restore justice or to extend the reach of just laws, should only be made when and if deemed necessary. Otherwise, Zasius argued that "the power of the law will be

---

47 Zasius, "De iustitia et iure," col. 265.§.8–9, 'Proinde si ius aliquando non bene collimat ad scopum iustitiae, hominis defectus est, non virtutis iustitiae: quapropter iustitia semper est perpetua & constans voluntas.'

48 Ibid, col. 251.§.41, 'Colligitur, per summam, ius naturale intendi quibusdam gradibus. Primum est informe: secundum aliquam formam recipit: tertium est formatius propter communia principia sine discursu apprehensa & percepta: quartum adhuc intenditur in forma, quia adhibetur discursus variis quidem modis. Et si addas quintum, est formatissimum, scilicet ius civilie, quod praecise & perfecte est forma iustitae.'; and "1518 Preface [*Lucubrationes*]," 3, 'Ergo lex positiva defectu, & item mutatione, a iure naturali & gentium declinat.'

diminished, & those subject to the law will be agitated to rebellion, if frequent alteration is made."[49] Moreover, only those changes that were in concord with the universal and common principles that *ius gentium*, natural law, *ius*, and justice shared in common could enhance the stability of the law rather than diminish it.

8 Universal, but Not Unlimited: The Right to Resist and the Power to Punish

With *ius gentium* defined, Zasius turned his attention to an exploration of what followed from it. In so doing, he set aside Ulpian's definitions in D.1.1.1. and instead offered a substantive discussion of universal rights and obligations. To frame the discussion, he combined Pomponius' claim in D.1.1.2. that the universal obligations that followed from *ius gentium* included "religious duties toward God, or the duty to be obedient to one's parents and fatherland," with Florentinus' assertion in D1.1.3. that focused on,

> ... the right to repel violent injuries. You see, it emerges from this law (*ius gentium*) that whatever a person does for his bodily security he can be held to have done rightfully; and since nature has established among us a relationship of sorts, it follows that it is a grave wrong for one human being to encompass the life of another.[50]

Together, these rights (and obligations) were expressions of *ius* in its inherent sense, viz., a power to act or not act shared among all mankind, as well as expressions of *ius* in its objective sense, viz., justice in action.

Conjoined and coeval with man, rooted in natural law, and expressed through *ius gentium*: a properly trained jurist, who understood their origins, content, and history, could appeal to these universal rights and obligations to demonstrate why some customs and practices were just, whereas others were not. They could also use them to argue for placing limits—*de iure* if not *de facto*—on legal and political authorities within specific communities as well as to help moderate and manage relations in times of war and in peace between societies. Such rights and obligations extending from natural law

---

49 Zasius, "1518 Preface [*Lucubrationes*]," 3, 'Vis legis infirmabitur, & subditi ad rebellionem movebuntur, si frequens legum mutatio usurpetur.'

50 D.1.1.2. and D.1.3., respectively.

through *ius gentium* were, in short, at the very core of Zasius' theory of universal jurisprudence.

The task of lawyers and jurists was to manage the intersections—constantly in flux—between order and disorder, restraint and violence, and reason and passion within civil society. Precisely because all of these intersections were imbued with conflicts between rights and obligations, the duty of civil and legal authorities was to administer law and justice to create balance between individual interests and to promote the common good and security among all. This required an understanding that, although co-original, coextensive, and common among all mankind, the universal rights and obligations that extended from *ius gentium*, and thereby natural law, were not unlimited. Grasping the latter was particularly salient for those who were being trained to take up positions of civil, legal, and political authority since it would equip them with tools that they could employ to vindicate rights, adjudicate conflict, settle disputes, and reform unjust laws in a multiplicity of contexts. In addition, it would also inform them, by implication, of the limits of their own authority in doing so. Foundational to each was acquiring a nuanced understanding of the relation between the right to resist an injury and the power to punish, which were, for Zasius, conjoined.

To begin to explain how and why this was the case and what followed from it, Zasius instructed his students to "deduce that that rule, [namely] that it is permitted to repel force with force, is found even within animals, and thus has been placed in the first position of natural law ... and thus that rule is part of natural law and *ius gentium*."[51] Although shared among all living creatures, it was expressed in two different ways. Among animals, it was a matter of pure instinct, amounting to nothing less or more than self-preservation and the protection of offspring. For man, it was more than sheer instinct; it was a power,

51 Zasius, "De iustitia et iure," col. 253.§.11, 'Collige, istam regulam, vim vi repellere licere, etiam inveniri in animalibus, & sic esse iuris naturalis primo loco positi [D.1.1.3. with D.1.1.5], Et sic ista regula est iuris naturias & gentium.' The crucial part of the *Digest* that Zasius was referring to here was D.43.16.27. Zasius (and Alciati) used this definition of force (*vis*) to support their arguments about and their interpretations of *ius gentium*. It is significant that Zasius concentrated above all on, "it is permissible to repel force by force, and this right is conferred by nature," while Alciati (as shown in Chapter 6 of the volume) focused instead on, "From this it appears, he says, that arms may be repelled by arms." Focusing on different parts of this definition in Roman law enabled Zasius to make an argument that equated, essentially, to the rights of man and the rights of communities, and for Alciati to make an argument in which the same was done in relation to the rights of man and the rights of city-, territorial-, and empire-states. *Ius gentium* enabled the microcosm (man) to mirror the macrocosm (state) in their discussions of *ius* precisely because they chose to link it to *vis* through *ius gentium*.

the exercise of which required moderation to ensure that it was done justly, and thereby in a manner that was restrained rather than excessive.[52] As such, the act of using force to repel force had a moral content for man that was absent among animals; precisely because humans could choose to restrain their actions, meeting force with force was both "a right conferred by nature" and a duty grounded in natural law.[53]

While the obligation/duty to meet force with force followed from the first quality of natural law, namely self-preservation and protection of offspring, exercising this right (which entailed inflicting an injury to repel an injury) ultimately required the violation of the third quality of natural law. When exercised in defense, it also provoked the original aggressor to respond with additional force. If left unchecked, this right could lead to cascading violence, extending from the original moment of conflict to the overrunning of an entire community—primordial, civil, and international. Indeed, the exercise of this right to meet force with force had the tendency, as evidenced in the history of most legal traditions, to escalate until one party was annihilated, or all parties agreed to a truce, on account of the instability and insecurity resulting from exhaustion or stalemate.

However, prone to consider their own actions as justified and those of their opponents as unwarranted, such a suspension of hostilities often amounted to little more than a temporary and unstable peace. To move beyond it necessitated the pursuit of justice through restraint rather than revenge and satisfaction through violence. Or, as Zasius explained, "For the mind having become greatly excited [as a result of injury or insult] and inflamed, [he] does not recognize the law: which is why this entire matter ought to be placed into the judgment of good men, that is, just judges."[54] As the guardians of justice and security, good men and prudent judges possessed both the knowledge and the

52 In relation to this distinction Zasius discussed the difference between animals and man in detail. col. 253.§.11., "But they differ. Since with respect to men the guiding force of faultless guardianship is required and this is natural law put in the second place, in animals this moderation is not required." ('Sed differunt, quam respectu hominum requiritur moderamen inculpatae tutelae; & hoc est ius naturale secundo loco positum. In animalibus ista moderatio non requiritur.') That Zasius made this comparison is not surprising, given that this was a commonplace discussion within scholastic jurisprudence and theology. Nevertheless, it is worth pointing out because this distinction is essential to his understanding of *ius gentium* as the source of universal rights and obligations shared among all mankind, across time and space.

53 D.43.16.

54 Zasius, "De iustitia et iure," col. 253.§.12, 'Animus enim effervescens & inflammatus nescit legem: quare hoc totum in arbitrio boni viri, id est, iusti iudicis est ponendum.'

moral authority to vindicate the use of force in society, as well as to emphasize the necessity of its restraint. As the protectors of peace and stability, they also had the ability (and permission) to punish those who failed to exercise restraint, "provided [that] in each instance the punishment is not more severe, more aggressive, than what is good and what is fair."[55]

The right to resist force with force and the power to punish were in accordance with the original precepts of natural law concerned with self-preservation and the protection of offspring. Both were also related to the care of offspring, albeit in different ways. Although man was inherently inclined to exercise his right to resist an injury, he had to learn through direct instructions as well as observation how to temper this inclination with reason to ensure that, if he had to exercise force, he would do so justly. If it were not possible to learn to limit such behavior and to only exercise force in such cases when one's life or body was in direct and immediate danger, then sheer hostility and passion in the face of threats, real and imagined, could lead to unbounded violence. In relation to the power to punish, and the restraint required to exercise it, man also developed an understanding of this through observation and experience, not only in terms of his own discipline and correction by his parents but also in terms of the discipline and correction of others in society. Such punishment was authorized by the third quality of natural law, wherein man was prohibited from injuring, plotting, and stealing from one another. If there were no punitive consequences to such behaviors, then there could be no security and stability among men. Living in mutual company would be untenable, rendering civil society impossible.

The need to hold those who committed harm—violent or non-violent—accountable to justice not only underpinned the authority of those charged with such a responsibility (e.g., in the family, mutual company, and in civil society) but also helped man to understand his own obligations and rights as well as to trust those charged with ensuring that they were protected and respected. The latter, in turn, required that the punishments inflicted by judges were reasonable, restrained, and commensurate with the offense committed. If man were subject to penalties that were neither proportionate nor warranted, there could be no stability and security among men, only violence, mistrust, and hostility; hence, there could be no justice. If, however, such punishments were appropriate to the offense, and therefore in alignment with *ius*, viz., what is good and fair conjoined, then they served as examples of justice

55 Ibid, col. 253.§.14, 'Sic dominus iuste suum subditum impetit, castigat, iuris praesumptione … dum in eos non sit severior, truculentior, quam sit aequum & bonum.'

in action for Zasius. In this scenario, those who committed harm were obligated, in accordance with natural law, to accept their punishment: "if I am attacked justly, it is not permitted to resist."[56] If one resisted a just punishment, such action would call into question the authority of the judges, and the stability of society. In this case, Zasius held that if subsequent responses were proportionate, then those who resisted their punishment could be met with more force.

The ability of good men and just judges to vindicate rights and to punish offenders was grounded in *ius gentium*, which, as the fourth quality of natural law, infused their decisions with a moral and historical authority that reached far beyond the choice to consult them in order to settle specific or isolated disputes. As Zasius' theory of universal jurisprudence unfolded over the course of the lecture, it became clear that this theory of justice was grounded in restraint rather than consent. In other words, one could not simply decide that judges had no authority to determine their fate—acquitting, convicting, or sanctioning one's actions—if they did not like the outcome of a decision, nor could they act as judges in their own cases. Doing either would be evidence of following one's passion rather than reason. Moreover, it was not the case that just anyone could occupy as important positions as a lawyer, jurist, or judge within society. Only those who combined a knowledge of the relation between various types and origins of laws, rights, and obligations and a corresponding appreciation of the gravitas of their own actions and responsibilities could serve as stewards of justice and right.

To state that a good man or a just judge could make these determinations was one thing, but to show why and on what basis they could do so was quite another. Thus, with the right to resist force with force and the power to punish asserted in theory, Zasius' next task in the lecture was to teach his students how to discern a just action from an unjust one in practice. Through a series of hypothetical scenarios, moving from the level of the individual to that of the community, he put forth a list of instances in which the right to meet force with force was not only permitted but also mandated from a moral point of view. Moreover, there were no rights that did not have a corresponding obligation; rights and obligations, just as good and fair, were conjoined. To Zasius, there were additional rights and obligations that extended from *ius gentium* besides the right to meet force with force, including the right to engage in trade, commerce, etc., within and between societies. Yet, when explaining the rights and obligations that extended from *ius gentium*, Zasius focused, above

56 Ibid, col. 253.§.14, 'Nam si iuste invador, non liceret restistere.'

all, on defense, preservation, and protection of oneself, one's family, and one's society.[57]

9 *Jus Gentium* as a Cache of Universal Rights

In exploring actions on their most basic level, Zasius asked his students whether it was permissible to use force not only to defend oneself but also one's property.[58] According to *ius gentium*, he explained, this was permitted on the grounds that it was just to repel force with force, if it was commensurate with the threat encountered.[59] Not surprisingly, he agreed with all those who held that "it is even permitted to kill the nocturnal thief if he is met with a weapon," given the potential that such a thief would kill those he planned to rob.[60] Beyond justifying defensive and preemptive violence to protect one's life, this first question also solidified the link between the right to defend one's life and limb, which extended directly from natural law (primary *ius gentium*), to the right to defend one's property, which extended from the demarcation of 'mine and thine' (secondary *ius gentium*).

Did this power to resist an injury extend to the protection of others?[61] For Zasius, there was no doubt that this was the case in relation to family; but what about in relation to a neighbor, friend, or associate?[62] Here, too, in accordance with *ius gentium*, it was permitted to defend them provided that, in doing so, the use of force to repel the injury was "not an unlawful act, and a means of managing the action is being used."[63] In addition to exercising this right to defend, preserve, and protect persons and property on behalf of one's family, friends, neighbors, and associates, it was also permitted for one to summon

57 Ibid, col. 253.§.26, 'Notate ex textu commercia, hoc est, conventiones populares esse iuris gentium, quae commercia postea ad speciem reducuntur, scilicet emptiones, venditiones, locationes &c.'

58 Ibid, col. 254.§.20, 'An autem resistere liceat ob defensionem rerum mearum, si forte res mihi auferantur?'

59 Ibid, col. 254.§.20, 'Dic posse. Hoc enim certum & evidens est, quid si tuberis in bonus tuis, posse propria manu repellere turbantem.'

60 Ibid, col. 254.§.21, 'Furem etiam nocturnum occidere licet si cum telo inveniatur, alioqui non, sed ad iudicem ducendus.'

61 Ibid, col. 254.§.21, 'Sed quid si defendere pergo alium quempiam, non meum corpus, an liceat? Dic de agnatis & cognatis non esse dubium, quos naturae sanguinis affectio merito permovet.'

62 Ibid, col. 254.§.22, 'Sed quid de vicino, amico, vel sociis, an liceat eum defendere?'

63 Ibid, col. 254.§.22, 'Puto licere eos etiam defendere, dummodo non sit in actu illicito, & moderamen adhibeatur.'

others to come to their defense, as "naturally it matters that a man is of benefit to a man."[64] However, the right to resist force with force in any scenario was not unlimited, as it was not a universal right to revenge or to punish aggressors, but a universal right—shared across time and space—to defend one's life, limb, family, and property against injury, which could also be used to help others do the same, provided that the force was not excessive.

Shifting from the level of individuals and groups to the level of peoples (*gens*) and states, which also reflected man's historical progression, Zasius claimed that it was on account of man's right to repel force with force and his ability to call on others to help effect stability and security in the face of threats—proximate and remote—that "just war was introduced."[65] In the case of war, however, rulers determined if this right was exercised legitimately. Although Zasius (and Budé before him) held that rulers should be surrounded by good men and just judges to help them to manage the use of force, when, how, and to what end this force was used was dictated by rulers before, during, and after a conflict. The right of rulers to call men to arms extended from the customs and practices of *ius gentium*, most notably the founding of kingdoms and with it the establishment of territorial boundaries, possessions, and kingship; so, too, did the rulers' right to end hostilities and conclude peace. *Imperium*, in other words, was natural law in action, as well.[66]

The ability of emperors, kings, or princes to wage war in order to protect their realm and subjects—and to conclude treaties, agreements, and alliances with neighbors—was based in the need to protect communities from external threats as well as to promote relations of peace within and between them. The rights of war and peace were conjoined with the ruler's ability to sanction

---

64 Ibid, col. 254.§.22, 'Nam possum convocare vicinos, ut me adiuvent contra turbantem, vel inferentum vim rebus meis [D.1.1.3.] Et naturaliter inter est, hominem prodesse homini.'

65 Ibid, col. 254.§.23. '... ex hoc iure gentium, bella iuste esse introducta de iure gentium, quid diximus esse ius naturale quarto loco acceptum.'

66 Ibid, col. 254.§.23, 'Praetera colligitur ex eo iure gentium orta fuisse regnat,'; and 'Colligitur tertio, limites seu terminos territoriorum qui hic dicuntur agri, originem accepisse a iure gentium: quo tempore distincta sunt dominia, coepit esse meum & tuum.' Cf. D.2.1.3: 'ULPIAN, Duties of Quaestor, book 2: *Imperium* is simple or mixed. To have simple *imperium* is to have the power of the sword to punish the wicked, also called *potestas*. *Imperium* is mixed where it also carries jurisdiction to grant *bonomm possessio*. This jurisdiction also includes the power to appoint a judge.' For a discussion of *imperium* — including debates about what it meant and entailed for early-sixteenth-century humanist jurists in the realm of conflict—see Chapter 6 of this volume. For an alternative perspective, which suggests a relationship between *imperium* and popular sovereignty, see Daniel Lee, *Popular Sovereignty in Early Modern Constitutional Thought* (Oxford, Oxford University Press, 2016).

his magistrates' decisions to vindicate or punish the exercise of force between subjects in society, to help provide internal security and therefore to engender the pursuit of peace, justice, and common good within communities. The ruler's power to punish, the magistrate's obligation to apply the law, and the subject's obligation to abide by it extended from the distinction within *ius gentium* between 'mine and thine' and thereby the foundation of civil society.

In sum, all of these practices and claims—ranging from boundaries, kingship, and just war to the ability to settle disputes by good men and judges, along with their corresponding power to punish—were rooted in and expressed by the rites (practices) and rights (powers) that extended from *ius gentium*; so, too, were the rites and rights exercised by individuals and rulers.[67] None of them, whether in the hands of individuals, groups, rulers, or nations (*gens*), were boundless or unlimited; all had to be exercised in accordance with reason and restraint in order to be deemed just. What is more, for justice to be realized, stability and security to be established, and the common good of all to prevail, one also had to honor the obligations that extended from *ius gentium*, and thereby natural law within and between societies, in addition to the rights that extended from it.[68]

It is no surprise, then, that Zasius immediately turned his attention to the basic obligations shared among all humans, regardless of time and place. These obligations did not simply correspond with the rights that followed from *ius gentium*, but rather underpinned and predated them. Indeed, these obligations corresponded to the first three qualities of natural law. As such, he invited his students and readers to return to ideas and actions that he had painstakingly laid out, but from a different vantage point. Like a wanderer who had reached the farthest point of the rights that extended from *ius gentium*, he retraced his steps back to natural law and its precepts and, in the process, back to the definitions presented in the opening book and title of the *Digest*.

10 *Jus Gentium* as a Cache of Universal Obligations

The practices of everyday life revealed the extent to which the qualities of natural law underpinned and structured interactions among persons, groups, communities, and peoples throughout history. These obligations, especially

67 Ibid, col. 254.§.24, 'Crediderim tamen ab initio semper fuisse dominia separata, ut non referat: utri naturali iuri adscribas.'

68 Ibid, col. 254.§.28, 'Colligitur obligationes esse iuris gentium.'

those that followed from the third quality (promise-keeping, sociability, and the pursuit of peace) not only structured relations among people prior to the introduction of civil laws in a specific community but also permeated relations between communities that were not subject to the same civil laws.[69] As such, the careful study of shared practices, which fall under primary *ius gentium*, viz., reproduction, self-preservation, sociability, and promise keeping, placed in comparative and historical perspective, revealed the foundational and essential obligations that all mankind shared, across time and space, that made social, economic, and civic society possible; that is, the obligations according to the second, third and fourth part of natural law.[70]

Just as the nature of man, natural law, and *ius gentium* were twofold for Zasius, universal obligations were as well: "one part is according to the pure characteristics of nature [primary] and the other part is from certain natural instincts through moderated reason [secondary]."[71] Those that extended from pure nature included self-preservation, reproduction, and the protection of offspring, and were "common to animals as well as to man: & it will be accepted as [part] of the first and second part of the natural law, so that we are certainly grateful to those [parts of natural law] which benefit us."[72] However, those types of obligations peculiar to man on account of his reason, inherent and practical, were "bound more by rules" and were necessary to "protect agreements and verbal promises, which have been accepted to be in the second part of natural law: because moderated reason dictates that agreements must be kept."[73] Man's ability to fulfill and live in accordance with both kinds of obligations—those communicated by instinct and those understood by reason—was evidenced by the history and development of *ius gentium*. Demonstrated in practice and in breech, the fundamental link between the

---

69 Ibid, col. 254.§.28, 'Quod autem gloss fieri putat actionem esse de iure civili, non est verum: quia cum actio sit filia obligationis, non potest censeri diversa origine.'

70 Ibid, col. 254.§.29–30, 'Et non quae hic non loquaetur de obligatione civili, quae est verborum obligatio, sed de popularibus gentium & naturalibus, id est, iuris naturalis obligationibus secundum tertium & quartum locum iuris naturalis.'

71 Ibid, col. 254.§.30, 'Et ista naturalis obligatio est duplex. Quaedam remanet in puris naturalibus, & ex quodam naturae instinctu per moderatam rationem.'

72 Ibid, col. 254–5.§.30, 'imo ex simplici naturae instinctu proficiscitur: & ista est communis animalibus & hominibus, & erit iuris naturalis primo & secundo loco accepti, ut scilicet grati simus benefacientibus.'

73 Ibid, col. 255.§.31, 'Alia est astrictior, & plus habet vinculi ad civilia, videlicet pacta & verba promissa servare, quae sunt iuris naturalis secundo loco accepti: quia ratio moderata hoc dictat, ut pacta serventur.'

two kinds of obligations was man's propensity, inherent and learned, to fear God, to obey one's father, and to protect one's *patria*.[74]

Appearing to cast aside Pomponius' assertion in the D.1.1.2. that "religious duties toward God" were part of *ius gentium*, Accursius and all those who followed him argued that religion—and its corresponding obligations—extended directly from divine law.[75] While Zasius rejected Accursius' interpretation, it is worth pausing to place it into context. Accursius' rejection of Pomponius on this point made sense on at least two levels. First, in the context of Universal Latin Christendom only those religious duties that were directly revealed through the old and new testaments, and not through the customs, practices, and rites of any other religion or the ordinary practices of man, were deemed legitimate. Here again, for Zasius, the limitations and contradictions inherent in grounding universal jurisprudence in one religion and worldview would have been apparent insofar as for universal jurisprudence to be truly universal, it had to reach beyond the temporal and doctrinal confines of Latin Europe and Christianity.

Second, Accursius' rejection made sense because of how he previously interpreted Ulpian's assertion that natural law and *ius gentium* were not coextensive. Placing this, again, into the context of Universal Latin Christendom, if *ius gentium* was not understood as an expression of natural law, but was understood as entirely separate from it, then the idea that religious duties toward God extended from, or were evidenced by, *ius gentium* would have been an absurd claim. After all, from the perspective of traditional jurisprudence, religious customs and rites that were transmitted from generation to generation before—or after—divine law was given directly to man, were not considered to be grounded in the words of God, so much as the interests of man. If, however, one approached *ius gentium* as a quality of natural law, as Zasius did, then what was common among these religious rites—even as they varied over time—could be interpreted as evidence that God revealed aspects of his will and overall plan to all of mankind through inherent and practical reason. Approaching *ius gentium* from this standpoint, Zasius dismissed the idea that religious duties could not fall under the category of *ius gentium*, as well

---

74 Compare with Samuel Pufendorf, *De jure naturae et gentium*, 2 vols., ed. Frank Böhling, Samuel Pufendorf: Gesam- melte Werke, ed. Wilhelm Schmidt-Biggemann, vols. 4.1–2 (Berlin: Akademie Verlag, 1998).

75 Zasius, "De iustitia et iure," col. 252.§.1, 'Secundo colligitur religionem in Deum esse iuris gentium: quod intellige ut praedixi Glossae disceptat an sit iuris publici, cum sit sacramentum.'

as the commentaries that supported such an interpretation, by simply stating that: "for my part I do not see why this is being debated."[76]

Agreeing with Pomponius, Zasius stated that religious obligation stood "apart from state affairs concerns our fear of God," as evidenced by attention to the customs and practices embedded in *ius gentium*.[77] Imprinted by instinct and inherent reason, man came to understand his fear of God as a consequence of the progress of life. In the same way that man learned, by direct instruction and observation, how to use his reason to temper his passions over time, so too he learned how to fulfill his duties toward God. Just as man was subject to fail in the former case, he was also subject to fail in the latter one. This did not, however, diminish the fact that it was "important for us as individuals to fear God," nor did it weaken Zasius' argument that "this obligation is not some religious observance of the gods. Instead, it is the power of reason, rooted in mankind by nature, common even to those peoples among whom the sacraments have no place."[78] Universally, all of mankind was obligated to fear God before—and even outside of—the advent of the civil oaths, religious institutions, and revealed religion that commanded them to do so. In essence, because the fear of God was innate, and therefore co-original with natural law and *ius gentium*, all that followed from it was at the very foundation of religious doctrine and institutions in the first place: "hence Statius said, fear first of all in the world made gods."[79] As individuals and communities developed, they came to understand this fear differently, especially as customary practices transformed into, or were changed by, religious doctrine.

The second obligation that Zasius explicitly addressed was to obey one's parents, which was also co-original and coextensive in natural law and *ius gentium*.[80] Although innate, through direct instruction, observation, and experience, one came to understand why this was necessary as well as the consequences of not doing so. Over time, one also came to learn why they should fear their father, above all, as a consequence of him teaching them to live in agreement with natural law and disciplining them if they did not. While the power to punish and the responsibility to educate were grounded in natural

76 Ibid, col. 252.§.1, 'Equidem non video cur hoc disceptetur.'

77 Ibid, col. 252.§.1, 'Ergo nostra privatim inter est timere Deum.'

78 Ibid, col. 252.§.1, 'nec est sacramentum ista in Deum religio, sed est vis rationis per naturam in hominbus radicata, communis etiam gentilibus, in quibus non habent locum sacramenta.'

79 Ibid, col. 252.§.2, 'Vnde Statius dixerat: Primus in orbe deos timor fecerat.'

80 Ibid, col. 252.§.2, 'Tertio collige patriae & parentibus parendum fore: quod hic duae glossea colligunt: magis tamen obediendum patri quam matri ... & hoc facit patria potestas, quae non est in matre.'

law, the shared customs and conventions to affect such ends were embedded in and communicated by *ius gentium*. As societies developed, these customs and expectation were transformed into civil laws.[81] Moreover, the obligation to fear one's father mirrored the obligation to fear God, and both were reinforced with instruction and punishment. The same went for civil law and civil authority as societies developed.

The last obligation that underpinned and infused all of man's other duties in familial, primordial, and civil society was implanted in man by God, but it was understood as a result of by practical reason and developed because of social life. Connected to the first and second, but not equivalent to them, this third obligation was to obey the customs and laws of one's own community and, in so doing, to fulfill the obligation to protect one's *patria* from internal and external threats. Just as was the case with the fear of God and father, man came to understand this obligation through direct instruction and by observation. As a result, he came to understand why, as a subject to its authority, one's *patria* had the power to punish those who did not fulfill their duty to protect it as well as those who violated its customs, conventions, and laws. He likewise came to understand that the obligation to protect and the power to punish emerging from *ius gentium* was reflective of the power that his father, *patria*, and God exercised over him.

Once nations (*gens*) were established, and with them boundaries and borders patrolled and administered by laws and protected by force, all those who lived within such nations acquired the obligation to protect their *patria*—and the right to do so—in the same vein as they had to protect their family, neighbors, and associates when faced with immediate danger. Unlike one's family and friends, however, if one did not exercise this right (or, rather, did not fulfill this obligation), then they became a threat to the stability and security of society, and thus were subject to punishment:

> One must obey the *patria*, because we are born in a commonwealth … thus unless one gives aid to his community when it is in danger, he will destroy the laws of the *patria* … and just like the son who abandons his father in danger, or does not declare imminent danger to him, can be punished as a parricide, so too one who conceals dangers to his republic can be punished the same way.[82]

81 See Budé's discussion of Roman Stork Laws in Chapter 2 of this volume.

82 Zasius, "De iustitia et iure," col. 252.§.6, 'Colligitur quarto, patriae ideo parendum, quia reipublicae nascimur … Vnde nisi civis civitati subveniat periclitanti, patriae iura perdet … Et sicut filius qui deserit patrem in periculo, vel ei non indicat imminens periculum, puniri potest ut parricida, … ita & civis pericula civitatis dissimulans punitur.'

Drawing on both Bartolus and Baldus to great effect, the connection between the obligation to protect the *patria*—and the corresponding analogy to parricide if one failed to do so—provided Zasius' students with a clear link between the obligations that existed prior to mutual company and obligations that arose from it, something which, in turn, reinforced the connection between the obligations resulting from the first three qualities of natural law and the obligations that extended from its fourth quality, viz., *ius gentium*, in his theory of universal jurisprudence. These obligations, moreover, were directly connected to the rights that extended from *ius gentium*, which, in turn, extended from the first three qualities of natural law. Everything, for Zasius, was interlocked and interrelated organically, historically, and logically within his theory of universal jurisprudence.

11 The Limits of Slavery

As instructive as Zasius' account of the universal rights and obligations shared among all mankind was, one obvious question remained unaddressed: under what conditions, if any, could the universal rights and obligations that extended from *ius gentium*, and therefore natural law, be suspended, diminished, or abrogated by civil laws, institutions, and authorities? Rather than simply exploring this question through the lens of punishment (and the moral and legal limits placed on it), Zasius took it up in both his *De Iustitia et iure* lecture and in the 1518 *Preface* of his *Lucubrationes* in relation to a ubiquitous and persistent condition that was not co-original with natural law, but extended from *ius gentium*, namely slavery, and its analog servitude.[83] That he did so is not surprising given that Ulpian's definition of manumission, which directly linked *ius gentium* and slavery as well as natural law and freedom in *the Digest*, was placed by the Byzantine compilers between Florentinus' assertion of one's right to use force to preserve oneself and Hermogenian's assertion that wars—as well as the founding of kingdoms—followed from *ius gentium*.[84] While Alciati made much of the connection between the former and the latter by focusing on war (explored in part three of this volume), whereas Zasius—sharing some of the same concerns as Budé, but addressing them in a far more direct and substantive way—amplified the relationship between the two definitions by concentrating on the institution of slavery and the limits of servitude.

83 Zasius, "De iustitia et iure," cols. 255–6, and "1518 Preface [*Lucubrationes*]," 2.

84 D.1.1.3. through D.1.1.5.

In both his *De iustitia et iure* lecture and the 1518 *Preface*, Zasius' discussion of slavery lies between his reinterpretation of *ius gentium*, as a form of natural law and a cache of universal rights and obligations, and his discussion of civil law, as both an expression of justice and a departure from it. The analysis and interpretation within the lecture were as lucid and to the point as his treatment of slavery in the 1518 *Preface* was striking and dangerous. Folded within his broader presentation of *ius gentium* in the former and the reinterpretation of the relation between natural law and *ius gentium* in the latter, Zasius directly rejected Bartolus and Baldus' interpretation that those enslaved were under the total domination of their master, and thus property rather than persons before the law, with no rights or obligations. Here was yet more evidence to support his broader argument that civil law and justice had fallen out of joint at the hands of traditional jurisprudence.

Placing the definitions of slavery within the first pages of the *Digest* in comparison with those of Accursius, Bartolus, and Baldus, Zasius demonstrated that the institution of slavery was common, yet the conditions of servitude varied. Approaching slavery and servitude from a historical perspective revealed how and why the conditions of servitude—and the corresponding rights and obligations that underpinned and structured it—had been changed, for worse, to suit interests within specific societies. Studying slavery and servitude in comparative perspective illuminated what all forms of slavery shared and what distinguished them. Combining these methods would enable jurists to comprehend that while slavery and servitude were two expressions of the same thing, namely subjection, they were not equivalents.

This was the case even though they shared so many features in common. For example, slavery and servitude each extended from secondary *ius gentium* and thus expressed the baser nature of man, each had two forms (voluntary and involuntary), and each was considered just insofar as they were considered better than the alternative, whether it was death in the case of those who became enslaved because of war or starvation in the case of those who became unfree because of need. Nevertheless, the two institutions were not coextensive. Just as in the case of the distinction between public law and private law and primary and secondary *ius gentium*, they diverged from one another on account of the needs they fulfilled and the purposes they served. While, for example, slavery in times of war served as an alternative to violence for both the captive and the captor, servitude in times of peace served as an alternative to scarcity for both the lord and peasant/serf. In each case, the condition was interpreted, at least in theory, to be balanced as an exchange of one's life and liberty, albeit in differing degrees, and for stability and security, albeit of different kinds.

Beyond the reasons for entering such conditions of subjection, degrees of servitude also differed across time and space. These differences accounted for why there was no simple equivalent between a Roman slave and a German serf, even though traditional jurists who approached these categories logically rather than historically may have assumed there was. Indeed, slavery, as the Romans knew it, never existed in Germany.[85] What is more, exploring the institutions through a historical and comparative lens revealed that, over time, there had been different kinds of slavery within the Roman Empire, just as there were different forms of servitude within the Holy Roman Empire. Thus, one could no sooner remove slavery from one legal, political, economic, and social context and superimpose it on another, then one could assume that forms of servitude that existed in the sixth century—when the Roman *Digest* was compiled—were precisely the same forms that existed in the *Digest* when it was 'rediscovered' in the eleventh century (let alone the same forms that accompanied territorial-state and empire-state formation in the sixteenth).[86] This is worth emphasizing since it is not only what some scholastic jurists attempted to do amid the expansion of servitude and serfdom within Europe but also what they tried to do by expanding servitude and slavery beyond Europe—especially into the Atlantic.

Rejecting such impositions and, instead, approaching the institutions, customs, practices, and laws that were associated with servitude from a comparative perspective had the potential of illuminating what they had in common and how they might be brought into conversation as part of a shared legal tradition and a theory of universal jurisprudence. For example, although there was no direct correspondence between the Roman legal category of slave and the German one of unfree peasant, there was a category of persons within Roman law that the latter could be compared to: freedmen.[87] Despite the historical, geographical, and cultural distance between them, what made this possible was the fact that Roman freedmen and German unfree peasants could use the courts to seek legal remedies, they both had the right to enter contracts and thereby take on obligations, and they both could own property.[88] Moreover, both were permitted to exercise rights and fulfill obligations precisely because the civil laws that defined and regulated their legal status

85 See Sidney Bradshaw Fay, "The Roman Law and the German Peasant," *The American Historical Review* 16, no. 2 (1911): 234–54; and Peter Blickle, *Von Der Leibeigenschaft zu den Menschenrechten: Eine Geschichte der Freiheit in Deutschland* (Munich: C. H. Beck, 2003).

86 Ibid.

87 See *Institutes*, 1.5: Freedmen.

88 Bradshaw Fay, "The Roman Law and the German Peasant."

did not violate the principles and practices embodied within and communicated by *ius gentium*—as a form of natural law—by attempting to abrogate or demolish universal rights and obligations shared among all mankind, without distinction. This was not the case, Zasius argued, with those laws stemming from the errors embedded within traditional jurisprudence.

Seemingly convinced that *ius gentium* placed no limits on the actions of man, Accursius, Bartolus, and Baldus argued that the barbarity and violence of slavery extended from *ius gentium*, whereas the limiting of such violence, thus making the institution and the conditions of those subject to it less harsh and more just, extended from civil law.[89] This is not surprising if we remember that, in the context of traditional jurisprudence, both canon and civil law were understood as distant, yet significant expressions of God's will, while *ius gentium* was thought to have extended predominantly from the failings of man. However, when subjected to historical scrutiny, whether evidence-based or imagined, such an order of the laws proved problematic. Equally important, the introduction of new civil laws and the abrogation of older ones to enhance the power of political and legal authorities at the cost of those subject to them served as evidence that Accursius and all who followed him on this point were in error when they first, split good from fair, and then, natural law from *ius gentium*.

Indeed, Zasius—in line with his reinterpretation of *ius gentium*—rejected this interpretation, by asserting that "the power of the masters is not restricted from the civil law, although their excessive savagery is kept in check, lest they rage too greatly."[90] Conceding that legal mechanisms were embedded in and protected by civil laws to help prevent the excessive use of violence by a master or lord (or prince) was not a concession to Accursius' interpretation. Rather, in bearing Zasius' overall theory of universal jurisprudence in mind, these provisions and protections existed in civil law precisely because they were embedded in *ius gentium*, the fourth quality of natural law, and the material from which civil laws were made. Therefore, he declared that the restrictions on the use of excessive force "has come from *ius gentium*. For since excessive savagery

89 Zasius, "De iustitia et iure," col. 257.§.11, 'Item iuri gentium detrahitur quo ad dominicam potestatem: quia dominorum potestas in servos est restricta de iure civili, quae fuit ampliata de iure gentium, si Accursio credimus ... Mihi hoc exemplum non videtur tutum, licet Doctores communiter transeant: quia potestas dominorum non est restricta de iure civili, sed nimia eorum servitia est coercita, ne nimis saeviant: & hoc etaim (tacite saltem) fuit de iure gentium. Nam nimia saevitia cum sit contra ius naturale etiam in brutis animalibus, ut supra diximus, ergo fortius erit contra ius gentium: nec enim frustra dicitur servire a servando.'

90 Ibid.

is against natural law … it will be more strongly against *ius gentium*, for not in vain is it to be said that "to be a slave" comes from preserving."[91] The use of force, whether in defense or in punishment, had to be commensurate and restrained in order to be just. At the same time, it was clear that the condition of slavery and servitude and, by extension, other forms of legal (and political) authority appeared to be excessively harsh and unjust. If permissive use of such excessive violence could not be traced to *ius gentium*, then where did it come from? According to Zasius, it was "civil law"—not *ius gentium*—that "deprives, destroys, and annuls the status of the slave."[92]

To articulate this point in his 1518 *Preface*, in true humanist form, Zasius invoked the historical and moral authority of the Ancients and placed them in comparison. First, Zasius turned to Job, whose words served as evidence that among the Hebrews, "slaves were able to stand up against their masters by means of legal action, and therefore [slaves] were able to be obligated."[93] To show that slaves, in addition to having access to the courts, were able to enter into a variety of contracts and to inherit property, he referred to Tacitus, who "among the ancient Germans writes, that everywhere it was accepted according to the customs of the people, that slaves were able to acquire goods amongst themselves, and were not much different in this regard than freedmen."[94] Moving back in time, and from Rome to Greece, Zasius paraphrased Aristotle, who "relates in *Book IV* of the *Politics* that slaves, if they were wealthy by a small amount, could be chosen for administrative civil duties" to show that slaves were able to contribute to the common good, and in the process of doing so, take on new obligations (duties).[95] Linking these examples, Zasius demonstrated that, despite the perceptions of his contemporaries and predecessors, ancient slaves were indeed able to exercise rights and take on obligations; that their condition of subordination in one context did not demolish their ability to interact in others. Finally, Zasius borrowed from *Exodus* for evidence that

---

91 Ibid.

92 Ibid, col. 255.§.34, 'Sed ius civile enecuit, peremit, annullavit statum servi.'; and Zasius, "1518 Preface [*Lucubrationes*]," 2. 'Nec porro verum putamus, quod de iure gentium secundario (ut Bartulos nominat) servi status annihiletur.'

93 Zasius, "1518 Preface [*Lucubrationes*]," 2, 'Nam Job capituli xxxi colligis, servos contra dominos iudicio stare potuisse, ergo & obligari poterant denique servi dominis ab intestato, haeredes succedebant, si non extitissent filli.'

94 Ibid, 'Quod & Cornelius Tacitus apud veteres Germanos scribit, passim usu gentium receptum, ut servi subiipsis acquirerent, & non multum a libertis distarent.'

95 Ibid, 'Denique Philosophus libri IIII Politica capitulum XV, tradit servos, si paulo essent opulemtiores, ad munera civila administrativa eligi.'

the power one had over slaves was limited: "according to *ius gentium* servants and slaves are not able to be destroyed."[96]

If ancient slaves had not been entirely subject to the legal or physical domination of their masters, then why and how did it come to pass that they were held to be so in traditional jurisprudence? As with other instances in the 1518 *Preface* and in his lecture, the answer came down to the fact (for Zasius) that Accursius and his followers misinterpreted fundamental terms, categories, and institutions of Roman law, which included the fundamental aspect of servitude. They interpreted the assertion that "the slave was inherently his own property," and thus "he was able to be obligated by *ius gentium*," to mean that through the process of becoming a slave, whether by force or by choice, their ability—and right—to take on other obligations was suspended and even abolished.[97] Extending this to feudalism, it meant that when one entered a contract of servitude, whether tacitly or explicitly, thereby changing their status from free to unfree, they forfeited their ability—and rights—to take on additional obligations or even to fulfill preexisting ones.

According to Zasius, Accursius and others understood the contract of voluntary submission and servitude in this manner because they believed "freedom [originates] from natural law, but domination proceeds from *ius gentium*."[98] Placed in such a contrary relation would suggest that when people became enslaved, they did not only become unfree in terms of labor and fealty restrictions, but they lost their freedom altogether.[99] Yet, this interpretation could only stand if the power that advanced from *ius gentium*—on behalf of the masters—demanded that the rights (and obligations) of the enslaved be alienated and, further, that power and right were opposed to one another. Zasius rejected this position outright, stating that while domination, viz. power, authority, dominion, and rule, extended from *ius gentium*, "I do not think it is proper to infer from this that the status of the slave is abolished: since the domination of the lord does not require the demolition of the slave;" by extension, the rule of princes did not require the demolition of their subjects.[100]

96 Ibid, 'Exodus capituli xii quibus consequens est servos (eo salvo, quod sub domini manum subdebantur) de iure gentium non ita esse annihilatos.'

97 Ibid.

98 Ibid, 'Nec ad rem pertinent quod ibidem [D.1.1.4.] dicitur, libertatem naturali iure, dominationem vero ex iure gentium procedere.'

99 Zasius, "De iustitia et iure," col. 257.§. 11. See note 89 above.

100 Zasius, "1518 Preface [*Lucubrationes*]," 2, 'Sit sane ita, sicuti est: utraque tamen sunt legis naturalis, ut supra declaravimus, & licet dominatio iuris gentium esse dicatur, ex hoc tamen non puto iuste inferri, quod igitur servi status annihilatus sit: cum manus dominica annihilationem servi non impellat.'

Again, for Zasius, it was the "civil law that deprives, destroys, and annuls the status of the slave," and not *ius gentium*.[101] The original condition that extended from—and was founded in—*ius gentium* did not negate the status of the person in servitude or their inherent rights and obligations, any more than it gave the lord unlimited and unrestrained power over them. Although the enslaved were subject to the authority of another, this did not mean that they were precluded from engaging in traditions, customs, and practices that extended from *ius gentium*, and thereby natural law. Likewise, in relation to political authority, the fact that cities or peoples (*gens*) who entered a (political) contract with a prince or emperor did not mean that they could not engage in other customs of *ius gentium*, such as commerce and trade, with subjects of a different ruler. Nor did it preclude them from practices that enabled them to live in accordance with—and fulfill the obligations of—natural law, justice, and the common good with their neighbors.

Just as a slave had only one master and a serf had only one lord, so too a subject had only one ruler. Yet, in accordance with natural law as expressed through *ius gentium*, each would still be able to have obligations with others, including family, friends, neighbors, and associates. They would also be able to make promises, engage in trade and commerce, take on debt, and practice their duties toward God, as well as to exercise their right to meet force with force and the power to punish in order to preserve and protect their family, community, and *patria* from threats. Even if these abilities were limited by contracts of subjection and protection, they could not be abolished. In the case of defense, those subject to a master would have access to the courts to vindicate their actions and to settle disputes over contracts and agreements. Regarding the power to punish, they would still be able to exercise force when necessary (albeit in a just and restrained manner), in order to preserve themselves, their family, and their associates from danger.

When masters, lords, or rulers used civil laws or legal authorities to diminish their subjects' ability to exercise such rights or to prohibit them from fulfilling obligations (e.g., through marriage, exchange, commerce, trade), then those civil laws and legal authorities not only ceased to be just but they also became dangerous. The same restrictions and reasoning applied to spiritual authorities as well. Neither secular nor sacred rulers could require persons under threat of penalty, punishment, and violence to do what they themselves could not do justly; they could not require their subjects (state) or their

101 Zasius, "De iustitia et iure," col. 255.§.34; and "1518 Preface [*Lucubrationes*]," 2. See note 92 above.

members (church) to violate natural law or, by extension, the universal rights and obligations that extended from *ius gentium* as the fourth quality of natural law. If no authorities could make unnatural demands on their subjects, then no civil laws could make unlimited power or total submission just. *Imperium*, in this respect, not only followed from *ius gentium* but it was also limited by it.

Akin to his interpretation of primary and secondary *ius gentium*, Zasius' interpretation of servitude also covered a spectrum of conditions. Rather than approaching the distinction between being under one's own power (*sui juris*) and being under the power of another (*alieni juris*) in simple binary terms, his depiction of the common practices and customs that extended from *ius gentium* suggested that ancient slaves and sixteenth-century unfree peasants were not entirely devoid of rights; even if their liberties were constrained in some instances, their rights could not be wholly abrogated. Put differently, chattel slavery, no matter what form it took, was unjust precisely because it violated the universal rights and obligations that extended from *ius gentium*, and thereby natural law and justice. Moreover, within a few sentences, Zasius stripped Accursius, Bartolus, and Baldus' interpretation of slavery of its historical, moral, and legal authority. His interpretation presented ancient customs and conventions of slavery and servitude as more just (closer to natural law) and, by implication, new civil laws (and civil authorities) that attempted to change these long-held practices as less just (more distant from natural law).

In both his lecture and his preface, Zasius' remarks on slavery and the relation between natural law, *ius gentium*, and civil law serve as apt examples of his methods in action. It also, once again, pointed out Accursius' error in defining *ius* into sharp relief for his students and his readers. This supported his overarching argument that it was imperative to restore Roman law to its original form and, in the process, to cleanse traditional jurisprudence of errors that, if left unchecked, would continue to turn law into a mechanism of power rather than a standard of justice.

12 The Trouble with Tyranny

Bold and compelling on its own terms, Zasius' rejection of abject slavery and servitude, especially in the context of his reinterpretation of the relation between natural law and *ius gentium*, amounted to a fundamental critique of civil laws that made the conditions of slavery and servitude increasingly harsh, sometimes putting the enserfed and enslaved under the unlimited power of their masters. Such attempts to turn people into chattel show the extent to which some legal and political authorities, namely those who departed from *ius gentium* and distorted the category of *ius*, used aspects of Roman law to augment the power, dominance, and dominion of masters over the enslaved, lords over vassals, and rulers over subjects. Such laws were created to expand economic, political, legal, and religious power. In this respect, Zasius' analysis of slavery as an institution extending from *ius gentium* and encompassing universal rights and obligations challenged the corruption of civil laws. It also presented a thinly-veiled critique of the corrupt political and economic changes across the German lands of the Holy Roman Empire, which were made under the guise of reform.

It was a thinly-veiled critique insofar as Zasius used the term *homines propria*—the Latin equivalent to the German *Eigenleute*, *Eigenmenschen*, or *Leibeigene*, all of which refer to indentured servitude, unfree peasants, and the enserfed. He did so while resorting to the term *servus* in the *Digest* and following the definitions of slavery therein.[102] His argument was not simply semantic, nor his concern esoteric. He thoughtfully linked his own, contemporary context to an ancient one. He then used Tacitus' assertions that slavery as the Romans understood it never existed in Germany in order to underpin the fact that he was by no means questioning the legitimacy, utility, or necessity of Roman slavery as historical fact but rather the changes to servitude and political power in his own time, which were making the condition of those subject to the authority of a master increasingly harsh and thus life for those living in servitude less and less tenable within the Holy Roman Empire.

From at least the turn of the sixteenth century, attempts to consolidate economic authority and power on the part of lords over their peasants were unrelenting. They also mirrored the efforts of emperors, princes, and cities to expand their power over those subject to their jurisdiction throughout the Holy Roman Empire. As civil laws were used to augment the authority of rulers in the name of stability and security, the ability of communities to engage in common practices—such as determining their own relations of trade and commerce with their neighbors (proximate and remote)—became increasingly restricted and regulated. At the same time, the rights of individuals to use courts to redress the imposition of new taxes or property arrangements by their lords became increasingly limited. Over time, communities lost their ability to engage in practices that promoted their own common good, and their long-held rights and obligations were increasingly ignored. Indeed, the specter of unlimited authority and tyranny—sanctioned and underpinned by civil laws and institutions—seemed to be expanding across the Empire. This

102 See Blickle, *Von der Leibeigenschaft zu den Menschenrechten*.

process was exacerbated by calls for legal and economic reforms throughout Europe in the latter decades of the fifteenth century, when those trained in accordance with traditional jurisprudence were charged with transforming—and codifying—unwritten legal traditions into written ones.

For example, serfdom intensified in southwest Germany in the early sixteenth century, in response to agrarian crises, with temporal authorities (e.g., free cities, manorial lords, regional lords, princes) and ecclesiastical authorities reasserting, expanding, and centralizing their power over the countryside and even over wage-laborers within cities.[103] These authorities instituted restrictions on the freedom of movement and the marriage of peasants, curtailed the use of common arable lands and woodlands, and allowed for an increase in certain fees and work requirements imposed on the enserfed and peasants as well as on wage-laborers. These measures resulted in increased revenue and power for cities, lords, princes, and the emperor. At the same time, they were met by resistance—legal and violent—by peasants, a development which culminated with the Peasants' War of 1524–1525 across Germany.

Although there were several instances of rebellion, revolt, and outright war by peasants, the urban poor, and even the nobility throughout the Germanies prior to and during the religious Reformations that began in 1517, those that erupted in the mid-1520s were particularly relevant to Zasius. The peasants' revolt in Freiburg led to the cancellation of his lectures and nearly caused the university to close. Zasius' physical safety was at risk as well; at one point, he witnessed his own house being hit by a cannon shot.[104] These experiences no doubt impacted the content of his lecture, and they may even account for why his 1518 *Preface* was missing in later editions of his *Lucubrationes*: as innocuous as the preface might have appeared to some readers in 1518, the critiques would have been too direct after 1525.[105] Even so, the extent to which Zasius was arguing either on behalf of the peasants or for the burghers against the clergy, patricians, and lords remains unclear. What was clear, however, was his sustained defense of the customary rights and obligations that extended directly from *ius gentium* as a form of natural law that were subject to change, corruption, and

---

103 Ibid.

104 Rowan, *Ulrich Zasius*, 158.

105 See Peter Blickle, *The Revolution of 1525: The German Peasants' War from a New Perspective* (Baltimore, MD: John Hopkins University Press, 1981); Peter Blickle, ed., *Resistance, Representation, and Community: The Origins of the Modern State in Europe* (Oxford: Clarendon Press, 1997); Tom Scott, "Peasant Revolts in Early Modern Germany," *The Historical Journal* 28, no. 2 (June 1985): 455–68; and Tom Scott, *Freiburg and Breisgau: Town-Country Relations in the Age of Reformation and Peasants' Wars* (Oxford: Clarendon Press, 1986).

diminished by those whose interests were advanced by limiting the actions and rights of others.

This emphasis on customary rights and obligations was also evident in the appeals to and uses of collective memory by peasants throughout the Germanies to counter the introduction of new taxes, work requirements, and restrictions on everything from the freedom of movement to marriage. For example, as Peter Blickle had shown, some peasants responded to these changes by going to court, and successfully argued that although the civil laws had changed, their customary rights had not.[106] They did so in some instances by showing the contradictions that arose from conflicts in law as different kinds of authorities extended their powers over them. In other instances, they did so by claiming their rights with reference to tacit promises and explicit agreements. As a result of seeking legal remedies, rather than violent ones, some were able to limit the power that a lord had over them, whereas others were able to break free of some obligations altogether on the basis that previous customs, practices, and rights, like the freedom of marriage, had been violated by the creation of new laws. Such instances of unfree peasants using the courts rather than resorting to violence seemingly echoed Zasius' rejection of slavery and servitude as conditions in which those subjected to the authority of others were devoid of universal rights and obligations shared among all, without distinction.

Again, Zasius' argument was based on the fact that he did not consider slavery to be a natural condition; it was neither co-original with natural law nor with man's natural obligations and rights. He, just as Budé, followed—and agreed with—Ulpian's characterization of slavery in Book One, Title One of the *Digest*, namely, that freedom was man's natural condition whereas slavery was not.[107] Slavery and, by extension, all forms of servitude extended from war, viz., captivity and convention, over time. It had, in other words, a history. As an institution created by man, regardless of whether it extended from necessity and thereby fell under the category of secondary *ius gentium*, it could not be used as evidence that those subject to it were stripped of their ability and capacity to exercise the same universal rights and obligations as the rest of humankind. Although enslavement and enserfment changed one's legal condition before the law, neither negated one's status as a person (man *qua* man). Moreover, the condition of slavery annulled neither a person's instincts nor their ability to temper their actions with reason, nor did it nullify their capacity to live in accordance with the inherent principles, precepts, and qualities of natural law. Although it could—and did—place restrictions on movements,

106 See especially Blickle, *Von der Leibeigenschaft zu den Menschenrechten*.
107 D.1.1.4.

labor, and the ability to enter contracts, it did not—and could not—strip away one of the fundamental characteristics of man *qua* man, namely that of dignity or the existence of inherent natural rights and obligations. For humanist jurists like Zasius, the universal attributes of dignity, rights, and obligations were gifts from God and shared by all of mankind across time and space, thus they could not be rescinded by an act of man. This did not mean, however, that Zasius thought everyone within a civil society had the same civic and legal rights. In fact, at the same time as he emphasized universal rights and obligations that extended from *ius gentium*, he also argued for the limitation—and even expulsion—of some based on perceived violations of long-held customs and agreements as well as on those who were not Christian.[108] In other words, civil laws reflected the mores of a specific community (sacred or secular), whereas *ius gentium* reflected the universal rights and obligations of all mankind.

Nevertheless, civil laws that sought to deprive those in a state of slavery and servitude of their basic universal rights and obligations not only violated long-held customs of *ius gentium*, but they also violated natural law, justice, and right. For Zasius, such laws did more than split good and fair as a matter of utility or necessity, they also violated *ius* as both justice and right by attempting to do something that even the customs and practices of secondary *ius gentium* did not: place slaves and serfs under the absolute and unlimited power of their masters and lords. Civil laws could not deprive a person of the universal rights and obligations that extended from natural law, as communicated through *ius gentium*, nor could one's status as persons before the law—customary, civil, or canon—be abolished, nor could the long-held customs and agreements that underpinned everyday practices or political arrangements be changed to increase the economic and political power of lords, princes, popes, or emperors. Even though the civil laws of a specific territory (e.g., cities, imperial and otherwise, and principalities) could punish and expel, they could not do so without cause. To determine whether such cause was just or unjust—and thus in accordance with a rule of law—required the expertise and knowledge of properly trained jurists.

108 For a detailed discussion of Zasius' first published work, "De Iudaeis Quaestiones tres" (1508), wherein he explored the legal questions attended on the baptism of Jewish children against the will of their parents see Steven W. Rowan, "Ulrich Zasius and the Baptism of Jewish Children," *The Sixteenth Century* Journal 6, no. 2 (1975): 3–25. Although Zasius included a scathing attack on Jews in this treatise—providing clear evidence of his anti-Judaism—he ultimately appeared to argue that when addressed simply as a question of law "true forced baptism was illicit," while simultaneously acknowledging his agreement with moral and religious arguments for baptizing Jewish children without their parents' consent.

In this context of change, and resistance to it, it was necessary for those receiving training in universities to acquire a proper understanding of the ways in which the customs and institutions embedded in *ius gentium*, as well as the rights and obligations that extended from it, could not be abrogated by civil laws. Thus, if they understood how and why *ius gentium*—and all that it entailed—could be used to bring unjust civil laws and civil authorities back into alignment with justice and right, then they could use it to reform unjust laws and to protect just ones. It was also necessary for those not matriculating in universities, either because they had already completed their studies or because they were being trained through apprenticeships, to acquire such an understanding of *ius gentium* through Zasius' published works. Without recourse to a proper understanding of the relation between *ius* and *ius gentium* (as the fourth quality of natural law), power—not justice—would continue to diminish the moral authority of law and of those who administered it.[109]

13 Implications of Zasius' Re-interpretation of *Jus Gentium*

Zasius' emphasis on *ius gentium* in his lecture on the first title of the *Digest* and in his 1518 *Preface* reflected the context and concerns of his time and provided his students and readers with insights and tools that they could use to foster stability in an era of rapid change. Instead of presenting a theory of universal jurisprudence as a system permeated by artificial binaries—splitting good from fair; justice from *ius*; public from private justice; justice from utility; public from private law; natural law from *ius gentium*; and primary from secondary *ius gentium*—Zasius set out to show how and why all of these aspects of jurisprudence were related to—and indeed were various expressions of—the same thing: justice and right. Understanding that all of these categories existed on a spectrum rather than in opposition to one another would enable properly trained jurists to determine how to reform laws that had missed the mark of justice and to ensure that new laws met the criteria of good and fair conjoined.

Making such determinations required jurists to draw on collective memory and specialized knowledge to place customs and laws into historical and comparative perspective. In the absence of a single legal structure, or 'national' law, across the Holy Roman Empire or even the German lands, understanding the origins, function, and extent of *ius gentium* could provide lawyers and jurists with foundational and fundamental criteria to administer law, and thereby

109 Rowan, "Ulrich Zasius and the Baptism of Jewish Children"; and Rowan, *Ulrich Zasius*.

justice, as well as to advise princes, lords, and cities as they underwent multiple levels of legal reform and change. Aware that many of his students would be tasked with effecting legal reforms, Zasius effectively brought *ius gentium* from the periphery of civil jurisprudence into its center; he presented *ius gentium* as something that they could use to help shore up existing practices that were just and to reform those that were not.

By focusing on *ius gentium*, as the fourth quality of natural law, "the law of nations common among all mankind," as well as a cache of universal rights and obligations, Zasius offered a theory of universal jurisprudence that could help lawyers and jurists to manage and to navigate the relations among and between peoples that extended far beyond the parameters—religious and geographical—of Universal Latin Christendom. In the context of early calls for religious reformation, of the violence and instability that such calls unleashed, of the various economic transformations, and of state and empire-state formation within the Empire from the late fifteenth century, Zasius presented a theory of jurisprudence that could help to effect and moderate the legal and political re-formation of the Germanies, the Empire, and even Europe at large, which was already well underway by the early decades of the sixteenth century and would continue to change the face of the continent and beyond.[110]

At the same time, it is important to recognize that Zasius' discussion of *ius gentium* was limited by local contexts and concerns, and that his attention to the rights and obligations that extended from it was aimed at providing his students conceptual tools that they needed to reform civil laws, customs, practices, and institutions within the Germanies above all else. To explore the extent to which *ius gentium*, as a form of natural law and a source of rights and obligations, was reinterpreted in a broader context—that is, between kings, emperors, and city-states beyond the Germanies and in relation to the rights of war and peace in particular—we need to turn our attention to the works of Alciati, who pushed the definitions, distinctions, and ideas he drew from both Budé and Zasius into new directions.

Unlike Budé, who was writing in response to calls for legal reforms in France, and Zasius, who was writing in the context of training those who would effect legal reforms in Germany, Alciati's appeal to and redefinition of

110 The term re-formation draws out the changes that encompassed legal reform within states, as much as the negotiation of boundaries and borders between them, as all the major powers and significant political entities in central and southern Europe came into conflict—first over Naples and then over Milan—from 1494 onwards. The use of the term re-formation of Europe is not meant as either a play on, nor an alternative to, the religious changes of that followed from the (Protestant) Reformation or the (Catholic) Counter-Reformation.

the fundamental categories of Roman law was more directly informed by the instability, uncertainty, and violence that embroiled nearly all of Europe in a series of conflicts from 1494 through 1559. Despite the fact that Budé and Zasius were also writing in the context of conflict and war and not just of reform, the necessity and urgency to understand the foundation and limits of rights, obligations, and law took on a far more practical, pragmatic, and urgent tone in Alciati's case. Alciati himself was never subject to only one political entity, as Budé was to the King of France or Zasius was to the Holy Roman Emperor, nor was he even bound to a single *patria* or community. Just as Zasius adopted and adapted Budé's restoration of *ius* as the art of what is good and fair conjoined, before fundamentally departing from his understanding of the relation between *ius* and *ius gentium*, so too did Alciati. Addressing fundamentally different questions, however, Alciati also rejected aspects of Zasius' theory when he attempted to decouple the link between *ius* and justice on the level of states, while maintaining it on the level of man. Thus, while the so-called fathers of humanist jurisprudence might have shared an understanding of *ius* that signified objective justice and the inherent dignity of man, none of them shared the same understanding of *ius gentium*. While Zasius interpreted it as an extension of natural law, and thus as the source of universal obligations and rights shared by all mankind, Alciati interpreted it—almost solely—through the category of violence, viz., the right to meet force with force among persons and states. It is that understanding that permeates Alciati's work and thus the remaining chapters of this volume.

PART 3

Andrea Alciati: Jus, *Violence, and* Imperium

CHAPTER 5

Self-Evident Truths and Demonstrable Facts

Power, Politics, and Persuasion

1 Lawyer First, Humanist Second

Although the third member of 'le grande triumvirate' of legal humanism studied, taught, and practiced law within the same broad context of crisis and reform as Budé and Zasius, the manner in which Andrea Alciati approached it and articulated his interpretations to audiences across Europe allowed him to distinguish himself from both men in fundamental ways.[1] Already by 1515, his determination to draw on lesser-known and newly-discovered sources and to employ more analytical methods to place these sources into their proper textual and historical contexts enabled him to demonstrate a more nuanced understanding of Roman law and Roman history than his counterparts.[2] Even so, his focus on the significance and meaning of terms tended to render his work more antiquarian than Budé's in some instances, whereas his methods of interpretation made aspects of his work even more abstract than Zasius' in others. Even so, the way Alciati interpreted the first title of the *Digest* was, in the end, closer to the "Practical Jurisprudence," viz., *usus modus pandectarum* in Germany, than to the more cumbersome theoretical approach that Zasius brought to his lecture on the same title.

Despite his interest in historical context and his emphasis on placing legal principles and practices into historical perspective, the specific questions Alciati explored in his lectures, orations, treatises, and emblems often betrayed his pressing concern with issues and problems shaping his present, especially those directly affecting the stability of territories in Northern Italy. Indeed, for all of its historicity and innovation, Alciati's work tended to be far more personal, political, and presentist than one might expect, given his insistence on

---

1 Roberto Abbondanza, "Jurisprudence: The Methodology of Andrea Alciato," in *The Late Italian Renaissance, 1525–1630*, ed. Eric Cochrane (London: Macmillan, 1970), 77–90; and Roberto Abbondanza, "La vie et les oeuvres d'Andre Alciat" in *Pedagogues et juristes: Congres du Centre d'Etudes Superieures de la Renaissance de Tours: été 1960*, ed. Pierre Mesnard (Paris: J. Vrin, 1963), 93–106.

2 For extensive biographical information on Alciati see John MacDonell and Edward Manson, eds., *Great Jurists of the World* (Boston, MA: Little, Brown, and Company, 1914), 58–82; Viard, *André Alciat*; and Kelley, *Foundations of Modern Historical Scholarship*.

 | DOI:10.1163/9789004528451_007

the necessity to explore ideas, texts, and people in their proper historical contexts. Nevertheless, precisely because he drew on the past with an eye to the present, Alciati was able to push some of the definitions and ideas developed by his legal humanist peers into new, and potentially dangerous, directions.

Although he accepted Budé's two-fold definition of *ius*, viz., 'what is good and fair conjoined' and as an attribute of man *qua* man, Alciati emphasized, above all, *ius* as the right to meet force with force, among persons and peoples—something Budé's work did not imply, let alone assert. Moreover, whereas distinctly local contexts and issues limited Zasius' interpretations, Alciati's theory of *ius gentium* was far more international in scope. As such, he effectively applied Zasius' understanding of *ius gentium* as the source of universal rights and obligations not simply to cities, principalities, and regions within a single empire—albeit with disparate jurisdictions—but also to the relations between rulers, viz., the Holy Roman Emperor, the King of France, and the Papacy, among others, across and beyond Latin Christendom. This approach enabled him to forward a theory of *ius gentium* that could be used to restrain (or at least to defend resistance to) those who tried to expand their possessions and power beyond their borders and territories through war—something that Zasius did not explicitly explore, even though his theory implied it.

Alciati's choice to adopt and adapt some, but not all, of Budé's and Zasius' innovations ultimately allowed him to disentangle natural law from *ius gentium*. In turn, this enabled him to demarcate the limits of each. Precisely because natural law was an expression of objective *ius*, viz. a universal attribute of justice, it could serve as a *de iure* check on tyranny. Likewise, because *ius gentium* was an expression of inherent *ius*, viz., a universal attribute of man *qua* man, it could serve as a *de facto* check on *imperium*.[3] The inverse, however, was not possible, as natural law could not be used to justify actions between city-states, kingdoms, and empires, nor could *ius gentium* be invoked to buffer or critique civil laws within them.[4] Operating in different realms and on

3 For detailed discussions of *imperium*—including debates about its source and its limits—spanning from Ancient Rome through eighteenth century see Berman, *Law and Revolution I*; Pennington, *The Prince and the* Law; Canning, *Ideas of Power in the Late Middle Ages*; Anthony Pagden, *Lords of All the World: Ideologies of Empire in Spain, Britain and France c.1500–1800* (New Haven, CT: Yale University Press, 1995); and Davies, *Periodization and Sovereignty*.

4 Alciati, "Oratio in laudem iuri civilis, principio studii cum Avenione profiteretur [1518]," in *Omnia opera*, vol. 3, 506–11; and Andrea Alciati, "Bona fides," in *De verborum significatione* (Lyon: Sebastianum Gryphium, 1535), cols. 306–8. It is worth noting here that his interpretation of *bona fides*, as presented in D.16.3.31, draws on ancient sources—Herodotus and Cicero, above all, and Bartolus and Baldus—to explore whether the validity and expediency of good faith agreements should be judged by civil law alone or in accordance with

divergent levels of society, these two types of law nevertheless remained inextricably linked by *ius*, a fact which exemplified the essential and fundamental equality of all persons, peoples, and nations vis-à-vis one another.[5]

Starting with the common underlying assumption that man was as inclined to live in mutual company as he was to pursue his own self-interests, Alciati set forward a theory of universal jurisprudence to argue that people's universal right to defend and preserve themselves, their community, and their property rendered all persons and rulers as equals.[6] This premise was not merely a self-evident truth but a demonstrable fact for Alciati. Observable across time and space, all persons, peoples, and nations—no matter if in the heat of the moment, in the theatre of war, or in the ritual of honor—shared the universal right to repel force with force.[7] Moreover, whether one attributed the origin of this right to God, nature, or reason, the right to exercise such force, as well as the obligations attendant upon doing so, underpinned and permeated his theory of universal jurisprudence.

While solely a matter of self-preservation when used against beasts, the justification for exercising this right among men entailed the recognition of one's opponent or adversary as equal—as someone with the same right to meet force with force.[8] If the exercise of such force by one resulted in the injury or death of another, then it was necessary for whoever committed the injury to account for why he did so to the community in which he lived. Hence, even though the universal right to meet force with force extended from the necessity of self-defense, the vindication of its use had to meet the requirements of justice. The exercise of force had to be in accordance with the rule of law

ius gentium as well. To explore this, Alciati offered a series of examples—ranging from settling disputes over primogeniture to whether the actions of a father and husband, if found guilty of a capital crime, should extend to his children and wife. For our purposes, the most interesting part of this brief discussion of good faith is Alciati's response to the question as to whether one could be forced to turn over evidence against another, if their plans (even nefarious ones) were shared in secret. To which Alciati simply states: "Equity says no, because I would be violating the conferred trust, & the concealment of secrets is in accordance with natural law, which can be denied by no civil constitution." [col. 307–8: æquitas negat, quia datam fidem violarem, & arcanorum occultatio iuris naturalis est, quod nulla civili constitutione tolli potest]. Alciati likewise emphasized the importance of good faith in *Emblem* 12: Plans ought not to be divulged and *Emblem* 13: One ought not to yield, even under torture. Appendix.

5 Alciati, "De iustitia et iure," col. 1.

6 Ibid, cols. 1–3.

7 Alciati, "De iustitia et iure," especially cols. 12–4; and Andrea Alciati, *Duello* (Venice: Appresso Comin da Trino di Monferrato, 1562).

8 Alciati, "De iustitia et iure," cols. 1–8.

within civil society to protect peace, to ensure security, and to promote the common good of all rather than simply the self-interest of one.

To justify the exercise of this right—to ensure that any injury or death that extended from it was not a sheer act of passion, tyranny, terror, or power—required wise men and, later, jurists to hear accounts and explanations offered by those who wielded it. Upon hearing the accounts, it was the responsibility of these men to determine not only if the act was necessary but also if it was just.[9] For Alciati, the latter required that such men understood, first, how and why this universal right extended from and related to customs common among all mankind, viz., *ius gentium*; second, how it was, in turn, sanctioned by natural law; and third, why and how the community had the right to sanction or punish its use. All of this demanded an understanding of *ius*, or right, not only as an expression of justice in action but also as a distinguishing attribute of man *qua* man. It likewise required an understanding of the relation between justice and right as well as justice and law that illuminated how they diverged from one another.

Such illumination was necessary because when the right to meet force with force—held by peoples as well as by persons—was exercised by one community against another, the question of justice could not be vindicated by wise men or by judges. Indeed, for Alciati, the exercise of force—offensive and defensive—between communities was not a question of justice at all; it was, instead, a question of necessity.[10] This was the case because justice required the existence of a rule of law, yet there was no rule of law outside of civil society nor between peoples, nations, or empires; there was only *ius gentium*.[11] Using the rhetoric of moral philosophy or historical precedent to dress up necessity as justice might persuade subjects and allies to accept such actions as warranted. It did not, however, change the fact that force, not justice, had been exercised. Given that all empires, nations, and peoples had the right to

9 Alciati, "De iustitia et iure;" and Alciati, *Duello*.

10 Alciati, "De iustitia et iure," cols. 9–12. For good discussion of just war within scholastic thought see Frederick H. Russell, *The Just War in the Middle Ages* (Cambridge: Cambridge University Press, 1975); and Kretzmann, Kenny, and Pinborg, *The Cambridge History of Later Medieval Philosophy*.

11 Indeed, Alciati's interpretation of enemies in relation to war was strikingly like ideas underpinning Thomas Hobbes' *Leviathan* [1651], especially Chapters 18. (Cambridge: Cambridge University Press, 1991); see also Carl Schmitt's *The Nomos of the Earth in the International Law of Jus Publicum Europaeum* [1950], trans. G. L. Ulmen (New York: Telos Press Publishing, 2006). It should be noted that Schmitt's *Nomos* discussed Alciati and Zasius on multiple occasions, acknowledging their historical importance as well as critiquing some of their ideas, while still recognizing their innovations and contributions to *ius gentium*.

meet force with force grounded in *ius gentium*, the question that needed to be addressed was not whether the exercise of such a right was just—a question that permeated scholastic just war theory—but whether those who exercised this force to wage war had the right to do so.[12] Leaving the question of justice aside in his *De iustitia et iure* lecture, and thus approaching it in an entirely different manner than Budé or Zasius had done, Alciati set out to explore whether the exercise of force by communities vis-à-vis one another was licit or illicit and how that determination could be made by properly trained jurists and advisors.

The latter made it possible to explore whether the community who inflicted harm—defensively or offensively—had the essential and universal right to do so. This, in turn, could help to determine if they were equal in status as an enemy against an adversary or if they were subject to the command and authority of another power. Indeed, by focusing on the right of self-defense exercised by superior and inferior princes, Alciati explored the relation between rulers in times of war in such a way as to suggest that their status as enemies rendered them equals *de facto*, even if they were not yet regarded as such *de jure*.[13] Short of developing a full-fledged theory concerning the rights of war and peace, Alciati's investigation into who had the right to meet force with force in the realm of dukes, princes, kings, and emperors nevertheless contributed to the 'laws of nature and nations' genre of political thought that lies at the foundations of modern international law. By avoiding the entanglements and pre-suppositions of scholastic just war theory altogether, precisely when one might expect him to draw on them, Alciati ultimately offered his students and readers an alternative theory of right that was rooted in the necessity to resist harm—passively and actively—as well as an explanation as to why the exercise of such a right was held equally by all manner of persons, peoples, city-states, kingdoms, and empires.

For modern readers, grounding a theory of universal jurisprudence on such a universal right is bound to seem familiar, and, indeed, even normative, precisely because it tends to underpin modern political and legal theory, interpretation, and practice, domestically and internationally. In the early-sixteenth century, however, making this claim was a rather dangerous endeavor, especially since it emphasized an essential equality between persons, peoples, and nations, and, by extension, princes, kings, popes, and emperors. This was certainly the case for men like Alciati, whose ability to teach and practice law was

12 Alciati, "De iustitia et iure," cols. 9–12.

13 Alciati treated this directly in the "De iustitia et iure," and indirectly in his *Duello*.

wholly dependent on earning the support, respect, and admiration of the very entities whose authority could be limited by such a theory.

While Alciati drew on Roman and post-Roman interpretations of natural law, *ius*, and *ius gentium* in his lecture on the first title of the *Digest*, the way he approached this title was remarkably different than one might expect. He not only departed from his humanist peers and scholastic predecessors but he also diverged from the manner and methods of interpretation that he advocated in both his teachings and publications. As a result, Alciati's contemporaries, no less than modern readers, would be hard-pressed to make sense of this lecture without reference to his other works and the contexts in which he crafted them.

As part of broader effort to understand his theory of universal jurisprudence, arguably the most essential works to consider are the orations he delivered while teaching at Avignon at the start of his teaching career and at Bologna in the middle of it, wherein he set forth his understanding of the art of justice and the stability of the rule of law to his students.[14] At the base of each oration stood an argument for the essential equality of man, in terms of his capacity of learning and his status vis-à-vis one another in nature as well as the need to respect such equality, at least formally, within civil society by establishing a rule of law. Alciati also expressed these ideas in his *Emblems*, wherein he linked aspects of his theory of jurisprudence and of human nature by pairing images with epigrams, thus enabling him to not only draw on the past but also to comment on his present while articulating his understanding of the relation between right, law, and justice.[15]

In addition to exploring how he communicated his ideas across different genres, encountering the orations and the emblems also allows modern readers to observe one particular aspect of Alciati's method in action, namely his *extensio* (extension), whereby Alciati attempted, by implication, to draw out how particular actions or laws reflected—or departed from—universal

14 Alciati, "Oratio in laudem iuri civilis, principio studii cum Avenione profiteretur [1518]," in *Omnia opera*, vol. 3: 506–11; and Alciati, "Oratio Andreae Alciati, dum Boniniam [1537]," in *Omnia opera* (Basel: Insingrinius), vol.3: 1051/52–1055/56. As was the case for Zasius (see Chapter 3 of this volume), these speeches fit under the category of declamations, viz., fully written out to be delivered in a specific setting, even though they are called orations in Alciati's *Omnia opera*.

15 See Andrea Alciati, "Alciato's Book of Emblems: The Memorial Web Edition in Latin and English," Translated by William Barker, Mark Feltham, Jean Guthrie, and Allan Farrell. http://www.mun.ca/alciato/index.html.

principles such as justice and right.[16] Encountering traces of his *extensio* in his orations and emblems, as well as bearing in mind his *Duello* (or little book on dueling), allows us to observe the extent to which he set out and applied ideas concerning the basis of authority and the necessity of its constraint in a variety of contexts.[17] It also helps to provide additional insights and explanations of key concepts that underpinned and structured his lecture on the first title of the *Digest* more broadly, especially in relation to how he linked the right to meet force with force among persons and the right to wage war among rulers in order to delineate justice from right as well as to show how they were related.

Bringing all of the above together makes it possible for us to view Alciati's theory of universal jurisprudence from multiple perspectives, to explore how he used it to address contemporary issues and problems for multiple audiences, and to see the implications of his ideas in historical context. It also allows us to observe how consistent Alciati's conceptions were, despite the variability of patrons, authorities, and jurisdictions he was subject to at various points of his career. Precisely because Alciati's conception of natural law, *ius*, and *ius gentium*—as presented in his very short lecture on *De iustitia et iure*—was so directly informed by the world he lived in, it is useful to consider how his life and work intersected with, and was shaped by, the Italian Wars that began in 1494, when Ludovico Sforza, the Duke of Milan (r. 1494–1499) invited the King of France, Charles VII (r. 1483–1498) to claim the kingdom of Naples. Particular attention to the contested status of Northern Italy as these wars unfolded in combination with Alciati's career also highlights the ways in which his fortunes in war and in peace were directly and indirectly tied to the ambitions of the Houses of Sforza, the Valois, the Habsburg, and the Medici over the course of the early-sixteenth century. All of these houses were engaged in shoring up and establishing dynastic and territorial claims by arms and by law, both across and beyond the Italian Peninsula and before, during, and after the advent of the religious wars within Europe—and the imperial conquest and expansion beyond it. Caught between duchy and city-state, emperor and king, and amid persistent wars and brief periods of peace, Alciati's career in context serves as a reminder that the task of defining and understanding *ius* and *ius gentium* always carried risks in the sixteenth century, and therefore required meticulous modes of argument.

---

16 Alciati, "De iure et iustitia," cols. 3–4.

17 Alciati, *Duello* (Venice: Appresso Comin da Trino di Monferrato, 1562).

2 Law and Violence: Alciati's Career in Context

In 1508, the same year that Budé launched his relentless attack against traditional jurisprudence, Alciati began attending lectures on Roman law at the University of Pavia, located in southwest Lombardy and about twenty miles from Milan.[18] That same year, the League of Cambrai—consisting of Pope Julius II (Giuliano della Rovere, 1443–1513), Louis XII of France, Holy Roman Emperor Maximilian I, King Ferdinand II (1475–1504) and Queen Isabella I (1451–1504) of Spain, and the Duke of Ferrara, Alfonso I (1476–1534)—joined together to wage war against the Republic of Venice, which had been steadily expanding its territory across Northern Italy and along the Adriatic coast since the conclusion of the Italian War of 1499–1504.[19] Destroying the Venetian army at the Battle of Agandello on May 12, 1509, the League of Cambrai effectively rendered the Republic of Venice harmless. Thereafter, Pope Julius II shifted his attention to limiting the influence of another power that was shaping the political and military landscape of Italy.

Breaking his 1508 agreement with France against Venice, Julius II created a new alliance in 1510. This time he joined forces with the Republic of Venice and the Swiss Cantons to wage war against France. By October 1511, this Holy League, which soon expanded to include England, Spain, and the Holy Roman Empire, supplanted the League of Cambrai. The League was so effective that, by October 1512, the Swiss were able to wrest Milan from Louis XII, who had held it since 1499, and place it back into the hands of the Sforza family. This swift success, and with it the possibility that all of Italy could become its spoils, led the Republic of Venice to change sides. Rather than fight with the Holy

18 Unless otherwise noted, the biographical information on Alciati has been taken from MacDonell and Manson, *Great Jurists of the World*; Abbondanza, "La vie et les oeuvres d'Andre Alciati;" Viard, *André Alciati*; and Kelley, *Foundations of Modern Scholarship*.

19 For an in-depth discussion of the Italian Wars and their effect on culture, politics, technology, as well as territorial state- and empire-state formation throughout Europe see Burckhardt, *Civilization of the Renaissance in Italy*; H. G. Koenigsberger and George L. Mosse, *Europe in the Sixteenth Century* (London: Longmans, 1968); Garrett Mattingly, *Renaissance Diplomacy* (New York: Dover Publications, 1988); Eugene F. Rice and Anthony Grafton, *Foundations of Early Modern Europe* 1460–1559, 2nd ed. (New York: WW Norton, 1994); Christine Shaw, *Italy and the European Powers: The Impact of War, 1500–1530* (Leiden: Brill, 2006); David Potter, *Renaissance France at War: Armies, Culture and Society, c.1480–1560* (Suffolk: Boydell & Brewer Ltd., 2008); Michael Edward Mallett and Christine Shaw, *The Italian Wars, 1494–1559: War, State and Society in Early Modern Europe* (New York: Pearson, 2012); and John Gagné, *Milan Undone: Contested Sovereignties in the Italian Wars* (Cambridge, MA: Harvard University Press, 2021).

League against France, it now joined France to fight against the League on the condition that France and Venice would split Northern Italy between them.

In 1511, the same year that the Holy League was formed, and thus one year before France lost possession of Milan, Alciati left Pavia to take up the study of law at the University of Bologna, the oldest Roman law faculty in Latin Europe.[20] Whether the tumults that led to the reinstatement of the Sforza family in Milan had affected Alciati's decision to move to Bologna is not clear, especially given that the University of Bologna was as vulnerable to the ravages of war as the University of Pavia. Ceded to the Papacy by Rudolf I of Germany in the thirteenth century, the Romagna region had a long history of being subject to the dispositions and ambitions of popes and emperors, powerful ducal families (like the Ferrara), eager Republics (like Venice and Florence), as well as to claims by France and Spain. Indeed, when Alciati moved to Bologna in 1511, the Romagna region was as engulfed in the Italian Wars as Lombardy. In fact, it was a series of defeats suffered by the Pope at the hands of the French in Romagna that prompted Julius II to break from the League of Cambrai and create the Holy League in the first place.

Thus, instead of leaving Pavia on account of recent wars, it is more likely that Alciati left for Bologna because he was tired of pouring over interpretations of law by scholastic jurists rather than engaging with the original texts of Roman law. Although the law faculty of the University of Bologna privileged the works of the Doctors, most notably Bartolus and Baldus, it was nevertheless possible to access handwritten copies of the Roman *corpus* as well as texts and fragments that reached beyond it. Soon after his arrival, Alciati was able to set aside the commentaries and glosses that permeated traditional jurisprudence and, instead, take up the study of Justinian's *Institutes* and *Code* in the humanist manner, viz., by returning to the original sources (*ad fontes*) in order to place them into their proper historical, textual, and philological contexts. Once given the opportunity to apply his talents and to pursue his interests directly to the study of Roman law at Bologna—rather than merely study scholastic interpretations of it at Pavia—Alciati thrived.

In 1515, the same year that Francis I (1494–1547) ascended to the French throne and routed the Swiss at Marignano, effectively changing the tide of the war against the Holy League in France's and Venice's favor, Alciati published

20 For an in-depth discussion of the University of Bologna's place in the history of European jurisprudence see Berman, *Law & Revolution I*; Charles Radding, *The Origins of Medieval Jurisprudence, Pavia and Bologna, 850–1150* (New Haven, CT: Yale University Press, 1988); Brundage, *The Medieval Origins of the Legal Profession*; and Herzog, *A Short History of European Law*.

his *Annotations on the Last Three Books of Justinian's Code*.[21] His choice to focus on the lesser-known parts of the *Code*, which dealt predominately with the administrative aspects of law and governance, and to use his immense knowledge of ancient literature and language in doing so, provided him with the perfect opportunity to demonstrate the value of humanist methods in action. Anticipating detractors, his 1515 *Annotationes* also presented an occasion for him to defend his work against those who did not think it was "appropriate for one and the same man to know the laws and to profess the *studia humanitatis*."[22] Not only did the *Annotationes* allow Alciati to demonstrate the flaws in such an opinion but it also enabled him to show how drawing on history, moral philosophy, poetry, grammar, and rhetoric to interpret—and expand—the texts of Roman law could put an end to the perpetuation of well-worn errors within traditional jurisprudence.

Applying methods and sources of the *studia humanitatis* to lesser-known books within the *Code* also shed light on the meaning of the terms within Roman *corpus* more generally, making it possible to better grasp how the specific language of the law conveyed its proper meaning and, in turn, what that meaning conveyed about the society that created such laws. After all, Alciati argued, words were the correlates of intention as much as they were of things and actions. His application of humanist methods to the *Code* also demonstrated how the meaning of legal terms, as well as the laws and the society they reflected, could change over time at the hands of university-trained jurists. As commonplace as all of this may be today, especially among historians, philologists, and legal scholars, this was a radical departure from the traditional methods of teaching law, namely the *mos italicus*.[23] Moreover, the fact that Alciati was able to do all of this—to write *Annotationes* on the last three books of Justinian's *Code* and, in so doing, place them into their broader historical and linguistic contexts—in about a month's time and one year before he earned his Doctor of Law degree, showed that the methods and sources of *studia humanitatis* were more efficient, and even more practical,

21 Andrea Alciati, *In tres posteriores codiciis Justiniani libros, Annotationes* [1515], in *Paradoxorum* (Basil: [Hercules Gallicus], 1523), cols. 240–76. [Hereafter: Alciati, "1515 *Annotationes*"].

22 Alciati, "1515 *Annotationes*," cols. 240, 'Auguror tamen, quin potius videor, quantos in meum caput crabrones excitem: quum exploratum mihi sit, increbuisse eam inter recentiores iuris civilis sectatores opinionem, ut eiusdem esse negent, & leges scire, & humanitatis studia profiteri.'

23 For a narrative description of the *mos italicus* see Chapter 1 of this volume.

than combing through centuries of cumbersome, convoluted commentaries and glosses on Roman law.[24]

As a result, Alciati's 1515 *Annotationes* provided evidence for humanists, like Budé, that cleansing the stables of traditional jurisprudence could be done rather quickly, if undertaken by someone who could combine humanist and legal training. Indeed, Budé hoped that Alciati would soon turn his new critical and historical methods to the *Digest* in order to help finish the broader project of restoring the entire *corpus* of Roman law, thus purging it of the mistranslations and errors introduced by Accursius and all those who followed him. However, when Alciati circulated, and later published, his works that drew on and directly intersected with the *Digest*, the result was entirely different from what Budé had hoped. Within a decade, it became clear that Alciati had no intention of simply continuing the work of Budé; instead, he set out to surpass it.[25]

Upon earning his Doctor of Law in 1516, the same year that the Treaty of Noyon brought the war between the Holy League and France to a close and placed all of Northern Italy in the hands of France and Venice, Alciati returned to Milan to practice law.[26] Throughout this period, Milan was firmly in the hands of Francis I, given that Charles I of Spain (1500–1558) recognized France's claim over it in exchange for the Valois ceding their claim over Naples to the Habsburgs. Over the course of the next two years, thanks to Lombardy's relatively stable condition, Alciati not only found plenty of legal work but also began his search for a university position. He was finally able to secure his first teaching position at the University of Avignon in 1518.

24 In the 1515 preface/dedication letter of "In tres posteriores codiciis Justiniani libros, annotatiunculae," Alciati declared the following: "if this work may have been completed by us in a short time, (for we have not worked on it longer than a half-month), nevertheless I have used the greatest zeal and unfailing care in such a way that that which was able to be lacking on account of time has been made up for by diligence." Thus, the text that made Alciati famous throughout Europe was written in roughly fifteen days.

25 Within fifteen years of Alciati's publication of his 1515 *Annotationes on Justinian's Code*, Alciati and Budé were bitterly at odds. One of the most contentious moments of their relationship came when Budé's accused Alciati of plagiarism, arguing that much of Alciati's 1530 *De ponderibus et mensuris* was lifted from Budé's 1514 *De asse*. Such accusations of plagiarism were not one-sided, though. Indeed, after Budé published a revised edition of his *Annotationes* in the 1530s, Alciati accused Budé of plagiarizing his *Annotationes* of 1518. See Kelley, *Foundations of Modern Scholarship*; Delaruelle, *Etudes sur l'humanisme français*; and Viard, *André Alciat*.

26 Although scholars do not agree on which institution granted Alciati his doctorate, most follow Roberto Abbandonza, who claims that Alciati received his Doctorate from Ferrara in 1516.

Avignon, like Milan and Bologna, had long been embroiled in tensions and conflicts between secular and spiritual rulers. By the time Alciati arrived, it had been under the purview and jurisdiction—at least nominally—of the Kings of France since the late-fourteenth century, viz., after the Papacy returned to Rome. However, religious tensions compounded by long-standing political ones had the capacity to break such arrangements, especially if they could be used to defend the faith and to expand the power of authorities, including popes, within Europe as much as beyond it, viz., the crusades. Indeed, when Alciati took up his position at Avignon, the possibility that religious conflict and dynastic squabbles might disrupt an already fragile peace was increasingly being tested.

As early as 1517, persistent tensions between the empire and the papacy were strained even further by an attack launched by Martin Luther (1483–1526)—a German monk, humanist, university professor, and subject not only of Emperor Maximilian I but also of Elector Frederick III of Saxony (1463–1525)—against Pope Leo X's (Giovanni di Lorenzo de' Medici, 1475–1521) expansion of the sale of indulgences to pay off his debts as well as other corruptions within Church doctrine. Nevertheless, even as Luther's criticisms started to resonate across Europe, both the status quo at Avignon and the Treaty of Noyon continued to hold. The latter was possible, in no small part, because the death of Maximilian I in 1519 had made nearly every secular and spiritual leader in Latin Europe divert their attention—and their money—to the election of the next Holy Roman Emperor.

Meanwhile, the Church, or at least the Papacy, was in clear crisis, as Luther's calls for reform resounded throughout Saxony and beyond; no matter who was elected as Holy Roman Emperor, the fate and fortunes of the Medici family, the Papal States, and all of Europe would be affected. As such, Pope Leo X had to choose carefully whom he would support. If he chose to back Frederick III, who remained Luther's patron and protector, then he would inadvertently empower rather than shut down calls for reform and various other forms of religious and political dissent from within German lands. This choice, no matter if Frederick won or not, could ignite rebellion in the Empire and, with it, Northern Italy, and the Papal States. If, instead, he backed the weakest of the four candidates, the self-nominated Henry VIII, this would have placed Leo at odds, and likely in military conflict with, nearly all of Europe. Supporting such an inconsequential power as England (at the time)—allied with Spain through marriage and nearly always at war with France—would also raise questions as to why he did not simply back one of the other two candidates standing for election, both of whom were far more powerful and had far more to lose in terms of both territory and influence than either Henry VIII or Frederick III.

If Leo chose to back the Habsburgs by supporting Maximilian's grandson Charles I of Spain, who had already amassed territories and titles that spanned from the Low Countries to Southern Spain as well as most of Italy and the Spanish Americas, then nearly all Latin Christendom would come under a single secular ruler. This, in turn, would leave France practically surrounded by territorial domains under the dominion of a single family and its allies by marriage.[27] Surrounded by enemies—potential and real—France would have been left with little choice but to wage war against the Empire, Spain, and the Papal States. However, if Leo backed Francis, and Francis won, the ongoing peace between Francis I and Leo X could be more secure, Charles I's power could be held in check, and the religious dissent within the Empire could be snuffed out.[28] Even if Francis lost the bid to become Holy Roman Emperor, supporting the Valois for election might ensure that Francis would come to Leo's aid if he found himself at war with Habsburg Spain and the Empire. Strategically, it made the most sense for Leo to back Francis I, despite the recent wars with France across Italy.

In the end, it was Charles, with the help of the Fugger family, who was able to outspend—or outbribe—Francis, regardless of the auspices of Leo and the deep pockets of the Medici. Elected Holy Roman Emperor in 1520, Charles I became Charles V, with territories stretching from Peru to Naples. Soon thereafter, realizing how much he had to lose if Charles were to turn on him, Leo switched alliances and, by 1521, was once again at war with France. Given what was to come, the span between the two wars (1516 to 1521) was one of the most stable and peaceful periods of the early-sixteenth century insofar as it concerned the relations between the Papacy and France on the one hand, and the stability of both Avignon and Milan on the other.

Upon his arrival in Avignon in 1518, Alciati was granted the title of 'extraordinary professor' (*regens extraordinarius*) and, with it, the right to confer degrees.[29] Initially, Alciati was determined to teach law in accordance with humanist methods, with particular emphasis on history and philology. However, students who wished to continue to learn Roman law according

27 For a detailed discussion of Charles' ascension to the Spanish throne as well as his election as Holy Roman Emperor see Geoffrey Parker, *Emperor: A New Life of Charles V* (New Haven, CT: Yale University Press, 2019).

28 For a detailed discussion of Francis' bid for Holy Roman Emperor, beyond its treatment in the historiography on the Italian Wars cited above (note 19), see R. J. Knecht, *Renaissance Warrior and Patron: The Reign of Francis I* (Cambridge: Cambridge University Press, 1994).

29 MacDonell and Manson, *Great Jurists of the World*, 70.

to scholastic methods protested and boycotted his lectures. As a result, he adjusted—yet did not abandon—his methods, which ultimately enabled students, especially those who had no prior exposure to studying the law with recourse to the sources and methods of the *studia humanitatis*, to gradually expand the scope of their studies. Moderating his teaching in such a way as to help them acquire the skills necessary to reach beyond well-worn texts and points rather than expecting them to do so from the outset, proved to be a success. Within two years, Alciati was drawing audiences estimated at around eight hundred—students old and young, as well as common and noble—to his lectures.[30]

By early-1520, when his initial contract was renewed at Avignon, Alciati was drawing praise from all quarters of Europe. Such acclaim was in response to his innovative lectures on Book 50 of the Roman *Digest*, entitled *De verborum et significatione* (*On the Significance and Meaning of Terms*) as well as the publication of his *Paradoxorum* (*Paradoxes in Civil Law*), which he had begun to compile when he was merely seventeen.[31] In the former, he set out the basic contours of his methods, including the four principal ways to explore the meaning and significance of words before applying his *extensio*, namely by 1) tending to the original and literal meaning of the terms used; 2) investigating customary usage by placing the terms under investigation into their historical context; 3) determining whether the author followed the literal or conventional use or if they adapted or extended the terms to express something new; and 4) interpreting the terms by placing them in the broader context of the overall text to arrive at an author's intended meaning.[32]

Alciati crafted what might be called a critical and expanded historical dictionary of Roman legal terms by combining and applying the above methods to Book 50 of the *Digest* (also called *De verborum significatione*). This work

30 Viard, *André Alciat.*

31 Alciati, *De verborum significatione libri quatuor* [1523] bound in Alciati, *Omnia opera*, vol.4. Within this text, Alciati emphasized, above all, the meaning of legal terms within a legal context—in many instances, within the very specific wording of a particular law itself, especially as the same word or term could very well mean different things in the context of different laws. Alciati was also very concerned with how the specific wording of the laws were intended and understood by the legislators, jurists, and advocates.

32 Alciati, "Commentaria de verborum significatione [1539]," In *Opera Omnia*, vol. 4.; col. 1025, 'Cum inventa sint verba, ut dicentis intentionem exprimant, merito eius voluntas in primis spectanda est. Cognoscitur autem ex eo, quod verba ipsa indicant. Et quatuor modis accipiuntur: ex proprietate, ex usu, ex abusione, & per interpretationem.'

served as virtual explanatory glossary to the text as a whole.[33] Whereas in his *Paradoxorum*, he applied these same four steps as well as his *extensio* to what appeared to be contradictions within Roman law in order to clarify why some laws, terms, or practices appeared to be inconsistent but were not.[34] Moreover, drawing out how the language of law changed over time to meet particular challenges and to solve specific problems, and thus interpretations and understandings of it, enabled him to demonstrate how the underlying principles to which they referred, or embodied, had remained constant, thus revealing the universal aspects that they shared.

Each work, especially the *Paradoxes*, impressed Zasius so much that he declared in a letter to one of his former students, Bonifacius Amerbach (1495–1562), "that a mighty reformer of the study of Roman law had arisen," and "expressed his readiness to fight under Alciati's flag."[35] Moved by such a powerful endorsement, Amerbach, who had started his legal studies at Freiburg in 1513 but never completed them, soon moved to Avignon to study under Alciati.[36] While there, Amerbach was able to help transform the mutual admiration of Alciati and Zasius into a regular correspondence between them, as well as to introduce Alciati, by letter, to Erasmus, who—like Budé and Zasius—had already been singing his praises to other humanists across Europe.[37] In addition to becoming part of a broader 'republic of letters' while in France, Alciati also had the opportunity to meet Budé in person, five years after he had first drawn Budé's attention with his *Annotationes on the Last Three Books of Justinian's Code*.

After three short years at Avignon, Alciati had become such a respected and well-known humanist jurist in Europe that Erasmus deemed him an essential member of 'le grande triumvirate' of humanist jurisprudence, alongside Budé and Zasius.[38] By this time, he had also gained the attention and admiration of

33 For an in-depth and systematic analysis of the various modes and the ways that jurists approached and interpreted Book 50 of the *Digest* from the thirteenth through the sixteenth centuries see MacLean, *Interpretation and Meaning in the Renaissance*.

34 Alciati's *Paradoxorum* [1523] was, as he explained to his readers, already compiled by 1517, though he began writing them ten years earlier, when he was merely fifteen years old.

35 MacDonnell and Manson, *Great Jurists of the World*, 71.

36 For more information on Boniface Amerbach see Kisch, *Erasmus und die Jurisprudenz seiner Zeit*; Gilmore, *Argument from Roman Law*; Rowan, *Ulrich Zasius*; and Virginia Woods Callahan, *Andreas Alciatus and Boniface Amerbach: The Chronicle of a Renaissance Friendship* (Tempe, AZ: Medieval & Renaissance Texts & Studies, 1988).

37 Kisch, *Erasmus und die Jurisprudenz seiner Zeit*.

38 Maffei, "Les débuts de l'activité de Budé, Alciat et Zase;" and Kisch, *Erasmus und die Jurisprudenz seiner Zeit*.

Francis I, to whom (as the Duke of Milan) he was a subject and to whom (as the King of France) he was a guest. Although Alciati was not yet in his direct employ, Francis' familiarity with his work—thanks in part to his royal secretary, Budé—would prove to be significant to Alciati's fortunes in the coming decades.

Despite his success at Avignon, by the end of 1521 Alciati had decided to leave. This decision was based not on the renewed fighting in Italy between all the major players in European politics but rather on the terms of his renewal at Avignon, which he deemed insulting. Considering his international reputation and his popularity among students, he thought that the university should pay him more; whereas the university, which had been shut down intermittently due to outbreaks of the plague, thought that he should be willing to take a reduction in pay if or when such a calamity happened again. Rather than agree to such terms, Alciati returned to Milan and resumed practicing law, all the while continuing his studies of ancient literature, philology, and history. He also continued to look for teaching positions, but this became increasingly difficult as economic, political, and religious crises unfolded across the continent.

Alciati was able to complete the first collection of his *Emblems* in 1522, in spite of the instability, uncertainty, and violence that was unfurling across Lombardy—associated with the Italian Wars that recommenced after Charles V's election as Emperor—and of the time and energy he devoted to his legal practice.[39] This little book consisted of an array of adages and epigrams, which touched on history, moral philosophy, rhetoric, and politics, along with corresponding images that were meant to convey lessons on virtue and vice, war and peace, and law and justice.[40] Although Alciati crafted some of these adages and epigrams, most of them were drawn from the ancients; the same was true for the images. Once this work was printed, however, Alciati did not think that the quality of the images properly signified the meaning of the words that accompanied them.

39 Henry Green, *Andreae Alciati Emblematum fontes* (Manchester: Published for the Holbein Society by A. Brothers, 1870), Introduction.

40 For a discussion of the relation between some of Alciati's *Emblems* to his legal texts, see Peter M. Daly, ed., *Andrea Alciato and the Emblem Tradition: Essays in Honor of Virginia Woods Callahan* (New York: AMS Press, 1989); specifically see the contributions by Konrad Hoffman, "Alciato and the Historical Situation of Emblematics," 1–46; and Peggy M. Simonds, "Alciati's Two Venuses as Letter and Spirit of the Law," 95–126. See also Holger Hoffman, *Studien zur Emblematik des 16. Jahrhunderts* (Utrecht: Haentjens Dekker & Gumbert, 1971); and Peter Goodrich and Valérie Hayaert, eds., *Genealogies of Legal Vision* (London: Routledge, 2015).

Alciati's insistence on this point is significant insofar as he was adamant that the *Emblems* meet the same standards as his legal texts, enabling his readers to interpret them properly. In the case of the *Emblems*, readers needed to fully understand the meaning and significance of an author's words in historical and textual contexts in order to grasp the author's intention in writing them, and, conversely, readers needed to grasp the significance of the images attached to the adages and epigrams, so to properly understand what the author meant to convey by selecting them. While in some cases Alciati's meaning was direct, in others it was implied. In each, the clarity of the images was crucial; they had to reflect or speak directly to the adages, otherwise it would have been near impossible for readers to decipher their meaning—explicit or implicit—in, political, social, and moral contexts.

Once he saw the poor quality of the images in the printed text, Alciati cancelled production and tried to destroy as many copies as he could. Notwithstanding Alciati's efforts, copies of this first collection survived in circulation among his friends.[41] As the readership of the surviving printed copies—as well as of the manuscript—expanded, this first collection of the *Emblems* served as a more effective means for Alciati's methods of interpretation to reach a broader audience than his legal texts, largely on account of their form. The *Emblems* also afforded him a medium to comment on the events unfolding before him, namely the wars that began about the same time as he returned to Milan.

In 1521, in the wake of Charles V's election as Holy Roman Emperor and Pope Leo X's subsequent decision to break his allegiance with France against Spain to join Charles against France, Francis allied with the Republic of Venice in a series of battles and skirmishes that ultimately drew all of Europe into another war. Although Francis I and Charles V were initially focused on territories in northern Europe, particularly the Low Countries, the violence soon moved to Northern Italy when Francis chose to defend his claim over Milan and expand his power across Italy. In response, Charles V took Milan by force in 1521 and, by 1522, reinstalled the Sforza family to power. Over the next three years, Francis I continued to assert his claims in Italy with little success. Then, in February 1525, in what turned out to be an ill-fated attempt to retake Milan, Francis was defeated by Imperial troops at the Battle of Pavia. His subsequent imprisonment by Charles V ended with the Treaty of Madrid, whereby Francis withdrew his claims to rule in Italy, Flanders, and Burgundy. Within weeks of

41 Green, *Andreae Alciati Emblematum fontes*, Introduction.

his release, however, Francis reneged on this treaty, and the next set of Italian Wars commenced.

Fearing the growing power and expanding territory of the Habsburgs, Pope Clement VII (Giulio di Giuliano de' Medici, 1478–1534) created the League of Cognac in 1526, whereby the Papal States, France, the Republics of Venice and Florence, the Duchy of Milan, and England all became allies in a war against the Holy Roman Empire and Spain. Within a year, however, the superiority of Imperial and Spanish forces became clear. Indeed, in the wake of the sack of Rome, the siege of Naples, and the defeat of Genoa, all in 1527, there was no question of Charles' ability to dominate all of Italy if he chose to do so. Still, it took two more years until Francis I agreed to the 1529 Treaty of Cambrai, which removed France from the League of Cognac. As a result of this treaty between Charles and Francis, combined with Pope Clement VII's subsequent imprisonment by Imperial troops, it was clear that the emperor had won the war.

Remaining in Milan throughout the above events, Alciati resumed work on his emblems, many of which were (direct and indirect) commentaries on the inability of the Italian dukes and princes to keep foreign powers from tearing Italy apart.[42] He also continued to practice law in Milan, while seeking another teaching position. The University of Padua, the second oldest Roman law faculty in Latin Europe, was especially attractive to Alciati because it was a focal point of innovation. It was founded by a group of professors and students who had left Bologna, as early as 1222, to have more academic freedom in what they studied and, more importantly, in how they studied it. Those who taught there had a degree of academic freedom and flexibility that was absent elsewhere as Charles V was tightening his grip over Northern Italy.[43]

Had Alciati secured an appointment at Padua, he would have been able to continue to teach Roman law according to the methods and sources of the *studia humanitatis*, something that was still looked down upon by students at traditional law faculties like Pavia and throughout most of Italy. The problem

---

42 See specifically Alciati's *Emblem* 10: Treaties; *Emblem* 39: Harmony; *Emblem* 42: What stands firmest cannot be overthrown; *Emblem* 43: Hope is near; *Emblem* 134: The tomb of Giangaleazzo Visconti, first Duke of Milan; *Emblem* 143: From Albutius to Master Alciatus, persuading him to withdraw from the conflicts of Italy and to teach in France; *Emblem* 144: The prince, ensuring the safety of his subjects; and *Emblem* 166: Something evil, from an evil neighbor. Appendix.

43 See John Herman Randall, *The School of Padua and the Emergence of Modern Science* (Padova: Antenore, 1961); John Kenneth Hyde, *Padua in the Age of Dante* (Manchester: Manchester University Press, 1966); Agostino Sottili, *Humanismus und Universitätsbesuch: die Wirkung italienischer Universitäten auf die studia humanitatis nördlich der Alpen* (Leiden: Brill, 2006); and Grendler, *The Universities of the Italian Renaissance*.

with drawing on the methods and sources of the *studia humanitatis* as part of the broader study of Roman law was that it seemed esoteric and impractical to those who were training to simply practice law rather than to become legal scholars. Seeking more than mere credentials like his students at Pavia, students at Padua would have likely been far more prepared for and open to his methods of teaching and interpretations. Though not removed from the tumults or violence, moving to Padua—which was just west of the Republic of Venice—would have protected Alciati from the direct impact of the wars he had endured while in Milan. For example, his house and library were severely damaged in 1523 by French troops, and again in 1526 by Spanish mercenaries.[44] However, unable to secure a different position in Italy, Alciati returned briefly to Avignon in 1528, in hopes of finding a teaching position in France, thus escaping the escalating violence at the hands of Imperial troops as they advanced north.

Then, in 1529 (the same year that he signed the Treaty of Cambrai), Francis I personally called Alciati to the University of Bourges and invested him with a teaching position.[45] This was the break that Alciati had been hoping for. Given that most of the students at Bourges had pursued humanistic studies before taking up the study of law, Alciati could finally teach it as he saw fit. Alciati's presence at Bourges, combined with Francis I's embrace of legal reform and his tolerance—for the time being—of religious reformers, elevated the reputation of the university. Although Alciati remained Catholic and criticized Luther for his attacks, he still drew several reform-minded students to his lectures on account of his critical and innovative methods of teaching law as well as his interpretations of the relation between justice, law, and right.

From the outset at Bourges, Alciati's lectures drew students from all over France, including John Calvin (1509–1564), Theodore Beza (1519–1605), and François Hotman (1524–1590), all of whom would later apply aspects of Alciati's methods and teaching in their own commentaries concerning law, authority (religious and secular), and tyranny over the course of the sixteenth century.[46] Other students included Hugo Donnelus (1527–1591), François Connan (1508–1551), and Jacques Cujas (1524–1590), who, after completing

44 Virginia Woods Callahan, "Andrae Alciati" in *Contemporaries of Erasmus: A Biographical Register of the Renaissance and Reformation*, eds. Peter G. Bietenholz and Thomas B. Deutscher (Toronto: University of Toronto Press, c.1985–1987), Vol. 1, 24–26; MacDonell and Manson, *Great Jurists of the World*; and Viard, *André Alciat.*

45 Alessandro Grimaldi, *Funeral Oration January 19, 1550, for Andrea Alciati*, trans. Henry Green (Manchester: Holbein Society by A. Brothers, 1871), 6; and Viard, *André Alciat.*

46 Witte, *The Reformation of Rights.*

their studies with Alciati, would push humanist jurisprudence into a far more historical direction—in particular, by applying legal hermeneutics to the study of French customary laws and codes in addition to Roman ones.[47] What is more, from time-to-time Francis I also attended Alciati's lectures,

> That one praise is not least among many, so to have charmed the mind of my auditor, that the royal majesty in person, has appeared to lower the fasces, the ensigns of his power, in honor of myself, while sitting on the throne of jurisprudence.[48]

It was amid such audiences that Alciati claimed to have reintroduced philology into the classroom after its long absence. Although he had been teaching in accordance with the same methods used at Avignon as early as 1518, it was his time at Bourges—and the influence he had on the next generation of legal humanists in France—that solidified what became known as the *mos gallicus*; this was the French manner of teaching and interpreting the law which was grounded primarily in the sources and methods of humanism and was thus distinct from the *mos italicus*, which was grounded primarily in the sources and methods of scholasticism.[49]

The fact that the French manner of interpretation extended from the teachings of an Italian jurist highlights the confluence of humanistic studies and legal interpretation at the University of Bourges in particular, and among jurists across Europe more generally. Indeed, what distinguished the *mos gallicus* associated with Alciati from the earlier methods employed by the French humanist Budé was the fact that Alciati and his followers were university-trained experts in Roman law, who systematically applied these methods in order to earn their degrees. Many of these students, after completing their studies, proceeded to refine these methods in their capacities as professors of law, magistrates, and religious reformers (Protestant and Catholic). Although the same could be said for those applying humanist methods to the study of law in Germany, what distinguished the *mos gallicus* from the those employed by German jurists like Zasius was that Alciati focused more on placing Roman law in textual context in order to understand its particular meaning, and how it

47 Kelley, *Foundations of Modern Scholarship*; Berman, *Law and Revolution II*; and Herzog, *A Short History of European Law*.

48 Henry Green, *Andrea Alciati and His Books of Emblems* (London: Trübner and Co., 1872), 9.

49 For a primer and comparison see Chapter 1 of this volume and Kelley, "Civil Science in the Renaissance: Jurisprudence Italian Style"; and Kelley, "Civil Science in the Renaissance: Jurisprudence in the French Manner."

changed historically, rather than on using abstract methods of historical imagination to fill gaps within it and to account for why it changed over time.[50]

Finally free from many of the frustrations that he encountered in Milan (the constant prospect of war) and Avignon (the matriculation of underprepared students), Alciati completed the next edition of his *Emblems* in 1531.[51] This edition not only met Alciati's expectations of clarity, but it also expanded his exposure to audiences across Europe. This 1531 edition, printed in Latin, was a further exercise in ensuring the quality of the print and the arrangement of the emblems, even though Alciati had little control and input over how the printers ultimately reformatted and reimagined it. Soon after the 1531 edition was published, for example, printers and publishers, taking advantage of the popularity of the *Emblems*, began to produce a variety of (pirated) versions, ranging from pocket-sized collections to large folio volumes, and in the original Latin as well as in French, German, Spanish, and Italian translations.

Then, in 1533, after three productive years of teaching at the University of Bourges, Alciati returned to Milan at the request of Duke Francesco Maria Sforza (1495–1535). Aware of his reputation and indeed counting on it to help draw students to the University of Pavia, Sforza invested Alciati with both senatorial rank and a teaching position.[52] As a subject to Sforza, who had been installed by the Emperor Charles V in 1521, this was an offer that Alciati could not refuse. As it turned out, due to ailing health, Alciati was happy to return south. However, he suspected it would necessitate a moderation of his methods of teaching to suit the expectations of Italian students. Lamenting this prospect, Alciati wrote a stanza that betrayed his pessimism of what was to come once he crossed the Alps,

> Thou loving city Bourges! Thee loving, unwillingly I leave;
> Through summers five the land wast thou inhabited by me.
> Now need there is from wether sheep to sucking calves to go,—
> Therefore farewell! And happy wool-gathering be to thee.[53]

Alciati was not wrong. Although his reputation as a brilliant jurist and humanist had permeated Northern Italy, many of his students bemoaned his methods

50 For more information on the students of Alciati, specifically those at the University of Bourges, see Kelley, "Law;" Viard, *André Alciat*; Abbondanza, "Jurisprudence: The Methodology of Andrea Alciato;" and Witte, *The Reformation of Rights*.

51 Green, *Andrea Alciati and His Books of Emblems*, Introduction.

52 Grimmaldi, *Funeral Oration*, 6.

53 Green, *Andrea Alciati and His Books of Emblems*, 15. See also *Emblem* 143:From Albutius to Master Alciatus, persuading him to withdraw from the conflicts of Italy and to teach in France. Appendix.

and wished, instead, to continue to study in accordance with the Italian manner (*mos italicus*), rather than the new French one (*mos gallicus*).

At Pavia, he moderated his teaching methods for his students, especially for those who lacked previous exposure to ancient languages and literature. He also renewed his work on yet another edition of his *Emblems*. Published in 1534, this edition featured even cleaner and clearer woodcuts than the previous one, enabling a more direct interpretive link between image and text. In addition to his teaching and his *Emblems*, Alciati published legal treatises in Latin and Italian. All of his work drew praise from humanists across Europe—ranging from Budé and Zasius to Erasmus and Thomas More (1478–1535). This attention by well-placed and connected peers made him hopeful that he would eventually be able to land a better teaching position within Italy or perhaps return to southern France.

With few viable options to leave Lombardy in the early-1530s, Alciati remained at the University of Pavia for about five years, even as the number of students matriculating were dropping as tensions, and then open conflict, drew the Holy Roman Empire and France into yet another war. In 1535, the same year that Alciati published a new edition of his *De verborum significatione*, Thomas More was executed for treason in England, Zasius died of natural causes in Freiburg, and Francesco Maria—the last remaining member of the Sforza family and the duke who had called Alciati back to Milan—also died. Since the duke left no undisputed heir, representatives of Charles V soon took over Milan. Initially, neither the people of Milan nor its Italian neighbors objected, or at least there were no major revolts or invasions to suggest otherwise. However, when Charles V bequeathed Milan to his son Phillip (1527–1598), the reaction of one neighboring power was swift.

In 1536, six months after Sforza's death, France invaded Italy. Francis I's aim was to reinstate his claim to the Duchy of Milan and, in the process of doing so, to claim Genoa and Asti (located just east of Turin). From the outset, this war reached beyond Italy into France, when, in response to Francis' bid to take Turin on the way to Milan, Charles V invaded Provence. Charles' ambition to retain his dominance in Europe, however, exposed the limits of his forces rather than of their strength. Within the first year, French armies in alliance with anti-Imperial interests in Italy stopped the advance of Imperial forces and Spanish mercenaries at nearly every turn. If that were not enough, the Ottoman Empire, in alliance with France, pulled Charles to fight on two fronts.[54] French armies helped keep Charles from advancing on Marseille and

54 For more information on this alliance and its reception in Europe, in addition to the historiography above (note 19), see Knecht, *Renaissance Warrior and Patron;* Christine

Avignon, whereas Ottoman forces helped ensure that France kept newly conquered Genoa and surrounding territories. Unable to take Aix-en-Provence or to keep France from advancing in Italy, Charles opted for peace in 1538. While the Truce of Nice enabled Charles to turn his attention to civic and religious troubles within the German lands, it did little for Francis other than to recognize Turin as a possession of France.

By the end of this war, and on account of how the uncertainty and instability of it affected enrollments at Pavia, Alciati was able—after much haggling—to secure a three-year position in Bologna. Indeed, Alciati had been there, teaching Roman law according to the moderated version of the *mos gallicus*, for about a year by the time the Truce of Nice was concluded. Alciati's ability to land a position at Bologna, and his insistence on teaching Roman law using humanist sources and methods while there, suggests that even if the *mos italicus* continued to be the dominant mode of teaching, study, and interpretation in Italy—three decades after Budé launched his attack in the 1508 *Annotations*—legal humanism had in fact managed to make an imprint on the institution that was considered to be the birthplace of civil (Roman) jurisprudence.

To convey the importance of Alciati's presence at Bologna, it is worth noting that students who matriculated in the law faculty, from about 1537 to 1540, would have been expected to attend Alciati's lectures at least for a brief time. Indeed, to leave Bologna without having attended lectures given by one of the most famous humanist jurists in Europe during this period was tantamount to not having been at Bologna at all. However, in line with his experiences at nearly every university where he taught, except for Bourges, those students who attended his lectures and lacked expertise in the *studia humanitatis* to follow them were especially critical of Alciati's teaching manner and methods. They implored him to teach Roman law in accordance with the traditional scholastic methods and texts—to do what they were used to—rather than expect them to do something innovative, viz., to study Roman law in historical context.

Seemingly holding students at Bologna to higher standards than those he taught at Pavia, Alciati refused to yield to their demands. Rebuffing his refusal, these students continued to complain as the term wore on. Unhappy with this stalemate, Alciati started looking for a teaching position at another university.

Isom-Verhaaren, *Allies with the Infidel: The Ottoman and French Alliance in the Sixteenth Century* (London: I. B. Tauris, 2011), John Julius Norwich, *Four Princes: Henry VIII, Francis I, Charles V, Suleiman the Magnificent and the Obsessions that Forged Modern Europe* (New York: Atlantic Monthly Press, 2017); and Parker, *Emperor*.

News of such a search, which, if successful, would have terminated his three-year contract, prompted civil authorities to threaten confiscation of his property if he left.[55] University officials also appealed to Pope Paul III (Alessandro Farnese, 1468–1549) to help them to convince Alciati to keep his good-faith agreement and to finish out his time at Bologna. Fortunately for Alciati, by the end of his first year, newer students began to embrace the *mos gallicus*, while older students gradually—if begrudgingly—adapted to it.

Over the following two years, his lectures became more popular with students already at Bologna at the same time as they drew new students to the university. His fame and influence at Bologna, however, was never able to match what he had enjoyed at Bourges. This was the case, in part, because the climate attendant on reform—religious and legal—had changed dramatically, across all of Europe and over the last 20 years. This trend made it difficult to attract reform-minded students, like those whom he had encountered in France, into Italy or vice versa.

Indeed, by the late-1530s and early-1540s, Francis I—who was open to such reformers in the early stages of the Reformation—had begun to distrust and then to persecute Protestants, especially after the Affair of the Placards in October 1534. Moreover, by the time Alciati arrived at Bologna, printing—the lifeblood of humanism—had been censored throughout Europe and even in France, despite the fact that Francis was an early patron of humanistic ideas and learning. Moreover, as part of Francis' increasing persecution of Protestants, Calvin and other reformers had already been driven into exile.[56] It should be no surprise that, by the 1540s, the situation in Northern Italy—under the domain and power of Charles V, as the defender of the Catholic faith—had become even less tolerant. Indeed, as conservative and reactionary as France was under the Valois by the late-1530s, it paled in comparison to what has happening—in terms of efforts to shut down dangerous ideas and resistance to authority—across the domains of the Habsburgs.[57]

Luckily for Alciati, throughout the 1530s and 1540s his methods of teaching—also applied and explained in his publications—were no longer

55 MacDonell and Manson, eds. *Great Jurists of the World*, 75.

56 See Witte, *The Reformation of Rights*.

57 For a good compendium that covers much of the turmoil and change extending from both the Italian wars and the European Reformation see Thomas A. Brady, Jr., Heiko Augustinus Oberman and James D. Tracy, eds., *Handbook of European History, 1400–1600* (Grand Rapids, MI: William B. Eerdmans Publishing Company, 1984). For a monograph, see Diarmaid MacCulloch, *Reformation: Europe's House Divided 1490–1700* (New York: Penguin Books, 2004).

'new', even though they still had dangerous implications if applied critically. Indeed, to teach at the most important university in Northern Italy—and quite possibility the most important faculty of Roman law in all of European Christendom—had, in effect, sanctioned Alciati's methods, theories, and, by extension, his publications, despite the fact that they were imbued with arguments for limited authority and the right to (active and passive) resistance on the one hand, and arguments for equality before the law among persons and equality in war among rulers on the other.[58] Although the degree to which these ideas were sanctioned by his patrons remains unclear, what is clear is that, by his second year at Bologna, his ability to draw large audiences to his lectures and to increase his European-wide readership had attracted the attention of rulers across Northern Italy.

In 1540, the same year that Budé died, Charles v recalled Alciati from Bologna to the University of Pavia, to help draw students back to Lombardy.[59] Then, in 1542, the same year that Paul III brought the Inquisition to Italy, Alciati was called to teach at the University of Ferrara (just northeast of Bologna) by Duke Ercole II d'Este (1508–1559).[60] Over his time at both institutions, the possibility of working with Alciati (among others) had reinvigorated the law faculties, which helped to put the universities on a more stable footing, despite the festering tensions between the powers in Europe.

The same year Alciati was called to Ferrara, Francis I—once again allied with the Ottoman Empire—waged an offensive war against Charles v. Under the pretense of reclaiming Milan, and thereby Lombardy, Francis intended to rout Imperial troops in the Low Countries (to expand France in the North), in Tuscany (to support a bid by republican exiles to take Florence and the region from Charles), and in Provence (to wrest Nice from the Empire). None of this proved successful, and indeed—courtesy of an alliance between Charles v and Henry VIII—Francis almost lost much of his northern territories; at one point Imperial and English troops made it to within 60 miles of Paris.

In 1544, after two years of fighting, Charles and Francis accepted the terms of the Treaty of Crépy. This treaty essentially reinstated the terms of the 1538 Truce of Nice, thus once again freeing Charles to redirect his attention to problems within the Holy Roman and Spanish Empires. Meanwhile, England and France continued to be locked in conflict. By September 1545, French troops,

---

58 Alciati, "De iustitia et iure," in *Omnia Opera*, Vol. 1: cols. 1–14.; Alciati, "Bona fides," in *De verborum significatione*, cols. 305–13; and Alciati, *Duello*.

59 MacDonell and Manson, *Great Jurists of the World*; Viard, *André Alciat*; and Grimaldi, *Funeral Oration*.

60 Ibid.

under the command of the Dauphin, were able to push English troops back to Calais and to the port of Boulogne. At the same time, the English were able to hold off French fleets from invading the English mainland. In 1546, Henry and Francis ended the war with the Treaty of Ardres, which—after a protracted stalemate—freed each to redirect their attention to other conflicts and affairs. That same year, before leaving Ferrara, Alciati oversaw the publication of the first official Italian edition of his *Emblems*, more than twenty years after he had completed the first collection in Milan.

The conclusion of the wars, between Charles and Francis and later between Francis and Henry, effected relatively little change to the territorial and dynastic map of Europe. However, the costs of war had forced Charles, Francis, and Henry to contend with increased civil tensions and unrest, which were amplified by calls for and reactions against the Protestant Reformation; by the 1540s, these had convulsed the Holy Roman Empire, France, and England to differing degrees and for different reasons.[61] To make matters worse, the pillaging of the Italian coasts by Ottoman troops triggered the indignation and shock that accompanied the alliance—for the second time—between France with the Ottomans against Christian rulers. All of these issues left much of Europe in an even more unstable condition than it had been in 1542, when the wars had started.

Indeed, by the conclusion of the war in 1546 an intense sense of crisis—religious, economic, social, and political—was felt throughout all quarters of Europe. One response was to continue to effect legal reform in the hopes of stabilizing civil society amid division, insecurity, and uncertainty. A key part of this was to continue efforts to revitalize universities across Europe, especially the law faculties whose principal task was to train those who would be charged with legitimizing, managing, and applying civil laws and procedures to effect stability. Just as it had been in the past, as the need for councilors and advisors to serve the interests of empires, kingdoms, principalities, republics, and duchies grew in the wake of war, so too did the universities.

By the 1540s, however, it was no longer enough to train students to effect the kind of legal reforms called for by Maximilian I and Louis XII in the late 1490s. Instead, all European powers needed educated professionals who could manage—and even govern—modern administrative states whose territories and trading networks were not only spanning the globe but also becoming increasingly—albeit to varying degrees—secular in their attempts to

61 For a comprehensive narrative history of the impact of the Reformation across Western Europe see MacCulloch, *Reformation*.

control confessional strife and conflict. In the face of such conflicts, which were provoked—often inadvertently—by attempts to reduce the impact and influence of religion on political and legal institutions, the demand for jurists continued to grow, especially for those who understood the relation between justice, law, and right in civil contexts and the relation between *ius gentium* and *ius* in international and global ones.

In 1547, one year after the most recent Italian wars concluded and the same year that both Francis I and Henry VIII died, Charles V once again called Alciati back to Pavia.[62] Charles did so to renew the law faculty and to help train students to implement legal and political reforms. While at Pavia, Alciati oversaw new editions of his *Emblems*, one published in 1548 and the other in 1549. These two editions, unlike unauthorized editions created by printers and publishers, contained the same number of emblems (201) and were arranged, by Alciati, in precisely the same order, thereby becoming the standard editions.[63] These editions included, just as the previous ones had, Alciati's emblems that were critical of the wars that shook Italy throughout his lifetime, as well as some that spoke to aspects—in muted form—of the Reformation.[64] Untouched by the index, inquisition, or royal censors, the emblems continued to be of interest to broad audiences, in part because they remained timely in the midst of upheaval, uncertainty, and crisis but also because they had been translated into nearly every European vernacular by the 1540s. Shortly after he oversaw the last two Latin editions of his *Emblems*, and after three years of teaching, "with a constant crowd of learned men from all quarters gathering around him," Alciati died on January 12, 1550.[65]

Buried in Pavia, Alciati's career was summed up by his epitaph, "He completed the whole circle of learning, and was the first to restore the study of laws to its ancient dignity."[66] Such assessment and admiration was also expressed by Alessandro Grimaldi, who, in speaking about Alciati's passing, asserted "Voice, strength, words will fail me if I should wish to declare aloud how miserable,

62 MacDonell and Manson, *Great Jurists of the World*; Viard, *André Alciat*; and Grimaldi, *Funeral Oration*.

63 A total of 212 *Emblems* were included in 1621 edition, the standard edition for the scholarship. A full facsimile of the 1621 text (as well as twenty-one other editions in Latin, French, German, Italian, and Spanish) is available from *Alciato at Glasgow*, http://www.emblems.arts.gla.ac.uk/alciato/index.php. All of the *Emblems* included in this volume are taken from the 1621 edition.

64 For example, see *Emblem* 103: That which is above us, is nothing to us. Appendix.

65 Grimaldi, *Funeral Oration*, 7.

66 Green, *Andrea Alciati and His Book of Emblems*, 25.

how wretched, how bitter to us may the death of this man be."[67] A sentiment that Grimaldi—in typical humanist manner—went on to express in loquacious form, by providing a lengthy description of Alciati's life and career for his auditors (and readers), embellished throughout by the eloquence of grief:

> Already I seem to myself to hear Jurisprudence, mourning and cast down, to break forth into these words: Where is the resplendent brightness? Where the assured protection? Where Andrea Alciati, my only safety? Where is he, who, by the elegance of speech, began to increase me when I was lessened, and by the greatness of his genius, by the gravity of his judgments, and by the power of his eloquence, has strengthened me when I was weakened, defended me when I was tossed and driven about by many injuries, came to assist me when thrown headlong, drew me forth from the waters when sinking, and raised me up when afflicted and lost?[68]

Celebrated in Germany and France as well as heralded as one of the greatest humanists of his age across Europe, it took nearly his entire career—from the publication of his 1515 *Annotations* to his last teaching appointment in Italy—to receive such praise within his homeland; when it came, it was only as a result of his death. Ironically, such commemorations of Alciati's influence by Grimaldi and others served to validate legal humanism and, with it, the *mos gallicus*, on university-based jurisprudence in the heart of Northern Italy—where it was even suggested that it was the preferred manner of teaching and interpretation by the end of Alciati's career.

Later attempts were made to celebrate Alciati's impact on university development, reputation, and identity in a variety of ways. Whether in narratives, monuments, or exhibits, these enabled each institution to incorporate Alciati into their histories, so to render his methods as far more welcome—even traditional—than they were at the time.[69] In the process of folding his contributions into the longer history of these institutions, his ideas and methods became normative rather than innovative. As a result, the dangerous

---

67 Grimaldi, *Funeral Oration*, 7.

68 Ibid.

69 If one visits the University of Avignon, Pavia, or Bologna, for example, nearly all the public exhibits and markers that commemorate the university's founding, mission, and history note the importance of Alciati's presence, though none are as grand or impressive as the placement of Alciati's tomb (the façade) in a courtyard that celebrates professors of law, medicine, and the sciences at the University of Pavia.

implications of his ideas in context and the impact of his teaching were tamed and muted to emphasize his contribution to their respective legal traditions, which reached back to 1361 at Pavia, 1303 at Avignon, and 1088 at Bologna; the history of the University of Bourges was much shorter: it was founded by the Valois in 1463 and closed during the French Revolution. Enveloping Alciati into such histories is significant, in no small part, because little dulls originality or silences criticism more than wrapping them into narratives that emphasize continuity over change, and thereby tradition over novelty.[70]

Such public orations, commemorations, and histories likewise effaced the criticisms Alciati endured from students and peers—particularly in Italy—as well as his persistent arguments in the face of such detractors. His drawing on the *studia humanitatis* in order to understand and interpret Roman law was a necessary component of understanding and applying legal precedent and principles in practice. Equally justified was his steadfast insistence that it is was neither an esoteric nor a frivolous endeavor to study history, rhetoric, and philology as part of one's legal training, but rather a necessity since, without doing so, one could scarcely understand the fundamental and universal principles that underlay and permeated all of jurisprudence—Roman or otherwise—and therefore the rule of law and justice.

By removing his work—and even his life—from context these commemorations also tended to mute one of the most consistent and salient features of Alciati's work, namely the defensive stance he took regarding his methods, choices, and interpretations throughout his career. From the preface of the 1515 *Annotationes on the Last Three Books of Justinian's Code* to his combative orations delivered at various universities and to the last edition of his *Emblems*, Alciati anticipated—and later responded to—critics, real and imagined. In so doing, he persistently argued that while they might take issue with his application of the methods and sources of the *studia humanitatis* to the study and interpretation of Roman law, they could not deny that in doing so he had contributed to their quest to restore Roman law as the Romans knew it.

Nor could they deny—at least in his estimation—that if the study of Roman law remained confined to the Byzantine *corpus* of Roman law and the commentaries and glosses on it rather than studying it within its broader historical contexts, then there would be little opportunity to properly comprehend the nature of jurisprudence as well as the universal principles that underpinned

70 This also applies to Budé (whose statue at the College de France marks his influence as founder), and to Zasius (traces of whom are sprinkled throughout Freiburg, including streets named after him and his tomb in the Münster).

and structured it. Moreover, given that correcting errors in the law required revision to legal education, they could no sooner deny—without impunity—that humanist methods and interpretations were essential to the overall project of legal and political reform, then they could deny that limiting their gaze to canonical texts and scholastic interpretations had the tendency to stall them. Such an influence was not only exemplified by his legal treatises and *Emblems* but also amplified by his orations with which he called students to the study the law in the humanist manner in the first place.

3 The Art of Justice, the Power of Speech, and the Necessity of Jurists

Alciati's orations *In Praise of the Law*, delivered at Avignon in 1518 and Bologna in 1537, shared three principal aims.[71] First, they were meant to convince returning students that if they took up the study of Roman law with him, and thus were willing to study new sources and adopt new methods associated with the *studia humanitatis*, then they would be able to accomplish something far more worthy and essential than if they continued to study law in the scholastic manner. To accomplish this, he assured them that he would help them to achieve success, regardless of their previous experience or natural talent:

> Come now, strive, all of you, with all your strength such that you may traverse this obscure way through so many troublesome footpaths, in order that you may arrive at that very goal as soon as possible, in which you may taste all sweet and agreeable things. Let them prepare themselves for this occupation, who are superior in fame, who are superior in wealth, let not those of low birth despair, let them confirm that they themselves are poor, this art extends in accordance with equity to everyone, who shall have applied the utmost labor to learning it. [72]

71 Alciati, "Oratio in laudem iuri civilis, principio studii cum Avenione profiteretur [1518]," in *Opera omnia*, vol. 3, 505/6–511 [Hereafter: "Avignon Oration"]; and Alciati, "Oratio Andreae Alciati, dum Bononiam [1537]," in *Opera Omnia*, vol. 3, 1051/1052–1055/1056 [Hereafter: "Bologna Oration"].

72 For example, Alciati, "Avignon Oration," 510, 'Cum ergo tot proposita praemia huius disciplinae studiosis videatis, agite, omnes totis viribus adnitimini, ut per tot laboriosos tramites hoc caliginosum iter superetis, & ad metam ipsam quamprimum perveniatis, in qua omnia dulcia, omnia iucunda degustetis. Huic negocio accingant se, qui nobilitate, qui divitiis praepollent, non desperent ignobiles, confirment seipsos pauperes, omnibus haec ars ex aequo patebit, qui in ea perdiscenda plurimum operae impenderint. Aluit semper honos artes, nullaque tam barbara aetas fuit, in qua docti viri inprecio non essent.'

Second, they persuaded new students of the benefits of pursuing a law degree rather than a degree from another faculty within the university. For this, he explained why, once they completed their studies, his students would not only surpass their peers in knowledge but they would also "obtain the most honored offices from kings and occupy principal place among citizens."[73] Third, and most importantly, his orations informed students that the study of law—Roman or otherwise—was not merely the study of texts, commentaries, and opinions but also the study of justice. To this end, he focused on the origins of law, the intentions of the lawgivers, and the importance of its interpreters over time; in so doing, he laid out the fundamental aspects of his theory of universal jurisprudence that underpinned his lectures.

While both orations fit within the broader genre of the humanist rhetoric to instruct, entice, and move listeners to action—in this case, to convince students to willingly reject the bad habits of traditional jurisprudence and to adopt new ones—the criticisms within them and the scope of each ultimately distinguished Alciati's speeches from those delivered by his counterpart in Germany, namely Zasius. Indeed, Alciati's disparaging and defensive tone, which was muted in the Avignon oration when compared to the outright scathing remarks in the Bologna one, stemmed from his frustrations with humanist and scholastic jurisprudence throughout his career. As such, exploring them in tandem and as complements to one another rather than treating them in sequence illuminates both the persistence of Alciati's critiques of his predecessors and his disenchantment with his peers.

For example, he offered his humanist peers an alternative mode of study and interpretation, viz., a method of legal hermeneutics drawing on the sources associated with the *studia humanitatis*, as presented in his 1515 *Annotationes*. However, by the time he took up his first teaching position at Avignon in 1518, very little had changed even though humanists continued their calls for reform. A decade after Budé first launched his attack against scholastic jurisprudence and Zasius had begun teaching in accordance with humanist methods, the primary focus of study at the universities remained the same. Instead of trying to recover Roman law as the Romans knew it, humanist jurists—as much as scholastic ones—continued to focus on the same reduced texts of Roman law, notably the fragments compiled in the *Digest*. They did so rather than seeking out the original texts from which such fragments were drawn so that Roman

73 Alciati, "Avignon Oration," 510, 'quam ob causum amplissima dignitate eius sectatores culti, magnos magistratus, summas dignitates, honestissima officia a regibus impetrant, primum in civitatibus locum obtinent ...'

law could be expanded and understood beyond the confines of the Byzantine compilation.

In light of this narrow, well-worn focus, Alciati lamented in his oration at Avignon that the profession as a whole not only suffered from glaucoma but also—just as bad doctors—continued to "always apply the same salve for whatever kind of affliction of the eyes."[74] Rather than pursue such a practice, he assured them that he "resolved to imitate them in regard to this matter least of all" because "I have always determined [it] to be a characteristic of an unhappy, ungrateful temperament to depend on the words of others, and to put together nothing of one's own."[75] He did not want to pick up where their previous professors left off or to continue to teach the same old texts, or even to build on the work of other humanist jurists. Alciati had in mind to do something different. He endeavored instead to focus on lesser-known texts to help his students acquire both a broader—and more nuanced—perspective on and understanding of Roman law than they could acquire if they chose to study with someone else.

If he was frustrated by the lack of progress in 1518, his 1537 oration at Bologna betrayed his sheer annoyance with having to repeatedly defend his methods against both scholastic and humanist detractors. Replacing the metaphor of glaucoma with a historical account of the study of Roman law, he complained that after Bartolus' and Baldus' innovations in the fourteenth century, "nothing appears to be said with very many words,"[76] especially among those who continued to deny the utility of drawing on the sources and methods of the *studia humanitatis*, including the art of eloquence. Rejecting the habit of repeating well-worn points, and certainly those based on misinterpretations and error, Alciati announced that he would not dare "to elevate those things—which are now accepted everywhere—by surrendering my own [interpretations]."[77]

After roughly twenty years—since taking his first teaching position at Avignon—of responding to critics who questioned the value of eloquence

74 Ibid, 507, 'Quo sit, ut plerunque eadem a docentibus pro suggestu audiantur, qui, sicut mali medici solent, qualicunque oculorum aegritudini idem semper collyrium imponunt.'

75 Ibid, 'Quos ego hac in re minime imitari constitui, cum quod infelicis, ingratique ingenii semper existimavi de aliorum verbis pendere, nihilque de suo conferre, tum quod non istorum more multa, sed pauca & utilia disserere melius duxi.' See also *Emblem* 164: Against detractors and *Emblem* 180: It is sacrilege for scholars to malign scholars. Appendix.

76 Alciati, "Bologna Oration," 1057/1058, 'nihilque plerisque dictum videtur.'

77 Ibid, 'Nec enim ausim ego adversus torrentem niti, & quae iam ubique recepta sunt, traditionibus meis elevare.'

within legal studies, Alciati simply asserted to his Bologna audience: "I have had enough and more than enough to do with those who permit our discipline to be handed down by the illiterate."[78] Had such men, humanist and scholastic, been able to show that his manner of interpretation and teaching over the course of his career—and with it, his focus on language—resulted in more errors and confusions, then he would have taken them seriously. However, since they were disparaging his work without offering constructive comments, he dismissed them by claiming that "they cannot lodge a complaint against a generous salesman, that he has handed over more ornate and polished goods than he was obligated to do by the law of purchase."[79]

Turning away from his critics in favor of making a case for breaking new ground, Alciati proclaimed in both orations—and indeed, in most of his works—that if students and readers adopted his methods and tended to his interpretations, then they would be able to acquire a fuller understanding of law and a better knowledge of justice. The latter would result from the exposure to a variety of texts, in full and in fragments. With his guidance, Alciati's students would be able to grasp the original meaning and intent of specific laws at the time of their creation, as well as how the language of the law—and interpretations of it—was adapted and changed throughout history. This would grant them new insights into how specific bodies of law effect and reflect changes within discreet societies at specific times, thus revealing the timeless and universal principles shared between all peoples, across time and space. Studying law in this way would not only make them better jurists and advisors but it would also make them more virtuous, and therefore better men.[80]

At the start of his teaching career at Avignon, Alciati did not indicate which texts they would explore with him (beyond the *Digest*), nor did he offer the students a sense of how they would proceed throughout the year under his direction. Instead, he assured them that no matter what texts they studied they would not be set aside "until I have arranged them in relation to the

78 Ibid, 'Satis mihi & super negotii cum illis fuit, qui non nisi illiteratis literis tradi disciplinam nostram patiuntur.'

79 Ibid, 'Non iniusta eorum esset postulatio, si ideo me legum difficultates minus explicare ostenderent: sed cum nihil mihi reliqui ad summam diligentiam in eis declarandis faciam, non possunt liberali venditori obiicere, quod ornatiores, politioresque venalitios tradiderit, quam ex lege emptionis deberet.'

80 For in-depth discussions of the power of eloquence for humanists see Gray, "Renaissance Humanism;" Seigel, *Rhetoric and Philosophy*; Hankins, *Renaissance Civic Humanism*; and Hankins, *Virtue Politics*.

highest summit of these arts" with the greatest skills.[81] He promised them, in effect, that even though working with him would be challenging and require a lot of effort on their part, it would also require him a great deal of exertion and effort to ensure that they benefited from the opportunity to study with him. As open-ended as this first oration was, however, by the time he delivered the one at Bologna, Alciati announced within it that those who chose to study with him would spend the entire year focusing on a single category of law, namely contracts (with an emphasis on obligations).[82] The distance between the two orations, in terms of focus and specificity, accented Alciati's unwavering determination to help students—no matter their long term goals—to explore and understand practical applications of law. Likewise, it highlighted his interest in categories, precepts, and principles that spanned innumerable contexts within public and private law as well as arrangements between peoples, states, empires that encompassed everything from the rights of war to the conditions of peace. In sum, it reflected his interest in pragmatic and practical jurisprudence as much as his interest in the history of different types of obligations.

By engaging with all manner of contracts within civil society, ranging from marriage to commerce to constitutions, students could gain a better understanding of the importance and role of promise-keeping and the consequences of bad faith (and cavillation) within families, between neighbors, and among citizens and subjects at large. Moreover, approaching the study of contracts both thematically and historically would aid them in comprehending the central place held by obligations and, by extension, rights within and between societies over time. All of this would give them ample experience, examples, and resources to draw upon for crafting and enforcing agreements, contracts, and treaties after the completion of their studies. Collectively, the above would empower his students to sharpen their understanding of justice as much as it would facilitate their mastery of law, customary and civil as well as public and private. Thus, attention to the relation between justice and law, and, indeed, his underpinning theory of universal jurisprudence, was as central to

81 Alciati, "Avignon Oration," 511, 'Consoletur ergo unusquisque seipsum, & spe plenus nobiscum haec studia aggrediatur, ego illi praevius per aspera, per devia, per omnes anfractus adero, nec mihi ipsi satisfactum putabo, donec in summo huius artis culmine eum constituero.'

82 Alciati, "Bologna Oration," 1057/58, 'Interpretabimur hoc anno tractatum, qui de verborum obligationibus inscribitur: cuius utilitas toties a mairoibus nostris praedicata, iterata, inculcataque est, ut minime commendatione nostra amplius indigeat.'

his overall argument in these orations as it was to calling students to the study of law or defending his methods of teaching and interpretation.

To explain the relation between justice and law in the Avignon oration, Alciati appealed to his auditors' collective memory, religious understanding, and historical imaginations to shed light on how laws were first communicated to humankind, and how and why man adopted the rule of law, and thereby justice, by entering civil society in the first place.[83] Alciati also appealed to the collective memory of those at Bologna. Yet, instead of inviting them to exercise their historical imaginations, he invoked what he deemed to be historical fact to illuminate why and how the words, texts, practices, and institutions of Roman law came to serve as the basis for the rule of law for much of Europe.[84] In the former case, it was the power of eloquence that persuaded man to submit to the law and, in the process, to agree to the consequences of breaking it—ranging from monetary to physical penalties, up to and including marked, broken, and severed limbs as well as hanging and decapitation. In the latter case, it was the power of justice that drew entire societies to do the same.

A fundamental premise of Alciati's theory was that without law there could be no justice. Therefore, he needed to account for both the origins of law and what had existed before it and beyond it.[85] He did so in a concise manner in the Avignon oration by resorting to ideas that would have been quite familiar to his audience, on account of the biblical tradition as well as the classical one. For example, after asserting "justice is the entire source of laws,"[86] Alciati next appealed to a common secular and religious trope:

> Indeed this very knowledge of the laws, transported from the gods themselves of earlier peoples to men, they judged ought to be taken up with a certain well-deserved form of divine worship, handed down like a certain outstanding gift from Jove to mortals, receiving its sinews from justice, its intellect from prudence, its execution from bravery: (a gift) which if these divine virtues should be absent from it, would not now be called "laws"

83 Alciati, "Avignon Oration," 507–508.
84 Alciati, "Bologna Oration," 1056/1057.
85 Alciati, "Avignon Oration," 507–510.
86 Ibid, 507, 'Adeste ergo, & diis faventibus, benignas nobis aures praestate. Dicendum in praesentia est de legibus, quarum origo omnis & fundamentum est iustitia.'

> but "means of execution of men," or "treasonous acts," or anything else you like, rather than laws.[87]

As such, Alciati implied that all the rules, institutions, and actions that were called 'laws' before this gift were merely customary and conventional practices devoid of justice, whereas those that extended from the laws passed down to man from God(s) had at least a glimmer of justice within them, even if—as a result of corruption in the hands of man—they were not fully permeated by it.

If justice and law were gifts from gods, then neither law nor justice was inherent to man from his origins. In this way, Alciati's interpretation presented in the Avignon oration departed nearly wholesale from Budé's *Annotationes* and Zasius' *De iustitia et iure* lecture.[88] Initially inaccessible to man via reason, inclination, or experience, Alciati suggested that the only means by which one could acquire the knowledge of justice and obtain a means to pursue it was through direct instruction by a divine legislator. As such, the moment law and justice were revealed to man, through speech, stood as a distinct break with the past and served to shape everything that came after. Just as important, the moment held additional moral authority because it signified man's dignity and his place in the universe; the gods gave man, and man alone, justice. The moment also imbued law with historical authority; it marked the origins of law, after which man would never be without access to law and justice again.

Those men who initially received the knowledge of law and justice from the gods had disseminated it to the communities in which they lived. Once adopted, the law was passed down and further articulated from generation to generation through the art of speech and the technology of writing. Over time, adopting, upholding, enforcing, and expanding the rule of law as part of the pursuit of justice became a shared moral and historical tradition among humankind. This history, however, was neither linear nor progressive nor without interruptions, nor was the rule of law *de facto* applicable to all

87 Ibid, 'Ipsam vero legum prudentiam ab ipsis maiorum gentium diis in homines transfusam, divino quodam cultu merito excipiendam existimavere, a Iove ipso ceu praecipuum quoddam donum mortalibus traditam, a iustitia nervos accipientem, a prudentia intellectum, a fortitudine executionem: cui si divinae virtutes hae absint, non iam leges dicuntur, sed hominum carnificinae, sed seditiones, & quodvis potius aliud, quam leges.'

88 Budé's account of the origins of law and civil society is treated in Chapter 2, whereas Zasius' account is treated in Chapter 4.

forms of—and relations between—human society, even if it was ever present *de jure* since it had first been handed down to man. In practice, the rule of law— since it required a common authority like judges or courts to enforce it—only existed within civil societies, not between them.[89] Likewise, Alciati held that the rule of law could not exist within any community where power and violence was unlimited—whether in the form of tyranny or in the context of war—or where those subject to it did not agree to place their necks under its yoke, implicitly or explicitly.[90]

After briefly accounting for how man came to know the law (a story that corresponded as much with the Old Testament as it did with origins stories in ancient Roman and Greek philosophy) Alciati advanced a theory on how communities came to adopt the rule of law in the first place,

> For it could not have come to pass, that he who had more power, and excelled in strength toward everyone else, was willing to descend to the law without [the use of force] and submitted himself to be made equal to those weaker than he, unless it had been singled out by the eloquence of some great orator and had been persuaded by reasons.[91]

In so doing, he turned to the very discussion within Cicero's *De inventione* that Zasius had used in his 1508 oration at Freiburg, even as he departed from the latter's interpretation.[92] Whereas Zasius had admonished those who placed far too much emphasis and importance on eloquence in legal studies, Alciati emphasized the power of eloquence to persuade man to live in civil society. Indeed, no matter if accounting for how law was first communicated to man (its origins) or how man communicated law to others over time (its history), understanding the role of eloquence as a means to teach, entreat, and move man to understanding and action was central to Alciati's overall theory of jurisprudence.[93] Without eloquence, there would be no vehicle by which man could be convinced to consent to the rule of law.

89 Cf. Hobbes, *Leviathan* [1651], especially Chapters 17 & 26.

90 The allusion here is to capital punishment, by hanging or beheading, in which case the power of the law is made manifest by the rope or blade of the executioner.

91 Alciati, "Avignon Oration," 508, 'Nec enim fieri potuit, ut qui plus posset, atque viribus in caeteros praecelleret, ad ius sine vi vellet descendere, patereturque se imbecillioribus aequari, nisi magni alicuius Oratoris eloquentia allectus, rationibusque persuasus esset.'

92 See Chapter 3 in this volume.

93 In addition to the "Avignon Oration."

FIGURE 5.1

***Emblem* 99**[94]
Art aiding nature

As Fortune on her sphere, so Mercury sits upon his cube:
he presides over the arts, she over chance events.
Art is made against the force of fortune;
but when fortune is bad, it often requires the help of art.
Therefore, eager youths, learn the good arts,
that have with them the advantages of certain fate.[95]

94 Image from André Alciati, *Andreae Alciati Emblemata cum commentariis Claudii Minois I.C. Francisci Sanctii Brocensis, & notis Laurentii Pignorii Patavini. Novissima hac editione in continuam unius commentarii seriem congestis, in certas quasdam quasi classes dispositis, & plusquam dimidia parte auctis. Opera et vigiliis Joannis Thuilii Mariaemontani Tirol … Accesserunt in fine Federici Morelli … Corollaria & monita, ad eadem Emblemata. Cum indice triplice.* (*Patavii: Apud Petrum Paulum Tozzium, 1621*). Hereafter: Alciati, *Emblemata.*

95 Translation from Barker, et al., "Alciato's Book of Emblems: The Memorial Web Edition in Latin and English."

FIGURE 5.2

***Emblem* 181**[96]

Eloquence, surpassing strength

His left hand holds a bow, his right carries a rough club,
and the Nemean lion cloaks his naked body.
Is this therefore the likeness of Hercules?
That he is old and his temples hoary with age suggests otherwise.
What of his tongue, pierced with light chains,
by which he cleaves the ears of men and draws them to him without difficulty?
Don't the Gauls say that with his tongue, not with his might,
Alcides excelled in providing nations with laws?
Arms yield to the toga, and he who is powerful in speech
draws to his wishes even the most resistant hearts.[97]

96 Image from Alciati, *Emblemata*.

97 Translation from Barker, et al., "Alciato's Book of Emblems: The Memorial Web Edition in Latin and English."

Quoting nearly word-for-word from Cicero, who in turn drew from Plato and Aristotle, Alciati explained how "in that first moment of human affairs men were uncivilized" and, as a consequence, mankind "roamed through the mountains and fields, in the manner of beasts."[98] Such men, living in this condition, were "neither mindful of divine worship, nor of human affairs." This unsociable manner meant that "everyone directed everything by force alone in accordance with the strengths of the body." Humans lived in this natural state until a "wise man, aided with the arts of eloquence called them together by means of eloquent speech, and advised them how much usefulness mutual association and civil pursuits carried in themselves." Through this speech, "human kind was made gentle and tame, trust [*fides*] was cultivated, competition in [giving] mutual benefits arose," and, over time, "rustic habits were cast off, and better manners were accepted."[99]

Indeed, it was only by appealing to man's reason—and self-interest—through persuasive speech that it had "come to pass, that one who had more power, and excelled everyone else in strength was willing to yield to the law" and submit "himself to be made equal to those weaker than he."[100] Without such instruction, which included appeals to man's imagination of what was possible, man would not have been convinced that they had more to gain by adopting the rule of law than by living without it, and thus they would not have considered themselves to be equally subject to its procedures and punishments by joining together in a civil society administered by civil law.

Regardless of whether man was naturally inclined to live in mutual company or not, only the knowledge of law and justice could have drawn man to make such a choice to quit one condition—characterized by brute force and strength—and to take on another—characterized by law and justice. Only those instructed and convinced of the benefits of living under law in tandem

---

98 Alciati, "Avignon Oration,"508, 'Et ut ab eloquentia incipiamus, tradunt antiqui autores, in primaeva illa rerum humanarum infantia fuisse homines insociabiles, qui per montes agrosque passim, & bestiarum more vagarentur, non divinae religionis, nec humani officii memores, quique omnia sola fortitudine pro viribus corporis administrarent, donec sive Mercurius (ut Plato & Aristides credidit) sive quilibet alius vir sapiens eloquentiae artibus adiutus, accommodata oratione eos congregavit, quantumque in se utilitatis mutua conversatio, & studia civilia haberent, admonuit.'

99 Ibid, 'Sic humanum genus mite & mansuetum effectum est, sic fides culta, sic mutuis officiis certatum, & exutis agrestibus illis moribus, melio res accepti.' Compare with *Emblem* 181: *Eloquence, surpassing strength.* Appendix.

100 Ibid, 'Nec enim fieri potuit, ut qui plus posset, atque viribus in caeteros praecelleret, ad ius sine vi vellet descendere, pateretur que se imbecillioribus aequari, nisi magni alicuius Oratoris eloquentia allectus, rationibusque persuasus esset.' and 'Quae omnia eloquentiae debemus.' Cf. Cicero, *De Inventione*.

could choose to adopt a rule of law and to live in civil society since doing so would require them to agree that if they violated such laws, then they should be punished.[101] It was this choice to adopt the rule of law that gave rulers and jurists the moral authority to enforce it when violated and to protect it when subverted. Moreover, given man's propensity to pursue vice and depart from virtue, there would always be a demand for those who (1) understood law, (2) could enforce it fairly, and (3) knew how to carefully institute changes or reforms when necessary. If knowledge of the law and justice were to cease, then security and stability among men would cease. Echoing both Cicero and Budé, Alciati argued that without law (and lawyers and jurists to administer them), no one would know what was his, what was another's, and avarice and vice would reign everywhere.[102] To ensure the latter, there was—and always would be—a need for properly-trained jurists who understood the origins, essence, and purpose of justice and right.[103]

Alciati touched on this point directly in his oration at Bologna. Here, too, he was addressing an audience for whom his account of the origins of law (as a gift from God) as well as the act of calling men to adopt and follow these laws through elegant and persuasive speech (a common motif in ancient and contemporary sources) would have been quite familiar. In addition, he could also appeal to the collective memory and understanding of his audience in relation to the significance of Roman law at the University of Bologna. Given the prominence of Bologna in legal studies both in Italy and throughout Latin Europe, it would be nothing short of redundant for him to try to convince his auditors of the importance of studying civil law there. Instead, he simply asserted that "since we are speaking about embracing those very studies, which excel all others, I will not beat about the bush."[104] This did not mean, however, that there

---

101 Alciati, *Emblem* 172: A Just Revenge and *Emblem* 175: One Sins, The Other is Punished. Appendix.

102 Alciati, "Avignon Oration,"510, 'Si hi de medio tollerentur, exploratum nemini esse posset, quid suum, quid alienum, quid a patre accecepturus, quid liberis porro relicturus foret, nihil denique inter mortales aequi bonique relinqueretur, discordiarum semina undique pullularent. Fugerent de civitate omnes virtutes, omnes bonae artes contaminarentur, vis & avaritia ubique regnarent, innocentes nusquam tuti essent: quibus omnibus malis sola haec legalis scientia frena imponit: haec in facinorosos omnes severe animaduertit, divin umque iudicium exequitur, bonos praemiis invitat, oppressos calamitatibus erigit." Cf. Hobbes, *Leviathan* [1651], especially Chapter 13.

103 Cf. with Zasius' emphasis on the historical and moral role of jurists in society in Chapter 3 of this volume.

104 Alciati, "Bologna Oration," 1051/1052–1053/1054, 'Si ad id capessendum vos adhortarer, quod ambiguae esset utilitatis, vel a quo animi vestri abhorrerent, tum & mihi diligenti insinuatione esset opus, & summum oratorem res ipsa expostularet: sed cum de ipsis

was no need to convince students that matriculating in the law faculty would be more consequential for them than if they sought degrees in other faculties, namely theology and philosophy. To demonstrate why earning a law degree would not only amount to time better spent but also present more opportunities to secure employment and garner respect, Alciati made a historical argument.

Alciati pointed out that one could trace the history of law and the importance of its study back to the ancients—something that was not the case for theology. This did not mean, of course, that the theologians-in-training had no concern for sacred things, only that "among the Ancients there was no special profession of the theologians."[105] Rather than splitting the two, they combined the study of the sacred with the study of law because the latter was also the study of justice, which was a gift from the gods. Turning immediately to another discipline, he acknowledged that while the study of law was as tied to philosophy—particularly the "debates about ethics and civil association"—as it was to the sacred, no one who wished to learn how to write, interpret, and apply legal decrees and doctrines (*decreta ius*) did so by pouring over the works of Plato and Aristotle.[106] Instead, they studied how jurists and lawyers created, interpreted, and administered law over time by studying legal texts, decisions, constitutions, and opinions. Alciati's point was not to question the value of philosophy or theology so much as it was to reinforce something that his audience already knew, namely that the study of Roman law was of more import for aspiring advisors, councilors, and administrators, in that it provided a blueprint to apply law and not simply an opportunity to think about it. Taking exception to humanists like Budé with this comment, he assured his auditors that he had something far more practical to offer them.

The question remained: why should they study with him? More specifically, why should they study law by combining the *studia humanitatis*—including the works of Plato and Aristotle—with legal hermeneutics, which required

studiis amplectendis tractemus, quae omnium sententia praecellunt, praeconium aliquod non est necessarium.'

105 Alciati, "Bologna Oration," 1053/54, 'Apud veteres nulla fuit praecipua Theologorum professio, sed legali doctrinae iunctum ipsi existimarunt.'

106 Ibid, 'Cuius prima potentior pars Iureconsultorum praecipua est: nempe illa, quae de moribus & civili conversatione disputat'; and 'Quantum autem Iuresconsulti nostri & veteribus & magni nominis philosophis praecelluerint, eo argumento satis ostenditur, quod Platonis & Aristotelis, qui curiose prolixe que de legibus & civili conversatione scripserunt, nemo libros in eum usum recepit unquam, ut secundum eorum decreta ius diceret.'

attention to sources that reached far beyond legal fragments and texts. Why would this be more useful to them than studying the theories of ethics or theological doctrines? After all, Alciati's methods would have appeared just as esoteric as those employed within the faculty of philosophy and theology, to those who simply wanted to practice law rather than become legal scholars and university professors. Alciati's answer reinforced his previous points on the importance of Roman law in history as well as on the need to place Roman law in historical context—two things that they could do if they worked with him.

In the process of doing so, he made an argument that would have resonated with those already familiar with Engelbert of Admont's (c. 1250–1331) *De orate et fine Romani imperii* (*On the Rise and End of the Roman Empire*) written between 1307 and 1310, when Henry VII of Luxemburg was preparing for his expedition to Italy. Educated at Padua, Englebert, according to Antony Black, was "the first to ground the argument for empire on the new range of political concepts and arguments available from Aristotle" as well as on ideas from Plato, Cicero, the New Testament, Roman history, and St. Augustine to support his overall argument that "Roman rule (*imperium*) over them was tolerable, modest and fair."[107] Indeed, just as Engelbert asserted that,

> the Roman Empire acquired other kingdoms and dominions through voluntary subjection ... subjection by force became subjection by consent (*voluntatem*), so that they obeyed and were subject no longer through coercion but voluntarily, and they accepted of their own will the Roman laws which had been impressed upon them[108]

Alciati announced that those who wished to study the rule of law, and thereby justice, should study Roman law historically because, as the jurists say,

> not only the Roman provinces, but [even] hostile peoples, have deemed it worthy to observe [Roman law]; and [even] those who overthrew the Roman Empire with their arms gladly submitted to Roman laws, on account of their equity, power, keenness, and majesty. Just as today the Goths, the Alans, the Vandals, who have settled in Spain, as well as

107 Black, *Political Thought in Europe*, 93.

108 Ibid, 94. Black included a note that one should compare this statement by Engelbert with those within Thomas Hobbes' *Leviathan*, especially Chapter 20.

> the Oruli, Burgundians, and Franks, who occupy Gaul, ascribe to our [Roman] law.[109]

Yet, if one continued to study Roman law in the scholastic manner—as timeless rather than in historical perspective—then one could not study how Roman law became the very model for a rule of law for peoples within and across Europe in the first place. The importance of Roman law, in this context, extended from its longevity, which could be studied and understood by tending to the history and development of the law as the Romans knew it, and how those who adopted it came to understand and adapt its principles to fit new contexts and to reform existing customs and legal traditions.

That so many peoples and nations—even those who were the enemies of Rome—willingly adopted it upon seeing it in action confirmed the moral authority of Roman law; it was not only an extensive and useful body of law but also an embodiment of justice and right for Alciati. Therefore, students who took up the study of Roman law with him, precisely because they would be drawing on sources and texts that reached beyond the commentaries and glosses, would have the opportunity to develop an understanding of justice and right that extended far beyond the text or question at hand. They would develop, in short, an understanding of the universal jurisprudence that Roman law reflected and embodied throughout its history, as applied by the Romans and by those who were convinced—by word or by action—of the benefits of adopting it.

After asserting the importance of one aspect of the *studia humanitatis*, viz., the study of history, Alciati turned once again to the problem of eloquence. While he agreed with those who held that eloquent arguments about justice by those who lacked legal training (like Budé) could be dangerous, he nevertheless argued that seeking to join the knowledge of justice with eloquence was a noble pursuit; that all aspects of the *studia humanitatis* were important to the proper understanding of law.[110] In so doing, he posed a rhetorical

---

109 Alciati, "Bologna Oration," 1053/54, 'At Iureconsultorum nostrorum responsa, Romanasque leges, non Romanae solum provinciae, sed hostiles quoque populi observare non sunt dedignati: & qui Romanum imperium armis everterunt, Romanis tandem legibus propter earum aequitatem, vim, acumen maiestatem libentissime cervices submisserunt. Sic hodie Gotthi, Alani, Vandali, qui in Hispania consedere: sic Oruli, Burgundi, Franci, qui Gallias tenent, iuri nostro dant operam.'

110 Alciati, "Ampliss Voro Francisco a Turonbe Archiepiscopo Biturig (Dedication)," in *De verborum significatione*, [1] 'recte hunc tractatum ab eo percipi non posse, qui ab humanioribus studiis abhorreat: sicut nec vice versa, qui hasce solas literas profiteant, nisi idem iuris quoque civilis disciplina præcellat: oleum & operam hisce in responsis interpretandis perdit.'

question to his students: "What is more dangerous than to permit there to be in the *res publica* the sort of man, who, by his skill with words, drives simple men in whatever direction he pleases and exerts via verbal fiction a tyrannical [influence] over their minds?"[111] In response to his own question, he echoed the Athenians, who believed that the use of eloquence should be banned from judicial proceedings on account of its potency to render innocent men guilty and guilty men innocent.[112] However, the latter did not require that the study of rhetoric ought to be banned from legal studies; as long as it did not overshadow substance, there would be no need to abandon the form.[113]

"For," as Alciati argued at Avignon, "the law is not the words themselves or that written on parchment or engraved on bronze," rather the law is that which is "dictated by justice, led by equity and proclaimed by good counsel."[114] Moreover, unless eloquent and persuasive speech was joined to the knowledge of law and justice, it could neither "serve trust [*fides*], nor cultivate justice, nor end feuds."[115] Indeed, in cases when eloquence was not "joined to justice, it was the cause of the disaster in the commonwealth (*Reipublicae*), it was the cause of all evil things."[116] At the same time, if law had not been joined to eloquence, then man would have never been called into civil society. As powerful as eloquent speech could be to urge students and men to action, only when it was joined to the knowledge of law and justice could it help "make a man honest,

111 Alciati, "Bologna Oration," 1053/54, 'Quid pernisciosius, quam in republica sinere, qui verborum arte simplices homines quamlibet in partem arbitratu suo impellat, & fictio sermonis lenocinio, quandam quasi tyrannidem in animos exerceat?'

112 Ibid, 1053/54–1055/56, 'Viderunt id Athenienses, qui nullos affectus actori moveri permiserunt. Videre & Lacedaemonii, qui huiusmodi viros de civitate sua eiecerunt. Viderunt melius, perfectius, absolutius Iurisconsulti nostri, quorum sententiam omnis posterior aetas approbavit, qua ubique inductum est, solis legibus quancunque litem dirimi, non affectibus tantum sublatis, sed omni prorsus rhetorico colore, ne veritati quicquam tenebrarum ullius facundia possit offundi.'

113 Ibid, 1055/56, 'Nec a me haec dicuntur, quod Rhetoricae minus faueam, eiusque luminibus velim obstruere: sed ut adeo eam legalibus studiis coniungi ostendam, ut sine illis nullo modo recte consistat.'

114 Alciati, "Avignon Oration," 507, 'Neque enim verba ipsa, & quod vel membranis scribitur, vel aere figitur, Lex est, sed quod iustitia dictante, aequitate praevia, bono consilio profertur, verum Legis nomen habet.'

115 Ibid, 508, 'Quae eloquentiae gloria cum nostra hac arte communis proculdubio est: nec enim fidem servare, iustitiam colere, simultates abolere, sub legibus esse, eloquentiam magis, quam professionem hanc nostrum respicit, ut inde apertissime deprehendi possit, studia haec simul iuncta esse, & ab antiquissimis usque temporibus invicem suffragantia, & quorum alterum altero indigeat.'

116 Ibid, 'Nam & eloquentia, nisi iustitiae annexa fuerit, Reipublicae calamitatis, omniumque malorum causa est.' See also *Emblem* 53: Against Flatterers. Appendix.

sincere, and uncorrupted."[117] Therefore, those who studied legal texts without also studying the art of justice were merely learning how to play with words, whereas those who joined the study of rhetoric with the study of law were learning how to direct man's actions, and advise princes, to promote virtue, security, and the common good.[118]

Integrating the methods that tied eloquence to justice in his emblems with his oration at Avignon, Alciati briefly shifted his focus from the power of spoken words to the power of images. Moving from law to justice, Alciati explained that the Stoic philosopher Chrysippus (279–206 BCE) was the first who managed to portray Justice perfectly "with a powerful glance," which captured the "acute light in her eyes."[119] Justice could see everything and everyone clearly; nothing obscured her vision. Alluding to his previous remarks about the legal profession suffering from glaucoma and his insistence that the language of law must be studied from a much wider perspective, this elegant and powerful image crafted by Chrysippus taught man that it was "necessary that a judge be of uncorrupted judgment, sacred, stern, unyielding against the wicked, to be terrifying with the power and majesty of his fairness and his truthfulness."[120]

117 Ibid, 509, 'Neque enim veteres illae tritaeque altercationes, de universo, de materia, de ideis, de causis, de inani, de motu, caeteraque huiusmodi, seu physica, seu metaphysica respiciant, quicque habent ad veram sapientiam pertinens, cum propter incertitudinem, tum quod ea sola vera est Philosophia quae probum, syncerum, incorruptum hominem efficit: quae utilitas minime de eis decertationibus habetur.'

118 Ibid, 509, 'merito Iurisconsulti caeteros omnes excellunt, qui non solum sibi sciunt prospicere, sed etiam sui muneris id praecipuum habent, ut alios quoque tueantur, bonoque consilio confirment.'; and 509–10, 'hi humani foederis vincula sacrosancta continent, hi pacis studia amplectuntur, resectis vitiis cives ad bonam frugem perducunt.'

119 Ibid, 508, 'Is iustitiae imaginem ita expressit, ut puellari virginis forma, aspectu vehementi, luminibus oculorum acerrimis conspiceretur.' In addition to this description of justice, it is also useful to note that early Roman coins also depicted justice without her eyes covered. It was not until about the sixteenth century that justice became blind, represented by a blindfold. For a discussion of the transformation of the image of justice see Costas Douzinas and Lynda Nead, eds. *Law and the Image: The Authority of Art and the Aesthetics of Law* (Chicago: University of Chicago Press, 1999); and H. Bianchi, "The Scales of Justice as Represented in Engravings, Emblems, Reliefs, and Sculptures of Early Modern Europe," in *Images et représentations de la justice du XVIe au XIXe siècle*, ed. Georges Lamoine (Toulouse: University of Toulose-Le Mirail, 1983).

120 Alciati, "Avignon Oration," 508, 'quod videlicet Iudicem incorrupto esse iudicio, sanctum, severum, contra improbos inexorabilem, vi & maiestate aequitatis, veritatisque, terrificum esse oporteat.'

FIGURE 5.3

Emblem **145**[121]
On the senate of a good prince

Here, before an altar to the gods, sit statues with their hands cut off,
and the foremost among them has no sight.
These symbols of the highest authority
and of the sacred Senate were devised by the men of Thebes.
Why are they sitting down?
Because it behooves grave judges to be of calm demeanour,
and not to waver frivolously.
Why do they have no hands?
So that they should take no bribes,
or let themselves be swayed by promises or gifts.
But the Prince is blind.
Because the steadfast Senate carries out
what he has decreed without emotion, with his ears alone.[122]

121 Image from Alciati, *Emblemata.*
122 Translation from Barker, et al., "Alciato's Book of Emblems: The Memorial Web Edition in Latin and English."

Under the Thebans, Alciati continued, the image of the rule of law was adapted, although the message conveyed was the same. For example, the Thebans sculpted statues of their magistrates as having no hands and closed eyes in order to show "without doubt what the nature of justice is, such that it may not be corrupted, neither by begging, nor by prayers, nor [that] it would yield to another's will."[123] Just as justice placed all on an equal footing with her powerful gaze, so too were jurists placed on an equal footing with their closed eyes. Depicting such men with their eyes closed reinforced, rather than diminished, their ability 'to see' what was just and unjust because their vision, unlike those of jurists who suffered glaucoma, was not obstructed by a narrow focus or by the symbols of power, wealth, or majesty. Drawing his audiences' attention to the personifications of justice and judges helped Alciati to emphasize the immense responsibility and importance of jurists as representatives of the rule of law within civil society.

These images painted with words also enabled him to discuss the benefits of trying to see the law differently—in this case with one's mind—that accompanied approaching the study of law and justice as well as the importance of elegant and eloquent persuasion. The first step was to free their mind's-eye of the obstructions attendant on studying law by merely reading traditional sources and employing well-worn methods, which might cause them to lose sight of justice altogether. As important, shifting the way they looked at law also had the capacity to ensure students were not blinded by the authority of those whom they worked for or by the splendor of the patronage they might receive in exchange for bending the law to fit the interests of power rather than justice.

This appeal to the ancient images of jurists in the Avignon oration also served to remind his audience that from the moment man was persuaded to quit his original/natural condition and enter civil society—or, as he stressed in the Bologna oration, from the moment a community agreed to adopt the rule of the law—wise and learned men were called upon to enforce, protect, and administer it. That such men had existed among the ancients spoke to the stability of the rule of law itself, as well as to the need for men who studied, taught, and practiced it. It also reminded students—through a direct link to justice—that "jurists excel all the rest" in all respects.[124] They did so because,

123 Alciati, "Avignon Oration," 508, 'Quapropter memoriae traditum est, magistratuum statuas a Thebanis ita solere formari, ut sine manibus essent, principum vero clausis oculis: nimirum eam iustitiae naturam esse ostendentes, ut incorrupta sit, nec precio, precibusve, aut alienae ulli voluptati cedat.'

124 Ibid, 509.

from the time law was first revealed to man and subsequently passed down throughout history, those wise men who understood that it concerned the "the sacred chains of human alliances" within society and the "the studies of peace" between them had always been in demand.[125] Indeed, even "extraordinary princes endeavor nothing without these men," as "not only are the toils of peace set in order by their arbitration, but also a good many wars are suppressed."[126]

With these words, Alciati ensured his audiences that if they took up the study of law with him, they would be properly trained to both administer justice within society and to advise cities, princes, kings, and emperors of the obligations they had to their subjects and of their rights vis-à-vis other rulers. This promise was not limited to those who attended his orations at Avignon and Bologna. Throughout his career, Alciati assured students that he would help them to administer and practice law properly, an essential training if they aspired to serve as advisors, councilors, and jurists to the greatest rulers and republics of the age.

If students heeded Alciati's call in these orations, they would have encountered something quite different than what was promised when they attended his lectures. The was especially the case when it came to his very brief, yet novel lecture on *De iustitia et iure*, wherein Alciati set aside much of which was contained within this first title of the *Digest* to concentrate instead on the interpretations of this title by Bartolus and Baldus. Indeed, rather than trying to assess the meaning and significance of fundamental and foundational categories and terms of Roman law as the Romans had intended, understood, and applied them, Alciati focused on the relation between *ius* and *ius gentium*—especially in terms of the right to meet force with force—within traditional jurisprudence. What is more, instead of delving into the necessity of law, as his scholastic and humanist counterparts did, he focused on the ubiquity of violence.

Placed within the broader context of the Italian Wars, it is not difficult to imagine why Alciati opted to explore violence and the ways in which it could be tamed by the rule of law within civil society, nor why he chose to focus on the rights of war and peace between civil societies. At the same time, given his insistence on studying the texts closely, we might side with those frustrated

125 Ibid, 509–10.

126 Ibid, 'quam ob causum amplissima dignitate eius sectatores culti, magnos magistratus, summas dignitates, honestissima officia a regibus impetrant, primum in civitatibus locum obtinent, principes ipsius vox & consilium existimantur, sine his nihil egregii principes moliuntur, ipsi etiam multa sine illis: eorum arbitratu non solum pacis opera digeruntur, sed etiam plerunque bella discutiuntur.'

students who attended his lectures expecting a historical-legal explanations of fundamental concepts within Roman law, only to find he offered us something quite different in his *De iustitia et iure* lecture. Before indulging in such speculation, however, it's worth remembering two things: first, we only have a record of the lecture as written not as ultimately delivered. And second, those who were present at his lecture in Avignon or Bologna—or any of the other universities Alciati taught at over his long career—would have had the opportunity to ask him questions to gain clarification about a specific point and even how various aspects of the lecture fit together. We, on the other hand, must rely on his *extensio*, that is, we have to read his lecture in the context of the Italian Wars and his own turbulent experiences (as this chapter laid out), if we wish to understand why rather than exploring *ius* as a criterion of justice or equity, Alciati predominantly focused on *ius* as an inherent right to meet force with force among persons and the right to wage war among states.

CHAPTER 6

The Tenacity of Violence and the Parity of Right

Alciati's [Re-] Interpretation of Jus *and* Jus Gentium

1 Equality through Enmity: War-Making as State-Making[1]

Situated on the spectrum between a 'mirror for princes' advice book and a 'law of nations' treatise, Andrea Alciati's short lecture on the first title of the *Digest* was fundamentally different from what one would expect based on his insistence on bringing specific aspects of the *studia humanitatis* to bear on legal interpretation. In his orations and in other published works, he claimed that he would attempt to restore the definitions and terms of Roman law to how the Romans (Ancient and Byzantine) knew them and to reach beyond traditional interpretations to lesser-known texts in the process. Yet, when Alciati expanded his discussion beyond the precise terms and definitions within the *Digest*, he turned to the well-worn fourteenth-century commentaries of Bartolus and Baldus. And, despite his emphasis on the importance of placing legal terms into historical context—to decipher their original meaning as well as show how their sense changed according to time, use, and intention—Alciati's *De iustitia et iure* lecture was nearly devoid of such analysis. Nevertheless, his overall treatment of this title, especially his use of *extensio*—the method of demonstrating, by implication, how a particular word, term, or law reflected universal principles—invited his students to adopt a broader and far more critical perspective on the assumptions underpinning traditional jurisprudence.

This was the case, in part, because Alciati's examination of the relation between *ius* and *ius gentium* in his lecture explored one of the most pressing questions of his immediate context, namely who held the right to wage war and to contract peace on their own accord; that is who held pure *imperium* and who did not.[2] That question, in turn, required addressing several others,

1 This is a play on Charles Tilly, "War Making and State Making as Organized Crime," in *Bringing the State Back In*, eds. Peter Evans, Dietrich Rueschemeyer, and Theda Skocpol (Cambridge: Cambridge University Press, 1985), 169–87.

2 The literature on this subject is vast. See especially Canning, *The Political Thought of Baldus*; Canning, *Ideas of Power in the Late Middle Ages*; Davies, *Periodization and Sovereignty*; Fasolt, *The Limits of History*; Kalmo and Skinner, eds. *Sovereignty in Fragments*; Julia Costa Lopez, "Merum Imperium and Sovereignty in the Later Middle Ages." *International Studies Review*

 DOI:10.1163/9789004528451_008

including where such rights ultimately originated and what the recognition of them signified. All of this entailed a critical engagement with the distinctions between proximate and remote causes of violence, just and unjust wars, and superior and inferior rulers. The latter distinction became increasingly important and problematic in the wake of the decades of war that followed Charles VIII's invasion of Italy in 1494. This was especially salient since alliances with and against popes, emperors, and kings had altered the status—as allies and enemies—of nearly all 'inferior' rulers across the peninsula, ranging from principalities to city-states—in practice (*de facto*) even if not yet in principle (*de jure*).[3]

Indeed, it was the increasing use of a special legal status to justify obtaining dynastic titles and lands by force that was eroding traditional distinctions between superior and inferior princes.[4] This occurred in two directions simultaneously. First, in respect to allies, superior rulers rendered inferiors as equals in the realm of war and peace when they joined them in defensive leagues through oaths and treaties. Second, as the Italian Wars unfurled, superiors rendered inferior rulers equals when they engaged them as enemies on the field of battle. No matter the size of the territory or how they held dominion over it (e.g., election, inheritance, appointment, conquest), the act of tacitly acknowledging that lesser dukes, princes, and republics could fully exercise *imperium* vis-à-vis one another, fundamentally challenged conventions anchored by the premise of inequality and, with it, the hierarchy of sovereignty that underpinned scholastic, viz., traditional, jurisprudence.[5]

Such temporary alliances undoubtedly had the potential to create permanent problems. Would, for example, a small republic or commune aligned with an emperor out of necessity retain their standing as an ally and, by implication, as a fully autonomous entity with the same rights to declare war and to sue for peace (*sui iuris*) as the emperor once the danger passed? Would a duke or prince in league with a king or pope be content to forgo their strategic importance, their aggrandized status, or their dynastic ambitions after the war, or would they expect to be rewarded with new titles, lands, and powers? Given

20, no. 3 (2018): 10–4; Maiolo, *Medieval Sovereignty*; Pennington, *The Prince and the Law*; Pagden, *Lords of All the* World; Skinner, *Foundations of Modern Political Thought I & II*.

3 See Mallett and Shaw, *The Italian Wars, 1494–1559*.

4 These changes were not new to the sixteenth century. They had spanned centuries and served as a common reference point and underpinning of European jurisprudence since at least the eleventh century.

5 The term 'hierarchy of sovereignty' is adopted from Canning, *The Political Thought of Baldus*; and Black, *Political Thought in Europe*.

how fickle alliances were and how unstable the Italian peninsula and much of Europe was, what guarantees could rulers and princes of smaller territories—not to mention independent city-states, communes, and republics—have to assure them that they would not simply be annexed by emperors, popes, or kings when their cooperation was no longer needed? These kinds of questions stirred jurists like Alciati to develop a new theory of state over the long sixteenth century (1492–1618); one that could reach beyond the legal limits, boundaries, and inequalities that had underpinned and justified the superior status of feudal, dynastic, papal, and imperial authorities across post-Roman Europe for nearly half a millennium.[6]

Considering how deeply entrenched such hierarchies of power were in traditional understandings of the foundational categories of Roman law, Alciati's interpretation of *ius gentium* as a marker of equality among rulers of empires, kingdoms, and city-states, was rife with dangerous implications. For example, adjustments that diminished the standing of superior rulers with respect to their inferiors in the realm of war and peace had the potential to be applied—by analogy— to a whole range of relations among persons and peoples. Inviting his students to see the law and jurisprudence differently—as a spectrum of power rather than a hierarchy of authority—he encouraged them to question long-held assumptions underpinning feudal-sovereignty.[7] Moreover, if new theories could render all legitimate rulers, secular and spiritual, as equivalent in rights, then it stood to reason that the same applied to those subjected to their jurisdictions. If, in other words, the foundational categories within Roman law, which were understood as reflecting universal and timeless principles by humanists like Alciati, rendered all sovereigns—feudal and otherwise—as equals in the realm of war and peace, then would it not also make all subjects and citizens of empires, kingdoms, or *civitas* equal as well?

Raising such questions—both directly and indirectly—within the interlocking and overlapping contexts of territorial consolidation, the Italian Wars, the Protestant and Catholic Reformations, and European Expansion had the potential to destabilize the foundations and justifications for power and

6 The year 1492 is stated because the Italian Wars followed on the heels of the Reconquest of Granada, the Expulsion of the Jews from Spain, and the onset of European incursion into Africa as well as the Atlantic and Indian Oceans on an unprecedented scale, which, when combined, played into how the Italian Wars unfolded.

7 The amalgamation feudal-sovereignty refers to the blurred boundaries and shifting understanding of power in this period. It captures both dependence and independence in a radically shifting world that was emerging in the early-sixteenth century. For a discussion of the blurred lines between feudalism and sovereignty, which also draws on the work of sixteenth-century humanist jurisprudence, see Davies, *Periodization and Sovereignty*.

authority that not only elevated some above others based on birth and office (elected and inherited) but also on the basis of religion, wealth, and culture (as well as age, gender, hue, and geography). The point here is not, of course, that legal humanists argued that all markers of difference—political, economic, or otherwise—were meaningless, nor that they implied that such markers should be eradicated from society wholesale. Rather, Alciati and his peers, Budé and Zasius, effectively called all manner of inequalities embedded in the *ius commune* into question and offered a vision of society in which a more elastic and pliable conception of *ius gentium*, as a repository of universal rights and obligations shared by all persons and peoples, could serve as a check against the exercise of arbitrary power, grounded in feudal customs, relationships, and laws, that justified the domination and subjection of some to ensure the liberties and freedoms of others.

In so doing, Alciati offered his students and readers an understanding of the basis and limits of political and legal authority that fundamentally challenged and, in some cases, rejected traditional hierarchies of power at precisely the moment that new kinds of city-, territorial-, and empire- states were emerging within and beyond Europe. Thus, rather than explore how and why *ius* was an expression of natural law in his *De iustitia et iure* lecture, Alciati chose to explain how and why *ius*, as a fundamental right held by all persons and peoples, was anchored in *ius gentium*. This required, at base, an understanding that any moral authority within *ius gentium* had emerged directly from *ius*, in its most rudimentary form, rather than through the lens and apparatus of a full-fledged theory of justice.

To this end, Alciati arranged his lecture thematically around three discrete, but analogous and familiar scenarios where *ius*—as the right to meet force with force—was exercised, namely in homicide (self-defense and commissioned), war (defensive and offensive), and dueling (recompense and satisfaction). This emphasis on force enabled Alciati to articulate a theory of universal jurisprudence in which the category of *ius gentium*, and the practices that fell under it, demarcated various types of rulers (e.g., kings, emperors, princes, dukes, and republics) as equivalent within the realm of rights, even if they retained markers of difference in the field of politics. As important, Alciati's understanding of *ius gentium* echoed beyond his lecture and into his treatises on dueling as well as in select *Emblems* to reach audiences well beyond the universities where he taught. Together, they reveal that Alciati's illumination of the limits of majesty (*majestas*; *majeste*) and the attributes of *imperium* led him to anticipate some of the most salient features and principles of modern sovereignty (*sovereinete*) that were bounded by—and grounded in—the historical authority of *ius gentium*.

2 Changing the Subject: Alciati's Radical Departure from His Humanist Peers

Studying law amid the Italian Wars, Alciati's students—whether in Italy or in France—did not need a definition-by-definition explanation of the first title of the *Digest* or an understanding of how and why the scholastic Doctors failed to understand aspects of basic terms and ideas (Budé). Furthermore, they did not need to engage in logical supposition, historical imagination, or theoretical interpretation to decipher the principles embedded within it in order to reform local statutes, laws, and customs (Zasius). What they required, instead, was an understanding of why, despite sharing the same foundations, *ius* and *ius gentium* effected different ends and operated in different domains. Indeed, they had to be able to apprehend why *ius gentium* served as a marker of equality and a cache of rights between states, while also representing the sinew that connected natural law to civil law and, by extension, private and public law within states.[8]

Hence, rather than open his lecture by defining justice or by explaining the tripartite division between natural law, *ius gentium*, and civil law, Alciati began with Hermogenian's definition preserved by the Byzantine compilers in D.1.1.5:

> As of a consequence of this *ius gentium*, wars were introduced, nations differentiated, kingdoms founded, properties individuated, estate boundaries settled, buildings put up, and commerce established, including contracts of buying and selling and letting and hiring (except for certain contractual elements established through *ius civile*).[9]

Framing his lecture with this definition suggests four things. First, that Alciati likely assumed—given his high expectations for his students and readers—that his audience was already aware of (if not well versed in) the other definitions in the first title, and even that the most astute among them were already familiar with Budé's and Zasius' interpretations of basic terms and fundamental ideas within their treatment of the first book and title of the *Digest*. Second, that he agreed with his humanist peers that *ius* was both an objective measure of justice (what is good and fair, conjoined) and an attribute—or

8 Although the former was at the heart of his lecture, the latter was expressed more directly in his short treatise on *Bona Fides*, also well as through a series of discrete, but related, examples that were also represented in a few of his *Emblems*. See Appendix to this volume.

9 D 1.1.5. For an in-depth discussion of on Hermogenian's definition see Kaser, *Ius gentium*.

faculty—of man *qua* man (as a marker of man's dignity and universal inherent rights and obligations), and therefore could be used to critique civil laws and civil authorities that missed the mark of justice. Third, that even if he agreed with some aspects of Budé's and Zasius' understanding of *ius gentium*, he did not accept their interpretations wholesale. By invoking this definition of *ius gentium*, Alciati signaled his break from Zasius by informing his students that if they wished to truly understand the relation between *ius* and *ius gentium* as well as *ius gentium* and *iustitia* (justice), then it was necessary to tend more carefully to what followed from it rather than from whence it originated. Otherwise, one might conclude that *ius gentium* was a type of natural law and thereby a direct expression, albeit muffled, of justice rather than something that could be used when placed in its proper context in order to amplify it.

Finally, Alciati's choice to frame his lecture with *ius gentium* indicated that his attention would reside on the rights of war and peace. As such, he reinforced the promise that he had set forth in his orations and other published works: to offer a practical understanding of the aspects of Roman law to his readers and students that they could use to help navigate and mitigate a world rife with uncertainty and insecurity. At the same time, it revealed his intention to use this lecture to contribute to ongoing debates, as framed by his Italian predecessors, about the scope, nature, and limits of political and legal authority between competing powers across the Italian peninsula.[10] It indicated, in other words, his desire to take Bartolus' and Baldus' treatment of *ius gentium* to task in ways that his humanist counterparts, writing from beyond a distinctly Italian context, could not. This choice also indicated that—despite employing similar methods and sharing some ideas and vocabulary—his interpretations of *ius* and *ius gentium* would no sooner stand as a culmination or synthesis of Budé's or Zasius' ideas than their interpretations could have anticipated his. Different contexts called for different emphases, understandings, and interpretations of justice and right.

10 Walter Ullman, *A History of Political Thought: The Middle Ages* (New York: Penguin, 1965); Ernst Kantorowicz, *The King's Two Bodies: A Study in Mediaeval Political Theology* (Princeton, NJ: Princeton University Press, 1967); Pennington, *The Prince and the Law*; David Abulafia, *The Western Mediterranean Kingdoms, 1200–1500: The Struggle for Dominion* (New York: Longman, 1997); Ryan, "Bartolus Of Sassoferrato and Free Cities"; Canning, *The Political Thought of Baldus*; Canning, *Ideas of Power in the Late Middle Ages*; and Fasolt, *The Limits of History*.

3 The Trouble with *Imperium*: Alciati's Novel Departure from His Scholastic Predecessors

The stakes were high in challenging traditional accounts (Italian and otherwise) of how basic categories of Roman law either fit together or came into conflict. Indeed, disentangling *ius gentium* from natural law on the one hand and from justice on the other, as Alciati did, was at odds with the assumptions that had underpinned just war theory (*ius bellum iustum*) and, with it, distinctions that were central to medieval and early-modern political and legal thought, including the division between pure and mixed *imperium*.[11] After all, scholastic interpretations had underpinned debates about the foundations and extent of *imperium*, and, by extension, attempts to demarcate the boundary between licit and illicit violence, for centuries.

Although all rulers, large or small, effectively shared the same rights when it came to protecting the common good within their domains, they did not share the same rights vis-à-vis one another. For example, superior rulers held pure *imperium*, and thus had the right to wage both offensive and defensive wars *sui iuris*, whereas inferior rulers merely held mixed *imperium*. Because inferior rulers were *alieni iuris*, they were required to seek permission from their superiors to wage offensive wars—or at least be able to justify their actions after the fact. While there were many levels of inferior rulers within empires, kingdoms, and the Catholic Church, at the summit of each stood a superior who claimed to be subject to none but God within their own domain—and, in some cases, even beyond it.

Determining precisely who was *sui iuris* proved to be an extraordinarily complicated task, even for legal experts.[12] There was no consensus as to which ruler was wholly independent from others, particularly when it applied to the relations between secular and spiritual princes. Likewise, there were no ready

11 Russell, *The Just War*; Jonathan Barnes, "The Just War," in *The Cambridge History of Later Medieval Philosophy: From the Rediscovery of Aristotle to the Disintegration of Scholasticism, 1100–1600*, eds. Anthony Kenny, Eleonore Stump, Jan Pinborg, and Norman Kretzmann (Cambridge: Cambridge University Press, 1982), 771–84; Jens Bartleson, "Double Binds: Sovereignty and the Just War Tradition," in *Sovereignty in Fragments*, 81–95; James Turner Johnson, "Then and Now: Medieval Conception of Just War Versus Recent Portrayals of the Just War Idea," in *Medieval Foundations of International Relations*, 117–31; and Skinner, *Foundations of Modern Political Thought. Volume 1*.

12 Walter Ullman, *Law and Politics in the Middle Ages: An Introduction to the Sources of Medieval Political Ideas* (Ithaca, NY: Cornell University Press, 1975); Tierney, *The Idea of Natural Rights*; Canning, *The Political Thought of Baldus*; Pennington, *The Prince and the Law*; Fasolt, *The Limits of History*; and Maiolo, *Medieval Sovereignty*.

means to determine how and why those subject to the authority of one superior, viz., the pope, were not equally bound to the authority of another, viz., the Holy Roman Emperor or the kings of France, Spain, and England. With no clear line of demarcation between spiritual and temporal authority, attempts by scholars to provide a systematic account as to who had *imperium*—and what kind—ultimately produced a tangled web of discordant opinions, arguments, and theories that mirrored and, in some cases, amplified conflicts among those who insisted that they alone were entirely independent of the power of another.

Distinctly juridical debates about the source and limits of *imperium*, pure and mixed, reached back to at least the Investiture Controversy, which began in the Germanies in 1076 before extending to France and England, and finally ending, for the Empire, with the Concordat of Worms in 1122. Due to their ambitions to shore up their respective authority, Pope Gregory VII and Holy Roman Emperor Henry IV came to blows—with words and armies—over the essential attributes of feudal-sovereignty, including the right to invest offices and collect tithes and taxes in areas under their jurisdiction; the right to punish and pardon their subjects (and, in the case of the Papacy, to relieve subjects of their obligations to a feudal lord); and the right to wage offensive and defensive wars to maintain their prerogatives within their domains.[13]

One aspect of the dispute between Gregory VII and Henry IV centered on who held *imperium* over whom. Was, for example, the emperor subject to the pope's authority, or vice versa? To whom did lesser rulers and commoners owe their allegiance when their secular and spiritual leaders came into direct conflict? Could the pope, as the spiritual leader of Latin Christendom, depose the emperor for refusing to bend to his will? Could an emperor take up arms against a pope when, by exerting his authority in secular matters, he affronted the Holy Roman Emperor's regalian rights? These questions, and many others, affected what Berman called the first legal revolution, which saw all sides in the dispute—regardless of whether it extended to realms beyond the empire and outlasted the original protagonists—attempting to settle questions about the nature, scope, and limit of authority by seeking precedents in Roman, canon, customary, and feudal laws, traditions, and statutes.[14]

It was during this controversy that a copy of Justinian's *Digest* was 'found' in Pisa; a copy that prompted the systematic study of Roman law, first among

13 For a more detailed discussion of this dispute and its impact on the history and development of the Western legal tradition see Chapter 1 of this volume, especially *Reform, Revolution, & Rediscovery*.

14 Berman, *Law and Revolution I*.

scholars in Italy and then across Latin Christendom, with the creation of the first universities in the *Regnum Italicum* since the fall of Rome.[15] Serving as centers of legal studies, these new universities (beginning in Bologna, which claims its lineage reaches back to 1088) became focal points for the intensive study of canon law as well. In each case, students and teachers alike applied similar scholastic methods to bring the principles and ideas underpinning both Roman and canon law into concord or, failing that, to be able to explain their divergences.[16] These bodies of law were then used to help reform, or substantiate, the shared principles within existing customary laws (written and unwritten), including those that organized and legitimized feudal hierarchies and obligations. The combination of various aspects of Roman, canon, customary, and feudal law generated a new *ius commune*—or what Manlio Bellomo referred to as the common law of Europe—which was shared, to varying degrees, among all peoples within Latin Christendom.[17] Over the span of a century and in the wake of competing claims for *imperium*, scholars, notaries, and jurists (secular and sacred) created a legal framework that came to serve as the endoskeleton of a so-called Western legal tradition.

The scholarship by historians and political scientists that explores the complex history of medieval state- and city-state formation, along with the distinct attributes of feudal-sovereignty, is extensive, and thus can offer a far more engaged and nuanced account of disputes over *imperium*—mixed and pure, both in and beyond the eleventh century—than can be provided here.[18] Nevertheless, for our purposes, it is essential to remember that conflicts over *imperium* among emperors and popes as well as among a full spectrum of secular rulers continued to be marked by violence, ambiguities, incongruities, and confusions long after the Concordat of Worms was concluded in 1122. Moreover, from the twelfth century onward, university-trained jurists and lawyers were increasingly called upon to help disentangle a web of overlapping obligations and authorities—secular, sacred, and customary—that permeated all levels of society.[19]

15 Berman, *Law and Revolution I*; Grendler, *The Universities of the Italian Renaissance*; and Brundage, *The Medieval Origins of the Legal Profession.*

16 For a more detailed discussion of the development and application of scholastic methods to the study of Roman law see Chapter 1 of this volume, especially *Modus Docendi.*

17 Bellomo, *The Common Legal Past of Europe*; Padoa-Schioppa, *A History of Law in Europe*; and Herzog, *A Short History of European Law.*

18 See note 3 in Chapter 5 of this volume.

19 For a discussion of such instances, in the development of modern political and legal thought, see Skinner, *The Foundations of Modern Political Thought. Volume I*; Berman,

In their attempts to clarify who was subordinate to whom and why, jurists—lay and ecclesiastical—constructed a complex apparatus of conflicting theories of state (feudal, dynastic, administrative, etc.) that became increasingly incomprehensible to those who lacked formal training in Roman and canon law. Consequently, as the apparatus grew, so too did the need for rulers to seek the advice of experts to help them to implement these new legal frameworks in order to centralize and administer their domains.[20] To that end, many jurists used ideas, precedents, and structures from Justinian's *corpus* to rationalize and legitimize hierarchies of power that were alien to Byzantium and Ancient Rome. The fact that they did so, of course, is not surprising; after all, it made their specialized knowledge relevant and practical beyond a small circle of experts within the universities. What was surprising—due to its novelty at the time—was the extent to which some of the most powerful rulers of the age increasingly sought the advice, aid, and approval of these scholars (especially Doctors of Roman law) to shore up the legitimacy of their claims and to shape their legacy.[21] This not only elevated the status of the law faculties and the universities but also infused the dynastic and customary titles of emperor, kings, and princes with legal authority that reached well beyond customary practices and collective memory.

The demand for university-trained jurists and lawyers grew as attempts to ground authority in precedent, not simply force, increased throughout Latin Christendom. Legal scholars—canon and civil—had a notable and distinctive influence on diplomacy among and between popes, emperors, and kings on the one hand, and a direct impact on administration and governance within kingdoms, empires, and the church on the other. Consequently, as these university-trained jurists were called on to apply legal theory to solve political problems, the questions that shaped the study and teaching of law in the

Law and Revolution I & II; Black, *Political Thought in Europe*; Pennington, *The Prince and the Law*; Fasolt, "Visions of Order in the Canonists and Civilians"; Fasolt, *The Limits of History*; Tierney, *The Idea of Natural Rights*; Maiolo, *Medieval Sovereignty;* Canning, *Ideas of Power in the Late Middle Ages*; Pagden, *Lords of All the World*; Davies, *Periodization and Sovereignty*, and Koskenniemi, *To the Uttermost Parts of the Earth*, especially Chapter 1.

20 An example of this occurred at the Diet of Roncaglia, wherein Holy Roman Emperor Frederick Barbarossa (r. 1155–1190) sought the counsel and expertise of four jurists from Bologna to reclaim his regalian rights over Italy and thereby assert his sovereignty. This is explored in detail within Pennington, *The Prince and the Law*; Canning, *The Political Thought of Baldus;* and Maiolo, *Medieval Sovereignty.*

21 This is explored within Berman, *Law and Revolution I & II*; Black, *Political Thought in Europe*; Pennington, *The Prince and the Law*; Fasolt, "Visions of Order in the Canonists and Civilians"; Tierney, *The Idea of Natural Rights;* and Brundage, *The Medieval Origins of the Legal Profession.*

universities became more and more political. The fact that there was such a symbiotic relationship between law and politics should remind us, as modern readers, that (just as today) any boundaries that existed between political and legal thought (and action) were irregular, unstable, and indistinct throughout the late medieval and early modern eras.

This was especially the case across the Italian peninsula, which was the epicenter for the struggle for sovereignty among European rulers, from the eleventh to the mid-sixteenth centuries. Rooted in this context, even as he had promised otherwise, Alciati's *De iustitia et iure* lecture was influenced far more by local and regional politics and the interpretations of it by his scholastic predecessors than by Roman history. Given that most of his students and readers would have been quite familiar with the contours of local and regional history—from the start of Barbarossa's invasions in 1154 through the onslaught of the Italian Wars in 1494, and the perpetuation of them in the early-sixteenth century—he was free to invoke and engage aspects of this history without the burden of providing a narrative. Instead, Alciati used his lecture on the first title of the *Digest* as an opportunity to weigh-in on well-worn debates about *imperium* and to recast aspects of *ius gentium* in relation to *ius* and justice. In so doing, Alciati made a careful and nuanced argument, whereby he slowly led his students through a series of interlocking examples to demonstrate how precarious—and even futile—some of the distinctions and categories that structured traditional jurisprudence were, especially those concerning the rights of war and peace.

Drawing on a wide range of sources, including Accursius, Bartolus, and Baldus, Alciati deliberately and carefully assembled the scaffolding that supported his analysis of the relation between *ius* and *ius gentium*. However, instead of spending a lot of time or effort in placing the ideas and interpretations of these jurists in historical and textual context, he simply used them to advance his own argument—invoking them to mark points of departure rather than treating their arguments in full. Keeping this in mind is important for two reasons. First, Alciati frequently chastised others in his orations and published works for wresting ideas, words, definitions, etc., out of context because doing so resulted in errors steeped in anachronism, incongruity, and equivocation. Second, by ignoring his own advice, he effectively signaled his intention to provide a novel interpretation of this title rather than to merely restore the text to its original or to correct errors in scholastic glosses and commentaries dedicated to it. As such, whether he got Bartolus (or others) right is far less important than how he used them to mark out and to mask his innovations. The same goes for his methods in approaching both the *Digest* and commentaries on it; by approaching the texts as if they revealed a historical progression rather than a logical truth, he offered his students an understanding of *imperium* that was dependent on a parity of rights (linear), and not on a hierarchy of authority (vertical) shared by persons, peoples, and states.

4 *Jus* as Necessity in Action

Instead of following in the footsteps of his peers, who had begun to plot a new course through the first title of the *Digest*, Alciati opted to lead his students down the well-worn path of scholastic jurisprudence. He did so, in no small part, to demonstrate that no matter how straightforward a concept or an explanation might seem at first glance, when one looked at it more closely it often revealed more confusion than clarity.[22] In this respect, the first third of Alciati's lecture bears a closer resemblance in method to Petrarch's meandering *Ascent of Mont Ventoux* than to a typical lecture on law. Just as Petrarch, while seeking an easier route to the summit, followed imprints that only seemed to frustrate his efforts and require him to back track and begin anew, Alciati ushered his students and readers down a series of blind alleys and dead ends to emphasize the necessity of approaching the fundamental ideas within the *Digest* from a different direction and in a different manner. Given Alciati's appeal to what had become—by the sixteenth century—a typical trope or tactic in humanist rhetoric, namely, to present a seemingly insurmountable obstacle as something that could not be conquered without unyielding effort, his choice to mirror the same journey as Petrarch's in his *De iustitia et iure lecture* is not surprising. What is surprising is that Alciati treated aspects of just war theory as the main obstructions that had to be overcome; or, as alluded to in his Avignon *Oration*, the glaucoma that had to be surgically removed.

At the outset of this lecture, Alciati drew his students' attention to the fact that, even in light of the clarity of Hermogenian's words (*ad fontes*), when Bartolus treated it he initially chose to focus on what lay prior to *ius gentium* (*ab initio*) rather than on its specific consequences.[23] Rejecting Bartolus'

22 A case in point is the extensive scholarship produced by historians and political and legal theorists about the history and development of natural law, *ius*, and *ius gentium* from the ancient to the modern era, precisely because what the terms *ius* and *ius gentium* meant varied by context as well as by the design and intent of those who used them.

23 Alciati, "De iustitia et iure, lecture," col. 1, 'Ex hoc iure. Notat ex hoc textu Bartolu quod dictio Ex, principium temporis denotat. Sed certe istud non videtur, quod orobetur ex hac lege.' For a fascinating (and definitive) discussion of Bartolus' political and legal theory in relation to the cities in Northern Italy see Ryan, "Bartolus of Sassoferrato and Free Cities."

underlying assumption that *ius gentium* was primeval rather than a product of history, Alciati nevertheless used some of his interpretations to set the parameters of his analysis of *ius gentium*, and thus to demonstrate to his students the perils of abstracting cause from consequence and to show them the extent to which traditional interpretations of *ius gentium*, *ius*, and *imperium* were mired in confusion, ambiguities, logical inconsistencies, and moral suppositions. Even so, Alciati employed a straw man argument when he set out to explore Bartolus' choice—despite there being no explicit link in the original definition—to use Hermogenian's statement "As of a consequence of this *ius gentium*, wars were introduced …" to distinguish between proximate and remote causes of violence and war.[24] Although to modern readers (and perhaps even to Alciati's students) the distinction between proximate and remote cause might seem like a mere attempt at interpreting the definition through Aristotelian categories, or even a matter of semantics, it had direct implications for differentiating between licit and illicit violence, and, by logical—and moral—supposition, just and unjust war. Alciati's choice to start here, moreover, hinted to his students (and his readers) that the long-debated question of *imperium* in relation to the Italian peninsula was foremost on his mind.

At issue for Alciati was that, by ripping Hermogenian's words out of their original context, jurists were able to attribute a moral resonance to them that was otherwise absent. Not only was such an approach anachronistic but it also obscured the fact that not all licit actions were moral and, inversely, not all immoral actions were illicit. Consequently, arguments that anchored their claims for moral authority on the origins of particular actions or institutions tended to do little more than to reinforce these assumptions. If, for example, one set out to determine whether a war was just or unjust without first asking if war could even be explored in those moral terms, then any and all attempts to clarify the source of the war, including distinguishing between proximate and remote causes, enabled one to reaffirm that there was such a thing as a just war and that its cause was what made it just. The latter, not surprisingly,

24 Not only is there no mention of the relation between proximate and remote cause in Hermogenian's definition (D.1.1.5.) but also there is no explicit or direct link to the distinction between proximate and remote causes of violence in Bartolus' commentary on this first title of the *Digest*. For Bartolus' discussion see "De iustitia & iure, Rea.," in *Partem digesti veteris, Bartoli A Saxoferrato commentari* (Basel: Episcopius, 1588); and "De iustia et iure, Rubr." in *Bartolus a Saxoferrato super authenticis, & instit*, (Venice, 1580).

was directly linked to identifying who had pure *imperium* and, in turn, could yield evidence for a just cause for a just war.[25]

Informed by St. Augustine's discussion in *De civitate Dei* (*The City of God* (426 CE)), debates concerning just war within traditional jurisprudence tended to focus on two questions: (1) who had the right to wage war (*ius ad bellum*); and (2) how wars should be conducted (*ius in bello*). Although they were intrinsically linked, it was the former question, more so than the latter, that tended to draw medieval jurists' attention, not least because many were tasked with providing the moral and legal justifications for wars conducted by their rulers—ranging from disputes over dynastic claims to crusades. As a result, Alciati's efforts to depart from traditional arguments about just war—especially in relation to *imperium*—hinged on determining who had the right of war and who did not. Although some held, as Frederic J. Baumgartner tells us, that "the medieval theory of imperial title with its claim to universal jurisdiction included the concept that the emperor could neither declare war nor have war declared against him, because no other ruler was his equal," most medieval jurists, according to Antony Black, agreed that all *principes* (princes/rulers) had the right to do so. Indeed, Black explained, the dominant interpretation in medieval jurisprudence was "that the declaration of just war belonged to *any autonomous ruler* on the grounds that he had no superior to whom to appeal in pursuance of his claim."[26] The idea that not all such rulers were *sui iuris*, and thus had the right to wage war on their own accord, re-entrenched feudal hierarchies and distinctions between superiors and inferiors—between those who held pure *imperium* and those who did not—in the realm of *ius gentium*. In doing so, jurists also attributed wars waged by superior princes moral authority, making their actions practically unimpeachable.

Although more often implied rather than stated outright, the logic underpinning the above runs as follows. If wars were waged by those who had pure *imperium*, then the proximate and remote causes of the war—no matter if offensive or defensive—were grounded in their authority to conduct war, thus the war was just by definition, viz., precisely because the one who

25 The discussion of just and unjust war in the following section is informed by Black, *Political Thought in Europe*; Russell, *The Just War*; and Chris Covell, *The Law of Nations in Political Thought: A Critical Survey from Vitoria to Hegel* (New York: Palgrave McMillan, 2009).

26 Frederic J. Baumgartner, "Declaring War in Sixteenth-Century France," *The Journal of the Historical Society* (Boston, MA) 7, no. 1 (March 2007): 85–110, 94; and Black, *Political Thought in Europe*, 90. *Emphasis added.* For an in-depth analysis of canonist and civilian discussions see Russell, *The Just War*. For an account that ties the medieval interpretations to contemporary debates see Bartleson, "Double Binds: Sovereignty and the Just War Tradition."

commissioned it had the right to commission it. For superior rulers, when they ordered their inferiors—those who only held mixed *imperium*—to conduct war on their behalf, their command was deemed as just, and thus so too was the war. It is more complicated, however, when jurists shifted their attention to rulers who only held mixed *imperium*, and thus only had the right to wage defensive wars *sui iuris* and not offensive ones.

Attempts to determine whether an offensive war waged by an inferior ruler could be classified as just on account of a remote cause, rather than a proximate one, could give rise to a series of loaded questions with dangerous implications. Should, for example, an offensive war initiated by a ruler with mixed *imperium* be deemed illicit by default or was such an assessment open to debate after the fact? If such an offensive war was deemed illicit, then did that also mean that the war was unjust? What if it was waged in the name of God or the common good? Could it, after it was concluded, be deemed necessary, licit, and just? If the answer was yes, then by whose authority and on what grounds? If the answer was no, then did that, in turn, mean that such wars, even if cloaked in moral intentions and aimed at moral ends, were unjust? Put another way, could the consequence of the war and the ends to which the war was waged render the cause less important if those with mixed *imperium* waged offensive wars on what they deemed to be moral grounds? Did might make right?

Given how tightly interlocked such questions were, and the extent to which their responses could challenge the fundamental suppositions that underpinned *imperium* and just war theory, jurists tended to offer answers that reinforced the hierarchy of feudal-sovereignty they were deployed to illuminate rather than question it. Yet, while the assumption that all licit wars were just wars and all unjust wars were illicit wars did not make sense to Alciati, it also did not reflect reality, especially when applied to the shifting alliances, offensive and defensive violence, and the rising status of inferior rulers, viz., those who held mixed *imperium* across Italy. Hence, if jurists and lawyers wanted to break free of the suppositions and circular reasoning that underpinned these traditional interpretations, then they would have to do so by asking new questions; instead of focusing on whether a specific war was just or unjust, they needed to shift their inquiry (as Alciati did) to explore whether such a determination was even useful.

Using the first part of his lecture to highlight the distinction between proximate and remote cause by Bartolus, Alciati then presented his argument about *imperium* by simply accenting the very first component, in sequence and time, of Hermogenian's definition of *ius gentium*. To do so, he utilized scholastic methods rather than humanist ones, especially when organizing his discussion by implicitly bringing Aristotle's four causes to bear on his interpretation.

Meanwhile, he left the material cause (*ius gentium*) aside, in favor of the formal cause (war). He did so to mark his departure from all of the Doctors, including Bartolus, who argued that exploring the efficient causes of war (proximate and remote) could illuminate its final cause or purpose, namely justice, and to altogether question the validity and veracity of just war theory in no uncertain terms. He did this in three interconnected ways over the course of his *De iustitia et iure* lecture.

First, in his discussion of homicide, Alciati alleged that Bartolus' conclusions about war and its relation to *ius gentium* rested on a false supposition, namely that there was a clear distinction to be made between proximate and remote causes of violence. Second, in his discussion of licit/illicit war, Alciati questioned whether such a distinction, even if it could be made, had any role to play in determining who had the right of war and, by extension, who had *imperium*. Third, by invoking brigandage and slavery, Alciati challenged the traditional assumption concerning how war and justice were related and, in the process, emphasized the centrality of *ius*—the subjective/inherent right to meet force with force, rather than an objective category of justice—in distinguishing between licit/legitimate and illicit/illegitimate violence. As it turned out, for Alciati, *ius* in the former sense was not only the material, formal, and efficient cause of *ius gentium* but also its final cause. In effect, protecting *ius* was the source of *ius gentium*, and therefore *ius gentium* legitimated—or justified—the exercise of *ius*.

Upon briefly highlighting the errors within scholastic jurisprudence, Alciati redirected his students' attention to an exploration of the meaning and significance of words (*ad fontes*) in context.[27] Utilizing his *extensio*, he examined Hermogenian's definition of *ius gentium* with recourse to Florentinus' understanding in D.1.1.3 that "the right to repel violent injuries. You see, it emerges from this law (*ius gentium*) that whatever a person does for his bodily security he can be held to have done rightfully."[28] Next, just as Zasius did, Alciati used the definition of force (*vis*) by Ulpian in D.43.16.27 to advance his own interpretation of *ius gentium*: "Cassius writes that it is permissible to repel force by force, and this right is conferred by nature. From this it appears, he says, that arms may be repelled by arms."[29] Linking all of the above highlighted the fact that all persons (as well as kingdoms, republics, empires, peoples) shared at least one right in common, across time and space. Indeed, the right to meet force with force, when necessary and even if it meant killing or destroying

27 Alciati, "De iustitia et iure," col. 2.

28 D.1.1.3.

29 D.43.16.27.

one's opponent, "originated from *ius gentium*. For such *ius* permitted anyone to ward off an injury."[30] Moving from persons to peoples, Alciati continued, "wars are started in order to ward off injury and protect ourselves and our property."[31] Therefore, the right to ward off injuries with force was "the proximate and the immediate cause of war."[32]

Without making any reference to, or gesture toward, assigning a remote cause either to self-defense (by persons) or war (by peoples), Alciati ultimately encouraged his students to consider the possibility that what lay prior to and followed from *ius gentium*—at least in terms of its most fundamental institution—were one and the same, namely *ius*. Expressed differently, the origin of war, viz., efficient cause, and the sake for which it was waged, viz., the final cause, were identical; each were grounded in the same universal right to preserve and protect life and property with force when necessary.[33] This did not mean, however, that the exercise of such rights by individuals was equivalent to the exercise of these rights by states. Among the most essential differences between the two was that the right of self-defense among persons was rooted in the moral authority of natural law, whereas the right of war among states was not. In essence, Alciati replaced Ulpian's trifurcation with a bifurcation. Rather than attempting to explain how natural law, *ius*, and *ius gentium* were related, Alciati offered an interpretation wherein the question as to how *ius* and natural law were connected was an entirely different question than how *ius* and *ius gentium* were related. This freed him from both Budé's conflation of *ius* and *ius gentium* and Zasius' interpretation of *ius gentium* as the fourth quality of natural law. Moreover, it enabled Alciati to argue that rulers not only had the right (*ius*) to defend against immediate danger (proximate cause) but they could also use force (*vis*) to attack potential threats to their security (remote cause). As a result, the parity of right that existed between persons mirrored the parity of force between rulers, yet not without significant distortions.

What is noteworthy here is the absence of any discussion of justice, dignity, or even natural law within Alciati's initial explanation of *ius gentium*; not because it set him apart from his scholastic predecessors but rather because it revealed his divergence from his humanist peers. Although Zasius also paired *vis* with *ius gentium* in his lecture on the same title of the *Digest*, he only did so after he explained that *ius* was justice in action and that *ius gentium* was

30 Alciati, "De iustitia et iure," col. 2.§.4, 'Ista vero propulsatio iniuriae orta est ex iure gentium, nam tale ius permisit, ut quilibet iniuriam propulsaret.'

31 Ibid, 'Et sic propulsatio iniurie est causa proxima, & immediata belli.'

32 Ibid.

33 Cf. Hobbes, *Leviathan* [1651], especially Chapter 13.

natural law in action. Moreover, his assertion that *ius* was justice in action was anchored in Budé's understanding of *ius* as a fundamental characteristic of man *qua* man, and therefore his dignity and an expression of objective justice. Even in light of the vast differences in interpretation between Budé and Zasius, they both nevertheless held that the moral authority of *ius gentium*, on account of its relation to *ius*, was rooted in natural law, which was, in turn, an expression of justice. The latter is partly how they were able to argue that total subjection (viz., abject slavery and servitude) was akin to tyranny, precisely because it violated one's dignity and *ius*—as a criterion of universal justice and as a universal and inherent right of all mankind. Yet, all of the above was missing from Alciati's *De iustitia et iure* lecture thus far. Even if we concede that he imparted some moral meaning to the right of self-defense by emphasizing the necessity to resist injury, as well as to preserve life and property, there is nothing in his discussion to suggest that *ius gentium* had moral content or moral authority, beyond his initial definition of *ius* as the right to meet force with force.

Keeping this absence in mind is essential, especially given the fact that Alciati's next task was to explain why, despite the fact that all persons and all people had the right to repel force with force, the right of war was not merely the right to self-defense. Before fleshing out the distinction between the two, however, Alciati approached the problem of remote and proximate cause from another perspective; first in relation to violence, then in relation to commerce. Rather than venturing an abstract understanding of justice, he emphasized the necessity to understand why and how *ius gentium* was grounded in the tangible necessity of *ius*.

5 Homicide, Commerce, and War: Meticulous Meditations on Proximate and Remote Cause

Using homicide to disentangle Bartolus' distinction between proximate and remote cause in relation to *ius gentium*, Alciati asked his students whether one person who commissioned another to kill a third person should be held as responsible for the act as the one who committed it.[34] In this scenario, the

---

34 Alciati, "De iustitia et iure," col. 3.§.8. This is an extensive discussion which begins with: 'Quod condemnato ex homicidio non prosit pax, ut non comprehendat eum, qui est condemnatus: quia mandavit fieri homicidium & haec opinio videtur magis aequa, pro qua facit, quia damnatus ex mandato homicidii ... Contrarium tamen puto esse verius: & sic, quod tale statutum compraehendat tam condemnatum ex homicidio, quam ex mandato homicidium.'

person who committed the act was the proximate cause of the murder, whereas the one who commissioned it was the remote cause. Alciati explained that even if the strict letter of civil law only required that the person who carried out the murder be punished, the person who solicited the act should also be held liable. After all, the deed would not have taken place without the order.[35] Who ordered the act and to what end, however, could complicate an otherwise straightforward determination as to whether such an act was deemed as just or unjust or, indeed, if the act had any moral significance at all.

If, for example, the person who solicited the homicide was not a ruler, and thus did not have the right to command such violence, then—no matter what excuses might be offered otherwise—the assassination would not only be illicit but it would also be unjust. It would be unjust because it was premeditated, and thus the result of a remote rather than proximate cause; it would be illicit because only rulers had *imperium*, viz., the right to command violence, lethal or otherwise. If the person who solicited the act was a ruler, then neither he nor his subject could be held culpable, given that a ruler had the right and responsibility to commission acts of violence—offensive and defensive—to preserve and protect his life, the safety of his subjects, and the security of his realm. This did not mean, however, that the ruler would not be held responsible for the order, as all rulers were responsible for their commands. Nor would it mean that the action was just. Indeed, the question as to whether a ruler's command or the assassin's actions were just would be irrelevant; what mattered was whether the command and actions were necessary.

If rulers did not have the ability to command others to exercise force in punishing criminals, putting down rebellions, and eliminating threats, then they could not fulfill their obligations to preserve and protect their subjects. Likewise, if those who were commissioned to perform such acts—ranging from executioners to soldiers—could not do so without fear of being punished, then rulers would be unable to provide stability and security for those who lived within their domains, which, in turn, existed as a consequence of *ius gentium*. The ability to wage war and—in keeping with Alciati's example—to authorize violence when necessary, was not only an expression of *ius gentium* but also a marker of *imperium* insofar as, once "nations were differentiated" and "kingdoms [were] founded," force could be used to preserve and protect both.[36] Here, the authority of *ius gentium* was not based on an objective sense

35 Alciati conveyed this more explicitly in *Emblem*: 174, The fault belongs alike to the wrongdoer and the persuader and *Emblem* 175, One sins, the other is punished. Appendix.

36 D.1.1.5.

of justice or natural law; instead, it was based on the exigency of *ius*—the right to meet force with force in order to protect and preserve oneself, one's family, community, subjects, and domains.[37] The exercise of *ius* by rulers (and those who acted on their command) was grounded, first and foremost, in necessity and not justice.

By implication, in the realm of *ius gentium*, attempts to determine whether one could commission assassinations, decree punishments, or order their subjects to war were not questions of justice, but rather questions of right. Efforts to distinguish the proximate and remote cause of such violence, whether in the form of punishment or war, necessitated a means to differentiate between those who had *imperium* and those who did not. Moreover, to discern who had *imperium* required the ability to determine who had the right to give an order. This also applied to the case of a commissioned homicide, which obscured rather than clarified the line between proximate and remote cause. Why? Whether or not the act was licit or illicit, or just or unjust, the person who commissioned the act and the person who committed it were equally relevant to what followed from it. This example enabled Alciati to suggest that no matter how promising Bartolus' focus on causes rather than consequences might seem at first sight, when explored through the lens of a commissioned homicide it led to a dead-end at best, and to a logical quagmire at worst.

To dig out of this morass, Alciati asked his students to think about the relationship between origins and consequences by turning their attention away from the extraordinary actions (homicide) and toward the ordinary ones (commerce). The same impulse that had driven jurists, including Bartolus, to explore violence and war through the lens of proximate and remote causes also led them to consider commerce—"including contracts of buying and selling and letting and hiring"—in the same manner.[38] Once again, rather than acknowledge that there was a historical sequence in which institutions emerged as a consequence of *ius gentium*, Bartolus and others appeared to assume that commerce, like *ius gentium*, was primeval. Rejecting this, Alciati's sought to demonstrate why reasoning, from consequence to cause, tended to introduce disparities, inconsistencies, and anachronisms into traditional jurisprudence from another vantage point. In this instance, rather than reach beyond the text to homicide, Alciati set out to unearth the embedded history within Hermogenian's definition, by excavating the meaning and significance of the sequence of his words.

37 Alciati, "De iustitia et iure," col. 2.§.4.

38 D.1.1.5.

Although initially signaling his intent to provide a logical proof, or syllogism, to support his claim "whatever is the cause of the cause is also the cause of the caused," Alciati ultimately offered his students a historical understanding of *ius gentium* that amplified the futility of viewing it through this lens of cause, proximate or remote.[39] He effected this sleight of hand by asserting, first, that the distinction between mine and thine was caused immediately by *ius gentium*, and second, that, over time, the individuation of property caused the establishment of commerce, viz., buying, selling, obligations and the like.[40] Yet, at first glance, one might assume that, on the basis of these statements, "*ius gentium* was the cause of commerce."[41] Put differently, if *ius gentium* was the immediate cause of the establishment of property, and property was the immediate cause of commerce, then it stood to reason that *ius gentium* was at least the remote cause of commerce. Such an assumption, however, would be wrong, Alciati asserted, because the supposed link between *ius gentium* and commerce was "present by accident in this case."[42] Commerce and *ius gentium* were not coextensive, nor was there a logical correlation between them. Commerce emerged over time from *ius gentium*, and *ius gentium* encompassed far more than commerce.

Even when Alciati followed Bartolus' meaning, rather than arguing against him by conceding that a certain kind of commerce could be considered as "substantially present" in *ius gentium* from the beginning, this did not change the fact that what followed reflected the progress of life—practices associated with commerce emerged from necessity.[43] Not only did arguing backwards, from commerce to *ius gentium*, imply that commerce emerged as a result of providence rather than by accident, but it also tended to diminish the scope and complexity of human actions and ingenuity. Pressing Alciati's point further, we might conclude that just as one cannot limit the scope and content of the genus of commerce with reference to the single species that falls under it, one cannot limit *ius gentium* by interpreting it through a single institution that followed from it. To do so, in either case, would take the consequence for cause,

39 Alciati, "De iustitia et iure," col. 4.§.13–15, 'quicquid est causa causae, est etiam causati: probatur hoc modo: Per ius gentium causatum est immediate meum & tuum: ex quo causato orta postea sunt commercia: scilicet emptiones & venditiones, & obligationes, & similia: & tamen hic dicitur, quod ius gentium causavit commercia …'

40 Ibid.

41 Ibid.

42 Ibid, §.16, 'Istam tamen regulam sane intellige, ut fallat in his, quae in causato insunt accidentaliter, nam illa non dicuntur orta ex causa causae: secus est, si insint substantialiter, & hoc modo intelligenda sunt, quae ponit Bartolus.'

43 Ibid.

rather than explore it on its own terms, and it would narrow the scope of *ius gentium* dramatically. By implication, it would also make it possible to conflate moral justifications for actions—like war or buying and selling—with the actions themselves, thereby funneling aspects of *ius gentium* through moral categories that were, for Alciati, otherwise alien to it.

Unlike Zasius, who argued that *ius gentium* was a form of natural law, and thus had to account for why the institutions that followed from it had less or more justice, Alciati did not make much of the distinction between primary and secondary *ius gentium*, beyond using it to mark his departure from traditional jurisprudence, within his lecture. It was not necessary for him to make such a distinction, in no small part, because he did not claim that *ius gentium* was an expression or quality of natural law, and, as such, he did not have to explain why institutions that fell under *ius gentium* seemed to be in direct violation of natural law. Nor did Alciati, like Budé, set out to provide an explanation of justice and all that followed from it. As such, Alciati aptly directed his students away from exploring the morality—or lack thereof—of *ius gentium*, and explored it, instead, through the lens of necessity. Buying, selling, and leasing were neither inherently good nor bad. They were simply necessary; they enabled persons and peoples to live in mutual company and to exchange goods within and across societies that existed as a consequence of *ius gentium*.

Moving from private concerns and day-to-day activities (commerce) to public affairs and extraordinary events, Alciati shifted his attention to questioning the moral assumptions accorded to Hermogenian's definition in relation to war. In so doing, he used two opinions within Accursius' *Gloss*—just as Bartolus did in his commentary on this title—to set up his point of departure from scholastic jurisprudence. The first opinion, as Alciati explained it, anchored the distinction between a licit and illicit war in the sequence of causes—legitimate war followed immediately from (primary) *ius gentium*. In contrast, illicit war followed from man's subsequent actions (viz., secondary *ius gentium* in the *Gloss*).[44] Here, the remote cause of war stemmed from man's wickedness and thus was inherently unjust, which implied, in turn, that licit wars—because they were anchored in *ius gentium*—were just. It also implied that only one side in any given conflict waged a legitimate war,

44 Alciati, "De iustitia et iure," col. 5.§.24–25, 'quod bella licita sint orta ex iure gentium immediate: illicita vero occasionaliter, & sic mediate. nam eo ipso, quod datur ex una parte bellum licitum, ex alia est illicitum, quod ideo est illicitum: quia ita mens hominium est, vt ad malum semper prona sit.'; and 'bella licita importet causam proximam: quo ad illicita, importet remotam.'

and thus had a 'just cause' that followed immediately from (primary) *ius gentium*. The second opinion held that "all wars were permitted according to *ius gentium*."[45] Hence, if one wished to determine whether a war was just, they needed to look at its outcomes, which assumed that the consequence of any war could reveal the intentions behind it. Attention to the ends of war, in other words, could illuminate whether the war was just or unjust. If a war was waged to increase power and wealth, then it could be deemed unjust. If, on the other hand, a war was waged to simply ensure safety and security, then it could be deemed just.

In the latter example, it did not matter if the war was offensive or defensive. What did matter were the intentions of those who waged it. Therefore, despite framing all wars as licit, this second opinion nevertheless held that there was a strict dichotomy between just and unjust wars just as the first opinion did. The problem with both of these opinions, for Alciati, was that they not only failed to acknowledge that wars were comparable to legal disputes in which both sides pressed their claims equally—and justly—until the case was concluded, but they also evaded the most important question that needed to be considered.[46] This question was whether or not the party conducting a war—no matter if it was aimed at expanding their domain or defending it—had the right to do so.[47] These opinions neglected to entertain whether the parties concerned had *locus standi*, viz., the right to press their case by arms (rulers) or by law (persons), in the first place.

Alciati preferred the second opinion—that "all wars were permitted according to *ius gentium*"—to the first, even though it did not address the fact that no matter why a particular war occurred, it would always be just in the eyes of those who were commanded to fight it. Or, as Alciati put it, "war conducted by a *princeps*, whether from an unjust cause or from a just one, [was] always

45 Ibid, col. 5.§.26, 'qoud imo de iure gentium omnia bella errant licita.'

46 Ibid, col. 6.§.28, 'Sed in iudicio, quando lis contestata est, & partes iurarunt de calumnia, quam vis necessarium sit, quod altera iniuste litiget: tamen ex quo lex praesumit utranque partem esse in bona fide, ideo dicuntur iuste litigare interim donec iudicetur. Sic in nostro casu bella ipsa sunt ex utraque parte licita, ratione dubietatis. Unde potest sic distingui, quod autem sumus in dubio, quae pars foveat iustitiam: & tunc utraque pars dicitur iuste litigare, ratione dubietatis.'

47 Much of what follows in Alciati's discussion was also at the center of Alberico Gentili's discussion of just war in his *De iure belli libri tres*, published between 1588 and 1589. Whereas Alciati's discussion has been overlooked, modern scholars have identified Gentili's theory as groundbreaking, and even revolutionary. See Koskenniemi, *To the Uttermost Parts of the Earth*, especially Chapter 3, for a recent example of the latter.

called just as regards [his] peoples."[48] This would be the case, he continued, even if an emperor's actions were deemed unjust by his enemies. Although this was not a particularly innovative stance, the implications of his shift in perspective, from enemies to subjects, were insofar as this discussion was concerned. If wars conducted by emperors—and other superior rulers—were licit per *ius gentium*, and if all the wars waged by rulers were just to their subjects, then all wars were not only licit but they were also—in following the language of traditional jurisprudence—just. Yet, herein lay the problem for Alciati. If all wars were just because all wars were licit, then any attempt to draw the line between just and unjust wars, and with it the whole body of jurisprudence that supported just war theory, was not simply flawed, but nonsensical. Further, attempting to classify a war as just or unjust also carried with it moral distinctions that, while essential to civil and especially criminal law, had no bearing in the realm of *ius gentium*, and therefore no bearing on war or who had the right to wage it.

Recall, for example, Alciati's comments on homicide, wherein he made it clear that responsibility and culpability, although related, were not the same thing. If the person who solicited the act was not a ruler, then he was as accountable for the deed as the person who committed it; after all, the homicide would not have occurred unless it had been ordered. Each party used unauthorized violence to accomplish its desired ends, both committing an injustice by perpetrating a crime. If, however, the person who commanded another to kill a third were a ruler, then—despite being responsible for the killing—neither he nor the assassin would be guilty of committing a crime. The ruler had the right to authorize such violence to preserve and project his domain. This scenario, in which no injustice was committed because no crime was committed, was analogous to war; the ruler had the right (and responsibility) to authorize violence and was responsible for the outcome, yet in neither case was he nor his subjects guilty of breaking the law (civil or moral). Indeed, all acted in accordance with the customs and conventions that followed from *ius gentium*, whereby all wars, waged by those who had the right to do so, were licit. Nevertheless, the analogy breaks down, once again, when applied to the question of whether a war was just because the question of justice in relation to war elided the more pressing concern of how to ascertain who had the right of war and who did not.

48 Alciati, "De iustitia et iure," col. 5.§.26–27, 'Confirmo istam opinion, nam bellum inductum a principe sive a causa iniusta, sive iusta, semper dicitur iustum quo ad populos & quo ad effectus liciti belli.'

6 Slavery as a Marker of *Imperium*

For Alciati, determining whether a ruler had *imperium*, viz., the right and responsibility to wage war against external threats and to punish internal ones, required attention to two criteria, above all.[49] One criterion was the extent to which those claiming *imperium* were recognized—implicitly or explicitly—as legitimate rulers by others who held it; the other was the extent to which rulers exercised other rights and customs that followed from *ius gentium*, including enslaving captives in the realm of war and exercising clemency in the realm of civil society. Violent acts committed at the hands of or by the commands of those who did not fit either criteria were illicit and unjust, whereas violent acts committed at the hands of or by the commands of those who fit at least one of the criteria above were neither illicit nor unjust. This did not mean, of course, that rulers could act or direct others to act with impunity. It did mean, however, that, when it came to war, legitimacy was grounded in right, even when what followed from *ius gentium* was not always deemed as morally good or just. Carefully laying the ground for the novel aspects of his argument, Alciati had already provided his students with the tools they needed to comprehend why justice and right diverged from one another—at precisely the point that one might expect them to coalesce—in his initial discussion of commerce; these were the same tools that he then used when exploring slavery as a consequence of war, and thus a product of history and a marker of *imperium*.[50]

In terms of understanding commerce as a historical rather than a moral phenomenon, Alciati emphasized that there was no direct or immediate link between *ius gentium* and commerce. Moreover, *ius gentium* and commerce stood at opposite ends of Hermogenian's definition, "as of a consequence of this *ius gentium*, wars were introduced, nations differentiated, kingdoms founded, properties individuated, estate boundaries settled, buildings put up, and commerce established, including contracts of buying and selling and letting and hiring."[51] Therefore, if we read this definition the way that Alciati and his humanist counterparts suggest we should, as a historical account of

49 Recall D.2.1.3: ULPIAN, Duties of Quaestor, book 2: *Imperium* is simple or mixed. To have simple *imperium* is to have the power of the sword to punish the wicked, also called potestas. *Imperium* is mixed where it also carries jurisdiction to grant *bonomm possessio*. Such jurisdiction includes the power to appoint a judge.

50 For an excellent discussion of the relation between the markers of sovereignty and our understanding of the modern state see Denis Baranger, "The Apparition of Sovereignty," in *Sovereignty in Fragments*, 47–63.

51 D.1.1.5.

the development of society and the progress of life, then it would be anachronistic to suppose that commerce—and all that followed from it—extended directly from, or was coöriginal with, *ius gentium*. Nor could we suppose that there was a right to commerce, in and of itself, from *ius gentium*, given that such a right arose from the individuation of property, which resulted from war and the founding of kingdoms. The same historical sequence held for slavery; as it resulted from wars that emerged from *ius gentium*, which followed from *ius*. Here it is instructive to remember that just as the specific forms and types of commerce resulted unintentionally from *ius gentium*, for Alciati, the same held for slavery. The right to enslave captives did not extend directly from *ius*, so much as it extended by accident from wars that followed from *ius gentium*. Furthermore, the ability to enslave captives signaled *imperium*, even as *imperium* encompassed more than the ability to enslave captives.

Although we could make a relatively straightforward argument that commerce was necessary, we would have to look outside of the definition—and even outside of human action—to assert that either commerce, or a specific species of it, were just. The same rings true for the case of slavery. Precisely because slavery, like commerce, was a product of human actions, any argument that attempted to claim that it was an expression of justice rather than a consequence of war would have to look well beyond the text at hand, not only because slavery was not mentioned by Hermogenian but also because the status of slavery (as an institution that springs from war as well as an institution within civil society) among Romans was a legal one, and not a natural one. Nor was slavery a result of moral depravity for the Romans, even if it was the product of war. Moreover, all of the institutions that were mentioned explicitly in Hermogenian's definition of *ius gentium* emerged historically and, as a result, took their shape as practice, convention, and necessity required—including manumission as a practice that emerged from *ius gentium*, according to Ulpian in D.1.1.4. Indeed, Ulpain's brief discussion of manumission provided a historical explanation for the division of persons according to free (natural law), unfree (*ius gentium*), and freed (civil law).[52] Hence, to treat slavery as if it were always present or as a natural consequence of *ius gentium* rather than something that emerged by accident would be (as far as Budé, Zasius, and Alciati were concerned) to treat it anachronistically and thus not as an artificial (man-made) condition that could be entered into, freed from, or restricted by customs and agreements among states and by laws and procedures within in civil society. In addition, viewing slavery—or *ius gentium* more generally—through the lens of morality would be to miss the point, at least as far as Alciati was

52 See for example, D.1.1.1; D.1.1.4; In., I.II.2, In., I.V. Freedmen.

concerned, since slavery resulted from wars that stemmed from *ius gentium*, and thus signified *imperium* (which was neither a natural nor moral condition). Alciati deemed *imperium* as neither morally good nor bad; although *imperium* followed more directly from *ius gentium* than slavery, the exercise of it, too, was born of necessity, and not justice.

Second, although all wars were conducted by those who had the right to wage them, the right to enslave captives was not a matter of justice, but rather of necessity (viz., enslaving enemies restricted their capacity to commit further harm against their captors); this meant recognizing that captivity in war did not imply that slavery was just, nor that there was a right to enslave in and of itself. Here, remembering Alciati's discussion of homicide is once again instructive. Although commanding a subject to kill another (e.g., by assassination, by waging war, by punishment) might appear as just to the subject, justice had nothing to do with it. Such a command, however, would be licit if given by those who had the authority to do so. And, commanding one to kill in one discrete context—when necessity required it—could never be tantamount to declaring or suggesting that killing in and of itself was just. If killing were just, this would imply a universal right to command or commit homicide; it would also suggest, by analogy, that the right to enslave—a right limited to those who were authorized to do so—was universal. Not only would such statements be absurd but they would also undermine the claim that the right to use (and command) violence was restricted to rulers, and thus served as markers of *imperium*. All this invited the question: how could one determine who had the right to command licit acts of violence? The response that Alciati offered was rather straightforward: one could determine whether a ruler had the right of war by observing the extent to which those they commanded to fight practiced the other rights and customs that extended from *ius gentium*, such as enslaving captives. The reasoning went as follows: in accordance with *ius gentium*, soldiers had the right to enslave their prisoners, and this right was demonstrated by its observance by the vanquished as well as the victor.

Those who had the right of war stood vis-à-vis one another as enemies. They stood as equal in their right—albeit not always in their ability—to wage war against one another. It was only after a war had ceased, and peace was contracted, that the vanquished could be placed into a subordinate position to the victors. This was the case, in part, because the parties who engaged in war as equals likewise entered the peace as equals, even if the terms of the contract changed the status of each. All of this meant that if those subject to a prince who had the right of war recognized those who defeated them as enemies, then they recognized them as equals. If they were equals, then it necessarily followed that either both were exercising violence unjustly or that both had a right to wage war. In the former case, those exercising illicit violence—including killing and holding others in captivity—were bands of brigands, pirates, and criminals, whereas in the latter case those exercising licit violence were rulers (superior and inferior) and thus had the right of war, at least defensively.[53]

7 Rulers and Brigands; Superior and Inferior Princes

Individuals who commanded or committed acts of violence against persons without the right to do so were criminals; those who banded together to commit crimes in tandem—by force or by theft—were bandits, pirates, and robbers. No matter if such bands of brigands were made up of one's own subjects or of another ruler's subjects, their actions rendered them liable to punishment by all. If rulers could not exercise force against these bands without impunity, then they would be unable to provide security and stability for those under their domain, thus rendering their subjects and themselves susceptible to unchecked, unlimited, and arbitrary violence, viz., tyranny. These rulers would, in other words, lose their capacity, authority, and legitimacy to rule. Using force to resist and punish these criminals, however, was not the same as waging war against them. Brigands were not enemies. As Alciati explained to his students, in accordance with both Ulpian and Bartolus, "it is clear, that one party is waging war unjustly, & then those pressing suit unjustly are not called enemies, but rather brigands."[54] His choice to use the phrase 'waging war unjustly' was important if we recall that, as far as Alciati was concerned, all wars waged by those who had the right of war were licit. In other words, he was not using this language to distinguish between just and unjust wars, but rather licit and illicit violence.

Despite the inequalities embedded in feudal-sovereignty within and between states in times of peace, when it came to the realities of war, all enemies were equal; "For," Alciati asserted, "the word *hostire*, among the ancients, signifies being equal to another."[55] Calling such men brigands not only signified their status as criminals but it also emphasized that their leaders—despite any claims they might make to the contrary—were not rulers, and thus they

53 *Digest*, 49.15.19 informs Alciati's distinction between enemies and brigands as demonstrated below, especially: "The enemy are those on whom the Roman people has publicly declared war, or who themselves [declare war] on the Roman people; others are termed robbers or bandits."

54 Alciati, "De iustitia et iure," col. 6.§.28, '… clarum est, quod una pars iniuste belligerat, & tunc illi iniuste litigantes, non dicuntur hostes, sed potius latrunculi.'

55 Ibid, col. 6.§.28, '… nam verbum Hostire, apud antiquos significat aequum esse.'

not only lacked the right to command their subordinates to fight but also did not have the authority to enslave captives. In no way were "their vassals and other soldiers ... obligated to follow, or offer aid to them [brigands]," whereas subjects were obligated to help their rulers to defend and protect their *patria* against brigands.[56]

As clear-cut as the dichotomy between rulers and brigands was in the abstract, when applied to sort out feudal and customary relationships and obligations, it laid bare several embedded hierarchies of power and authority. Alciati used Baldus' assertion to emphasize the futility of such an argument: "when one defends himself, even illicitly, his vassal is obligated to help him: not however, when he wishes to commit an offence."[57] This statement, when explored through the lens of *imperium,* magnified the difference between superior and inferior princes that Alciati was inviting his students to think about in new ways, in particular, by straddling the line between committing an illicit act and exercising offensive force. Even though inferior rulers were neither ordinary persons nor brigands, Alciati treated Baldus' comparison as if it implied that inferior rulers who authorized offensive force were comparable to persons who used force without authorization. In so doing, he suggested that there was a false equivalence embedded in the contrast. He then used Baldus' statement to challenge the idea that only those who held pure *imperium* had the right to wage defensive and offensive wars *sui iuris* as well as to emphasize his rejection of the assumption that those holding mixed *imperium* could be compared to brigands commissioning offensive acts of violence.[58] This was meant to prepare Alciati's students to follow the implications of his novel interpretation of *imperium,* as he continued to unfold his argument about *ius gentium* for them.

Baldus' implied comparison between brigand and inferior rulers was problematic for three basic reasons. First, it rested on the supposition that an ordinary person who exercised force to repel an immediate injury in self-defense was not necessarily deemed as a criminal, whereas if that same person were

56 Ibid, col. 6.§.28, 'Unde quando tales belligerantur, non tenentur vassalli & alii milites eos sequi, nec illis auxilium impendere.' Compare with Zasius' discussion of obligations, also extending from *ius gentium,* in "*Jus Gentium as a Cache of Universal Rights & Obligations*" in Chapter 4 of this volume.

57 Ibid, col. 6.§.28, '... ut quando se defendit, etiam illicite, teneatur vassallus eum adiuvare: non autem quando vult offendere.'

58 Here again the key definition was provided by D.2.1.3: 'ULPIAN, Duties of Quaestor, book 2: *Imperium* is simple or mixed. To have simple *imperium* is to have the power of the sword to punish the wicked and this is also called *potestas. Imperium* is mixed where it also carries jurisdiction to grant *bonomm possessio.* Such jurisdiction includes the power to appoint a judge.'

to use force to attack or cause harm to another, then he was "called a brigand in the act of committing an offense."[59] Such a determination, however, depended on legal proofs aimed at discovering both the intentions and the causes of such violence, as presented by or on behalf of two or more parties in court. In this scenario, each side met one another as equals before a rule of law administered by experts whose tasks ranged from determining culpability (lawyers and jurists) to enforcing punishment (bailiffs and executioners). However, the legal apparatus and political authority that made all of the above possible within states did not exist between them. Inferior rulers did not meet one another in a court of law with fixed rules and penalties grounded in *ius commune*, natural law, or shared understandings of justice. They met, instead, in the realm of diplomacy and war, which was not only in flux and uncertain but also grounded in the necessity of right.

Second, the contrast between defensive and offensive force stood in direct opposition to a point that Alciati had already emphasized for his students, namely that as far as one's subjects were concerned, all wars waged by their rulers were just because their ruler had a right of war; this was a matter of perspective and a matter of necessity.[60] Distinctions as to whether or not their rulers were deemed inferior or superior princes by others—or what that even meant in terms of their capacity to command and commission violence—were incidental concerns for their subjects; what mattered was that the wars waged by their rulers were licit because they had the right and responsibility to preserve and protect their domain. All wars waged by those who had *imperium*—pure or mixed—were just from the point of view of those subject to them. Those exercising violence but lacking *imperium* were merely bands of brigands, pirates, and robbers.

After choosing select examples from Bartolus, the *Gloss*, and Baldus to illustrate the ubiquity of weak analogies, inconsistencies, and sleights of hand that were embedded within traditional jurisprudence, Alciati announced his intention to treat the problem of just/unjust wars in a third way.[61] In other words, having guided his students down a meandering path, overgrown with dense weeds, Alciati finally led them into the clearing. Adjusting his language to accommodate the commonplace assumption that wars could be illicit to

59 Ibid, col. 6.§.28, '… nam quando se defendit, tunc non potest dici latrunculus, sed quando offendit. latrunculus dicitur in actu offendendi.'

60 Ibid, col. 6.§.27. See note 48 above.

61 Ibid, col. 7.§.28–29, 'quare ego tertio modo respondeo, quod est verum quod bella, tam licita quam illicita, introducta sunt ex iure gentium, quo iure etiam introducta sunt latrocinia, furta & similia.'

demonstrate, once again, the problems inherent in reasoning backwards—from species to genus, from consequence to cause, and from ends to intention—he declared that: "wars, whether licit or illicit, have been introduced from *ius gentium*."[62] He then announced that it was "on account of this *ius*," viz., the right to repel injury with force from which *ius gentium* emerged, that "even acts of brigandage, theft & similar things have been introduced."[63] That forbidden acts, like theft, followed from *ius gentium*, he continued, should not be astounding since, after all, "there are many great things, from which occasionally at least wicked things are born."[64] To support his point, Alciati made use of a potent and common example by noting that God made disease and demons. That something wicked and harmful was created by the epitome of justice did not diminish the fact that God was also the source of all righteousness and virtue. Moving from the divine to the human, he applied this same reasoning to property by claiming that although the individuation of property had been a source of conflict and war, it was nevertheless a good thing on account of its utility; the same could be said for *ius*, which was good because it enabled one to repel injuries and injustice to their person, property, and *patria*, even though it required—in extreme cases—the exercise of lethal force, viz., homicide and war.[65]

Pushing off from cause to consequence, in addition to killing one's enemy, which was necessary but not good, the use of force to preserve and protect one's domain and subjects necessitated the ability to hold one's enemy in servitude, even though captivity—in and of itself—was not good. Slavery was, instead, invented to preserve fairness among enemies, who, by definition (as rulers) could not settle their disputes by laws because there was no law between them, only peace and war.[66] As such, slavery was deemed a lesser-evil, not only because it was an alternative to killing but also because it was a condition that, unlike death, was not permanent. As with any legal status, the condition of slavery was flexible and open to change within many civil law

62 Ibid.

63 Ibid.

64 Ibid, col. 7.§.29, '... nec istud debet esse mirum, nam & daemones & morbi facti fuere a Deo, & febres inventae saltem occasionaliter, & tamen Deus optimus est ... Sic etiam in iure gentium illud ius invenit distinctionem dominiorum, unde postea orta sunt bella & alia illicita, multa enim optima sunt, ex quibus saltem occasionaliter mala nascuntur.'

65 Ibid, Compare with Zasius discussion of obligations, which also extended from *ius gentium*, in Chapter 4 of this volume.

66 Alciati, "De iustitia et iure," col. 7.§.30, '... nam ideo est, quia cum sit in dubio, quae pars victoriam de iure habitura sit, ideo ratione aequalitatis servandae istud fuit introductum, quae aequalitas oritur propter dubium.'

traditions, including the Roman ones. More importantly, in the broader context of *ius gentium*, the ability to enslave one's captives was not a right held by all but rather a custom that could only be exercised by those who exercised force at the command of those who held *imperium*. In order to make this point abundantly clear to his students, Alciati invoked Ulpian, who not only held that slavery emerged from *ius gentium* but also explained that "a person who is captured by brigands is not the brigand's slave, nor does he need postliminium."[67]

Even though slavery indicated a right of war in the realm of *ius gentium*, many attempted to argue its necessity in civil society by appealing to civil law; they often employed slippery-slope fallacies to divert the attention of their readers. For example, rather than explore slavery as a consequence of war among peoples, they argued for its utility in ensuring civic stability.[68] Among those who made such dubious arguments, according to Alciati, was the fourteenth-century French jurist Johannes Faber (d. 1350), who even went so far as to claim that if captives were not enslaved, then "it would follow that they [could] possess goods: and thus such goods would remain in the power of the enemy."[69] It was this kind of reasoning that tended to confuse the issue because conquered peoples were not equivalent to captured soldiers and, when the war was concluded, such peoples were no longer enemies or captives, but subjects. Nevertheless, Faber went on to argue that it was necessary to enslave captives so that they could be barred from offering testimony in court: "For if they were free, the enemies would be able to make them witnesses in their own manner;" that is, they would be able to use the courts to challenge—or at least to undermine—the laws, authorities, and norms established by the new rulers.[70] While Alciati agreed with Faber's initial point, he rejected his premise as well as his conclusion.

According to Alciati, the reason why testimony offered by enemies was not valid stemmed from the fact that they were enemies and captives, and not subjects and citizens. Hence, Alciati explained, even if they offered it "without force"—and more so when they testified as a result of fear—their word should not be trusted, given that as long as they were enemies or captives they remained bound to the civil laws and civil authorities of their *patria*, and

67 See D.49.15.19. for a full definition and description of postliminium.

68 Alciati, "De iustitia et iure," col. 7.§.30, '... aliam rationem adsignarunt, scilicet quod ius civile istud introduxit ex quadam necessitate: quia si remanerent domini, non servi, sequeretur, quod haberent bona: & sic talia bona remanerent in potestate hostium.'

69 Ibid.

70 Ibid, col. 7.§.31, 'Tertiam rationem adsignat ipse Ioanus Fabius quod ideo fiunt servi, non possint testari. Nam si essent liberi, possent hostes facere eos testari suo modo: vel etiam sine vi favore inimicorum hoc facerent ...'

not to the laws and norms of their captors.[71] If, however, those who fell under the authority of a new ruler through arms, marriage, or treaty were no longer counted as enemies in war, then their standing under the civil law changed. Consequently, questions as to whether they should retain their existing rights, viz., to own property and give testimony, and be allowed to continue to practice their existing customs (including religious ones) fell within the purview of civic jurisprudence—and even natural law—but not *ius gentium*.

In essence, Alciati rejected the implications that followed from assuming that enslaving captives was necessary to protect civil laws and institutions from harm. Likewise, Alciati rejected the idea that civil laws that restricted a captive's access to due process in civil society, even after they became subjects, were caused by *ius gentium*. Faber's argument not only confused practice with right, but it also had dangerous implications. For example, applying the same kind of backward reasoning as Faber did, one might even suggest that since brigands enslaved their captives, rather than killing them, that they had the right to do so and, by implication, that they also had the right of war. If kidnapping and enslaving one's opponents were an indication of right, would that mean anyone who kidnapped another and then placed them into slavery rather than killing them had the right to do so? As problematic as comparing captivity by brigands to kidnapping by ordinary persons might be to modern readers, so too, for Alciati, was Faber's argument about slavery. So too Baldus' comparison between ordinary persons and brigands on the one hand, and brigands and inferior rulers on the other; this was not simply because such comparisons rested on faulty analogies and dubious suppositions but also because they forced the question as to whether the practice of enslaving one's opponents or captives could be understood as the equivalent to having the right to do so. Again, does might make right? If so, then were the distinctions between just and unjust, licit and illicit, and legitimate and illegitimate violence, merely semantic? If right was anchored in practice, rather than practice being anchored in right, then would that not render debates about *imperium*, mixed or pure, superfluous? Throughout his lecture, Alciati answered the latter question with a resounding no. Only rulers who had the right of war could practice and sanction the customs following from it, including enslaving captives; neither brigands nor ordinary persons were rulers, and thus neither had pure or mixed *imperium*. At the same time as he reinforced the boundary between rulers and brigands, however, he invited his students to question the utility of distinguishing superior and inferior rulers. If, as Alciati suggested, all

71 Ibid, col. 7–8.§.31, '... nam quamvis regulariter metus, non annullet ipso iure, ut tale tradit ... tamen contractus factus cum principe per metum, est ipso iure nullus.'

enemies were equal and all enemies had the right of war, then, by extension, all rulers would be equal too.

After all, if one's legitimacy as a ruler depended—as the distinction between rulers and brigands suggested—on whether they had the right to wage war and enslave captives, and both served as markers of *imperium*, then what was the difference between inferior and superior princes? Were they both equally capable of enslaving captives and taking prisoners in war? Or was the ability to hold captives a right only held by those who had pure *imperium*? If so, did the assumed distinction between pure and mixed *imperium* render inferior princes without right? Or did it merely restrict their rights in relation to what kinds of war they could wage? Did it mean, in other words, that a subordinate prince only had the right to defend his subjects from internal threats, viz., those who committed crimes or urged rebellion? Or was he also allowed to protect his domain against external threats, including those posed by superior rulers?[72]

To explore these types of questions within his *De iustitia et iure* lecture, Alciati used one of the most significant and contentious debates about the nature, scope, and limits of *imperium* within Italian history. The debate centered on the attempt by Holy Roman Emperor Henry VII (r. 1312–1313) to hold Robert of Anjou, King of Naples (r. 1309–1343), accountable for the crime of *lèse-majesté* after he opposed Henry's sojourn into northern Italy and, with it, his temporary residence in Rome. Rather than examining the dispute between Henry and Robert as a historical case, Alciati used it to explore who was *sui iuris* in war and peace, thus enabling him to bring aspects of his novel interpretations of *ius gentium* and universal jurisprudence to bear on questions directly related to—and implied by—transformations affected not only in the distant past but also amid the Italian Wars.[73] In so doing, Alciati offered his students an interpretation of *ius gentium* that was not only far more applicable to the immediate tensions and conflicts between the Houses of Sforza, Valois, and Habsburg, but also wholly divergent from those offered by his humanist peers and scholastic predecessors.

---

72 These questions also underpinned Jean Bodin's *Six livres de la République* [1576]. Just as was the case for his legal humanist predecessors, the political and legal conflicts that permeated late-sixteenth century France, and Europe as a whole, directly informed his own theory of universal jurisprudence. What separated Alciati and Bodin was, above all, that the wars between the Empire and France, which tore apart Alciati's homeland, were not fueled by religious hate as much as by conflicts over territorial dominion.

73 In his lecture "De iustitia et iure," Alciati refers to Robert of Naples as Robert of Sicily throughout his discussion of *lèse-majesté*.

8 Universal Empire Rejected

After distinguishing between licit war (rulers) and illicit violence (brigands and rebels) in the first part of his lecture, Alciati turned his attention to the question of who, among a whole spectrum of rulers, had *imperium*. In the process, he compared the relation between protagonists in war to that of persons involved in both legal (court) and extralegal (duel) contests. Alciati's interpretation of *ius gentium* in the final sections of the lecture were informed by disputes between emperors, kings, and princes, and suggested that the distinction between superior and inferior rulers—and the hierarchy of sovereignty, viz., *imperium*, pure and mixed, that it was predicated on—was at best a misnomer and at worst a mere fiction. Having argued that all wars were licit and that all enemies were equal, Alciati's next task was to explore the extent to which all rulers—on account of *ius*, viz., the right to repel injuries with force—stood as equals in the realm of *ius gentium*, despite any degrees of difference in the realm of politics. This, in turn, allowed him to contend that well-worn suppositions underpinning political and legal thought, especially those that had been developed to structure a feudal world, were not only outdated but mistaken. To show this, Alciati approached the problem of *imperium* in the context of the dispute between Henry VII and Robert of Naples, which came to a head in 1313.

Unlike previous contests between emperors and popes in Italy, the dispute between Henry and Robert pitted rulers of different ranks directly against one another.[74] Henry (a superior ruler) and Robert (an inferior one) both claimed authority over areas of the Italian peninsula, and each stood as independent rulers within their realms.[75] Yet, as far as Henry was concerned, Robert committed the crime of *lèse-majesté* when he supported rebels in the north, blocked Henry's entrance into Rome by arms, and refused to yield to his demands.[76] What set Henry's claims against Robert apart from previous conflicts was that he attempted to try Robert for crimes that could only have been committed by someone who was wholly subject to his jurisdiction—something that Robert did not consider himself to be. Not surprisingly, Pope Clement V (r. 1305–1314) and King Phillip IV of France (r. 1285–1314) rejected Henry's claims. They believed that Henry lacked the standing to make such an accusation against an independent king, and agreed that Henry lacked

---

74 The narrative that follows was drawn from Pennington, *The Prince and the Law*, especially Chapter Five; David Abulafia, *The Western Mediterranean Kingdoms*, especially Chapter Six; and Jonathan Baumgartner, *Declaring War in Early Modern Europe* (New York: Palgrave Macmillan, 2011).

75 Hence, each held *imperium* according to D.2.1.3.

76 Pennington, *The Prince and the Law*, 167.

the authority—or even the cooperation of other rulers—to compel Robert to appear in court to answer to such charges in the first place.

This conflict forced jurists across the *Regnum Italicum* to confront fundamental questions regarding the scope and limits of *imperium* in new ways. Some of the questions that required their utmost attention included: could the emperor "bring a treasonous vassal to trial who was ultimately an independent king? Was the emperor truly the lord of the world? Could he exercise jurisdiction over kings?"[77] No matter how one answered such questions, the jurists' opinions would shape the political climate and the scope of jurisprudence for centuries. Just as in the Italian Wars, this conflict between superior and inferior rulers encompassed the ambitions of the various city-states, principalities, and kingdoms that spanned the Peninsula, as well as the kings and popes well beyond it.

A German king had not been crowned Holy Roman Emperor in Italy since 1220, when Frederick II (r. 1220–1250) was installed by Pope Honorius III (r. 1216–1227). Henry of Luxembourg, who was elected King of the Romans in November 1308, was determined to restore the tradition and the emperor's regalian rights in Italy. Robert of Naples, the king of the Angevin kingdom in Sicily and "the leader of the Guelph party in Florence and in other northern city-states," however, had other plans.[78] Although Pope Clement V, residing in Avignon, tried to broker peace between these two houses, an achievement which would have served his own interests in pacifying Sicily, Robert was determined to limit Henry's power from extending across the Alps.

After his coronation in Aachen as King of the Germans in January 1309, Henry, with the aid of Pope Clement V, put a plan in motion to receive the imperial crown in Rome by the end of the summer. Upon restoring Ghibelline exiles and trying to appease Guelph concerns, Henry received the iron crown of Italy in Milan by October 1310, while he was on his way to be coronated as emperor at (old) St. Peter's in Rome. Although Florence, Lucca, Siena, and Bologna—emboldened by Robert's support—entered into an alliance to prevent Henry from reaching Rome, it was Genoa, Pisa, and other imperial strongholds that helped to ensure his arrival in the spring of 1312. In addition to supporting rebellion and resistance to Henry's entrance into northern and central Italy, Robert had "sent his brother, John of Gravina, to Rome with a sizable army," in order to block Henry's coronation.[79] Nevertheless, Henry was crowned by Clement V's cardinals in the Basilica of St. John Lateran on June 29, 1312. Installed as Holy Roman Emperor, Henry sent envoys and letters

77 Ibid, 166.
78 Ibid, 166.
79 Ibid, 167.

to princes across Europe to announce that he—and he alone—was "King of kings and lord of lords."[80] He then set his sights on asserting his rule in Italy and exacting revenge against Robert.

On September 12, 1312, Henry issued a proclamation, which was nailed to the cathedral door in Arezzo, accusing Robert of treason against the Empire. This proclamation summoned Robert "to appear before him within three months to answer charges that he supported rebels in Lombardy and Tuscany, that his legates promoted treatises inimical to imperial interests, and that his brother and allies waged war on him in the streets of Rome."[81] In the meantime, Henry attempted, yet failed, to besiege Florence. By March, after returning to Pisa, Henry issued two decrees of condemnation against Robert, who had continued to support rebels across Tuscany and Lombardy. The first explained that those who committed treason could be tried in absentia. This statement was necessary not only because Robert had failed to appear before Henry but also because what Henry was attempting to do was unprecedented. The second answered the question of what a rebel was in order to establish the criteria for subjecting Robert to condemnation in the first place. Each, as Kenneth Pennington explained, were quickly incorporated into the jurisprudence aimed at understanding the *corpus iuris civilis*, and thereafter studied within the law schools. Indeed, by the time Alciati first matriculated at Pavia, this case had shaped debates about imperial authority for nearly two centuries.

On April 26, 1313, Henry promulgated an official judgment against Robert, condemning him "to be beheaded and his lands confiscated" for committing treason.[82] This judgment was necessary, Henry explained, because Robert's crimes were public and notorious, and therefore a direct affront to the emperor's authority and reputation. Despite his absence in the proceedings, the Imperial stance was that the sentence was legitimate because several witnesses had provided testimony of Robert's subversive actions. War ensued once again in early August, with Henry unable to assert his authority by arms in Tuscany. Although the direct conflict between the two rulers ceased when Henry died of illness on August 24, 1313, legal polemics and debates about the nature and limits of imperial power and the fundamental attributes of *imperium* continued to draw the attention of scholars in all quarters of Europe.[83]

Some argued that a prince could not deny a subject the right to due process since the right itself was grounded in natural law, as observed by *ius gentium*, viz., customs in common among all mankind, and confirmed by civil laws and

80 Ibid, 168.

81 Ibid, 169.

82 Ibid, 170.

83 Ibid, also see Chapter 5 in this volume.

constitutions. Others focused on the problem of jurisdiction by attempting to discern whether the Holy Roman Emperor was *de facto* the lord of the whole world (*dominus mundi*) or if he merely held that title *de iure*. If *de facto*, did this entitle the emperor to exercise legal authority beyond the boundaries and borders of the Germanies? If, moreover, the emperor was "King of kings and lord of lords," did that mean that he was a superior to all other princes, including the Kings of France, England, and Spain? If he was only lord over the world in name, were those kings and princes whom he regarded as his subordinates *sui iuris*, and therefore equal to him in the realm of war and peace? Or did they, on account of the minute size of their domains, occupy a lower status within a hierarchy of sovereignty?

The above questions were not new to the fourteenth century, although the contours of the dispute they attempted to address were.[84] Indeed, debates about the emperor's authority extended back to the Investiture Controversy in the eleventh century, and re-emerged with Barbarossa's (Frederick I, r.1155–1190) and Frederick II's (r.1220–1250) respective attempts to rule over Italy in the twelfth and thirteenth centuries. Beyond the *Regnum Italicum*, broader questions about the source and limits of sovereignty that permeated the conflict between Pope Boniface VIII (r. 1293–1303) and King Phillip IV of France (r.1285–1314) over taxation and territorial sovereignty as well as the stability and supremacy within the Church, had also stemmed from a long history of conflict.[85] These types of questions persisted into the early-sixteenth century, when Alciati explored them in his lecture, and they were no less urgent for his students in northern Italy than they had been for the students of Bartolus and Baldus.

9 *Imperium* Interrupted

With the previous example in mind, Alciati noted that Accursius held—in the *Gloss*—that all wars waged by the Holy Roman Emperor and, by implication,

84 More common were disputes between emperors and popes, emperors and cities, and popes and kings. The rich literature concerning the limits of *imperium* and the origins of *potestas* is exemplified in the works of Dante Alighieri (1265–1321), Marsilius of Padua (1275–1342), William of Ockham (1285–1347), Bartolus de Saxoferrato (1313–1357), and Baldus de Ubaldis (1327–1400).

85 Koskenniemi, *To the Uttermost Parts of the Earth*, especially Chapter One, wherein he explores the conflict between King Philip IV, called Philip the Fair, and Pope Boniface VIII over the taxation of clergy in France in detail.

all those waged by superior rulers, were licit, whereas wars initiated by "a prince recognizing a superior" without first securing his permission were illicit.[86] Here, rather than repeating his previous claim that all wars were licit, Alciati argued instead that all rulers, even if they recognized a superior, possessed "the right of the sword, both pure and mixed *imperium*."[87] To suppose otherwise would require evidence that the emperor alone could wage war *sui iuris*—in this case, inferring Barbarossa's reclamation of his regalian rights over Lombardy—and that *ius* and *ius gentium* could be restricted by fiat in the first place.[88] In regard to more recent history, as Alciati alluded in the lecture, this meant that both the Republic of Venice and the Duchy of Milan had a legitimate right to wage the Lombardy Wars (1423–1454), and also implied that in the dispute between Henry and Robert, the Emperor's claim of pure *imperium* neither diminished the fact that Robert had the right of the sword to defend and protect his realm nor did it suggest that the Emperor could limit Robert's ability to do so.[89] For an indication of Alciati's stance as to whether or not Robert stood as fully equal—and therefore as an enemy vis-à-vis Henry—rather than a rebel or brigand, his students had to follow the logic of his argument interspersed within a series of examples. It was necessary to do so, in no small part, because the way Alciati worked through and linked these examples had implications for how he viewed the status of a whole spectrum of rulers across the Italian peninsula in the sixteenth century, a perspective through which he invited his students to fundamentally rethink *imperium*.

Moving from the level of superior and inferior princes to those subject to them, Alciati asserted that even rulers like "the *capitaneus* of the Duke of Milan, & similar men," who had—like the Duke of Milan himself—"specifically recognized the Emperor" as their overlord, were able "to set war in motion against rebellious subjects" without delay, viz., without having to get permission from

86 Alciati, "De iustitia et iure," col. 8.§.31, '... ubi princeps recognoscens superiorem, non potest arma movere absque iussu superioris.'

87 Ibid, col. 8.§.31, '... ego puto, quod, opinioni Guli, sit vera, etiam si talis princeps recognosceret superiorem: dummodo sit ex his, qui habent ius gladii, & merum & mixtum imperium, quails est Marchio Mantuae & quilibit alius: vel ex his, qui habuerunt merum imperium ex privilegio Federici, quales sunt omnes civitates Lombardiae.'

88 Ibid, 'Sed non reperitur, quod princeps specialiter sibi reservaverit istam licentiam.'

89 Here, Alciati is adding his voice to a formative debate about the balance of power across the Italian Peninsula since the fourteenth century. For discussion of the debate and its implications for traditional jurisprudence see Ryan, "Bartolus of Sassoferrato and Free Cities;" Pennington, The *Prince and the Law*; Canning, *Political Thought of Baldus*; Maiolo, *Medieval Sovereignty*; Fasolt, *The Limits of History*; and Abulafia, *The Western Mediterranean Kingdoms.*

a superior.[90] Their ability to do so stemmed from the need to secure the realm from danger. If the Duke of Milan's subordinates were not granted the latitude to put down existential threats, then they could not preserve and protect the duke's holdings and subjects. Such agents were indispensable to superior and inferior rulers alike, given that stability of all nations and kingdoms was dependent on a ruler's dexterity to punish those who posed a credible threat to safety of the realm, both internally (rebels and criminals) and externally (brigands). In this respect, the ability for such proxies to act was comparable to the ability of deputies and delegates "[to] condemn a brigand to death, provided that he could not have done otherwise" when "an ordinary judge is absent."[91]

Alciati's choice of this analogy is telling for several reasons. First, it drew out relations of dependence at the same time as it carved out a sphere for independent action; the *condottieri* of inferior rulers and, by implication, inferior rulers themselves, could act on their own volition if they deemed it necessary. Second, it enabled Alciati to suggest that the agents of the Duke of Milan—as much as the agents of the emperor—had the ability to use force to defend their domains, just as individuals had the right to defend themselves, their family, and their property. In other words, all had the right to repel injury: the agents and deputies of rulers exercised force for the security of the realm (public), while individuals did so to secure their own welfare (private). Third, just as was the case in his initial definition of *ius* and *ius gentium*, Alciati established that the right to use defensive force was shared universally by all persons and, in turning his attention to the right to command offensive violence, that this was a right reserved for the few who had 'the right of the sword, both pure and mixed *imperium*.' As such, the comparison between military capacity "to set war in motion against rebellious subjects" and the ability of delegates "[to] condemn a notable brigand to death" corresponded with the exercise of *imperium* on behalf of one's superior, thus leaving wide-open the question of the right of war, while at the same time illuminating its necessity.[92]

Finally, the analogy between the proxy of a ruler and the delegate of a judge pressed Alciati's students to think about the various levels of authority from multiple perspectives, and to shift their attention from extralegal (putting down rebellion) and legal (capital punishment) concerns to the difficulty in determining who was subordinate to whom— *alieni iuris*—and, by implication, who was superior—*sui iuris*. The latter, in the context of the first

90 Alciati, "De iustitia et iure," col. 9.§.33, '... quando copia principis haberi non posset, nam tunc potest ille princeps inferior bellum movere in subditos rebelles ...'.

91 Ibid, col. 9.§.34, '... ubi si absit ordinaribus iudex, potest delegatus insignem latronem ad mortem damnare, licet alias istud non potuisset facere.'

92 Ibid.

discussion of Milan, was further complicated by the fact that neither the rebels nor the brigands were enemies, and thus the duke's agents did not wage war against them since to do so would have elevated their status from criminals to enemies. Instead, the duke's agents wielded the sword on behalf of their superior to punish them and to protect and secure the peace as well as the common good of the community. Alciati then redirected his line of questioning to the status of the Duke of Milan himself, albeit indirectly.

"At this point," Alciati announced to his students, jurists tended to ask: "if the King of France can set war in motion against another nation without the command of the emperor?"[93] Put differently, did the King of France, who at times happened to be the Duke of Milan as well, possess pure or mixed *imperium*? For Alciati, at issue in this discussion was Bartolus' contention that the Holy Roman Emperor—based on the *corpus* of Roman law—held authority over the entire globe in theory (*de iure*), albeit not in fact (*de facto*); this was a distinction that Baldus developed to great effect.[94] This distinction not only gave credence to the division between pure and mixed *imperium,* but it also tended to reinforce it insofar as offensive and defensive wars waged by those who held pure *imperium* were *prima facie* just, and wars waged by those who only had mixed *imperium* were not.[95] It was this very division that Alciati invited his students to reject, or to at least reimagine, in order to provide them with a means to address issues in the world in which they lived, rather than simply debate relations of power in the world that Bartolus and Baldus had attempted to explain. His respect for his Italian predecessors was not diminished in this approach. After all, Bartolus' and Baldus' influence on the history and development of law and jurisprudence extended from their ability to use Roman law to address contemporary problems—to transform it from a relic of history to "a living instrument and legal and political language for Europeans," something that Alciati was attempting to do as well.[96]

Nevertheless, rethinking and even abandoning some of these divisions and distinctions was necessary because they justified a hierarchy of rights within

93 Ibid, col. 9.§.35, 'quaerunt hic Doctor [Bartolus] utrum Rex Franciae possit indicere bellum alicui nationi absque iussu Imperatoris? Punctus est videre, vtrum recognoscat Imperatorem de iure in superiorem?'

94 See Pennington, *The Prince and the Law*; Canning, *The Political Thought of Baldus*; Maiolo, *Medieval Sovereignty*; and Fasolt, *The Limits of History*.

95 For just war theory, see Black, *Political Thought in Europe*; Russell, *The Just War*; and Covell, *The Law of Nations in Political Thought*. For a discussion of how and why ideas of just war were affected by the violence of the Italian Wars see Stephen D. Bowd, *Renaissance Mass Murder: Civilians and Soldiers During the Italian Wars* (Oxford: Oxford University Press, 2018).

96 Black, *Political Thought in Europe*, 127.

Universal Latin Christendom and underpinned a political and legal structure that was becoming increasingly suspect—in theory and in practice. This trend occurred in the wake of nearly constant war within and beyond Europe since the *corpus* of Roman law was recovered and amid the ongoing disputes between the King of France (and Duke of Milan) Francis I and the Emperor (and King of Spain) Charles V. To call these divisions into question without knocking down the edifice of European jurisprudence as it stood at the start of the sixteenth century was no easy task. Any attempt to rearrange the components of the tradition, let alone to challenge them, required a systematic reinterpretation of their core premises. Before one could reject the supposition that the division between pure and mixed *imperium* was tenable, one had to entertain the long-standing debate as to who warranted the moniker 'superior ruler' in the first place.

By summarizing Bartolus' and Baldus' explanations as to why the emperor was *de iure* above all the rest in order to rehearse arguments for and against the claim that the Holy Roman Emperor was the ruler of the whole world, Alciati asserted his position in no uncertain terms. When it came to the King of France's authority to conduct affairs of state, including offensive war, Alciati simply stated: "I think permission is not required."[97] Paying little attention to Bartolus' argument that "if someone were to say that the lord emperor is not lord and monarch over the entire world (*dominus et monarcha totius orbis*), he would be a heretic," Alciati explained that "the King of France does not recognize the [Holy Roman] Emperor as a superior," either *de facto* or *de iure*.[98] As such, Alciati not only rejected Bartolus' claim that, "if the King of France should recognize the [Holy Roman] Emperor *de iure* as superior, [it] would follow, that he [the King of France] would not be able to set in motion war without the permission of the emperor," he also rejected its implications, wholesale.[99] In so doing, he ultimately agreed with those who, like Pope Innocent III (r. 1198–1216), argued that "the king of France recognizes no temporal superior"—although

97 Alciati, "De iustitia et iure," col. 11.§.39, 'Sed ego puto, quod dato etiam, quod subsit illi, tamen non requiritur licentia, ut supra dixi, nam ista recognitio (ut dixi) parum operatur.'

98 Ibid, col. 10.§.36, '… In contrarium tamen, quod Rex Franciae non recognoscat Imperatorem in superiorem.' Bartolus translation quoted from Fasolt, *Limits of History* (2004), 172.

99 Ibid, col. 10.§.39, 'Tenendo ergo opiniones Bartolum & glossae quae est verior, scilicet quod rex Francorum recognoscat Imperatorem de iure in superiorem, sequeretur, quod non posset movere bellum absque licentia Imperatoris, secundum doctrinam Bartolus hic. Sed ego puto, quod dato etiam, quod subsit illi, tamen non requiritur licentia, ut supra dixi, nam ista recognitio (ut dixi) parum operatur.'

the Pope's claim was rooted in politics (election), whereas Alciati's was rooted in violence (war).[100]

In addition, if we follow the logic of the traditional jurisprudence then the claim that the king required permission to preserve and protect his domain would have been absurd to Alciati.[101] How could he truly be the King of France if he was required to seek another's permission before waging offensive war? Indeed, how could the King of France, the declared enemy of the Holy Roman Emperor throughout most of the Italian Wars, be subject to his authority, while at the same time be the emperor's rival? As ridiculous as the idea that the King of France would have to solicit permission from the emperor to wage war against him was, addressing the question as to the limits of the emperor's authority—*de iure* and *de facto*—was not without utility, especially since it would illustrate the equal status of two rulers in the realm of *ius gentium* as well as within their respective domains.

The fact that the King of France had the right to wage offensive and defensive war *sui iuris* against his enemies meant that he and the emperor were peers; they each held pure *imperium* and they each sat at the apex of political and legal authority within their respective domains. Their authority, for Alciati, was anchored in *ius* and *ius gentium*, as confirmed by the customs and practices of war. Asserting that the king was equal to the emperor, however, did not diminish the emperor's standing vis-à-vis others. Indeed, Alciati reminded his audience that the "universal power [of the emperor] is not obliterated on account of any singular power being diminished."[102] Furthermore, it did not diminish the King of France's authority over others. The subordinates of each, ranging from agents of force to deputies of law, still required their permission to command and commit offensive violence, even though such subordinates were able and expected to exercise defensive force in the face of an insurrection or rebellion and to enforce punishments and penalties to ensure the stability and security of the subjects and holdings of both France and the Empire.[103]

After abandoning Bartolus' and Baldus' interpretation of the Roman principle that the emperor was the 'lord of the whole world,' Alciati aligned himself with those who rejected the idea that there could be a single sovereign entity on earth who was superior to all others *de iure* or *de facto*. In the process

100 Pennington, *The Prince and the Law*, 176.

101 Cf. Bodin, *Six Books on the Commonweale* (*Six livres de la République*) [*1576*], *ed.* Kenneth Douglas McRae (Cambridge, MA: Harvard University Press, 1962).

102 Alciati, "De iustitia et iure," col. 11.§.37, 'Universitas enim non deletur per hoc, quod aliquid singulum diminuatur.'

103 Ibid, col. 9.§.33. See note 88 above.

of doing so, he set out a theory of sovereignty—although he did not use the term—that depended on the mutual recognition and independence of multiple rulers holding *imperium de iure* and *de facto*. In essence, he rejected a unilateral conception of authority that reflected a hierarchy of authority and power, opting instead for a multilateral one whereby power and authority were shared among equals. He at once affirmed the superior status of the King of France without diminishing that of the Holy Roman Emperor and argued that the king should respect the *imperium* of the emperor and vice versa—just as both should respect the *imperium* of the Pope (viz., the Papal States). Thereafter, Alciati worked through the implications of his novel interpretation of *ius gentium*—rooted in the parity of right and the equality of enemies—without calling, in one fell swoop, all traditional types or gradations of authority into question. Instead, he structured his argument by following a long-established line of inquiry: he invited his students to consider whether there were other secular rulers who also held *imperium* and thus stood as equals to the King of France and the Holy Roman Emperor in the realm of *ius gentium*.

Moving from kingdoms to republics Alciati asked: "What about the Venetians? Are they under the Emperor?"[104] Contrary to those who contended that Venice was removed from the (Byzantine) Emperor's *de facto imperium* on account of a privilege granted to expand their influence and trade, Alciati agreed with Bartolus' assertion that the Holy Roman Emperor could revoke the Republic's seemingly independent status at any time.[105] Although they operated as if they were free from the Holy Roman Emperor's *de facto* or *de iure* rule, the Venetians did so at his pleasure. In theory, they were required to obtain permission from their superior before setting offensive wars in motion, unless there was danger in delay. They were also able, like all inferior and superior rulers, to wage defensive wars in response to immediate and proximate dangers. "What about the King of Sicily?"[106] Although Sicily was considered "a fief [under the power of] the Pope," and, thus not part of the Holy Roman Empire, the King of Sicily should nevertheless respect the emperor's status as a superior ruler, with full *imperium*.[107]

104 Ibid, col. 11.§.40, 'Sed quid de Venetis? utrum subsint Imperatori?' The fact that Alciati chose to focus on Venice, rather than on Florence, suggests that the version of the lecture bound in his *Omnia opera* was delivered after 1530, when Florence became a Duchy.

105 Ibid, col. 11.§.40. Alciati also rejected Baldus' claim that since the city was on the sea, it was outside of the purview of the emperor, by arguing that if the sea is under the domain of the emperor, then the fact that Venice sits on it places it under his power.

106 Ibid, col. 11.§.41, '... quid de rege Siciliae?'

107 Ibid, col. 11.§.41, '... nam Sicilia est feudum Papae. Teneo contrarium per supra dicta. Non obstant praedicta iura: quia est verum, quod Rex Siciliae non dicitur esse sub Imperatore,

Insisting on this point, however, was not equal to the assertion that the King of Sicily was subject to the Holy Roman Emperor's authority. After all, Sicily was lost to the Empire when Manfred (r.1258–1266), the son of Frederick II, was defeated in the Battle of Benevento in 1266 by Prince Charles, Count of Anjou and Provence, who, in turn, was crowned as King of both Sicily and Naples (r. 1266–1285) by Pope Innocent IV. Precisely because the independence of Sicily was "confirmed by the pontiff," Alciati continued, the emperor could neither claim "power over such a King" nor expect to "be called his lord."[108] Sicily was, in other words, "under its own rule" since 1266, and even after it was claimed by the House of Aragon as early as 1282, as well as officially after the Peace of Caltabellotta at the conclusion of the War of the Vespers in 1302, when the kingdom was divided; the Island of Sicily went to Frederick III (r. 1295–1337) and hence the house of Aragon, whereas the peninsular territory of Naples went to Charles II (1254–1309) and hence the house of Anjou.

As such, upon referring directly to the attempt by Henry VII to punish Robert in 1313 for rejecting his authority and standing in Italy, Alciati asserted that "Robert King of Sicily [the peninsular part] was not under the power of the emperor in such a way that he could commit a crime of *lèse-majesté* against him—which is a crime no one can commit except those who are in reality subject to him."[109] Even so, the King of Sicily should respect the Holy Roman Emperor—rather than attempt to diminish him—in the same way that he respected the Pope, who confirmed his rule.[110] The implications of Alciati's argument were clear: Robert was not required to ask permission of the emperor (or the pope) to wage an offensive or defensive war. Robert was a ruler who held *imperium* and stood as an equal to his peers—the Holy Roman Emperor, the King of France, and the Pope—in the realm of *ius gentium*, that is, in the realm of war and peace. Moreover, Robert—just as his peers—was the highest authority within his domain (*princeps in regno suo*). This meant

quia Sicilia non sit Imperatoris; sed tamen tenetur eum honorare, & recognoscere in superiorem, ea saltem ratione, quod confirmatus est a pontifice, & quod Sicilia olim erat sua.'

108 Ibid, col. 11–12.§.41, 'Est bene verum, quod Imperator non tantum potestatis habet in talem Regem, ut dicatur eius dominus, & dicatur Sicilia esse regni sui ...'

109 Ibid, col. 12.§.41, 'Robertus Rex Siciliae non eo modo sub fuit potestati Imperatoris, quod in eum crimen laesae maiestatis commiserit, quod crimen non possunt committere, nisi hi, qui re ipsa sunt illi subditi: quasi dicat, bene subfuit, sed non eo modo facit, quia cum recognoscat Papem, debet etiam recognoscere Imperatorem, quia illa bona concessit Papae ...' When Alciati used the term King of Sicily, he was referring to the peninsula. For the sake of clarity, Naples will be included in parenthesis throughout the remainder of the chapter.

110 Ibid, col. 12.§.41.

that his subordinates and agents—as was the case in the discussion of the Duke of Milan—required his permission to exert offensive force unless there was danger in delay.[111]

Moving beyond the *Regnum Italicum*, Alciati asked his students if the King of England was *sui iuris* or did he require the permission of a superior before setting offensive wars in motion?[112] Alciati did not linger on this question long. He suggested the King of England was not subject to the emperor, *de iure* or *de facto*, and therefore had *imperium*. Given that his students would have been well aware of the long history of both Holy Roman Emperors and the Kings of France waging war against—and entering alliances with—the Kings of England, there was no need for Alciati to explain the idea that the present King of England held the same independent status the King of France, and thereby the Holy Roman Emperor. "What about the Kings of Spain?"[113] Were they similar to the kings of England and France? Or were they similar to the Republic of Venice, and thus required to seek the emperor's permission before setting offensive wars in motion? Or, instead, were they like the King of Sicily, viz., Naples, and thus able to wage war *sui iuris*? According to Alciati, some argued that the emperor held no authority over the Kings (and Queens) of Spain on account of the fact the rulers of Latin Christendom "lost that part of Spain occupied by infidels," whereas others argued that he did not wield authority over the kings precisely because their kingdoms were "recovered by the Spanish themselves, with their own blood without the emperor's help."[114] Both premises, Alciati continued, led many to the same conclusion, namely that the Holy Roman Emperor should not have anything to do with Spain and that Spain should not be counted as under his authority, *de iure* or *de facto*. Rejecting both the conclusions and the premises, Alciati argued: "Spain was subject to the Roman Empire ... . & although it was occupied by enemies *de facto*, & then was recovered by others, the right of the Emperor is not lost through this, if he did not regard it as abandoned."[115] As such, the status of Spain was comparable to Venice—and entirely different from France, England, and Sicily, viz.,

111 Ibid, col. 9.§.34, '... quando periculum esset in mora ...'

112 Ibid, col. 12.§.42. 'Quid de Rege Angliae?'

113 Ibid, col. 12.§.43, 'Quid de Rege Hispaniae?'

114 Ibid, col. 12.§.43, 'Quidam dicunt non recognoscere eum Imperatorem. nam quamvis Imperator sit dominus totius mundo, tamen cum eam partem Hispaniae ab infidelibus occupatam amiserit, cum etiam recuperata sit ab illis Hispanis proprio sanguine absque auxilio Imperatoris non debet Imperator de ea aliquid contingere.'

115 Ibid, col. 12.§.43, 'Puto contrarium per supra dicta, nam Hispania erat subiecta Romano Imperio ... & quamvis occupata fuisset ab hostibus de facto, & recuperata deinde ab aliis, per hoc non amittitur ius Imperatoris, si eam non habuit pro derelicta.'

Naples—insofar as whether Spain was under its own power or subject of the emperor depended entirely on the emperor's will, regardless of how they were treated by others or how they perceived themselves.

Just as was the case in his initial discussion of Milan, Alciati left his assessment of whether the Kings of Spain held pure *imperium* ambiguous; he did not add, as he had in relation to the other examples thus far, a conclusive statement about their status vis-a-vis the Holy Roman Emperor. The omission of a definitive answer makes sense in the historical and political contexts in which he lived and taught. Here it is useful to recall that both Spain and the Holy Roman Empire had been in the possession of the same family since Emperor Maximilian's son Phillip of Burgundy (d. 1506) became King of Castile in 1506, and, further, that Maximilian's grandson Carlos I, who became King of Spain in 1516 (r. 1517–1556), also became the Holy Roman Emperor Charles V in 1519.[116] Thus, attempting to determine whether Spain was under the power the Holy Roman Empire or was equal to it would have prompted questions about primogeniture, blood proximity, and marriage in relation to canon, private, and natural law, all of which were well beyond Alciati's task at hand, namely exploring the relationship between *ius* and *ius gentium* in order to challenge traditional interpretations of—or at least superimposed divisions within—*imperium*.[117]

Spain was not, of course, the only domain in which the distinction between pure and mixed *imperium* was muddled on account of dynastic claims by a single family or of problems stemming from (re)conquest. It was not the only case in which its ruler stood at the apex of power in two or more territories occupied by subjects who did not consider themselves to be of the same nation. Alciati himself lived in such a realm, and it should be of no surprise that he concluded this line of questioning by returning once again to Milan. This time, instead of discussing the capacity of his *capitaneus, condottieri*, or deputies to wield force on his behalf, Alciati posed the question: "What about the Duke of Milan?"[118] Did he require the permission of his superior to set wars in motion or was he *sui iuris*? Was he, in other words, a ruler who possessed 'the right of the sword, both pure and mixed *imperium*'? The answer, much like the discussion of both Sicily (Naples) and Spain, was dependent entirely on context.[119]

116 For a study on the Habsburg dynasty in the late-fifteenth century and Charles' place at the head of it in the sixteenth see Parker, *Emperor.*

117 It would have also drawn Alciati into the debates about what precisely *bonorum possessio* meant in the context of D.2.1.3., and how it should be interpreted vis-a-vis dynastic and territorial possessions in the realm of rulers.

118 Alciati, "De iustitia et iure," col. 12.§.43, 'Quid de duce Mediolani?'

119 See Shaw and Mallett, *The Italian Wars*; Knecht, *Renaissance Warrior and Patron*; Parker, *Emperor*; and Jane Black, *Absolutism in Renaissance Milan: Plenitude of Power under the*

For example, it seems likely that if Alciati was inquiring about Milan under the rule of the Visconti (1395–1447), then he would have deemed the duke to be a superior ruler in possession of full *imperium*. The Visconti—just as the Kings of England—were recognized as enemies in war and allies in peace by other superior (i.e., fully independent) rulers, including the King of France and the Holy Roman Emperor, and thus occupied a comparable status to them in the realm of *ius gentium*. Likewise, he would have surely recognized the ability of the Duke of Milan to set offensive wars in motion, even against the emperor himself, when his territory was in the possession of the Valois Kings of France—under Louis XII, from 1499–1512, and under Francis I, from 1515–1521.

Determining the duke's status when Milan was in the hands of the Sforza would have been more complicated. If he was referring to their first rule, initiated in 1450 with Francisco I (r. 1450–1466) claiming his right to rule based on marriage to Bianca Maria Visconti (c. 1425–1468) and on conquest, then it seems improbable that Alciati would have conceded that the duke not hold *imperium* or that he was subject to the *de facto* or *de iure* rule of the emperor. It stands to reason that the early Sforza, in this respect, were comparable to the Visconti, as well as Robert of Sicily (viz., Naples) and the King of England. If, however, he was referring to the second or third rule of the Sforza (1513–1515; 1522–1535), both of which were accomplished with the help—and, in the latter case, permission—of the Holy Roman Emperor, then it is likely that he would have deemed the duchy as subject to a superior prince and as unable to wage offensive wars without first seeking permission. This did not mean, however, that Alciati—form the perspective of subject to the Sforza—would not have recognized them *de iure* as holding full *imperium*, even if *de facto* they were deemed by others as inferior rulers. The same applied when Milan finally came under Habsburg rule in 1535 and remained so for the rest of Alciati's life—despite French claims to the contrary. In this respect, the latter Sforza—and certainly the Habsburg Dukes—were comparable to the Venetians and the Kings of Spain insofar as they were independent if the emperor chose to recognize them as such. All this suggests that, although the duchy was dependent when in the possession of France or the Empire, neither the king nor the emperor negated its independence in the past nor precluded it in the future.

As for Alciati's response to his question "What about Milan," he simply stated that the duke ought to respect the *imperium* of the emperor and that, like all other rulers, "the Duke of Milan is able to do, what the emperor is able to do" when it came to his own subjects.[120] In essence, he evaded a

Visconti and the Sforza 1329–1535 (Oxford: Oxford University Press, 2009). For a discussion of the dismantling of the Sforza at the hands of the French see Gagné, *Milan Undone*.

120 Alciati, "De iustitia et iure," col. 12.§.43, 'Sed an possit ea, quae potest Imperator, in suis civitatibus? Dic, quod sic.'

comprehensive answer to the question he posed for his students. Although Alciati clearly considered the Duke of Milan to be *princeps in regno suo*, the question over whether or not he was *sui iuris* and an equal to the Emperor and the Kings of France and England in the realm of *ius gentium* remained ripe for interpretation.[121] The open-ended aspect of the status of the Duke of Milan likely prompted speculation from students, readers, and even patrons, given that any definitive answer—no matter if Alciati held the duchy as *sui iuris* or *alieni iuris*—would have been pregnant with dangerous implications. Implications, already introduced, with his statement that all rulers, even if they had a superior, possessed 'the right of the sword, both pure and mixed *imperium*.'

Explicitly stating where the Duchy of Milan stood vis-à-vis the Holy Roman Empire and France in the realm of *ius gentium* might have invited conjecture as to whether superimposing the division between superior and inferior princes—and mixed and pure *imperium*—within Italy had any utility at all. This was especially true if the duke's standing was determined by whether the duchy was in the possession of France or under the auspices of the Empire or of Habsburg-Spain. In each case, the duchy would have been *alieni iuris*—albeit in different configurations—since, in theory, an offensive war would have to be authorized by either the King of France or the Emperor. The implications would have been even greater if the Duke of Milan was truly only *sui iuris* when the duchy was in the hands of the Visconti—and through conquest and primogeniture, the early Sforza—who were native to Lombardy. After all, if Robert King of Sicily (Naples) exercised pure *imperium* and stood as an equal to the emperor and pope, and the Visconti and the early Sforza (1450–1499) were *sui iuris* as dukes of Milan and also stood as equals in the realm of war and peace to the King of France and Holy Roman Emperor, then what about other so-called inferior rulers across Italy? If they were *sui iuris* in the past, could they once again become *sui iuris* in the near or distant future? If, in other words, the Italian Wars had robbed a multiplicity of entities across the peninsula of their standing and, with it, their full *imperium*, could they band together against the Holy Roman Emperor, the King of France, and even the Papacy to reclaim it? If so, then would each entity remain independent and stand as equal to one another once foreign armies were expelled?[122]

121 Innocent III, "Rex superiorem non recognoscens in regno suo est Imperator," Decretal Per Venerabilem, 1202.

122 Cf. Niccolò Machiavelli, *The Prince*, trans. Harvey C. Mansfield (Chicago: University of Chicago Press, 1998), Chapter 26; and Alciati, *Emblem* 134: The tomb of Giangaleazzo Visconti, first Duke of Milan, and *Emblem* 151: The republic set free. Appendix.

Having led his students to the brink of answering such questions by returning to Milan, Alciati shifted back to the King of France and the Holy Roman Emperor. Only this time, rather than focusing on their standing vis-à-vis one another, Alciati encouraged his students to think about their relation to one another's subjects. This tack amounted to an exploration of the inviolability of their domains and the obligation not to interfere with one another's subjects—two principles of sovereignty that modern scholars tend to consider innovative for the seventeenth century (so-called Westphalian) sovereignty despite their clear presence in the sixteenth century.[123] Shifting the perspective from interactions among rulers in the realm of *ius gentium* to the interactions that crossed the boundaries established by it enabled Alciati to continue down the meandering path that his series of examples laid open, without directly challenging the authority of his patrons and protectors. Posing a rhetorical question, Alciati invited his students to "suppose that a subject of the King of France inflicted an injury on a subject of the emperor." Would, then, the Emperor have cause to initiate war against France?[124] Unless the King of France compelled his subject "to make recompense" for his offense, the answer would be a resounding yes: the Emperor would be justified, Alciati argued, to respond to the injury with force.[125] Yet, the Emperor could only exercise force—and thereby conduct war—against the king—and thereby France as a whole—and not a single subject or area under the jurisdiction of the king. The emperor could not, for example, wage war simply against Milan, nor could the king defend only Milan if imperial troops descended into Northern Italy.

What if an emperor tried to settle such a dispute with a king's subject without force?[126] Regardless of whether the subject was a person or a territorial possession, if the emperor attempted such an arrangement, then it would be a direct affront to the king's *imperium*. If such an agreement tried to change the status of a person or possession—like Milan—from being subject to the king's authority to being subject to the emperor's realm, then it would be nothing

---

123 See especially Benno Teschke, *The Myth of 1648*; and Julia Costa Lopez, et al., "Forum: In the Beginning There Was No Word (for It): Terms, Concepts, and Early Sovereignty," *International Studies Review* 20, no. 3 (September 2018): 489–519.

124 Alciati, "De iustitia et iure," col. 12.§.45, 'Sed quaero hic: pone, unus subditus Regi Francorum fecit iniuriam uni subdito Imperatori, utrum iusta sit causa, ut Imperator possit bellum movere contra regem Francorum? dic, quod sic, nisi Rex cogat hunc subditum satisfacere … quod Imperatur non poterit facere remissionem, nec concordiam de iniuria illata subdito.'

125 Ibid, col. 12.§.45.

126 Ibid, col. 12.§.45.

short of stealing on the part of the emperor, and clear rebellion on the part of the subject. If such nefarious dealings were to come to pass, then the parties who negotiated them would be guilty of committing the crime of *lèse-majesté* against the king, and thus subject to capital punishment.[127] No subordinate, no matter what their status in society, could enter into an agreement with a foreign ruler to promote their own interests or security without committing treason; those who had authority to conclude any agreements with foreign rulers did so at the pleasure and command of the king. In addition to having the right to put down rebellion within his domain, the French monarch would also have the right to wage war against the Holy Roman Emperor.

Put another way, since the emperor's authority to contract agreements did not extend beyond his own domains or subjects, when he suffered an injury or insult from the subjects of the king, he had two choices: either enter an arrangement whereby the King of France would order his subordinate to make amends or declare war against France to get satisfaction. For Alciati, any other course would be considered illicit because it violated the boundaries of nations and kingdoms that followed from *ius gentium*. Conversely, it was also illicit for the King of France to exercise force against, or to attempt to enter an agreement with, a subject or territory under the authority of the emperor. As peers, they both stood at the apex of authority within their own realms, and therefore had the right to use violence to preserve and protect their domains and subjects from incursion and instability. However, they could not act unilaterally beyond them. Since they had the right of war, they each had the obligation to respect the *imperium* of the other. But what about the ability of subjects or territories, who were not entirely subject to the King of France or to the Holy Roman Empire, to make recompense for injury or to change their status? Did they also have the right to enter into agreements with kings and emperors or to use force against them?

Although Alciati was clear that all wars conducted by rulers were just from the perspective of their subjects, questions over whether it was licit for an inferior ruler to wage war against a superior ruler—to defend and protect his subjects from proximate and remote harm—remained open. So too questions concerning whether the inferior prince's subjects would be obligated to offer him aid if he exercised force against his superior, and thus help to defend their *patria* in the event of war. This was the second time that Alciati led his

127 It as possible, that Alciati was referring to Charles III, the Duke of Bourbon (1490–1527), who ultimately betrayed Francis I by serving in the army of Charles V, as he was referring to the Sforza in Milan. See Knecht, *Renaissance Warrior and Patron* and Parker, *Emperor*.

students to the threshold of such a discussion. Instead of providing a direct answer to such questions, he seemingly changed the subject. The first time occurred when he challenged Baldus' implied comparison of brigands and inferior rulers, illuminating the fact that all enemies were equal in war based on their right to conduct war in the first place. Now, just when they might have expected him to discuss the status of inferior rulers in the realm of *ius gentium* explicitly, Alciati shifted his attention to dueling to suggest that just as parties meet one another as equals on the field of combat, so too did all rulers in the realm of war and peace.

Alciati closed his discussion by asking whether duels were licit.[128] To address this question, he followed the same reasoning that he had used to determine if other practices that followed from *ius gentium* were licit, ranging from war, slavery, and commerce. With an emphasis once again on violence, his discussion of dueling was as fraught with dangerous implications for the broader process of rethinking divisions within *imperium* and hierarchies of sovereignty across Europe as was his initial discussion of war. Moving from war between states to duels between persons, Alciati seemingly shifted from the realm of sovereigns back to the realm of individuals. Yet, once again, the relation between inferior and superior princes was at the heart of his investigation. Alciati signaled this to his students by reminding them that dueling was neither an act of self-defense (a right of an individual) nor an act of war (a matter of *imperium*). It was, instead, a simple offense, remedied by rules of combat.[129]

10 Contests Among Equals: Dueling as an Analogy to War

Dueling was neither self-defense nor a response to an immediate and proximate injury. It was, instead, a delayed reaction to a remote cause, namely an offense or an injury inflicted by another in the past. Comparable to a legal case and their need for a third party to monitor the procedures of the process, adversaries in duels used force rather than words to press their cause.[130] Dueling was

128 Alciati, "De iustitia et iure," col. 13.§.46, 'Et an duellem sit licitum?'

129 Ibid, col. 13.§.48, 'quia hoc non est bellum, sed potius quaedam offensio simplex.'

130 Alciati explored the history and rules of dueling, drawing on Lombardy law in his *De singvlari certamine liber. Eiusdem consilium in materia duelli, exceptum ex libro quinto Responsorum* (Venice: Vicentium Vaugris, 1544). He presented getting permission to duel, and the act of dueling itself, as burdensome, ultimately suggesting that settling disputes through law was not only easier for those (elites) who suffered an indignity or injury that prompted them to seek permission to duel in the first place, but also because settling disputes by law was, in theory, open to everyone except sovereigns. Because sovereigns stood as equals vis-à-vis one another, they had to pursue a remedy through diplomacy and war.

a consequence of *ius gentium* and reflected customs and conventions developed to mediate conflict between persons after the founding of kingdoms and the individuation of property.[131] It depended, like commerce, on good-faith agreements that both sides would not only follow specific conventions but also respect the outcome. It was also a restricted practice, like enslaving captives, insofar as only those who met particular specifications were allowed to engage in it; parties who indulged in unauthorized contests of violence were criminals.

Dueling was analogous to war. In both, differences in status and rank—no matter how significant in ordinary circumstances—became immaterial during the contest. For Alciati, just as in ordinary legal disputes, duels and wars enabled opponents to press their cause until a conclusion was reached. However, both duels and wars existed beyond the parameters of the rule of law. War was extralegal, whereas dueling was extrajudicial; there were no laws in the realm of war, only rights; duels, as a relic of chivalric custom, were dependent on the impact of arms rather than on the assessments of juries or judges. Dueling and wars were also acts of last resort; they were events that signified the failure of diplomacy and negotiation between adversaries. Just as all enemies were equal in war, so too were the participants in a duel, yet the ability to engage in both served as a marker of status. In the case of duels, settling disputes by arms rather than law represented both the extraordinary nature of the dispute and the exceptional standing of all the participants. In respect to war, the right to wage it and the authority to commission and command others to fight it signified the special status of rulers and, with it, the capacity to wield *imperium*. Where the analogy broke down, for Alciati, was in relation to superior and inferior princes.

Remembering that the category of *ius gentium,* as defined by Hermogenius, concerned everything from the founding of kingdoms to the individuation of property as well as the waging of war and the contracting of peace, helps to illuminate why Alciati used dueling to further challenge long-held assumptions within traditional jurisprudence that distinguished the rulers who held full *imperium* from those who did not. Dueling, like all the customs that followed from *ius gentium,* was grounded in *ius*—the right to meet force with force. Unlike slavery, which clearly derived from war, and commerce, which followed from the individuation of property, dueling did not fit so easily into the historical progression or progress of life encapsulated by various definitions of *ius gentium* in Roman law. Was it a practice that extended all the way

131 D.1.1.5. 'Hermogenian, Epitome of Law, book 1: As of a consequence of this *ius gentium,* wars were introduced, nations differentiated, kingdoms founded, properties individuated, estate boundaries settled, buildings put up, and commerce established, including contracts of buying and selling and letting and hiring (except for certain contractual elements established through *ius civile*).'

back to war or did it emerge after kingdoms were founded? Was it a contest of rights or was it merely a custom of honor? Why did something that was neither self-defense nor war hold sufficient enough purchase for Alciati to challenge distinctions of difference that, while they may have made sense in theory, bore little resemblance to practice?

In his brief remarks on dueling, Alciati followed the same type of analysis that he used to open it. Hence, just as he questioned the utility of Bartolus' division between proximate and remote cause, the *Gloss*' distinction between licit and illicit war, and Baldus' contrast between brigands and rulers, Alciati invoked the customs and practice of dueling to establish a clear line between just and unjust exercises of violence. By asking whether dueling was licit, he recounted his disagreement with Baldus, who argued that dueling, unless "permitted from the license of the prince for a great cause," was illicit.[132] In addition to articulating how rare licit duels were, this statement emphasized the necessity for one to acquire the approval of their superior before they could engage in one. Such a claim would have surely reminded Alciati's students of a similar one in the *Gloss*, which he emphasized—and rejected—in his discussion of war, namely "a prince recognizing a superior cannot declare war without his superior's command."[133] As synonymous as these two assertions appeared to be, however, they described exercises of violence within two very different realms.

All persons, for example, who lived within civil society—whether in a commune, republic, duchy, principality, kingdom, or empire—were subject to a superior authority who held a monopoly over legitimate violence within their domains. Hence, any attempt by a subject to settle disputes by arms rather than through law and without first acquiring permission from a superior, served as an affront against the rule of law and to the authority of rulers. To take matters into one's own hands meant taking them out of the hands of one's sovereign, thus calling their *imperium* directly and indirectly into question and committing a crime of *lèse-majesté*. In the realm of sovereigns, however, there was neither a rule of law to subvert nor—as far as Alciati was concerned—a universal sovereign to affront. The determination to use force by rulers was not a challenge to sovereignty so much as it was an affirmation of it. Finally, unlike subjects within society, not all rulers were subject to superiors, and thus not all required permission before they could act. Those rulers who could not set offensive wars in motion without permission were not, strictly speaking, rulers

132 Alciati, "De iustitia et iure," col. 13.§.46, 'dic, qoud, non prout concludit hic Baldus ... quod de principis licentia permissum est ex magna causa.'

133 Ibid, col. 8.§.31. See note 86 above for Latin.

at all. Since they did not possess the right of the sword, they did not possess *imperium*, mixed or pure. They were proxies and delegates, who acted on the command of authority rather than on their own volition.

For Alciati, the problem with Baldus' definition of a licit duel and with discussions of dueling in the *Gloss* was that each viewed dueling through the lens of civil law, despite the fact that no matter how much "it was confirmed by the civil law," the custom extended from *ius gentium*.[134] Therefore, determining whether the practice was licit or illicit required a different approach. To underscore his point, he once again used commerce as an example. Discrete civil laws were developed over time to regulate and organize commerce and trade within societies, yet this did not negate the fact that commerce existed prior to—and crossed the boundaries of—such civil laws. Hence, although "purchase & leasing, & similar contracts are confirmed by the authority of the civil law, nevertheless they are of the *ius gentium*."[135]

Indeed, all institutions, conventions, customs, and practices that existed because of *ius gentium*—whether approved and developed by civil law or abridged and abrogated by it—nevertheless remained historically anchored in *ius gentium*. Some of those practices were immediately caused by *ius*, the right to meet force with force; some were remotely caused, developing over time to reflect current needs and interests. What made dueling appear to be more directly related to *ius* than other practices that followed from *ius gentium*, like commerce? The answer was relatively simple, namely the centrality of force and violence was not only at the epicenter of the practice but it was also at its periphery. Violence was, in other words, both the remote and proximate cause of everything that happened within a duel, just as in the case in war, from the moment preparations were made through to the end of the contest.

Alciati linked dueling to *ius gentium* and, in the process, distinguished it from war by explaining that dueling—despite its similarities—was not equivalent to war because it was not the act of a *princeps* reclaiming lost rights against an enemy or waging a defensive war. With this determination, Alciati brought to his students' attention the fact that "however much duels are regularly prohibited" by civil laws, "it escapes notice, that a duel might happen in defense of one's own affairs."[136] Moreover, duels were not limited to restoring honor

134 Ibid, col. 13.§.47–48, '... nam teneo, quod istud bellum sit de iure gentium, quamvis confirmatum sit a iure civili.'

135 Alciati, "De iustitia et iure," col. 13.§.48, 'Nam etiam emptio & locatio, & similes contractus confirmantur auctoritate iuris civilis, & tamen sunt iuris gentium.'

136 Ibid, col. 13.§.49, 'Et hinc est, quod quamvis duella regulariter sint prohibita ... quin duellem fieret pro defensione rerum suarum.'

and reputation, but they could also be over one's property. Here, it is important to consider that, while few persons were permitted to use arms to settle disputes, rulers were not precluded from using the duel rather than protracted war to settle conflicts. Just as for persons, if rulers met one another in a duel, no matter their rank or the size of their territory or armies, they met as equals on a level field to settle their affairs through a single combat. Nevertheless, the option to partake in a duel rather than in a war would not be without immense complications and consequences.

If, for example, Francis I had taken up Charles V's offer to settle the question of who possessed Milan by means of a duel, this would have created more problems than it solved.[137] Suppose that such a contest took place, would that mean that the inhabitants of the duchy, and all the land and possessions that they thought they owned, were the property of another all along? If this was so in the case of Milan, wouldn't that suggest that any territory within the domain of kings and emperors was not merely under their protection but also in their possession? Were the lives and fortunes of those who lived within these territories subject to the whims of superior rulers who could, at any moment, gamble them away by partaking in what amounted to a game of chance? If so, what rights, protections, and assurances, if any, would subjects have that could not be gambled away by their rulers? Were inferior rulers, who exercised authority over the territories that superiors dueled over, merely custodians and caretakers? Or did inferior princes, especially those recognized as *princeps in regno suo*, also have the right to engage in duels in defense of their own affairs or to defend their own possessions, even against superior rulers? Could the Duchy of Milan, in other words, assert its independence from both the emperor and the king by inviting them to a duel? And, finally, would an acceptance to the offer, by either party, signal that Milan was on equal standing with its opponents?

If we consider the latter question within the context of Alciati's lecture, it is reasonable to suspect that his answer would have been yes. An inferior ruler could challenge a superior ruler to a duel because duels—as responses to past offenses rather than present threats—were distinct from war and occurred among persons, and not nations, peoples, or kingdoms. Furthermore, duels were not acts of self-defense, wherein one party suddenly had to defend themselves or their *patria* from the onslaught of violence by an aggressor; they were premeditated rituals of violence between two consenting parties. Although one might argue that some wars followed conventions indistinguishable—on

137 Charles challenged Francis to a duel on several occasions. Although Francis sometimes agreed, a duel never transpired between them. Knecht, *Renaissance Warrior and Patron* and Parker, *Emperor.*

account of the highly-orchestrated customs and diplomacy—from dueling, even so, these conflicts engaged armies and mercenaries, not simply rulers. Moreover, since dueling was not war, the conditions of a duel were not open to change once the parties had stepped onto the field.[138] A duel between two rulers who claimed authority over Milan, for example, could not be used as a pretext by either side to settle an affair or to acquire a territory that lay beyond it, nor could such a duel change the status of other entities, like Florence or Venice. Duels, unlike wars, had clearly defined limits.

As important, the subjects of the combatants in a duel were neither required to help them to secure a victory nor could they be commanded or commissioned to help either opponent win the contest. Even so, what about Baldus' claim that a duel would be illicit if waged without permission from one's prince, viz., superior? Wouldn't that mean, even to Alciati, that an inferior ruler required permission from a superior before he could meet him with arms? While accepting a challenge from a subordinate was equivalent to granting him permission, the consequence would not change the cause; the fact would remain that the inferior initiated the duel, and thus, by implication, it was licit for an inferior to challenge his superior to meet as equals on a field of combat. This was possible because, no matter if they occurred between ordinary persons or rulers, duels were not intended to settle questions of justice, nor even of necessity; they were aimed at asserting and defending one's rights, restoring one's honor, or defending one's reputation. Duels were not equivalent to seeking justice by law or retribution by war, but they constituted something in between.

No matter how improbable it may have been for a king to accept a challenge to a duel from an emperor—let alone from an inferior ruler—to settle dynastic and territorial disputes, the fact remains that an inferior could set a duel in motion in response to a remote or prior injury, or in order to press their rights. Given that dueling was analogous to war, would this mean, by implication, that an inferior also had the right to set an offensive war in motion against other rulers, inferior or superior, in order to press their rights? If duels exemplified a parity of rights among participants, wouldn't wars signify a parity of rights among combatants? Finally, if an inferior ruler, in the context of a duel, could exercise both offensive and defensive force, then what implications might that carry for doing the same in war? These kinds of questions were invited, yet not explicitly entertained, when Alciati chose to conclude his lecture on the first

138 Alciati, *De singvlari certamine liber. Eiusdem consilium in materia duelli, exceptum ex libro quinto Responsorum.*

title of the *Digest* with a discussion on dueling, therefore limiting his overall analysis to the category and consequences of *ius gentium*.

As innocuous as his coverage of dueling might appear at first sight, when we interpret the broader contours of his discussion of *ius* as the right to meet force with force, its implications become clear. Before turning to dueling, Alciati asserted that inferior rulers—rather than being mere proxies—possessed full *imperium* in the realm of war, and therefore were not—strictly speaking—inferiors; they could wage offensive and defensive wars *sui iuris*, just as they could punish brigands and rebels without seeking permission. They could do so because any ruler who possessed the right of the sword, possessed mixed and pure *imperium*. His discussion of dueling took this one step further insofar as he suggested that it was the contest itself that rendered both sides equal, no matter who emerged as the victor or the cause—remote or immediate—that prompted it. No matter who won, the fact that both parties had the right to press their claim by arms remained the same. If we apply this same principle to war, all rulers, regardless of their distinctions in the realm of politics, stood as equals in the realm of force. As such, the question of justice in the realm of *ius gentium* was redeployed as a question of right. Furthermore, just as duels rendered opponents as equals, so too did war. Hence, if we follow his logic, the distinction between mixed and pure *imperium* when it came to war was academic. If all rulers had the right to wage war, then all wars waged by rulers, no matter if offensive or defensive, were licit. If all wars waged by rulers were licit, then none were illicit and the distinction between just and unjust wars was immaterial. The only wars that were unjust were not wars at all—they were acts of violence perpetuated by brigands, pirates, robbers, and rebels. Hence, to put down such violence required punishment, not a declaration of war.

In essence this lecture suggests that Alciati saw no hierarchy of sovereignty among rulers in the realm of *ius gentium*. When it came to *imperium*, what mattered was that all enemies were equal in their right to press their cause by arms—to wage both offensive and defensive war. Recognizing that communes, republics, principalities, and duchies were *sui iuris* in the realm of *ius gentium* did not diminish the sovereignty of emperors or kings. It suggested, instead, that all sovereigns, no matter the size of their domains, were equal in the realm of war and peace. Therefore, not only could all rulers defend their borders and boundaries by waging defensive and offensive wars but also no other sovereigns—no matter what their political status—could interfere with their subjects or their domestic affairs. Hence, no matter where rulers stood in relation to territorial size, political constitution, dynastic history, or influence, they all held the same rights because they were all rulers. They were, in sum, equally sovereign, and thus equally entitled to use force to defend and deflect proximate and remote threats to their authority, subjects, and domains. There was no hierarchy of sovereignty in the realm of *ius gentium*, only the binary: enemies who held the right of the sword and brigands and rebels who didn't.

11 The Practical Significance of Alciati's Novel Re-interpretation of *Jus Gentium* in Context

Although there is no indication of the specific years when Alciati presented his *De iustitia et iure* lecture, it stands to reason—given its brevity and timely content—that he delivered it on several occasions throughout his academic career. Bearing in mind Alciati's quest to ensure that his words were conveyed as clearly as possible, the final bound version likely reflects three decades of fine-tuning and adjustment just as in his publications. At the same time, the lecture also displayed his mastery of the use of analogy to communicate ideas that, if spoken too plainly, would have surely drawn rebuke from his protectors and patrons. When it is not possible to arrive at the intended meaning of an author's words directly, as Alciati tells us in his *Emblems*, such words should be interpreted and "understood according to context."[139] In Alciati's case, that context included the changing fortunes of Milan and, with it, of northern Italy throughout the first half of the sixteenth century. As such, remembering the ways in which his life was affected by the ambitions of some of the most powerful rulers of the age underscores the sense of urgency in his lecture and the issues at stake.

For example, at Avignon, Alciati would have presented this lecture in the wake of the Wars of the League of Cambrai (1508–1510) and the War of the Holy League (1510–1514), which began with the Papacy, the Holy Roman Empire, Spain, and France united against the territorial ambitions of Venice, and were concluded with the defeat of the Holy League—consisting of the Papal States, the Holy Roman Empire, England, and Spain—at the hands of Venice allied with the French. For one of the most respected and famous legal humanists of the time to explicitly argue, in the aftermath of such wars, that all inferior and superior rulers were equal in their capacity to exercise *imperium* in the realm of war and peace would have surely drawn attention from all quarters of Europe. Not only would it have implied that smaller states across the Italian peninsula had the same rights as the Holy Roman Empire, the Papal States, and Kingdoms of England and France in the realm of *ius gentium* but it also would

139 Alciati, *Commentaria de verborum significatione*, 1025, 'nisi non ita voluisse auctorem præsumamus: tunc enim ex coniectura restringuntur.'

have suggested that the well-worn distinction between inferior and superior rulers and states was problematic, if not wholly arbitrary. Extended beyond the confines of Italy and into the Germanies, France, or across the Atlantic, such a theory could be used to justify resistance in the hands of those rulers, princes, and governors who refused to bend to the will of those at the metropole, and wished instead to assert their right to oversee internal affairs (law and order) and to defend the integrity of their territories against incursions from other rulers (war and peace).

Delivered a decade later, while teaching—at the invitation of Francis I—at the University of Bourges, such an argument would have been even more dangerous, given the ever-shifting landscapes of violence and instability within and beyond Europe; this volatility was attendant on religious, economic, technological, and commercial changes that corresponded with the Italian Wars of 1521 to 1526. These wars pitted the newly-elected Holy Roman Emperor Charles V, allied with the Medici Pope Leo X, against France, and were immediately followed by the Italian Wars of 1526 to 1530, wherein France was allied with the Medici Pope Clement V, England, Venice, and Florence against the Holy Roman Emperor. After nearly a decade of war—extending well beyond northern Italy—the military might of Charles V was well established and appeared unstoppable. Both in the midst and aftermath of these conflicts, Alciati's interpretations of *imperium*, particularly those in relation to the emperor, surely pleased Francis I, and would have resonated among princes and rulers throughout southern, central, and northern Europe, viz., Burgundy and the Low Countries, who were growing weary of Charles' rule.

As Alciati's career progressed, and the violence of the sixteenth century increased, his interpretations would have become more, rather than less, perilous. No matter how pregnant with possibilities and ramifications the lecture might have been for students studying in Avignon or Bourges, when read at the University of Bologna—perhaps the most authoritative Roman law faculty in Europe—as well as at the Universities at Ferrara and Pavia, its implications would have taken on greater urgency and meaning. Nestled between the Italian Wars of 1536–1538, wherein Charles V revealed his ambitions to place all of Italy under the dominion of the Holy Roman Empire and Spain, and the start of the Italian War of 1542–1546, in which Francis I tried (and failed) once again to assert his authority and claims over the transalpine region of northern Italy, Alciati's explanations as to why there were no just wars, only rightful enemies, would have been clear to all rulers and states (large and small) across Southern Europe.

Just as salient was Alciati's argument that all enemies were equals in the realm of *ius gentium* in the same way that all participants, no matter their ordinary status, were equal on the field of a duel. This argument in his lecture—paired with his book on dueling—became increasingly relevant each time Charles V invited Francis I to settle the question of Milan by means of a single combat, emperor versus king, rather than by protracted war. So, too, was Alciati's interpretation of *ius gentium* and how it fit into a broader theory of universal jurisprudence, in that it rendered all rulers no matter their title and all states no matter their size equivalent in the realm of war and peace, as well as hinted at why, despite a long tradition of conflict, Christian monarchs and Muslim rulers—the Ottoman Sultan in the case of Francis I and the Safavid Shah in the case of Charles V—could join together as allies, and thereby as equals, to wage war against their common enemy with impunity.[140] If all enemies were equal in war, then all allies were equal as well. Hence, the parity of rights among rulers—and not the distinctions based in religion or politics—made the wars they waged licit. If one rejected—as Alciati did—the notion that there was a single sovereign who held authority over a universal empire, then no ruler who held the right to wage war and conduct peace was illegitimate; all rulers could stand, equally, as enemies or allies. Only those who lacked the right to wage war, like brigands, pirates, and rebels, committed and commanded violence that was illicit, and thus were subject to attack and punishment by legitimate rulers—without distinction of size, history, or constitution—around the globe.

Only after he returned to the University of Pavia—at Charles V's request—in 1547, would Alciati have an opportunity to present this lecture in a period of relative peace. Read with an eye to what seemed to be stable conditions in Milan, we might assume that Alciati simply fused a discussion of *imperium* and the rights of superior and inferior princes with his interpretation of *ius gentium* in order to make Roman law more accessible to his students. We might also assume, he appealed to contemporary issues and anxieties in order to help students make sense of ideas, structures, and language that might otherwise have seemed esoteric, antiquated, or insignificant to them. There is little doubt that such a pedagogical choice would have engaged his students' imagination. Even so, it would be a mistake to ignore the broader implications of his interpretations of *ius* and *ius gentium* for students matriculating at Pavia in the wake of war, especially when paired with Alciati's *Emblems* lamenting the destruction of Italy over the previous five decades.[141]

Reading the lecture without taking this lack of stability into account, or as a mere prelude to his other works, might, in turn, lead us to ignore Alciati's

140 See Mallett and Shaw, *The Italian Wars*; Knecht, *Renaissance Warrior and Patron*; Parker, *Emperor*; Norwich, *Four Princes*; and Isom-Verhaaren, *Allies with the Infidel*.

141 See Emblems 42, 143, 144, 164, and 166 in the Appendix of this volume.

explicit link between the rights of rulers to the rights of persons; this analogy highlighted the necessity of respecting the rule of law within communities as well as the rights of *imperium* between them—large or small, imperial or dynastic, republic or monarchy. If, instead, we read his lecture in the context of the Italian Wars, then it becomes abundantly clear that Alciati offered his students an innovative—and dangerous—understanding of the relation between *ius* and *ius gentium*, along with the relation between justice and right (*De iustitia et iure*), at precisely the time when traditional ideas, and the political structures that they underpinned, were breaking down.

Putting Alciati's interpretation of *ius* and *ius gentium* in context also prevents us from supposing that a lecture written for law students would have had, at best, a rather mundane influence on emerging ideas about power and politics. The variable contexts in which he taught reminds us of the centrality of law and jurisprudence—especially in relation to the rights of man, of rulers, and of states—to the fundamental re-formation of Europe, amidst wars that drew nearly every state, empire, and kingdom into conflict, over the course of the long sixteenth century.[142] Being mindful of the intended audience of Alciati's analysis, viz., law students, invites us to consider the central importance of the university in providing a formal legal education in Roman law to the broader process of early modern territorial-state and empire-state formation. At the same time, it prompts us to consider how fundamentally transformative new ideas and methods within legal theory could be—and how innovative and flexible legal education had to be—in the face of rapidly-changing landscapes of power, territories, and norms.

Consider, for example, that whether Alciati's students—in Italy or France—became diplomats or ambassadors abroad, served as advisors to rulers at home, or tended to the day-to-day administration of civil law as clerks, lawyers, and jurists, the interpretations of *ius* and *ius gentium* that they encountered while studying with him had the potential to help them to shape the apparatus of the state in far more significant ways than might appear at first glance. Alciati's treatment of *ius gentium*, his focus on violence, and his emphases on the distinctions between the rule of law and the customs of war provided his students with tools they could use to expand an emerging rule of law ensconced in reason and grounded in necessity, as well as to explain why such a rule—as a check on the avarice and ambitions of some at the expense of the security and common good of the many—was essential. In this respect, Alciati's interpretation of *ius* and its relation to necessity rather than to justice within his

142 Again, the term re-formation in this context is meant to emphasize dramatic political and legal transformations that accompanied state formation.

treatment of *De iustitia et iure* shared more in common with arguments aimed at critiquing changes in the realm of politics by Niccolò Machiavelli (1469–1527) in Florence or Thomas More in London than in the realm of jurisprudence by Guillaume Budé in Paris or Ulrich Zasius in Freiburg.

Yet, at the same time, the manner in which Alciati organized his lecture around the principle of force, especially the right to meet violence with violence, reminds us that his text was neither a critique of socio-economic and political thought affected by the creation of new laws and institutions (e.g., More's *Utopia*), nor was it a handbook that provided advice on how to hold a principality once it was gained (e.g., Machiavelli's *Prince*).[143] It also reminds us that Alciati neither wrote his lecture to be read by princes in private nor by kings in public. Instead, it was crafted for those being trained as lawyers and jurists whose task was to ensure that a rule of law—as opposed to a rule of force or fear—would be protected, respected, and maintained within civil society, with an eye to procuring peace and security between societies. Hence, his primary audience, just as Budé's and Zasius', were those who, after completing their legal educations, would be charged with steering the ship of state and, if necessary, maintaining an even keel, despite the whims of those at the helm.

Although he was not writing for princes, Alciati knew full well that both Francis I and Charles V were paying close attention to his work. Nevertheless, he set forth a theory of right that shed light on the limits of their power, both domestically and internationally. That he did so, even though he was—at various points in his life—subject to the power and patronage of each, makes his theory even more remarkable, especially given the extent to which he invited his students to question the very distinctions used to demarcate a hierarchy of rights that rulers like Francis and Charles relied upon in order to assert their authority across Italy.

Drawing on the works of Bartolus and Baldus, Alciati questioned traditional legal theories that had become accepted by some as political fact and were used to describe and defend gradations of power between rulers as well as hierarchies of status within civil society. Knowing, as he acknowledged in his orations, that many students who took up their studies with him were either ill-prepared or uninterested in studying law in accordance with humanist methods, Alciati made his lectures accessible to as many audiences as possible, including those whose interest in Roman law was merely novel. At the same time, he was also aware that delivering his interpretations clearly and directly for his students carried the risk of offending and affronting his patrons. To that

143 See Thomas More, *Utopia*, eds. George M. Logan and Robert. M. Adams, Rev. ed. (Cambridge: Cambridge University Press, 2002); and Niccolò Machiavelli, *The Prince*.

end, Alciati led his students through a series of examples that, when taken in isolation, appear at first to be dead ends, yet taken together, reveal a complex and nuanced theory of universal jurisprudence and a novel understanding of sovereignty.

12 *Jus* as a Marker of Equality in Humanist Jurisprudence

Given that Alciati's *De iustitia et iure* lecture focused on legitimate and illegitimate violence among rulers as well as a narrow definition of *ius* as the right to meet force with force, we might conclude that his broader understanding of justice and right sat adjacent to, rather than intersected with, the humanist jurisprudence of both Budé and Zasius. Not least because, as a consequence of using the lecture to challenge assumptions underpinning hierarchies of sovereignty, Alciati neglected the very definition of *ius*—as the art of what is good and fair, conjoined—that framed the overall interpretation of the same title by his peers. Likewise, Alciati omitted clear explanations of the moral relation between *ius* and natural law, of the link between natural law and *ius gentium*, or indeed any substantive analysis of the connection between *ius* and justice, beyond his assertion that all wars were licit, and thus, by implication, all enemies were just. These omissions followed from Alciati's choice to explore *ius* as a marker of *imperium*, rather than as an objective criterion of justice, a cache of universal rights and obligations, or an attribute of human dignity. His focus, in other words, on violence in the realm of *ius gentium* drew his students' attention away from the plight of persons within civil society, or at least it appeared so.

Yet, in effect, Alciati's lecture, read with his orations and *Emblems* in mind, offered a theory of universal jurisprudence that emphasized a parity of *ius* among sovereigns, which reflected, in turn, a parity of *ius* among persons. Thus, despite arriving at the question of *ius* from a different angle than his peers, Alciati's lecture nevertheless illuminated a foundational aspect of humanist jurisprudence shared by both Budé and Zasius. This particular aspect was that the basic equality of man, rulers, and states vis-à-vis one another was not a problem that needed to be explained away in order to justify inequality and subjection within and between civil societies; it was, instead, a basic fact that revealed further foundational aspects and principles of universal jurisprudence, including universal rights and obligations shared among and between all mankind. These aspects could be used to reform laws, institutions, and customs that missed the mark of justice by diminishing the standing and rights of some, so as to augment the liberty and power of others. Alciati's choice to focus on the relation between *ius* and *ius gentium* among persons and peoples enabled him to explore why it was that *ius gentium* provided a virtual prism through which the rights among persons were reflected in the 'laws of nations,' yet such a reflection was not without significant distortions.

For example, the equality—or parity—of the right to meet force with force among persons was preserved in civil society by the rule of law insofar as that if one's life, family, or property were in immediate danger, then one had the right to defend and protect it/them. After the fact, those who exercised such force had to explain their actions; they had to convince the community or judges that they had no other recourse than to respond to violence with violence, and that the violence that they exerted was commensurate with the threat they had faced, viz., they had to harm or be harmed; kill or be killed. In theory, the opportunity for subjects and citizens to have their actions weighed in accordance with the rule of law was supposed to ensure that, regardless of the political, social, and economic distinctions and inequalities that existed among members of the same community, everyone was accorded due process. If the use of force was warranted, so the theory went, the person—no matter their status—would not be punished; if the use of force was found to be unwarranted, then the person would be subject to punishment.

Even though the rule of law often reflected the ideal rather than the reality, it nevertheless served as an important mechanism of reform. Jurists who understood the rule of law properly could appeal to it in order to effect changes to practices, procedures, and institutions that departed from, or clearly violated, underlying principles such as justice and right. They could do so because the rule of law was not only the impetus for man to join civil society; it also underpinned the purpose of civil society itself: to enable mankind to secure peace and to pursue the common good. This could only be accomplished if everyone agreed to refrain from exercising force (*vis*) to respond to injury, and instead chose to pursue recompense through laws established by civic agreements, charters, or constitutions interpreted by properly trained lawyers and jurists who understood *ius* in all aspects.

The equality or parity of the right to meet force with force among and between nations (*gentes*), however, could not be restricted by such civic agreements, nor were the actions of states, peoples, or rulers subject to punishment or acquittal by judges, even if they sought to defend their actions as if they were. That relations between nations could not be restricted by the rule of law did not mean that there was an absence of political and legal theory—secular and religious—aimed at explaining why some rulers or nations were under the domain, and thereby subject to the authority, of other nations and rulers. Indeed, superimposing theories that were reflective of civil society or feudal arrangements on the realm of nations, or *ius gentium*, enabled scholastic jurists to construct a hierarchy in which some rulers were deemed superior whereas others were classed as inferior.

Yet, for Alciati, these distinctions violated aspects of *ius gentium* and tended to perpetuate a limited understanding of the relations among rulers, states, and peoples. Hence, no matter how useful it might have been to draw on aspects of feudal, canon, and customary law to explain Roman law to students, elites, and rulers across Europe in the wake of its rediscovery, this did not mean that such examples were void of errors. While recognizing that all rulers belonged to the same genus, scholastic jurists nevertheless separated them according to various species of power; by demarcating the limits of their authority, they classified some rulers as having greater political, legal, and moral significance than others. In so doing, jurists developed theories of jurisprudence that ultimately undercut the legitimacy of inferior rulers to defend their subjects and territories from attacks without seeking authorization from those who held pure *imperium*.

Although exceptions were possible in dire instances, if inferior princes used force to repel an injury, then they would have to make their case—through diplomatic channels—as to why it was necessary for them to do so without first asking for permission. Among the most glaring problems with all of this, for Alciati, was that the limitations and procedures attendant on such an arrangement undermined the ability of those deemed as inferior rulers to be in command of their own subjects and their ability to defend, protect, and even punish those within their jurisdiction. It also undercut the inviolability of their territorial jurisdiction and legal authority, thus making each of their subjects vulnerable to the whims, wishes, and actions of superior rulers. If one's ruler, whose authority underpinned and structured civil laws within a discrete society, was subject to the authority and command of another, then what assurances were there that any customs, agreements, and civic constitutions within any society would not be simply overturned at the whim of another ruler? At one and the same time, then, the distinction between superior and inferior rulers both invited and pressed the question of autonomy in relation to external boundaries and borders, as much as it did the internal arrangements and institutions among those who lived within those borders and boundaries.

Such distinctions, however, were not merely theoretical. In the realm of war, they established that a superior ruler could exercise force *sui juris*, whereas an inferior ruler—because under the control of another—could not. It was precisely this kind of division, made by jurists and scholars for centuries, that increasingly came into question in the wake of the Italian Wars, religious Reformations, and European conquest and expansion over the long sixteenth century. Indeed, if such a (feudal) distortion of rights was superimposed on the realm of *ius gentium*, then the long-term viability of the rule of law within an inferior prince's realm would become increasingly uncertain and thus unstable. Without the parity of rights in the realm of *ius gentium*, as held by all rulers alike, the choice of submitting to a rule of law—in essence, of placing life and limb under the protection of another in exchange for stability, security, and justice—could very easily become a bad bargain (as in the case of Milan) for all persons, peoples, principalities, duchies, and cities across Europe as well as in areas beyond it. The realm of *ius gentium* among rulers had to be grounded in the equality of rights, just as the realm of civil society had to be grounded in the equality of law; otherwise, it would cease to fulfill its function of providing persons with some semblance of predictability, stability, or security. The right to use force to protect their boundaries and subjects was as inviolable to rulers—no matter their size, constitution, or history—as it was for individuals to use force to protect themselves, their possessions, and their *patria*. Although the exercise of this right by persons could be restricted by laws and procedures within civil society, it could not be fully abrogated or abolished without affronting their dignity and thereby natural law. Whereas for sovereigns, even while constitutions limited their authority over their subjects, no treaty or agreement could abrogate or abolish their right of war without violating their *imperium* and thereby *ius gentium*.

Conclusion

The Re-formation of Europe and the Turn to Jus Gentium

About 500 years ago something remarkable happened: a crisis of authority across Europe, which had already been simmering for nearly five centuries, erupted into a fast and furious boil. Although we might deem Martin Luther's calls to reform the Catholic Church in the early decades of the sixteenth-century as the flashpoint that transformed discontent into a seething mess of conflict and rebellion, by doing so we risk mistaking the manifestations of a long-term change for its cause and the pleas for the renewal and restoration of the true church—and the true state—as new rather than as part of a much longer history of calls, emanating from all corners of post-Roman Europe to reform secular and religious institutions and practices that had missed the mark of justice. We also risk overlooking—or at least underemphasizing—the ways in which, by the turn of sixteenth century, the long and haphazard process of city, territorial, and empire-state formation had already begun to transform nearly every aspect of socio-economic, political, and religious life throughout Latin Christendom, a trend that required attention to, and reassessments of, long-held customs and laws as well as the accommodation and adaptation of new ones.

Moreover, fixing our gaze on the causes and consequences of religious transformations might cause us to lose sight of the ways in which a fundamental shift in political and legal thought and practice, particularly in the early decades of the sixteenth century, helped to transform Europe from a collection of feudal-states—whose authority was based in and sanctioned by the eternal plan of God—to an array of increasingly secular states and empires whose authority was evidenced by the nature of man and anchored in *ius* and *ius gentium*. It also prompts us to reconsider the assessment that the ideas articulated by the Peace of Westphalia in 1648—and the corresponding political and legal thought that sought to explain and justify them—was solely the product of the wars, religious and secular, civil and international, on land and at sea, that dominated the affairs of Europeans states and empires in latter half of the sixteenth- and the first half of the seventeenth century.[1]

1 See Bartleson, "Double Binds: Sovereignty and the Just War Tradition"; Costa Lopez, et. al., "Forum: In the Beginning There Was No Word (for It);" Davies, *Periodization and Sovereignty*; Jean Bethke Elshtain, *Sovereignty: God, State, and Self* (New York: Basic Books, 2008); Andreas

 | DOI:10.1163/9789004528451_009

This book invites readers to approach these changes not from the perspective of religious conflict or of the aftermath of the Eight Years' War (1568–1648) and Thirty Years' War (1618–1648), but from perspectives that preceded both. That is, it explores shifts in juridical thought in the context of the re-formation of Europe itself—or rather a particular manifestation of it—at the hands of Renaissance jurists, who put forward a theory of universal jurisprudence based in universal rights, shared by all of mankind regardless of time or place, that could be invoked to hold political and legal authorities—sacred and secular—to a higher criterion of justice in the early-sixteenth century.[2] Writing in a world shaped—less or more—by the Italian Wars, which began in 1494, humanist jurists developed theories of universal jurisprudence that were neither dependent on nor tied exclusively to Catholic or Protestant doctrine, so much as an understanding of basic categories within Roman law that, as far as they were concerned, had been misunderstood, misinterpreted, and corrupted for centuries at the hands of traditional, viz., university-based, jurisprudence.

The legal humanists at the center of this book so thoroughly reinterpreted terms, idioms, and categories preserved within the first title of Justinian's *Digest* that they fundamentally transformed them. In the process, they invented conceptual tools—although they would claim that they had merely recovered them—that we tend to identify with modern political thought anchored in the late-sixteenth and early-seventeenth centuries rather than stretching back to at least the end of the fifteenth. Together, as a result of addressing fundamental understandings of the sources and limits of political and legal authority, humanist jurists shifted their attention (and their readers' and students') away from the European *ius commune*, that is, the amalgam of civil, canon, feudal, and customary law, grounded in the authority of emperors, princes, and popes, that permeated scholastic jurisprudence for nearly four centuries, towards a conceptual understanding of the foundations of law and society grounded in the attributes and actions of man, wherein *ius* as a criterion of justice and foundation of universal right and *ius gentium*, the customs in common among all mankind, were both central.

Osiander, "Sovereignty, International Relations, and the Westphalian Myth," *International Organization* 55, no. 3 (2001): 251–87; and Teschke, *The Myth of 1648*.

2 The term re-formation draws out the changes that encompassed legal reform within states, as much as the negotiation of boundaries and borders between them, as all the major powers and significant political entities in central and southern Europe came into conflict—first over Naples and then over Milan—in the early decades of the 16th century. The use of the term re-formation of Europe is not meant as either a play on, nor an alternative to, the religious changes of that followed from the (Protestant) Reformation or the (Catholic) Counter-Reformation.

Throughout their works, Budé, Zasius, and Alciati were occupied with general queries concerning the origins and the nature of governance as well as particular questions of political and legal authority in France, Germany, and Italy. They consistently engaged with questions of rights—of persons and of nations (*ius gentium*)—in their discussions of Roman law before and throughout the Protestant and Catholic Reformations. Precisely because they—following in the footsteps of luminaries like Valla—were already using Roman law as a means to legitimize and to critique the expansion of political and legal authority before the onset of religious conflicts and wars, one can examine their works outside of the traditional confines of theology in which scholars tend to explore natural law, *ius*, and *ius gentium* in the long sixteenth century (1494–1618).[3] In addition to focusing, nearly exclusively, on worldly rather than sacred understandings of justice and right, Budé, Zasius, and Alciati also stepped back from traditional scholastic methods that were dominant in the Roman and canon law faculties in universities at the time.

Rather than attempt to reconcile the contradictions and discrepancies within the *corpus iuris civilis* by means of logical distinctions—using inductive and deductive methods as the scholastics had done—the fathers of humanist jurisprudence paired the study of Roman law with the methods and sources associated with the *studia humanitatis,* viz., the study of history, moral philosophy, grammar, philology, and poetry. In doing so, they used their historical imaginations, as much as textual and historical analysis, to show how and why aspects of civil jurisprudence changed over time to illuminate the universal and immutable principles, such as justice and *ius*—as a measure of justice, a marker of dignity, and a cache of rights and obligations—that underpinned it. In essence, they historicized Roman law and its sources, while simultaneously using it to justify their call for a wholesale reform of university-based jurisprudence (Budé), to argue for the necessity to bring specific civil laws and practices into conformity with justice and right (Zasius), and to argue for the parity of force among states—no matter their territorial size, dynastic history, political constitution, or religion—in the realm of nations (Alciati).

In addition to breaking from their scholastic peers and contemporaries by placing definitions of *ius*, natural law, and *ius gentium* into historical rather than theological, perspective, Budé, Zasius, and Alciati re-defined and re-interpreted these categories of Roman law, as well as the relationship between them, in ways that fundamentally departed from the Romans, the Byzantines

3 From the outbreak of the first Italian War in 1494 to the outbreak of the Thirty Years' War in 1618.

and the Ancients. Moreover, through their re-interpretation of the vocabulary of Roman law, these legal humanists brought the category of *ius gentium* into the core of their theories of jurisprudence, and thus offered an understanding of it that transcended the limits and confines of the *ius commune* that was central to their scholastic predecessors and peers. At the same time, Zasius and Alciati shared some common ideas, features, and tropes with fellow Renaissance jurists in Catholic Spain and France (e.g., Francisco de Vitoria and Jean Bodin) as well as their predominantly Protestant seventeenth-century successors in Northern Europe.

Indeed, there are several striking similarities between theories of justice and right by the 'grande triumvirate' of humanist jurisprudence, as explored in this volume, and the so-called fathers of modern international law, sovereignty, and right, including Alberico Gentili (1552–1608), Hugo Grotius (1583–1645), Thomas Hobbes, and John Locke (1632–1704). Some of these similarities stem from their shared background in the *studia humanitatis*; the legal humanists and these modern theorists employed similar historical and comparative methods and drew from a cache of common sources. These similarities can also be accounted for by the sheer fact that the ideas of the first generation of humanist jurists, especially Zasius and Alciati, were picked up, expanded, and adapted to address new problems in the wake of European incursions and expansions into the Atlantic as well as the turmoil of the reformation and religious conflicts within Europe by subsequent jurists, scholastic and humanist.

For example, a quarter century after Alciati's death, Bodin coined the term sovereignty and laid out its features in his *Les Six Livres de la Republique* (*Six Books on the Republic*) published in 1576. Moreover, Vitoria, in his lecture on *De Indis* (*On the Indies*) delivered at the School of Salamanca in 1539, more than two decades after Zasius was first appointed as professor of law at Freiburg and Budé published his *Annotationes*, presented a list of universal rights (*ius*) and corresponding obligations stemming from man's inherent dignity and anchored by *ius gentium*.[4] Each offered an alternative to the problems of *imperium* (mixed and pure), and both rejected outright the idea that slavery was natural, let alone a moral condition. Unlike Vitoria, however, neither the fathers of humanist jurisprudence nor those who followed them (like Bodin), used *ius gentium* to argue for just wars or to justify total domination of victors over the vanquished (abject slavery).

4 Bodin, *Six Books on the Commonweale* (*Six livres de la République*) [1576]; and Francisco de Vitoria, "De Indis," [1539], in *Vitoria: Political Writings*, eds. Anthony Pagden and Jeremy Lawrance (Cambridge: Cambridge University Press, 1991), 233–92.

That does not mean, of course, that Budé, Zasius, and Alciati were without their own prejudices based on religious, cultural, and geographical distinctions, nor did they claim to be paragons of virtue, humility, or toleration. However, they did approach the categories of Roman law by putting forward interpretations of justice and right that were rooted in—and structured by—conceptions of man *qua* man, without distinction. What is more, they argued—in their own separate ways and to different degrees—that the universal rights and obligations shared by all mankind could not be demolished by civil authorities or laws. Put differently, they held that despite the fact that one's rights and obligations could be restricted and diminished as a consequence of their actions (contracts, crime, or war), such rights and obligations could not be alienated altogether by consent or by force. No one, no matter their circumstances, could completely submit themselves to the power of another, nor could their rights and obligations be demolished or abrogated by law without violating justice and right. As such, any attempt to exercise unlimited power and force over another was neither a necessary feature of war nor a fundamental condition of slavery. It was, instead, abject tyranny; it violated *ius gentium*, natural law, and *ius*, and it was also an affront to one's dignity.

The fact that such theories might strike us as anticipating or resembling seventeenth- and eighteenth-century political thought, more so than following from medieval and early modern legal thought, should give us pause. Not least because it reminds us that there was/is no magic moment or singular narrative that can accommodate the complex—and messy—contradictions, surprises and contingencies of the history of dignity, let alone the history of rights (natural or otherwise). It also reminds us that the use of categories such as *ius* and *ius gentium* to critique and delimit slavery, tyranny, and domination (political, legal, and physical) were co-original with, rather than a mere reaction to, the re-formation and expansion of Europe from the late-fifteenth century onward.

•••

Even though the contours of the law and jurisprudence change over time, one constant within the European legal tradition—and the political thought that emerged with and from it—is the attempt to infuse *imperium*, and later sovereignty, with the moral and historical authority to command acts of violence (punishment and war) with impunity. As such, some of the similarities between sixteenth-century humanist jurists and their seventeenth-century successors—including an emphasis on universal rights, obligations, and dignity that transcend civil jurisprudence as well as the *ius commune*—can also be attributed to the comparable contexts in which they wrote; each explored the relation between natural law, *ius*, and *ius gentium* during periods rife with uncertainty, instability, and conflict, which cast questions of law and rights—among persons as well as peoples—into sharp relief.

Budé, Zasius, and Alciati wrote at a time when the Italian Wars were writ large but also in an age when the authority and ideal of Universal Latin Christendom—which was always challenged and had never been truly realized—was increasingly being curtailed within the territorial jurisdictions of independent sovereign entities, viz., states. Seventeenth-century theorists wrote in an age characterized by the transition of these early-modern sovereignties into modern empires. Throughout this period, from the late-fifteenth century through to the late-seventeenth century, Europe confronted rapid changes in economic, social, and religious life, as well as international and civil conflicts. It was in the context of these conflicts and changes—whether swift or slow—that the so-called fathers of legal humanism in the sixteenth century and the so-called fathers of international law and modern statecraft in the seventeenth attempted to define a common understanding of rights—of persons and of peoples—shared among all and by all to address local as well as international problems of authority.

Although no longer considered revolutionary, scholars continue to identify the theories of the seventeenth century as modern, innovative, and new based on their secular, rationalistic, individualistic, and minimalist aspects. For example, the turn away from theology in favor of human nature or natural man is characterized as a turn toward secular, viz., nonreligious, theories that justify and legitimize the inherent legal and political authority within civil society. These so-called secular theories—in this sense, theories that were increasingly anthropocentric rather than theocentric—were based on a few moral principles shared by all men and across time, culture, and space. These theories are therefore also denoted as minimalist and universal. As this book demonstrates, all of these so-called modern aspects, including the discussions of the relations among sovereigns, were already integral to the discussions of natural law, *ius,* and *ius gentium* in the works of Budé, Zasius, and Alciati—not in the sense that the legal humanists had invented them but rather because these features were present in the texts of Roman law that structured and underpinned university-based jurisprudence and thus critiques of it, as much as the practical applications of law in Europe, since its rediscovery and recovery in the late eleventh and early twelfth centuries.

The early-sixteenth-century legal humanists and their seventeenth-century successors alike turned to human nature, and not merely to theology, as the source of moral authority to ground their discussions of natural law, *ius*, and *ius gentium*. This turn to human nature was related to the advent of *studia humanitatis*; both the legal humanists and the seventeenth-century theorists applied methods and sources in similar ways to their discussions of political, legal, and moral authority. Moreover, through the application of alternative methods in their interpretations of Roman law, Budé, Zasius, and Alciati challenged traditional assumptions and conventions of the political and legal thought that they inherited from their predecessors. Indeed, the very aspects of natural law and natural rights theories that these early humanist jurists used in their departure from traditional jurisprudence are often identified by present-day scholars as modern, in no small part, because they cannot be explained with reference solely to scholastic jurisprudence.

Humanist jurists, like their seventeenth-century successors, were also led to identifying shared universal moral principles or precepts of natural law and *ius gentium* by comparing the laws and customs of a variety of peoples over time. Moreover, the process of identification through observation and comparison was common to the modern theories of the seventeenth century and to Budé's, Zasius', and Alciati's turn to the historical construction (actual and imagined) of law to identify a set of innate attributes and inclinations, that is, universal characteristics (e.g., reason, dignity, will, passions) universally shared among all mankind. Once identified—typically the very first steps of the theory—the legal humanists and modern theorists then abstracted from these universal attributes or inclinations a conception of man's natural condition—man *qua* man. It was this natural condition that was then extended, by analogy, to the state of nature (man's pre-political condition), civil society, and the realm of nations.

With reference to universal natural inclinations, both early-sixteenth-century legal humanists and seventeenth-century theorists provided historical accounts for why man quit his natural condition and entered—and indeed created—civil societies governed by civil laws. The historical fictions at the base of these theories were constructed on the basis of whichever natural attribute or inclination theorists chose to emphasize to account for (1) the original transition to civil society, and (2) the principles by which a specific type of political society should be governed. For example, Grotius (and Budé and Zasius before him) identified sociability as the most basic inclination in man; man entered mutual company because he had a desire to both help and interact with others. Hobbes (and Alciati before him), on the other hand, identified man's most basic inclination as fear, thus man's impulse to enter both civil and political society was based on his desire to quit the *bellum omnium contra omnes* and the necessity of security. In the end, however, these theories were less about natural man than they were explanations of the necessity for and the justification of particular forms of political and legal authority. The historical fiction of the state of nature was secondary in comparison to the historical fiction of the original moment—whether this was described as a gradual historical process (Grotius) or articulated in terms of a break with the past (Hobbes)—in which man agreed to live in accordance with civil laws and to be punished (e.g., financially, socially, and physically) if he violated them. The account of how man came to place his neck under the yoke of the law provides the historical justification for the existence of political authority in the theories, whereas the historical fiction of the state of nature—which reflects man's natural attributes and inclinations—provides the moral justification for the existence of legal authority in these theories.

As shown throughout this volume, the discussions of natural law, *ius,* and *ius gentium* by the first generation of legal humanists also offered their readers and students an account of the transition from the family to mutual company, and finally to civil society, based on man's natural attributes, which were minimal, secular/worldly, and universal. Once identified, these characteristics provided moral authority to legal authorities within civil society for the legal humanists, which, in turn, defined the limits of the political authority and jurisdiction of rulers, regardless of the type of state. For Budé and Zasius, the transition from mutual company to civil society was the result of a natural historical progression, and thus the moral authority of a civil society, governed and administered by laws, was rooted in man's natural inclination to live in mutual company to pursue security, peace, and the common good in tandem. In short, man was driven to live in civil society on account of his sociability paired with an innate sense of justice, viz., what is good and fair conjoined. For Alciati, on the other hand, the transition was the result of an intervention, a break from nature and the past, whereby only after men were persuaded by a wise man to pursue peace, security, and the common good in mutual company did they submit themselves as equally subject to the rule of law. He also held that it was man's choice to abandon his unsociable condition—a condition permeated by necessity rather than justice—that stood as the source of the moral authority underpinning legal and political institutions and practices within civil society.

Moreover, Budé, Zasius, and Alciati used their explanations for the transition from mutual company to civil society to either legitimize or critique the expansion of authority underway in the first half of the sixteenth century. They did so because the creation of new forms of legal authority —and the expansion of existing ones—introduced a historical problem into the study of law, namely, how to protect customary rights and obligations in the face of new laws and vice versa. This was the fundamental problem that legal humanists attempted to resolve in the early-sixteenth century, that modern theorists tried to account for in the seventeenth century, and what contemporary scholars of human rights (e.g., lawyers, philosophers, historians, and political scientists) are still trying to address today.

The contexts in which each of the legal humanists were writing—Budé in France, Zasius in Germany, and Alciati in Italy and France—likewise account for how they used categories of natural law, *ius,* and *ius gentium* to accept or reject changes in civil law and, by extension, customary laws in the early-sixteenth century. For example, Budé accepted the absolute—but limited—authority of the sovereign, and thus rejected what he deemed as attempts by professional lawyers, especially those trained in and following the teaching of Italian jurisprudence, to usurp the king's legislative power and privilege. To do so, Budé used the categories of natural law, *ius,* and *ius gentium* to contend that university-trained jurists had corrupted Roman law as well as customary laws to serve their own or their patron's ends. As a lawyer and city councilor in Germany, Zasius participated in the extension of the legal, political, and economic power of the city of Freiburg over its countryside, but seemed to reject the inverse, viz., the tightening of the emperor's grasp over legal, political, and economic structures within Freiburg. In either case, he used the fundamental categories of *ius* and *ius gentium*—a form of natural law, according to him—to make arguments for both the limits and the legitimacy of new civil laws as well as to criticize existing ones that had missed the mark of justice. Alciati, under the patronage of warring states in and beyond Italy, pressed for the recognition of limits and boundaries that existed—or should have existed—between different sovereign entities in relation to one another as well as between sovereigns and their own subjects. Pushing his theory into novel directions, Alciati also argued that the rights and customs practiced among men outside of civil society—before man agreed to become equally subject to the rule of law—mirrored the rights and customs practiced between sovereigns—who did not share a common civil law—in the realm of nations.

The application of Roman categories like natural law and *ius* (in the sense of one's right) to states and the explanations that posit the conditions of international society as being similar to—and even a reflection of—the conditions among individuals outside society are also characterized by modern scholars, especially historians that focus on the history and development of international law and rights (of persons and peoples), as an innovation by seventeenth-century theorists. With the imagined histories and speculative narratives of theorists like Grotius, Hobbes, and Locke (or Renaissance jurists like Bodin), these two periods of historical fiction at the basis of their theories of sovereignty, rights, and law operate on two corresponding levels: (1) a state of nature from which people implicitly contract into civil society, viz., through the conventions of *ius gentium*; and (2) an international realm in which states explicitly contract into conditions of war and peace, viz., the conventions of *ius gentium*. At either level, whether explicitly mentioned or not, the category of *ius gentium* proved central: it was a form of natural law known through right reason; it referred to customary law within communities; and it referred to the customs in common between communities, viz., between groups who do not share a common sovereign or the same civil law. This was the case for both seventeenth-century theorists and early sixteenth-century legal humanists, on account of the variable definitions provided within the first title of the *Digest*, which served as the centerpiece and foundation of juridical thought throughout the late medieval and early modern era. In other words, the source of the most revolutionary ideas of political thought stem from—and are rooted in—the interpretations of the vocabularies of Roman law and of university-based jurisprudence and its critics throughout the medieval and early modern eras. No matter if they are claiming to restore it, clarify it, or offer an alternative, it is the durability of *ius* and *ius gentium* that enables the flexibility in relation to rights and obligation among persons, within political constitutions, or in the realm of international commerce as much as war.

•••

As a consequence of their historicist, comparative, and philological methods, the fathers of legal humanism, especially Zasius and Alciati, used *ius gentium* to provide a predominantly secular, viz., nonreligious, legitimatization for—and critique of—the re-formation of Europe, which was underway by the turn of the sixteenth century. This occurred well before it became a criterion of justice for the actions by European powers beyond Europe in the mid- to late-sixteenth century and before it was used to define and delimit the actions and responsibilities of states, vis-à-vis one another, as a matter of public international law from the turn of the seventeenth century onward. That later theorists picked up and developed some of Budé's, Zasius', and Alciati's ideas and innovations is not surprising; after all, every generation reinterprets the tradition inherited from the past to address new problems in their present. What is surprising is the dominant stance in scholarship, at least among historians of political thought, that Renaissance humanists, and legal humanists in particular, were neither interested in nor contributed to the history and development of natural law, *ius*, or *ius gentium*.

Drawing attention to the transformation of *ius* and *ius gentium* at the hands of the first generation of legal humanists broadens our understanding of the history and development of political and legal thought by reclaiming its sheer contingency beyond the dominant narratives within the historiography.

Moreover, it also has the potential to help us better understand how a category of law that had relatively little significance within traditional (scholastic) jurisprudence came to be central to ideas, practices, and institutions that permeated civil and universal jurisprudence within and beyond Europe by the early decades of the seventeenth century.[5] The latter in turn, has implications for our understanding of the history and development of *ius gentium* before it was used to justify—and critique—European incursions and expansions across the world's oceans, or changes in laws and institutions associated with religious Reformation. It likewise invites us to consider how and why reinterpreting *ius gentium* offered theorists and jurists the possibility to explore questions of justice and right that transcended the vocabularies and jurisprudence hitherto associated with *ius commune.*[6]

Again, the impact of the Italian Wars, which involved all of the significant powers in Europe in various permutations from 1494 to 1559, and the emergence of the early-modern state—demarcated by territorial boundaries and delimited by legal jurisdiction rather than by dynastic claims and ties—challenged the stability, universality, and utility of the *ius commune*. The latter was the case, in no small part, because the *ius commune* had stemmed from an eclectic combination of customary practices shared among peoples across the continent and islands, and explained, underpinned, informed, and legitimated by drawing on Roman and canon law and, with it, medieval jurisprudence. All of this came increasingly into question over the sixteenth century in response to (1) the overall impetus towards legal reform to help effect political and economic stability within discreet communities, (2) the breakdown of Universal Latin Christendom with the advent of the Protestant Reformation in Europe, and (3) the direct confrontation with the brutality of European incursions and excursions into the Atlantic. Combined, though not necessarily contingent, these three processes revealed the limits of the *ius commune* tradition and the necessity to rethink aspects of it to address new problems in the sixteenth

5 Thanks to lively debate and corresponding research about the history, development, and significance of *ius gentium* from the ancient to the modern eras, our understanding of the category—its durability and malleability—has changed significantly over the last decade. See notes throughout this volume and the attached bibliography.

6 In much the same way that the modern idiom *ius cognens* (compelling norms from which no derogation is permitted by way of agreements) has been used to transcend the vocabularies and jurisprudence associated with the *ius publicum gentium* (international law among nations) that defined—and provided the legal framework for—European dominance in the late-nineteenth and early-twentieth centuries. See Martti Koskenniemi, *The Gentle Civilizer of Nations: The Rise and Fall of International Law, 1870–1960* (Cambridge: Cambridge University Press, 2002).

century. The turn to *ius gentium* at the start of the century and the articulation of the theory of sovereignty near the end of it by Renaissance jurists, humanist and scholastic alike, offered an alternative means to ground universal and civil jurisprudence that could bypass, and even overcome, the limits of the *ius commune*. This book sought to demonstrate how the so-called fathers of legal humanism contributed to the emergence of *ius gentium*—as an alternative to the *ius commune*—as the common law not simply of Europe, but of all mankind. And further, it argued that at the basis of their contributions was an emphasis on man's inherent dignity and the inviolable rights of all persons and sovereign states.

Even so, the aim of this book is not to replace one genealogy of rights, liberty, or freedom with another, nor to suggest that simply folding Budé, Zasius, and Alciati into the dominant historiography could serve as a means to bypass or efface the fundamental tensions that dominate debates about the history of freedom (republican and otherwise), the history of rights (natural and human), and the histories of international law and sovereignty.[7] It does, however, aim to broaden our understanding of the history and development of political and legal thought by reclaiming its diversity and complexity. In this respect, exploring discussions of the first title of the *Digest* by Budé, Zasius, and Alciati—writing from different contexts and with different aims—reminds us that the Renaissance, as a result of the application of new ideas, sources, and methods, changed the way we think about the relation between justice and right as well as the historical and moral authority of *ius* and *ius gentium*, as much as it did our understanding of music, art, and architecture. Nevertheless, the insights and ideas of humanist jurists have become so familiar and normative to us that we seem to have forgotten how innovative and transformative they once were. Recognizing their innovations, and exploring their jurisprudence, allows us to appreciate their reinterpretations of the basic categories of Roman law as neither prelude nor ephemera but, in fact, as crucial for shaping both the world we know and the methodologies of comparative and historical juridical thought that we employ in our efforts to better understand the history and development of legal traditions and, with it, the history and development of (human) rights, sovereignty, and international law.

7 The debates about the history of freedom in the early modern era, and the role of liberty and rights in that history is extensive, but the contours of the discussion are still dominated by the ideas and arguments presented in J. G. A. Pocock, *The Machiavellian Moment*; Skinner, *Foundations of Modern Political Thought I & II*; Skinner, *Liberty before Liberalism*; Tuck, *Natural Rights*; and Tierney, *The Idea of Natural Rights*. As for the dominant scholarship on *ius gentium* within the realm of international law, see Koskenniemi, *The Gentle Civilizer of Nations*; Martti Koskenniemi, *The Politics of International Law* (Oxford: Hart Publishing, 2011); and Martti Koskenniemi, *To the Uttermost Parts of the Earth*.

Appendix: Select *Emblems* by Andrea Alciati

FIGURE A.1. *Emblem 10.*

Emblem 10[1]
Treaties

Take, O Duke, this lute whose form is said to come from a fishing boat,
and which the Latin Muse claims as her own.
May our gift be pleasing to you at this time,
as you prepare to undertake new treaties with your allies.
It is difficult, unless the man is skilled, to tune so many strings,
and if one string is not well stretched, or breaks (which happens easily),
all the pleasure of the shell is lost, and the splendid song becomes absurd.
So the princes of Italy join together in alliances:
there is nothing for you to fear if your love remains harmonious.
But if anyone withdraws, then, as we often see, all that harmony diminishes into nothing.[2]

---

1 All images in this Appendix are from Alciati, *Andreae Alciati Emblemata*, 1621 Edition.

2 All translations of Alciati's epigrams are from William Barker, Mark Feltham, Jean Guthrie, and Allan Farrell, "Alciato's Book of Emblems: The Memorial Web Edition in Latin and English Andrea Alciati," http://www.mun.ca/alciato/index.html.

 | DOI:10.1163/9789004528451_010

FIGURE A.2. *Emblem 12.*

Emblem 12

Plans ought not to be divulged

In the dark lairs of Cnossus with their hidden threshold
and thick darkness, Daedalus shut up the monster.
This image the Roman phalanx carries into battle,
and these standards, with bull that's half a man, shine forth splendidly.
They warn us too that the secret plans of leaders ought to lie hidden.
A plan that's known harms its author.

FIGURE A.3. *Emblem 13.*

Emblem 13

One ought not yield, even under torture

Laeana, whom you see depicted on the Cecropian fortress,
was the lover of Harmodius (or do you not know this, stranger?).
So it is pleasing to show the keen spirit of this female warrior
in the form of a wild beast, for she actually bore its name.
Because she did not betray anyone by her testimony,
when she was twisted on the rack,
Iphicrates represented her as tongueless.

FIGURE A.4. *Emblem 39*.

Emblem 39
Harmony

When Rome prepared its leaders for civil war
and the land of Mars fell by its own powers,
it was the custom, troops coming together into the same place,
to offer right hands be joined in mutual giving.
This is the sign of alliance:
harmony has this as a sign, that whom love unites,
the hand itself may also bring together.

FIGURE A.5. *Emblem 42*.

Emblem 42
What stands firmest cannot be overthrown

Though father Ocean stir up all his waves and you,
barbarous Turk, drink the entire Danube,
even so you will never penetrate our shattered border
so long as the emperor Charles gives signs of war to foreign nations.
Thus sacred oaks stand with steadfast roots,
even though winds shake the dry leaves violently.

FIGURE A.6. *Emblem 43*.

Emblem 43

Hope is near

Our state is shaken by innumerable storms,
and there is only one hope for its future safety;
just like a ship in the middle of the sea which the winds grasp,
it now breaks up in the briny water.
But if the brothers of Helen, shining stars, appear,
good hope restores those downcast spirits.

FIGURE A.7. *Emblem 53*.

Emblem 53
Against flatterers

The chameleon is always gaping,
always breathing in and out the thin air it feeds on,
and it changes its appearance,
takes on diverse colours, except for red or white.
Likewise the flatterer feeds on an air of popularity,
and, open-mouthed, devours all;
he mimics only the dark habits of the Prince,
incapable of the pure and the chaste.

FIGURE A.8. *Emblem 103.*

Emblem 103

That which is above us is nothing to us

Prometheus hangs eternally on the Caucasian rock;
his liver is ripped apart by the talon of the sacred bird.
He might regret that he made man;
detesting potters, he condemns the flame lit by the stolen fire.
The breasts of wise men –
those who seek to know the conditions of heaven and the gods –
are gnawed by divers cares.

FIGURE A.9. *Emblem 134.*

Emblem 134
The tomb of Giangaleazzo Visconti, first Duke of Milan

Instead of a tomb place Italy, place arms and dukes,
and the sea which thunders up the twin gulfs.
Add to these the Barbarian attempting in vain to break through,
and bands of men bought at a price for fierce wars.
Yet the serpent-bearer standing on top may say:
who has placed me, a great man, over these tiny things?

FIGURE A.10. *Emblem 143.*

Emblem 143

From Albutius to Master Alciatus, persuading him to withdraw from the conflicts of Italy and to teach in France

The tree which supplied these fruits, a newcomer to our region,
came earlier from the eastern extremity of Persis.
It was improved by its migration, in that while once it yielded poisonous fruits
in its own country, here it bears us sweet ones.
It has a leaf very like a tongue, and fruit very like a heart.
Alciatus, learn from it how to live your life.
Far from your country you will be held in higher estimation;
for you are most wise in your heart and are no less vigorous in speech.

FIGURE A.11. *Emblem 144.*

Emblem 144

The prince, ensuring the safety of his subjects

Whenever the Titan brothers stir up the oceans,
then an anchor thrown out gives aid to the wretched sailors.
This the dolphin, devoted to mankind,
embraces so that it can fix more safely in the deepest seas.
How fitting that kings bear these insignia
mindful that they are to their people what the anchor is to sailors.

FIGURE A.12. *Emblem 151.*

Emblem 151
The republic set free

Upon the death of Caesar, as if liberty had been restored,
this coin was struck for Brutus' leading men.
In the foreground are daggers,
over which is set a cap of the kind
that slaves receive when they are freed.

FIGURE A.13. *Emblem 164*.

Emblem 164

Against detractors

Dolts brandishing whips and stupid schoolteachers
dare to vomit the bile of their impure hearts against me.
What should I do? Return the favour?
But will I not be said to have seized the clamorous cricket by one wing?
What use is it to banish insects with busy flapping?
More satisfactory to ignore what you can't destroy.

FIGURE A.14. *Emblem 166.*

Emblem 166

Something evil, from an evil neighbour

A flood carried away two jars, one of which was of metal,
the other earthen, made by the hand of the potter.
The former asked the latter if she wished to be borne along next to her,
so that as one they could withstand the rushing waters.
The clay jar replied: "Your concerns are of no consequence to me:
let not closeness bring me much bad fortune.
For whether a wave carries you against me
or me against you, I, being fragile, will break,
and you alone will survive."

FIGURE A.15. *Emblem 172.*

Emblem 172
A just revenge

While the Cyclops rests at the entrance to his deep-winding cave,
among his tender flocks, he sings to himself thus:
"Feed yourselves upon the grass! –
I will feed upon the Achaean comrades,
and last of all my stomach will digest Nobody."
The Ithacan heard this, and blinded the Cyclops.
See how punishment is visited upon the schemer.

FIGURE A.16. *Emblem 174*.

Emblem 174

The fault belongs alike to the wrong-doer and the persuader

In a hideous dungeon a victorious throng holds captive
a herald for sounding out battle signals on a trumpet.
He pleads before them that he does not strive in arms,
nor has he with savage sword pierced the side of any man.
To him they answer:
But in that you stir others to arms with the clangor of your instrument,
you, most fearful one, commit a greater sin.

FIGURE A.17. *Emblem 175.*

Emblem 175

One sins, the other is punished

As a young dog picks up a stone and worries it with his teeth,
inflicting no damage in return on the one who tried to strike him with it,
so men let their real enemies elude them,
and with bared teeth hunt down those not charged with any crime.

FIGURE A.18. *Emblem 180.*

Emblem 180

It is a sacrilege for scholars to malign scholars

O Procne, alas why do you savagely seize the chirping cicada,
and prepare for your young a ghastly meal?
Do you, prattler, hurt a prattler?
Do you, songster of spring, hurt a songster of spring?
Do you, a guest, hurt a guest?
And do you, winged and flying, hurt another just like you?
Then cast away your prey—for musical souls, it is a most dreadful crime that one should perish by the tooth of another.

Bibliography

Primary Sources

Accursius. *Digestum vetus sive pandectarum iuris civilis totus primus ex pandectis Florentinis, quae olim Pisanae dicebantur, quod eius fieri potiut, repraesenatus. Commentariis Accursi, & multorum insuper aliorum tam veterum quam neotericorum iurisconsultorum scholiis atque observationibus illustratus*. Paris, 1566.

Alciati, Andrea. "Alciato's Book of Emblems: The Memorial Web Edition in Latin and English." Translated by William Barker, Mark Feltham, Jean Guthrie, and Allan Farrell. http://www.mun.ca/alciato/index.html.

Alciati, Andrea. *Andreae Alciati Emblemata cum commentariis Claudii Minois I.C. Francisci Sanctii Brocensis, & notis Laurentii Pignorii Patavini. Novissima hac editione in continuam unius commentarii seriem congestis, in certas quasdam quasi classes dispositis, & plusquam dimidia parte auctis. Opera et vigiliis Joannis Thuilii Mariaemontani Tirol ... Accesserunt in fine Federici Morelli ... Corollaria & monita, ad eadem Emblemata. Cum indice triplice*. Patavii: Apud Petrum Paulum Tozzium, 1621.

Alciati, Andrea. "Ampliss Voro Francisco a Turonbe Archiepiscopo Biturig (Dedication)." In *De Verborum Significatione*, [1]. Lyon: Sebastianum Gryphium, 1535.

Alciati, Andrea. "Bona fides." In *De verborum significatione*, cols. 305–313. Lyon: Sebastianum Gryphium, 1535.

Alciati, Andrea. "Commentaria de verborum significatione [1539]." In *Omnia opera*, Vol. 4. Basel: Insingrinius, 1546.

Alciati, Andrea. "De iustitia et Iure (Lecture)." In *Omnia opera*, 1:1–14. Basel: Insingrinius, 1546.

Alciati, Andrea. *De Ponderibus et Mensuris*. Basel: Claudius Galenus, 1530.

Alciati, Andrea. *De singvlari certamine liber. Eiusdem consilium in materia duelli, exceptum ex libro quinto Responsorum*. Venice: Vicentium Vaugris, 1544.

Alciati, Andrea. "De verborum significatione libri quatuor [1523]." In *Omnia opera*, Vol. 4. Basel: Insingrinius, 1546.

Alciati, Andrea. *Duello*. Venice: Appresso Comin da Trino di Monferrato, 1562.

Alciati, Andrea. *Emblemata: cum commentariis, qvibvs emblematum omnium aperta origine, mens auctoris explicatur, & obscura omnia dubiaque illustrantur*. Antverpiae: Christophori Plantini, 1581.

Alciati, Andrea. "In tres posteriores codiciis Justiniani libros, Annotationes [1515]." In *Paradoxorum*, 240–76. Basel: [Hercules Gallicus], 1523.

Alciati, Andrea. "Oratio Andreae Alciati, dum Bononiam [1537]." In *Omnia opera*, 3:1051/52–1055/56. Basel: Insingrinius, 1546.

Alciati, Andrea. "Oratio in laudem iuri civilis, principio studii cum Avenione profiteretur [1518]." In *Omnia opera*, 3:506–11. Basel: Insingrinius, 1546.

Alciati, Andrea. "Alciato at Glasgow." Accessed April 23, 2021. https://www.emblems.arts.gla.ac.uk/alciato/.

Aristotle. *Nicomachean Ethics.* Translated by H. Rackham. Loeb Classical Library 73. Cambridge, MA: Harvard University Press, 1926.

Bartolus. "De iustitia et iure, Rubr." In *Bartolus a Saxoferrato super authenticis, & instit.* Venice, 1580.

Bartolus. *On the Conflict of Laws*. Translated by Joseph Henry. Cambridge, MA: Harvard University Press, 1914.

Bartolus. "De Guelphis et Gebellinis." In *Politica e diritto nel Trecento Italiano: il "De tyranno" dI Bartolo da Sassoferrato (1314–1357), con l'edizione critica dei trattati "De Guelphis et Gebellinis," "De regimine civitatis" e "De tyranno,"* edited by Diego Quaglioni; translated by Jonathan Robinson, 131–46. Florence: Leo S. Olschki, 1983.

Bartolus. "De iustitia & Iure, Rea." In *Partem digesti veteris, Bartoli A Saxoferrato commentari*. Basel: Episcopius, 1588.

Bartolus. "De Regimine Civitati." In *Politica e diritto nel Trecento italiano: il "De tyranno" dI Bartoloda Sassoferrato (1314–1357) con l'edizione critica dei trattati "De Guelphis et Gebellinis," "Deregimine Civitatis" e "De tyranno,"* edited by Diego Quaglioni; translated by Jonathan Robinson, 149–70. Florence: Leo S. Olschki, 1983.

Bartolus. *On the Conflict of Laws*. Translated by Joseph Henry. Cambridge, MA: Harvard University Press, 1914.

Bodin, Jean. *Six Books on the Commonweale* (*Six livres de la République*) [1576]. Edited by Kenneth Douglas McRae. Cambridge, MA: Harvard University Press, 1962.

Bordoni, Francesco. *Homicidii proditorii vindicatio, et restitutio in eum pristinum statum, in quo illud Bartolus constituerat, per r. p. f. Franciscum Bordonum Parmensem Tertij ordinis regularis santci Francisci theologum*. N.p.: apud Marium Vignam, 1667.

Budé, Guillaume. *Annotationes Gulielmi Budaei parisiensis secretarii regii in quatuor et viginti pandectarum libros ad Ioannem Deganaium cancellarium Franciae*. [Paris]: Ab Iodoco Badio Ascensio impressae, 1508.

Budé, Guillaume. *Correspondance. Tome I, Les Lettres Grecques-Adjectis Paucis e Latinis*. Translated by Guy Lavoie. Vol. 6. Sherbrooke, Québec: Université de Sherbrooke, n.d.

Budé, Guillaume. *De asse et partibus eius libri quinque*. [Paris]: Venundantur in edibus Ascensianis, 1514.

Budé, Guillaume. *De l'institution Du Prince*. [Paris]: Nicole, 1547.

Budé, Guillaume. *Epistolae Gullielmi Budéi, Secretarii Regii, Posteriores*. [Paris]: Iodoco Badio, 1522.

Budé, Guillaume. *Répertoire analytique et chronologique de la correspondance de Guillaume Budé: Thèse Complémentaire Présentée A la Faculte de Lettres de l'Universite de Paris*. Edited by Louis Delaruelle. Toulouse: É. Privat, 1907.

Cicero, Marcus Tullius. *De finibus bonorum et malorum*. Translated by H. Rackman. Rev. ed. Cambridge, MA: Harvard University Press, 2014.

Cicero, Marcus Tullius. *De inventione, de optimo genere oratorum, topica*. Translated by H. M. Hubbell. Cambridge, MA: Harvard University Press, 1949.

Cicero, Marcus Tullius. *De Legibus*. Translated by L. P. Kenter. Amsterdam: Hakkert, 1972.

Cicero, Marcus Tullius. *De Oratore*. Translated by E. W. Sutton. Vol. 3. Cambridge, MA: Harvard University Press, 1942.

Cicero, Marcus Tullius. *On the Commonwealth and On the Laws*. Translated by James E. G. Zetzel. Cambridge: Cambridge University Press, 1999.

Cicero, Marcus Tullius. *On the Ideal Orator (De Oratore)*. Translated by James M. May and Jakob Wisse. Oxford: Oxford University Press, 2016.

Cicero, Marcus Tullius. *The Nature of the Gods*. Translated by Peter G. Walsh. Oxford: Oxford World's Classics, 2016.

Cicero, Marcus Tullius. *The Republic and the Laws*. Edited by N. Rudd and J. G. F. Powell. Oxford: Oxford University Press, 2016.

Cicero, Marcus Tullius. *The speeches: pro lege Manilia, pro Caecina, pro Cluentio, pro Rabirio perduellionis*. Translated by Humfrey Grose-Hodge. London: W. Heinemann, Ltd., 1927.

Erasmus, Desiderius, Guillaume Budé, and Marie-Madeleine de La Garanderie. *La Correspondance d'Érasme et de Guillaume Budé*. Paris: J. Vrin, 1967.

"Foundation Charter of Cluny, 910." In *Select Historical Documents of the Middle Ages*, translated by Ernest F. Henderson, 329–33. London: George Bell and Sons, 1910.

Gelasius, "Letter of Pope Gelasius to Emperor Anastasius on the superiority of the spiritual over temporal power." In Colman J. Barry, *Readings in Church History, vol. 1: From Pentecost to the Protestant Revolt*. Westminster, MD: Newman Press, 1960.

Gregory VII, Pope. "Decree of March 7, 1080, Forbidding Lay Investiture." In *Select Historical Documents of the Middle Ages*, translated by Ernest F. Henderson, 365–66. London: George Bell and Sons, 1910.

Gregory VII, Pope. "Decree of November 19, 1078, Forbidding Lay Investiture." In *Select Historical Documents of the Middle Ages*, translated by Ernest F. Henderson, 365. London: George Bell and Sons, 1910.

Grimaldi, Alessandro. *Funeral Oration January 19, 1550, for Andrea Alciati*. Translated by Henry Green. Manchester: Holbein Society by A. Brothers, 1871.

Grotius, Hugo. *The Rights of War and Peace*, edited by Richard Tuck, from the edition by Jean Barbeyrac. 3 vols. Indianapolis, IN: Liberty Fund, 2005.

Henry IV, Holy Roman Emperor. "Letter to Gregory VII." In *Select Historical Documents of the Middle Ages*, translated by Ernest F. Henderson, 372–73. London: George Bell and Sons, 1910.

Hobbes, Thomas. *De Cive* [1642; 1651]. Cambridge: Cambridge University Press, 1998.

Hobbes, Thomas. *Leviathan* [1651]. Cambridge: Cambridge University Press, 1991.

Justinian. *The Digest of Justinian*. Translated by Alan Watson. 2 vols. Philadelphia: University of Pennsylvania Press, 1998.

Justinian. *Institutes*. Translated by J. A. C. Thomas. Amsterdam: North-Holland Pub. Co. 1975.

Machiavelli, Niccolò. *The Prince*. Translated by Harvey C. Mansfield. 2nd ed. Chicago: University of Chicago Press, 1998.

More, Thomas. *Utopia*. Edited by George M. Logan and Robert. M. Adams. Rev. ed. Cambridge: Cambridge University Press, 2002.

Pliny the Elder. *Natural History*. Translated by H. Rackham. Cambridge, MA: Harvard University Press, 1962.

Pufendorf, Samuel. *De jure naturae et gentium*. Edited by Wilhelm Schmidt-Biggemann. Berlin: Akademie Verlag, 1998.

Pufendorf, Samuel. *On the Duty of Man and Citizen According to Natural Law*. Edited by James Tully; translated by Michael Silverthorne. Cambridge: Cambridge University Press, 1991.

Vitoria, Francisco de. "De Indis." In *Vitoria: Political Writings*, edited by Anthony Pagden and Jeremy Lawrance. Cambridge: Cambridge University Press, 1991.

Zasius, Ulrich. *Apologetica defensio contra Ioanne[m] Eckium theologum, super eo quod olim tractauerat, quo loco fides non esset hosti feruanda. Videbis lector Eckium iura ciuilia non perspecte intellexisse. Defensa magni Erasmi assertio, quam in elegantiss. Scholijs super septimo Matthei capite docuit. Experiere lector, quàm omnino periculi plenum sit, in alienam excurrere professionem*. Basel: Ioannem Frobenium, 1519.

Zasius, Ulrich. "De Iudaeis quaestiones tres." In *Opera omnia*, 5:328–54. Lyon: Sebastianum Gryphium, 1508.

Zasius, Ulrich. "De iustitia et iure (Lecture)." In *Opera omnia*, edited by Johann Ulrich Zasius and Joachim Münsinger von Frundeck, Facsímil., 1: cols. 241–269. Lyon: Sebastianum Gryphium, 1550.

Zasius, Ulrich. "Paratitla, De iustitia et iure (Lecture)." In *Opera omnia*, edited by Johann Ulrich Zasius and Joachim Münsinger von Frundeck, Facsímil., 1: cols. 12–15. Lyon: Sebastianum Gryphium, 1550.

Zasius, Ulrich. "In laudem legum oratio." In *Lucubrationes*, 1–4. Basel: Ioannem Frobenium, 1518.

Zasius, Ulrich. *Neue Stadtrechte und Statuten der Stadt Freiburg im Breisgau [1520]*. Aalen: Scientia Verlag, 1968.

Zasius, Ulrich. *Opera omnia*. Edited by Johann Ulrich Zasius and Joachim Münsinger von Frundeck. Facsímil. 7 vols. Lyon: Sebastianum Gryphium, 1550.

Zasius, Ulrich. "Praefatio." In "primam digestorum, Sive Pandectarum Partem Paratitla." In *Opera omnia*, Facsímil., 1:cols. 13–14. Lyon: Sebastianum Gryphium, 1550.

Zasius, Ulrich. "Praefatio, de iustitia et Iure." In *Opera omnia*, Facsímil., 1:cols. 14–17. Lyon: Sebastianum Gryphium, 1550.

Zasius, Ulrich. "Praefatio, de origine legibus." In *Lucubrationes*, 1–4. Basel: Ioannem Frobenium, 1518.

Zasius, Ulrich. "Praefatio in Iuris Civilis Originem, Scholia." In *Lucubrationes*, 1–4. Basel: Ioannem Frobenium, 1518.

Zasius, Ulrich. *Questiones de parvulis Iudaeorum baptisandis*. Strassbourg: Grüninger, 1508.

Zasius, Ulrich. *Von wahrer und falscher Jurisprudenz: aus Schriften, Reden, und Briefen, 1507 bis 1526*. Frankfurt am Main: V. Klostermann, 1948.

Secondary Sources

Abbondanza, Roberto. "Jurisprudence: The Methodology of Andrea Alciato." In *The Late Italian Renaissance, 1525–1630*, edited by Eric Cochrane, 77–90. London: Macmillan, 1970.

Abbondanza, Roberto. "La vie et les oeuvres d'Andre Alciat." In *Pedagogues et juristes: Congres du Centre d'Etudes Superieures de la Renaissance de Tours: été 1960*, edited by Pierre Mesnard, 93–106. Paris: J. Vrin, 1963.

Abulafia, David. *Frederick II: A Medieval Emperor*. London: Allen Lane, 1988.

Abulafia, David. *The Western Mediterranean Kingdoms, 1200–1500: The Struggle for Dominion*. New York: Longman, 1997.

Ahmed, Ehsan. "Wisdom and Absolute Power on Guillaume Budé's Institution du prince." *Romantic Review* 96, no. 2 (2005): 173–85.

Anghie, Antony. *Imperialism, Sovereignty and the Making of International Law*. Cambridge: Cambridge University Press, 2005.

Armitage, David. *Foundations of Modern International Thought*. Cambridge: Cambridge University Press, 2013.

Armitage, David, ed. *Theories of Empire, 1450–1800*. Aldershot: Ashgate, 1998.

Ascheri, Mario. *The Laws of Late Medieval Italy (1000–1500): Foundations for a European Legal System*. Leiden: Brill, 2013.

Baciero Ruiz, Francisco T. "The Concept of Subjective Right and the Right to Private Property in Suarez and in Locke." *Anuario Filosófico* 45, no. 2 (January 2012): 391–421.

Bain, William. "The Medieval Contribution to Modern International Relations." In *Medieval Foundations of International Relations*, edited by William Bain, 1–26. London: Routledge, 2017.

Bain, William, ed. *Medieval Foundations of International Relations*. London: Routledge, 2017.

Baldwin, John W. *The Scholastic Culture of the Middle Ages, 1000–1300*. Lexington, MA: Heath, 1971.

Baranger, Denis. "The Apparition of Sovereignty." In *Sovereignty in Fragments: The Past, Present and Future of a Contested Concept*, edited by Hent Kalmo and Quentin Skinner, 47–63. Cambridge: Cambridge University Press, 2010.

Barker, William. *Contesting the Renaissance*. Oxford: Wiley-Blackwell, 2011.

Barnes, Jonathan. "The Just War." In *The Cambridge History of Later Medieval Philosophy: From the Rediscovery of Aristotle to the Disintegration of Scholasticism, 1100–1600*, edited by Anthony Kenny, Eleonore Stump, Jan Pinborg, and Norman Kretzmann, 771–84. Cambridge: Cambridge University Press, 1982.

Baron, Hans. *The Crisis of the Early Italian Renaissance*. Princeton, NJ: Princeton University Press, 1966.

Barraclough, Geoffrey. *The Crucible of Europe: The Ninth and Tenth Centuries in European History*. Berkeley: University of California Press, 1976.

Bartleson, Jens. "Double Binds: Sovereignty and the Just War Tradition." In *Sovereignty in Fragments: The Past, Present and Future of a Contested Concept*, edited by Hent Kalmo and Quentin Skinner, 81–95. Cambridge: Cambridge University Press, 2010.

Bartlett, Robert. *The Making of Europe: Conquest, Colonization, and Cultural Change, 950–1350*. Princeton, NJ: Princeton University Press, 1993.

Baumgartner, Frederic J. *Declaring War in Early Modern Europe*. New York: Palgrave Macmillan, 2011.

Baumgartner, Frederic J. "Declaring War in Sixteenth-Century France." *The Journal of the Historical Society* (Boston, MA) 7, no. 1 (March 2007): 85–110.

Baumgartner, Frederic J. *France in the Sixteenth Century*. New York: St. Martin's Press, 1995.

Beaulac, Stéphane. *The Power of Language in the Making of International Law: The Word "Sovereignty" in Bodin and Vattel and the Myth of Westphalia*. Leiden: Martinus Nijhoff Publishers, 2004.

Bellomo, Manlio. *The Common Legal Past of Europe, 1000–1800*. 2nd ed. Translated by Lydia G. Cochrane. Washington, D.C.: The Catholic University of America Press, 1995.

Beneš, Carrie E. *Urban Legends: Civic Identity and the Classical Past in Northern Italy, 1250–1350*. University Park, PA: Pennsylvania State University Press, 2011.

Berman, Harold J. *Law and Revolution I: The Formation of the Western Legal Tradition*. Cambridge, MA: Harvard University Press, 1983.

Berman, Harold J. *Law and Revolution II: The Impact of the Protestant Reformation on the Western Legal Tradition*. London: Belknap, 2004.

Besson, Samantha, and John Tasioulas, eds. *The Philosophy of International Law*. Oxford: Oxford University Press, 2010.

Bezemer, Kees. "Jacques de Revigny's Contribution to the Concept of Subjective Rights and the Origins of the Maxim 'Ex Facto Ins Oritur.'" *Tijdschrift Voor Rechtsgeschiedenis* 81, no. 1–2 (January 2013): 199–217.

Bianchi, H. "The Scales of Justice as Represented in Engravings, Emblems, Reliefs, and Sculptures of Early Modern Europe." In *Images et représentations de la justice du xvie au xixe siècle*, edited by Georges Lamoine, 7–12. Toulouse: University of Toulose-Le Mirail, 1983.

Bietenholz, Peter G., and Thomas B. Deutscher, eds. *Contemporaries of Erasmus: A Biographical Register of the Renaissance and Reformation*. 3 Vols. Toronto: University of Toronto Press, c.1985–1987.

Biggar, Nigel. "What's Wrong with Subjective Rights?" *History of European Ideas* 45, no. 3 (April 2019): 399.

Black, Antony. *Political Thought in Europe, 1250–1450*. Cambridge: Cambridge University Press, 1992.

Black, Jane. *Absolutism in Renaissance Milan: Plenitude of Power under the Visconti and the Sforza 1329–1535*. Oxford: Oxford University Press, 2009.

Black, Robert. "Italian Renaissance Education: Changing Perspectives and Continuing Controversies." *Journal of the History of Ideas* 52, no. 2 (1991): 315–34.

Blickle, Peter, ed. *Resistance, Representation, and Community: The Origins of the Modern State in Europe*. Oxford: Clarendon Press, 1997.

Blickle, Peter, ed. *The Revolution of 1525: The German Peasants' War from a New Perspective*. Baltimore, MD: Johns Hopkins University Press, 1981.

Blickle, Peter, ed. *Von der Leibeigenschaft zu den Menschenrechten: Eine Geschichte der Freiheit in Deutschland*. Munich: C. H. Beck, 2003.

Boisen, Camilla, and David Boucher. "The Medieval and Early Modern Legacy of Rights: The Right to Punish and to Property." In *Medieval Foundations of International Relations*, edited by William Bain, 148–165. London: Routledge, 2017.

Bouwsma, William J. "Lawyers and Early Modern Culture." *The American Historical Review* 78, no. 2 (1973): 303–27.

Bouwsma, William J. "Three Types of Historiography in Post-Renaissance Italy." *History and Theory* 4, no. 3 (1965): 303–14.

Bouwsma, William J. *The Two Faces of Humanism: Stoicism and Augustinianism in Renaissance Thought*. Leiden: Brill, 1975.

Bouwsma, William J. *The Waning of the Renaissance, 1550–1640*. New Haven, CT: Yale University Press, 2000.

Bowd, Stephen D. *Renaissance Mass Murder. Civilians and Soldiers During the Italian Wars*. Oxford: Oxford University Press, 2018.

Bradshaw, Brendan. "Transalpine Humanism." In *The Cambridge History of Political Thought 1450–1700*, edited by J. H. Burns and Mark Goldie, 95–131. Cambridge: Cambridge University Press, 1991.

Bradshaw Fay, Sidney. "The Roman Law and the German Peasant." *The American Historical Review* 16, no. 2 (1911): 234–54.

Brady, Jr., Thomas A., Heiko Augustinus Oberman, and James D. Tracy, eds. *Handbook of European History, 1400–1600*. Grand Rapids, MI: William B. Eerdmans Publishing Company, 1984.

Breen, Michael P. "Law, Society, and the State in Early Modern France." *The Journal of Modern History* 83, no. 2 (2011): 346–86.

Brett, Annabel S. *Changes of State: Nature and the Limits of the City in Early Modern Natural Law*. Princeton, NJ: Princeton University Press, 2011.

Brett, Annabel S. *Liberty, Right, and Nature: Individual Rights in Later Scholastic Thought*. Cambridge: Cambridge University Press, 1997.

Brett, Annabel S., James Tully, and Holly Hamilton-Bleakley, eds. *Rethinking the Foundations of Modern Political Thought*. Cambridge: Cambridge University Press, 2006.

Brundage, James A. *The Medieval Origins of the Legal Profession: Canonists, Civilians, and Courts*. Chicago: University of Chicago Press, 2008.

Brunner, Otto. *Land und Herrschaft: Grundfragen der Territorialen Verfassungsgeschichte Österreichs im Mittelalter*. Dritte, Ergänzte Auflage. Veröffentlichungen des Instituts für Geschichtsforschung und Archivwissenschaft in Wien, Bd. 1. Brünn: R. M. Rohrer, 1943.

Bull, Hedley. *The Anarchical Society: A Study of Order in World Politics*. 4th ed. New York: Columbia University Press, 2012.

Burckhardt, Jacob. *The Civilization of the Renaissance in Italy*. Translated by S. G. C. Middlemore. New York: The Modern Library, 1995; reprint of 2nd ed., 1878.

Burns, J. H. *Lordship, Kingship, and Empire: The Idea of Monarchy 1400–1525*. Oxford: Clarendon Press, 1992.

Callahan, Virginia Woods. "Andrae Alciati." In *Contemporaries of Erasmus: A Biographical Register of the Renaissance and Reformation*. Edited by Peter G. Bietenholz and Thomas B. Deutscher. Toronto: University of Toronto Press, c.1985–1987, Vol. 1, 24–26.

Callahan, Virginia Woods. *Andreas Alciatus and Boniface Amerbach: The Chronicle of a Renaissance Friendship*. Tempe, AZ: Medieval & Renaissance Texts & Studies, 1988.

Cameron, Euan. *The European Reformation*. Oxford: Clarendon Press, 1991.

Camillo, Ottavio Di. "Interpretations of Humanism in Recent Spanish Renaissance Studies." *Renaissance Quarterly* 50, no. 4 (December 1997): 1190–1201.

Canning, Joseph. "Ideas of Empire in the Thought of the Late Medieval Roman Law Jurists." In *Empire and Legal Thought: Ideas and Institutions from Antiquity to Modernity*, edited by Edward Cavanagh, 280–99. Leiden-Boston: Brill Nijhoff, 2020.

Canning, Joseph. *Ideas of Power in the Late Middle Ages, 1296–1417*. Cambridge: Cambridge University Press, 2014.

Canning, Joseph. "Law, Sovereignty and Corporation Theory, 1300–1450." In *The Cambridge Companion to Medieval Political Thought, c.350–c.1450*, edited by J. H. Burns and Mark Goldie, 454–76. Cambridge: Cambridge University Press, 1988.

Canning, Joseph. "The Medieval Roman Law and Canon Law Origins of International Law." In *Medieval Foundations of International Relations*, edited by William Bain, 102–16. London: Routledge, 2017.

Canning, Joseph. *The Political Thought of Baldus de Ubaldis*. Cambridge: Cambridge University Press, 1987.

Cavanagh, Edward, ed. *Empire and Legal Thought: Ideas and Institutions from Antiquity to Modernity*. Leiden-Boston: Brill Nijhoff, 2020.

Celati, Marta. "Angelo Poliziano's Political Orations: The Humanist in Government." *The Modern Language Review* 115, no. 2 (2020): 317–37.

Celenza, Christopher S. "Ideas in Context and the Idea of Renaissance Philosophy." *Journal of the History of Ideas* 75, no. 4 (2014): 653–66.

Celenza, Christopher S. *The Italian Renaissance and the Origins of the Modern Humanities: An Intellectual History, 1400–1800*. Cambridge: Cambridge University Press, 2021.

Celenza, Christopher S. "Late Antiquity and the Florentine Renaissance: Historiographical Parallels." *Journal of the History of Ideas* 62, no. 1 (2001): 17–35.

Celenza, Christopher S. *The Lost Italian Renaissance: Humanists, Historians, and Latin's Legacy*. Baltimore, MD: Johns Hopkins University Press, 2004.

Chestnov, I. L. "Subjective Right in the Post-Classical Legal Science." *Теоретическая и Прикладная Юриспруденция* 2 (November 2019): 27–30.

Chittolini, Giorgio. "The 'Private', the 'Public', the State." *The Journal of Modern History* 67 (1995): S. 34–61.

Coleman, Janet. *A History of Political Thought: From the Middle Ages to the Renaissance*. Oxford: Blackwell Publishing, 2000.

Coleman, Janet, ed. *The Individual in Political Theory and Practice*. Oxford: Clarendon Press, 1996.

Costa Lopez, Julia. "*Merum Imperium* and Sovereignty in the Later Middle Ages." *International Studies Review* 20, no. 3 (2018): 498–502.

Costa Lopez, Julia, Benjamin De Carvalho, Andrew A Latham, Ayse Zarakol, Jens Bartelson, and Minda Holm. "Forum: In the Beginning There Was No Word (for It): Terms, Concepts, and Early Sovereignty." *International Studies Review* 20, no. 3 (September 2018): 489–519.

Covell, Chris. *The Law of Nations in Political Thought: A Critical Survey from Vitoria to Hegel*. New York: Palgrave Macmillan, 2009.

Crowe, Michael. *The Changing Profile of the Natural Law*. The Hague: Martinus Nijhoff, 1977.

D'Agostino, Francesco. *La Tradizione Dell'epieikeia Nel Medioevo Latino: Un Contributo Alla Storia Dell'idea Di Equità*. Milan: A. Giuffrè, 1976.

D'Entreves, A. P. *Natural Law: An Introduction to Legal Philosophy*. London: Hutchinson University Library, 1972.

Dahm, Georg. "On the Reception of Roman Law and Italian Law in Germany." In *Pre-Reformation Germany*, edited by Gerald Strauss, 282–315. New York: Harper and Row, 1972.

Daly, Peter M., ed. *Andrea Alciato and the Emblem Tradition: Essays in Honor of Virginia Woods Callahan*. New York: AMS Press, 1989.

Daston, Lorraine, and Michael Stolleis, eds. *Natural Law and Laws of Nature in Early Modern Europe: Jurisprudence, Theology, Moral and Natural Philosophy*. Aldershot: Ashgate Publishing Company, 2008.

Davies, Kathleen. *Periodization and Sovereignty: How Ideas of Feudalism and Secularization Govern the Politics of Time*. Philadelphia: University of Pennsylvania Press, 2017.

Davies, Kathleen. "Sovereign Subjects, Feudal Law, and the Writing of History." *Journal of Medieval and Early Modern Studies* 36, no. 2 (2006): 223–61.

Decock, Wim. *Theologians and Contract Law: The Moral Transformation of the Ius Commune (ca. 1500–1650)*. Leiden: Brill Nijhoff, 2012.

Delaruelle, Louis. *Études sur l'humanisme français: Guillaume Budé, les origines, les débuts, les idées maítresses*. Paris: H. Champion, 1907.

Descimon, Robert. "The Birth of the Nobility of the Robe: Dignity Versus Privilege in the Parlement of Paris, 1500–1700." In *Changing Identities in Early Modern France*, edited by Michael Wolf, 95–123. Durham, NC: Duke University Press, 1996.

Douzinas, Costas, and Lynda Nead, eds. *Law and the Image: The Authority of Art and the Aesthetics of Law*. Chicago: University of Chicago Press, 1999.

Drysdall, Denis L. "Alciato and the Grammarians: The Law and the Humanities in the Parergon Iuris Libri Duodecim." *Renaissance Quarterly* 56, no. 3 (2003): 695–722.

Dunbabin, Jean. "Government." In *The Cambridge Companion to Medieval Political Thought, c.350–c.1450*, edited by J. H. Burns, 477–519. Cambridge: Cambridge University Press, 1988.

Earenfight, Theresa. "Without the Persona of the Prince: Kings, Queens and the Idea of Monarchy in Late Medieval Europe." *Gender & History* 19, no. 1 (April 2007): 1–21.

Elias, Norbert. *The Civilizing Process*. Oxford: Blackwell, 2000.

Elshtain, Jean Bethke. *Sovereignty: God, State, and Self*. New York: Basic Books, 2008.

Fasolt, Constantin. *The Limits of History*. Chicago: University of Chicago Press, 2004.

Fasolt, Constantin. "Visions of Order in the Canonists and Civilians." In *Handbook of European History, 1400–1600*, edited by Thomas A. Brady, Jr., Heiko Augustinus Oberman, and James D. Tracy, 31–60. Grand Rapids, MI: William B. Eerdmans Publishing Company, 1984.

Fedele, Dante. "*Ius gentium*: The Metamorphoses of a Legal Concept (Ancient Rome to Early Modern Europe)." In *Empire and Legal Thought: Ideas and Institutions from Antiquity to Modernity*, edited by Edward Cavanagh, 213–50. Leiden-Boston: Brill Nijhoff, 2020.

Finnis, John. "Grounding Human Rights in Natural Law." *The American Journal of Jurisprudence* (Notre Dame) 60, no. 2 (December 2016): 199–225.

Finnis, John. *Natural Law and Natural Rights*. Oxford: Clarendon Press, 1980.

Floyd, Jonathan, and Marc Stears, eds. *Political Philosophy versus History? Contextualism and Real Politics in Contemporary Political Thought*. Cambridge: Cambridge University Press, 2011.

Fögen, Marie Theresa. "Learned Law and The Desire of Politics." In *Law and Learning in the Middle Ages: Proceeding of the Second Carlsberg Academy Conference on Medieval Legal History 2005*, edited by Helle Voft and Mia Münster-Swendsen, 29–40. Copenhagen: DJØF Publishing, 2006.

Folz, Robert. *The Concept of Empire in Western Europe from the Fifth to the Fourteenth Century*. London: Edward Arnold, 1969.

Freed, John B. *Frederick Barbarossa: The Prince and the Myth*. New Haven, CT: Yale University Press, 2016.

Frohen, Bruce P., and Kenneth L. Grasso, eds. *Rethinking Rights: Historical, Political, and Philosophical Perspectives*. Columbia, MO: University of Missouri Press, 2009.

Fubini, Riccardo. *Humanism and Secularization: From Petrarch to Valla*. Translated by Martha King. Durham, NC: Duke University Press, 2003.

Fubini, Riccardo. "The Italian League and the Policy of the Balance of Power at the Accession of Lorenzo de' Medici." *The Journal of Modern History* 67 (1995): S. 166–99.

Fukuyama, Francis. *The Origins of Political Order: From Prehuman Times to the French Revolution*. New York: Farrar, Straus and Giroux, 2011.

Gagné, John. *Milan Undone: Contested Sovereignties in the Italian Wars*. Cambridge, MA: Harvard University Press, 2021.

Garin, Eugenio. *Italian Humanism*. Translated by Peter Munz. New York: Harper and Row, 1965.

Garrisson, Janine. *A History of Sixteenth-Century France, 1483–1598*. New York: St. Martin's Press, 1995.

Gellner, Ernest. *Nations and Nationalism*. Ithaca, NY: Cornell University Press, 1983.

Gierke, Otto Friedrich von, and Ernst Troeltsch. *Natural Law and the Theory of Society, 1500–1800*. Translated by Ernest Barker. Union, N.J.: Lawbook Exchange, 2001.

Gilbert, Neal Ward. *Renaissance Concepts of Method*. New York: Columbia University Press, 1960.

Gilli, Patrick. "Humanisme Juridique et Science Du Droit Au XVe Siècle." *Revue de Synthèse* 130, no. 4 (December 2009): 571–93.

Gilmore, Myron Piper. *Argument from Roman Law in Political Thought, 1200–1600*. Cambridge, MA: Harvard University Press, 1941.

Gilmore, Myron Piper. "The Jurisprudence of Humanism." *Traditio* 17 (1961): 493–501.

Gilmore, Myron Piper. *The World of Humanism, 1453–1517*. 1952. Reprint, Westport, CT: Greenwood Press, 1983.

Godman, Peter. *From Poliziano to Machiavelli: Florentine Humanism in the High Renaissance*. Princeton, NJ: Princeton University Press, 1998.

Goebel, Julius. *The Equality of States: A Study in the History of Law*. New York: AMS Press, 1970.

Goffman, Daniel. *The Ottoman Empire and Early Modern Europe*. Cambridge: Cambridge University Press, 2002.

Goodrich, Peter, and Valérie Hayaert, eds. *Genealogies of Legal Vision*. London: Routledge, 2015.

Gouwens, Kenneth. "Perceiving the Past: Renaissance Humanism after the 'Cognitive Turn'." *The American Historical Review* 103, no. 1 (1998): 55–82.

Gozzi, Gustavo. "The Rights of Peoples and *Ius Gentium*: Their Origins in the Modern Age." In *Rights and Civilizations: A History and Philosophy of International Law*, edited by Gustavo Gozzi, 3–24. Cambridge: Cambridge University Press, 2009.

Grafton, Anthony. *Defenders of the Text: The Traditions of Scholarship in an Age of Science, 1450–1800*. Cambridge, MA: Harvard University Press, 1991.

Grafton, Anthony. "Humanism and Political Theory." In *The Cambridge History of Political Thought 1450–1700*, edited by J. H. Burns and Mark Goldie, 9–29. Cambridge: Cambridge University Press, 1991.

Gray, Hanna H. "Renaissance Humanism: The Pursuit of Eloquence." *Journal of the History of Ideas* 24, no. 4 (October 1963): 497.

Green, Henry. *Andrea Alciati and His Books of Emblems*. London: Trübner and Co., 1872.

Green, Henry. *Andreae Alciati Emblematum fontes*. Manchester: Published for the Holbein Society by A. Brothers, 1870.

Grendler, Paul F. *Schooling in Renaissance Italy: Literacy and Learning, 1300–1600*. Baltimore, MD: Johns Hopkins University Press, 1989.

Grendler, Paul F. *The Universities of the Italian Renaissance*. Baltimore, MD: Johns Hopkins University Press, 2002.

Gress, David. *From Plato to NATO: The Idea of the West and Its Opponents*. New York: The Free Press, 1998.

Grewe, Wilhelm G. *The Epochs of International Law*. Translated by Michael Byers. New York: Walter de Gruyter, 2000.

Haakonssen, Knud. *Natural Law and Moral Philosophy: From Grotius to the Scottish Enlightenment*. Cambridge: Cambridge University Press, 1996.

Hankins, James. *Renaissance Civic Humanism: Reappraisals and Reflections*. Cambridge: Cambridge University Press, 2003.

Hankins, James. *Virtue Politics: Soulcraft and Statecraft in Renaissance Italy*. Cambridge, MA: Harvard University Press, 2019.

Hartmann, Wilfried, and Kenneth Pennington, eds. *The History of Medieval Canon Law in the Classical Period, 1140–1234: From Gratian to the Decretals of Pope Gregory IX*. Washington, D.C: The Catholic University of America Press, 2008.

Haskins, Charles Homer. *The Rise of Universities*. Ithaca, NY: Cornell University Press, 1957.

Hatzimihail, Nikitas Emmanuel. "Bartolus and the Conflict of Laws." *Revue Hellenique de Droit International* 60 (November 2007): 12–79.

Headley, John M. *The Europeanization of the World: On the Origins of Human Rights and Democracy*. Princeton, NJ: Princeton University Press, 2008.

Headley, John M. "The Problem of Counsel Revisited Once More: Budé's *De asse* (1515) and *Utopia I* (1516) in Defining a Political Moment." In *Humanism and Creativity in the Renaissance*, edited by Christopher S. Celenza and Kenneth Gouwens, 141–70. Leiden: Brill, 2006.

Helmholz, Richard H. "Christopher St. German and the Law of Custom." *The University of Chicago Law Review* 70, no. 1 (2003): 129–39.

Henkins, Louis. *Age of Rights*. New York: Columbia University Press, 1990.

Herzog, Tamar. *A Short History of European Law: The Last Two and a Half Millenia*. Cambridge, MA: Harvard University Press, 2018.

Hoffman, Holger. *Studien zur Emblematik des 16. Jahrhunderts*. Utrecht: Haentjens Dekker & Gumbert, 1971.

Hoffman, Konrad. "Alciato and the Historical Situation of Emblematics." In *Andrea Alciato and the Emblem Tradition: Essays in Honor of Virginia Woods Callahan*, edited by Peter M. Daly, 1–46. New York: AMS Press, 1989.

Hunt, Lynn. *Inventing Human Rights: A History*. New York: W. W. Norton, 2007.

Hunter, Ian, and David Saunders. *Natural Law and Civil Sovereignty: Moral Right and State Authority in Early Modern Political Thought*. New York: Palgrave, 2002.

Hyde, John Kenneth. *Padua in the Age of Dante*. Manchester: Manchester University Press, 1966.

Isom-Verhaaren, Christine. *Allies with the Infidel: The Ottoman and French Alliance in the Sixteenth Century*. London: I. B. Tauris, 2011.

Jardine, Lisa. "Lorenzo Valla and the Intellectual Origins of Humanist Dialectic." *Journal of the History of Philosophy* 15, no. 2 (1977): 143–64.

Johnson, James Turner. "Then and Now: Medieval Conception of Just War Versus Recent Portrayals of the Just War Idea." In *Medieval Foundations of International Relations*, edited by William Bain, 117–31. London: Routledge, 2017.

Kahn, Victoria, and Lorna Hutson, eds. *Rhetoric and Law in Early Modern Europe*. New Haven, CT: Yale University Press, 2001.

Kalmo, Hent, and Quentin Skinner, eds. *Sovereignty in Fragments: The Past, Present and Future of a Contested Concept*. Cambridge: Cambridge University Press, 2010.

Kantorowicz, Ernst. *The King's Two Bodies: A Study in Mediaeval Political Theology*. Princeton, NJ: Princeton University Press, 1967.

Kaser, Max. *Ius gentium*. Cologne: Böhlau Verlag, 1993.

Kearley, Timothy G. "The Creation and Transmission of Justinian's Novels." *Law Library Journal* 102, no. 3 (2010): 377–97.

Kelley, Donald R. "Civil Science in the Renaissance: Jurisprudence in the French Manner," *History of European Ideas* 2, no. 4 (1981): 261–76.

Kelley, Donald R. "Civil Science in the Renaissance: Jurisprudence Italian Style." *The Historical Journal* 22, no. 4 (1979): 777–94.

Kelley, Donald R. "Civil Science in the Renaissance: The Problem of Interpretation." In *The Languages of Political Theory in Early-Modern Europe*, edited by Anthony Pagden, 57–78. Cambridge: Cambridge University Press, 1987.

Kelley, Donald R. "*De Origine Fuedorum*: The Beginnings of a Historical Problem." *Speculum* 39, no. 2 (April 1964): 207–28.

Kelley, Donald R. *Foundations of Modern Historical Scholarship: Language, Law, and History in the French Renaissance*. New York: Columbia University Press, 1970.

Kelley, Donald R. "Guillaume Budé and the First Historical School of Law." *The American Historical Review* 72, no. 3 (April 1967): 807–34.

Kelley, Donald R. *The Human Measure: Social Thought in the Western Legal Tradition*. Cambridge, MA: Harvard University Press, 1990.

Kelley, Donald R. "*Jurisconsultus Perfectus*: The Lawyer as Renaissance Man." *Journal of the Warburg and Courtauld Institutes* 51 (1988): 84–102.

Kelley, Donald R. "Law." In *The Cambridge History of Political Thought, 1450–1700*, edited by J. H. Burns and Mark Goldie, 66–94. Cambridge: Cambridge University Press, 1991.

Kelley, Donald R. "The Rise of Legal History in the Renaissance." *History and Theory* 9, no. 2 (1970): 174–94.

Kelley, Donald R. "Vera Philosophia: The Philosophical Significance of Renaissance Jurisprudence." *Journal of the History of Philosophy* 14, no. 3 (1976): 267–79.

Kelly, Samantha. *The New Solomon: Robert of Naples (1309–1343) and Fourteenth-Century Kingship*. Leiden: Brill, 2003.

Kingsbury, Benedict, and Benjamin Straumann, eds. *The Roman Foundations of the Law of Nations: Alberico Gentili and the Justice of Empire*. Oxford: Oxford University Press, 2010.

Kisch, Guido. *Bartolus und Basel, Basler Studien zur Rechtswissenschaft*. Basel: Helbing and Lichtenhahn, 1960.

Kisch, Guido. *Erasmus und die Jurisprudenz seiner Zeit: Studien zum Humanistischen Rechtsdenken*. Basel: Helbing & Lichtenhahn, 1960.

Kisch, Guido. "Humanistic Jurisprudence." *Studies in the Renaissance* 8 (1961): 71–87.

Kisch, Guido. *Studien zur Humanistischen Jurisprudenz*. Berlin: de Gruyter, 1972.

Knecht, R. J. *Renaissance Warrior and Patron: The Reign of Francis I*. Cambridge: Cambridge University Press, 1994.

Knoche, Hans Jürgen. *Ulrich Zasius und das Freiburger Stadtrecht von 1520*. Karlsruhe: C. F. Müller, 1957.

Kochi, Tarik. "Conflicting Lineages of International Law: Cicero, Hugo Grotius and Adam Smith on Global Property Relations." *Jurisprudence* (Oxford, England) 8, no. 2 (May 2017): 257–86.

Koenigsberger, H. G., and George L. Mosse. *Europe in the Sixteenth Century*. London: Longmans, 1968.

Koschaker, Paul. *Europa und das römische Recht*. Munich: C. H. Beck, 1953.

Koskenniemi, Martti. *The Gentle Civilizer of Nations: The Rise and Fall of International Law, 1870–1960*. Cambridge: Cambridge University Press, 2002.

Koskenniemi, Martti. "'International Community' from Dante to Vattel." In *Vattel's International Law from a XXIst Century Perspective / Le Droit International de Vattel vu Du XXIe Siècle*, edited by Vincent Chetail and Peter Haggenmacher, 49–75. Leiden: Brill, 2011.

Koskenniemi, Martti. "International Law in Europe: Between Tradition and Renewal." *The European Journal of International Law* 16, no.1 (2005): 113–24.

Koskenniemi, Martti. *The Politics of International Law*. Oxford: Hart Publishing, 2011.

Koskenniemi, Martti. *To the Uttermost Parts of the Earth: Legal Imagination and International Power 1300–1870*. Oxford: Oxford University Press, 2021.

Koskenniemi, Martti. "Vitoria and Us." *Rechtsgeschichte/Legal History* 22 (2014): 119–38.

Koskenniemi, Martti. Vocabularies of Sovereignty—Powers of a Paradox." In *Sovereignty in Fragments: The Past, Present and Future of a Contested Concept*, edited by Hent Kalmo and Quentin Skinner, 222–42. Cambridge: Cambridge University Press, 2010.

Koskenniemi, Martti. "Why History of International Law Today?" *Rechtsgeschichte: Zeitschrift Des Max-Planck-Instituts Für Europäische Rechtsgeschichte* 2004, no. 4 (2004): 61–66.

Kretzmann, Norman, Anthony Kenny, Jan Pinborg, and Eleonore Stump, eds. *The Cambridge History of Later Medieval Philosophy: From the Rediscovery of Aristotle to the Disintegration of Scholasticism, 1100–1600*. Cambridge: Cambridge University Press, 1982.

Kristeller, Paul Oskar. *Renaissance Thought and Its Sources*. Edited by Michael Mooney. New York: Columbia University Press, 1979.

Kristeller, Paul Oskar. *Renaissance Thought: The Classic, Scholastic, and Humanistic Strains*. New York: Harper and Row, 1955.

Kuehn, Thomas. "The Renaissance Consilium as Justice." *Renaissance Quarterly* 59, no. 4 (2006): 1058–88.

Kunkel, Wolfgang. "The Reception of Roman Law in Germany: An Interpretation." In *Pre-Reformation Germany*, edited by Gerald Strauss, 263–81. New York: Harper and Row, 1972.

Kuttner, Stephen. "Revival of Jurisprudence." In *Renaissance and Renewal on the Twelfth Century*, edited by Robert L. Benson and Giles Constable, 299–323. Cambridge, MA: Harvard University Press, 1982.

Lee, Daniel. *Popular Sovereignty in Early Modern Constitutional Thought*. Oxford, Oxford University Press, 2016.

Liebenau, Theodor von. *Der Humanist Ulrich Zasius als Stadtschreiber von Baden im Aargau*. Lucerne: Kath. Schweiz Bll, 1898.

Liermann, Hans. "Humanistische Jurisprudenz." *Zeitschrift für Religions- und Geistesgeschichte* 28, no. 1–4 (1976): 262–5.

Lines, David A. *Aristotle's Ethics in the Italian Renaissance (1300–1650)*. Leiden: Brill, 2002.

Lines, David A. "Humanism in Italian Universities," In *Humanism and Creativity in the Renaissance*, edited by Christopher S. Celenza and Kenneth Gouwens, 327–46. Leiden: Brill, 2006.

Lobingier, Charles Sumner. "The Reception of the Roman Law in Germany." *Michigan Law Review* 14, no. 7 (1916): 562–9.

Longfield Karr, Susan. "'The Law of Nations Is Common to All Mankind': Jus Gentium in Humanist Jurisprudence." In *Morality and Responsibility of Rulers: European and Chinese Origins of a Rule of Law as Justice for World Order*, edited by Janne Nijman and Anthony Carty, 73–92. Oxford: Oxford University Press, 2018.

Longfield Karr, Susan. "'Often We Are Deceived, and We Suffer Glaucoma': Rethinking Legal Humanism in the History of the Western Rights Tradition." European University Institute Working Paper, 2010.

Longfield Karr, Susan. "Redefining Ius to Restore Justice: The Centrality of *Ius Gentium* in Humanist Jurisprudence." In *Reassessing Legal Humanism and Its Claims: Petere Fontes?*, edited by Paul J. du Plessis and John W. Cairns, 108–34. Edinburgh: Edinburgh University Press, 2015.

Luscombe, D. E. "The State of Nature and the Origin of the State." In *The Cambridge History of Later Medieval Philosophy: From the Rediscovery of Aristotle to the Disintegration of Scholasticism, 1100–1600*, edited by Anthony Kenny, Eleonore Stump, Jan Pinborg, and Norman Kretzmann, 757–70. Cambridge: Cambridge University Press, 1982.

MacCulloch, Diarmaid. *Reformation: Europe's House Divided 1490–1700*. New York: Penguin Books, 2004.

MacDonell, John, and Edward Manson, eds. *Great Jurists of the World*. 2 vols. Boston, MA: Little, Brown, and Company, 1914.

MacLean, Ian. *Interpretation and Meaning in the Renaissance: The Case of Law*. Cambridge: Cambridge University Press, 1992.

Maffei, Domenico. *Gli inizi dell'umanesimo giuridico*. Milano: Giuffrè, 1956.

Maffei, Domenico. "Les Débuts de l'activité de Budé, Alciat et Zase ainsi que quelques remarques sur Aymar Du Rivail." In *Pédagogues et Juristes: Congrès Du Centre d'études Supérieures de La Renaissance de Tours: été 1960*, edited by Pierre Mesnard, 23–9. Paris: J. Vrin, 1963.

Maiolo, Francesco. *Medieval Sovereignty: Marsilius of Padua and Bartolus of Saxoferrato*. Delft: Eburon Academic Publishers, 2007.

Mallet, Michael Edward, and Christine Shaw. *The Italian Wars, 1494–1559: War, State and Society in Early Modern Europe*. New York: Pearson, 2012.

Mann, Nicholas. "The Origins of Humanism." In *The Cambridge Companion to Renaissance Humanism*, edited by Jill Kraye, 1–19. Cambridge: Cambridge University Press, 1996.

Manoscalco, Lorenzo. "Interpretatio ex aquo et bono: The Emergence of Equitable Interpretation in European Legal Scholarship." In *Networks and Connections in Legal History*, edited by Michael Lobban and Ian Williams, 233–61. Cambridge: Cambridge University Press, 2017.

Martines, Lauro. *Lawyers and Statecraft in Renaissance Florence*. Princeton, NJ: Princeton University Press, 1968.

Martines, Lauro. *Power and Imagination: City-States in Renaissance Italy*. New York: Vintage Books, 1979.

Martines, Lauro, ed. *Violence and Civil Disorder in Italian Cities, 1200–1500*. Berkeley: University of California Press, 1972.

Mattingly, Garrett. *Renaissance Diplomacy*. New York: Dover Publications, 1988.

Mautner, Thomas. "How Rights Became 'Subjective'." *Ratio Juris: An International Journal of Jurisprudence and the Philosophy of Law* 26, no. 1 (2013): 111–32.

Mazzacane, Aldo. "Law and Jurists in the Formation of the Modern State in Italy." *The Journal of Modern History* 67, Supplement: The Origins of the State in Italy, 1300–1600 (1995): S. 62–73.

Mazzocco, Angelo. *Interpretations of Renaissance Humanism*. Leiden: Brill, 2006.

McGrade, A. S., ed. *The Cambridge Companion to Medieval Philosophy*. Cambridge: Cambridge University Press, 2003.

McGrade, A. S., ed. "Rights, Natural Rights, and the Philosophy of Law." In *The Cambridge History of Later Medieval Philosophy: From the Rediscovery of Aristotle to the Disintegration of Scholasticism, 1100–1600*, edited by Anthony Kenny, Eleonore Stump, Jan Pinborg, and Norman Kretzmann, 738–56. Cambridge: Cambridge University Press, 1982.

McManamon, John M. *Funeral Oratory and the Cultural Ideals of Italian Humanism*. Chapel Hill: University of North Carolina Press, 1989.

McNeil, David O. "Guillaume Budé." In *Europe, 1450 to 1789: An Encyclopedia of the Early Modern World*, edited by Jonathan Dewald. New York: Charles Scribner's Sons, 2004.

McNeil, David O. *Guillaume Budé and Humanism in the Reign of Francis I*. Geneva: Droz, 1975.

Meyers, E. M. "Le Conflit Entre l'équité et La Loi Chez Les Premiers Glossateurs." *Tijdschrift Voor Rechtsgeschiedenis* 17, no. 2 (1941): 117–35.

Miceli, Augusto P. "Forum Juridicum: Bartolus of Sassoferrato." *Louisiana Law Review* 37, no. 5 (1977): s. 1027–1036.

Mignolo, Walter. *The Darker Side of the Renaissance: Literacy, Territoriality, and Colonization*. Ann Arbor: University of Michigan Press, 1995.

Miller, Jon. *The Reception of Aristotle's Ethics*. Cambridge: Cambridge University Press, 2012.

Mills, Charles W. *The Racial Contract*. Ithaca, NY: Cornell University Press, 1997.

Monfasani, John, ed. *Language and Learning in the Renaissance: Selected Articles*. London: Variorum Reprints, 1994.

Monheit, Michael Leonard. "Guillaume Budé, Andrea Alciato, Pierre de l'Estoile: Renaissance Interpreters of Roman Law." *Journal of the History of Ideas* 58, no. 1 (January 1997): 21–40.

Moore, R. I. *The First European Revolution*, c.970–1215. Oxford: Blackwell, 2000.

Mousourakis, George. *Comparative Law and Legal Traditions: Historical and Contemporary Perspectives*. Cham: Springer International Publishing, 2019.

Moyn, Samuel. *The Last Utopia: Human Rights in History*. Cambridge, MA: Belknap Press, 2010.

Muldoon, James. *Empire and Order: The Concept of Empire, 800–1800*. New York: St. Martin's Press, 1999.

Murray, James M., Walter Prevenier, and Michel Oosterbosch. *Notarial Instruments in Flanders between 1280 and 1452*. Brussels: Palais des académies, 1995.

Nauert, Charles G. *Humanism and the Culture of Renaissance Europe*. Cambridge: Cambridge University Press, 2006.

Nauert, Charles G. "Humanism as Method: Roots of Conflict with the Scholastics." *Sixteenth Century Journal* 29, no. 2 (1998): 427–38.

Nauert, Charles G. "The Humanist Challenge to Medieval German Culture." *Daphnis* 15, no. 2 (January 1986): 277.

Nauert, Charles G. "Renaissance Humanism: An Emergent Consensus and Its Critics." *Indiana Social Studies Quarterly* 33 (1980): 5–20.

Nauta, Lodi. *In Defense of Common Sense: Lorenzo Valla's Humanist Critique of Scholastic Philosophy*. Cambridge, MA: Harvard University Press, 2009.

Nederman, Cary J. *Lineages of European Political Thought: Explorations Along the Medieval/Modern Divide from John of Salisbury to Hegel*. Washington, D.C: The Catholic University of America Press, 2009.

Neff, Joseph. *Udalricus Zasius: Ein Beitrag Zur Geschichte Des Humanismus Am Oberrhein: Als Beilage Zum Programm Fur Das Schuljahr 1889/1890 and 1890/1891*. 2 vols. Freiburg i. B.: Universitats Buchdruckerei von Chr. Lehmann, 1890.

Neff, Joseph. *Ulrich Zasius: Ein Freiburger Humanist*. Freiburg i. B.: Stoll & Bader, 1890.

Nijman, Janne, and Anthony Carty, eds. *Morality and the Responsibility of Rulers: European and Chinese Origins of a Rule of Law as Justice for World Order*. Oxford: Oxford University Press, 2018.

Nijman, Janne, and Anthony Carty, eds. "The Moral Responsibility of Rulers Going Back Beyond the Liberal Rule of Law for World Order." In *Moral Responsibility and the Rule of Law: European and Chinese Origins of a Rule of Law as Justice for World Order*, edited by Janne Nijman and Anthony Carty, 1–52. Oxford: Oxford University Press, 2018.

Norwich, John Julius. *Four Princes: Henry VIII, Francis I, Charles V, Suleiman the Magnificent and the Obsessions That Forged Modern Europe*. New York: Atlantic Monthly Press, 2017.

Norwich, John Julius. *A History of France*. New York: Atlantic Monthly Press, 2018.

Oakley, Francis. *Natural Law, Conciliarism, and Consent in the Late Middle Ages: Studies in Ecclesiastical and Intellectual History*. London: Variorum Reprints, 1984.

Oakley, Francis. *Natural Law, Laws of Nature, Natural Rights: Continuity and Discontinuity in the History of Ideas*. New York: Continuum, 2005.

Oakley, Francis. *Omnipotence, Covenant, and Order: An Excursion in the History of Ideas from Abelard to Leibniz*. Ithaca, N.Y.: Cornell University Press, 1984.

Oestreich, Gerhard. *Geschichte der Menschenrechte und Grundfreiheiten im Umriß*. Berlin: Dunker & Humblot, 1978.

Oestreich, Gerhard, Brigitta Oestreich, and H. G. Königsberger. *Neo-stoicism and the Early Modern State*. Cambridge: Cambridge University Press, 1982.

Orford, Anne, Florian Hoffmann, and Martin Clark, eds. *The Oxford Handbook of The Theory of International Law*. Oxford: Oxford University Press, 2016.

Osiander, Andreas. "Sovereignty, International Relations, and the Westphalian Myth." *International Organization* 55, no. 3 (2001): 251–87.

Osler, Douglas J. "Andreas Alciatus (1492–1550) as Philologist." In *A Ennio Cortese*, edited by Ennio Cortese, Domenico Maffei, and Italo Birocchi, Part 3: 1–7. Rome: il Cigno Galileo Galilie, 2001.

Osler, Douglas J. " Budaeus and Roman Law." *Ius commune* 13 (1985): 195–212.

Osler, Douglas J. "Humanist Philology and the Text of Justinian's *Digest*." In *Reassessing Legal Humanism and its Claims: Petere Fontes?*, edited by Paul J. du Plessis & John W. Cairns, 41–56. Edinburgh: Edinburgh University Press, 2015.

Osler, Douglas J. "Images of Legal Humanism." Surfaces 9, (2001). https://doi.org/10.7202/1065066ar.

Osler, Douglas J. "Towards a Legal-History Bibliography: A Census of 16th-Century Legal Imprints." *Ius commune* 15 (1998): 231–42.

Padoa-Schioppa, Antonio. *A History of Law in Europe: From the Early Middle Ages to the Twentieth Century*. Translated by Caterina Fitzgerald. Cambridge: Cambridge University Press, 2017.

Pagden, Anthony, ed. *The Languages of Political Theory in Early-Modern Europe*. Cambridge: Cambridge University Press, 1987.

Pagden, Anthony, ed *Lords of All the World: Ideologies of Empire in Spain, Britain, and France c.1500–1800*. New Haven, CT: Yale University Press, 1995.

Park, Katherine, and Lorraine Daston, eds. *The Cambridge History of Science: Volume 3, Early Modern Science*. Cambridge: Cambridge University Press, 2006.

Parker, Geoffrey. *Emperor: A New Life of Charles v*. New Haven, CT: Yale University Press, 2019.

Pateman, Carol. *The Sexual Contract*, 2nd ed. Stanford, CA: Stanford University Press, 2018.

Pennington, Kenneth. "Baldus de Ubaldis." *8 Rivista International Di Diritto Commune* 35 (1997): 35–61.

Pennington, Kenneth. "Law, Legislative Authority, and Theories of Government, 1150–1300." In *The Cambridge Companion to Medieval Political Thought, c.350–c.1450*, edited by J. H. Burns, 424–54. Cambridge: Cambridge University Press, 1988.

Pennington, Kenneth. "Lex Naturalis and Jus Naturale" *The Jurist* 68 (2008): 569–91.

Pennington, Kenneth. "Politics of Law in Western Jurisprudence." In *The Jurists' Philosophy of Law from Rome to the Seventeenth Century*, edited by Andrea Padovani and Peter Stein, 157–211. New York: Springer International Publishing, 2007.

Pennington, Kenneth. *The Prince and the Law 1200–1600: Sovereignty and Rights in the Western Legal Tradition*. Berkeley: University of California Press, 1993.

Pettit, Phillip. *Made with Words: Hobbes on Language, Mind, and Politics*. Princeton, NJ: Princeton University Press, 2008.

Pettit, Phillip. *Republicanism: A Theory of Freedom and Government*. Oxford: Oxford University Press, 1997.

Piirimäe, Pärtel. "The Westphalian Myth and the Idea of External Sovereignty." In *Sovereignty in Fragments: The Past, Present and Future of a Contested Concept*, edited by Hent Kalmo and Quentin Skinner, 64–80. Cambridge: Cambridge University Press, 2010.

Plattard, Jean. *Guillaume Budé (1468–1540) et les origines de l'humanisme français*. Paris: Les Belles Lettres, 1966.

Plessis, Paul J. du and John W. Cairns. *Reassessing Legal Humanism and its Claims: Petere Fontes?*. Vol. 15. Edinburgh: Edinburgh University Press, 2015.

Pocock, J. G. A. *The Machiavellian Moment: Florentine Political Thought and the Atlantic Republican Tradition*. Princeton, NJ: Princeton University Press, 2003.

Poel, Marc van der. "Oratory and Declamation." In *A Guide to Neo-Latin Literature*, edited by Victoria Moul, 272–88. Cambridge: Cambridge University Press, 2017.

Pollmann, Judith. *Memory in Early Modern Europe, 1500–1800*. Oxford: Oxford University Press, 2017.

Popovic, Petar. "The Concept of «Right» and the Focal Point of Juridicity in Debate between Villey, Tierney, Finnis and Hervada." *Persona y Derecho* 78, no. 1 (January 2018): 55–103.

Post, Gaines. *Studies in Medieval Legal Thought: Public Law and the State, 1100–1322*. Princeton, NJ: Princeton University Press, 1964.

Potter, David. *Renaissance France at War: Armies, Culture and Society, c.1480–1560*. Suffolk: Boydell & Brewer Ltd., 2008.

Radding, Charles. *The Origins of Medieval Jurisprudence, Pavia and Bologna, 850–1150*. New Haven, CT: Yale University Press, 1988.

Randall, John Herman. *The School of Padua and the Emergence of Modern Science*. Padova: Antenore, 1961.

Rice, Jr., Eugene F. *The Renaissance Idea of Wisdom*. Cambridge, MA: Harvard University Press, 1958.

Rice, Jr. Eugene F., and Anthony Grafton. *Foundations of Early Modern Europe 1460–1559*. 2nd ed. New York: W. W. Norton, 1994.

Ricker, Leo Alexander. *Freiburg: Aus der Geschichte einer Stadt*. Reprint. Freiburg i Br: Verlag Rombach, 1982.

Ridder-Symoens, Hilde de, ed. *Universities in Early Modern Europe*. Cambridge: Cambridge University Press, 1996.

Ridder-Symoens, Hilde de, ed. *Universities in the Middle Ages*. Cambridge: Cambridge University Press, 1992.

Robichaud, Denis J. J. "Competing Claims on the Legacies of Renaissance Humanism in Histories of Philology." *Erudition and the Republic of Letters* 3, no. 2 (January 2018): 177–222.

Robinson, Jonathan. "Ockham, the Sanctity of Rights, and the Canonists." *Bulletin of Medieval Canon Law* 31, no. 1 (2014): 147–204.

Rowan, Steven W. *Ulrich Zasius: A Jurist in the German Renaissance, 1461–1535*. Frankfurt am Main: V. Klostermann, 1987.

Rowan, Steven W. "Ulrich Zasius and the Baptism of Jewish Children." *The Sixteenth Century Journal* 6, no. 2 (1975): 2–35.

Rummel, Erika. *The Humanist-Scholastic Debate in the Renaissance and Reformation*. Cambridge, MA: Harvard University Press, 1995.

Russell, Frederick H. *The Just War in the Middle Ages*. Cambridge: Cambridge University Press, 1975.

Ryan, Magnus. "Bartolus of Sassoferrato and Free Cities: The Alexander Prize Lecture." *Transactions of the Royal Historical Society* 10 (2000): 65–89.

Sarat, Austin, Lawrence Douglas, and Martha Merrill Umphrey, eds. *Law without Nations*. Stanford, CA: Stanford University Press, 2011.

Scattola, Merio. *Das Naturrecht vor dem Naturrecht: Zur Geschichte des >ius naturale< im 16. Jahrhundert*. Tübingen: Max Niemeyer Verlag, 1999.

Schiera, Pierangelo. "Legitimacy, Discipline, and Institutions: Three Necessary Conditions for the Birth of the Modern State." *The Journal of Modern History* 67 (1995): S. 11–33.

Schlesinger, Rudolf B. "The Past and Future of Comparative Law." *The American Journal of Comparative Law* 43, no. 3 (1995): 477–81.

Schmidt, Paul Gerhard. *Humanismus im Deutschen Südwesten: Biographische Profile*. 2nd ed. Stuttgart: Thorbecke, 2000.

Schmitt, C. B. *Aristotle and the Renaissance*. Cambridge, MA: Harvard University Press, 1983.

Schmitt, Carl. *The Concept of the Political*. Translated by George Schwab. Chicago: University of Chicago Press, 1996.

Schmitt, Carl. *The Nomos of the Earth in the International Law of Jus Publicum Europaeum* [1950]. Translated by G. L. Ulmen. New York: Telos Press Publishing, 2006.

Schoeck, Richard J. "Humanism and Jurisprudence." In *Renaissance Humanism: Foundations, Forms, and Legacy*, edited by Albert Rabil, 310–26. Philadelphia: University of Pennsylvania Press, 1988.

Scott, Tom. *Freiburg and the Breisgau: Town-Country Relations in the Age of Reformation and Peasants' War*. Oxford: Clarendon Press, 1986.

Scott, Tom. "Peasant Revolts in Early Modern Germany." *The Historical Journal* 28, no. 2 (June 1985): 455–68.

Seigel, Jerrold E. *Rhetoric and Philosophy in Renaissance Humanism: The Union of Eloquence and Wisdom, Petrarch to Valla*. Princeton, NJ: Princeton University Press, 1968.

Shaw, Christine. *Italy and the European Powers: The Impact of War, 1500–1530*. Leiden: Brill, 2006.

Simonds, Peggy M. "Alciati's Two Venuses as Letter and Spirit of the Law." In *Andrea Alciato and the Emblem Tradition: Essays in Honor of Virginia Woods Callahan*, edited by Peter M. Daly, 95–126. New York: AMS Press, 1989.

Simonds, Roger T. "The Teeth of the Law: Legal Interpretation in the Italian Renaissance." *Explorations in Renaissance Culture* 8 (January 1982): 97–106.

Simone, Franco. *Culture et politique en France á l'époque de l'humanisme et de la Renaissance*. Turin: Accademia Delle Scienze, 1974.

Skinner, Quentin. *The Foundations of Modern Political Thought. Volume 1: The Renaissance*. Cambridge: Cambridge University Press, 1978.

Skinner, Quentin. *The Foundations of Modern Political Thought. Volume 2: The Reformation*. Cambridge: Cambridge University Press, 1978.

Skinner, Quentin. *From Humanism to Hobbes: Studies in Rhetoric and Politics*. Cambridge: Cambridge University Press, 2018.

Skinner, Quentin. *Liberty before Liberalism*. Cambridge: Cambridge University Press, 1998.

Skinner, Quentin. *Visions of Politics*. 3 vols. Cambridge: Cambridge University Press, 2012.

Skinner, Quentin, and Martin van Gelderen, eds. *Freedom and the Construction of Europe*. 2 vols. Cambridge: Cambridge University Press, 2013.

Skinner, Quentin, and Martin van Gelderen, eds. *Republicanism: A Shared European Heritage*. 2 vols. Cambridge: Cambridge University Press, 2002.

Sottili, Agostino. *Humanismus und Universitätsbesuch: die Wirkung italienischer Universitäten auf die studia humanitatis nördlich der Alpen.* Leiden: Brill, 2006.

Stein, Peter. "Legal Humanism in Legal Science." *Tijdschrift Voor Rechtsgeschiedenis/ Legal History Review* 53, nos. 3–4 (1986): 297–306.

Stein, Peter. "The *Ius Commune* and its Demise," *The Journal of Legal History,* vol. 25, no. 2 (August 2004): 161–167.

Stein, Peter. *Roman Law in European History*. Cambridge: Cambridge University Press, 1999.

Stenner, Paul. "Subjective Dimensions of Human Rights: What Do Ordinary People Understand by 'Human Rights'?" *The International Journal of Human Rights* 15, no. 8 (December 2011): 1215–33.

Stintzing, Johann August Roderich von. *Ulrich Zasius: Ein Beitrag zur Geschichte der Rechtswissenschaft im Zeitalter der Reformation*. Basel: Schweighauser, 1857.

Strauss, Gerald. *Law, Resistance, and the State: The Opposition to Roman Law in Reformation Germany*. Princeton, NJ: Princeton University Press, 1986.

Strauss, Gerald. ed., *Pre-Reformation Germany*. New York: Harper and Row, 1972.

Strayer, Joseph R. *On the Medieval Origins of the Modern State*. Princeton: Princeton University Press, 2005.

Te Brake, Wayne. *Shaping History: Ordinary People in European Politics 1500–1700*. Berkeley: University of California Press, 1998.

Teschke, Benno. *The Myth of 1648: Class, Geopolitics and the Making of Modern International Relations*. London: Verso, 2003.

Thieme, Hans. *Kaiser Maximilian I im Leben und in den Werken von Ulrich Zasius*. Geneva: Publication du centre Européen d'Études Burgondo-Médianes, 1963.

Thieme, Hans. "Les Leçons de Zasius." In *Pédagogues et Juristes: Congrès Du Centre d'études Supérieures de La Renaissance de Tours: été 1960*, edited by Pierre Mesnard, 31–8. Paris: J. Vrin, 1963.

Thieme, Hans. "L'oeuvre juridque de Zasius." In *Pédagogues et juristes: Congrès Du Centre d'études Supérieures de La Renaissance de Tours: été 1960*, edited by Pierre Mesnard, 39–48. Paris: J. Vrin, 1963.

Throne, S.E. "Statuti in the Post-Glossators." *Speculum* 11, no. 4 (1936): 452–61.

Tierney, Brian. *The Idea of Natural Rights: Studies on Natural Rights, Natural Law, and Church Law, 1150–1625*. Atlanta, GA: Scholars Press, 1997.

Tierney, Brian. "Natural Law and Natural Rights: Old Problems and Recent Approaches." *The Review of Politics* 64, no. 3 (2002): 389–406.

Tierney, Brian. "Natural Rights in the Thirteenth Century: A Quaestio of Henry of Ghent." *Speculum* 67, no. 1 (January 1992): 58–68.

Tilly, Charles. "War Making and State Making as Organized Crime." In *Bringing the State Back In*, edited by Peter Evans, Dietrich Rueschemeyer, and Theda Skocpol, 169–87. Cambridge: Cambridge University Press, 1985.

Troje, Hans Erich. *Humanistische Jurisprudenz, Studien zur Europäischen Rechtswissenschaft unter dem Einfluss des Humanismus*. Internationale Bibliothek der Wissenschaften. Goldbach: Keip Verlag, 1993.

Tuck, Richard. *Natural Rights Theories: Their Origin and Development*. Cambridge: Cambridge University Press, 1979.

Tuck, Richard. *Philosophy and Government, 1572–1651*. Cambridge: Cambridge University Press, 1993.

Tuck, Richard. *The Rights of War and Peace: Political Thought and the International Order from Grotius to Kant*. Oxford: Oxford University Press, 1999.

Tully, James. *Public Philosophy in a New Key*. 2 vols. Cambridge: Cambridge University Press, 2008.

Ullman, Walter. *A History of Political Thought: The Middle Ages*. New York: Penguin, 1965.

Ullman, Walter. *Law and Politics in the Middle Ages: An Introduction to the Sources of Medieval Political Ideas*. Ithaca, NY: Cornell University Press, 1975.

Vernengo, Roberto J. "Human Rights and Axiological Inconsistencies." *Law and Philosophy* 8, no. 1 (April 1989): 65–82.

Viard, Paul-Émile. *André Alciat, 1492–1550*. Paris: Société anonyme du Recueil Sirey, 1926.

Villey, Michel. *Le droit et les droits de l'homme*. Paris: Presses universitaires de France, 1983.

Villey, Michel. "*La genèse du droit subjectif chez Guillaume d'Occam*," *Archives de philosophie du droit* 9 (1964): 97–127.

Villey, Michel. "Les origines da la nation de droit subjectif." *Archives de philosophie du droit* 2 (1953–4): 163–187.

Vinogradoff, Paul. *Roman Law in Medieval Europe*. Oxford: Clarendon Press, 1929.

Vogt, Helle, and Mia Münster-Swendsen, eds. *Law and Learning in the Middle Ages: Proceedings of the Second Carlsberg Academy Conference on Medieval Legal History 2005*. Copenhagen: DJØF Publishing, 2006.

Watson, Alan. "Aspects of Reception of Law." *The American Journal of Comparative Law* 44, no. 2 (1996): 335–51.

Wauters, Bart. "Aquinas, *ius gentium*, and the Decretists." *Journal of the History of Ideas* 81, no. 4 (2020): 509–29.

Weiss, Roberto. *The Dawn of Humanism in Italy: An Inaugural Lecture*. London: H. K. Lewis, 1947.

Whitman, James Q. "The Lawyers Discover the Fall of Rome." *Law and History Review* 9, no. 2 (1991): 191–220.

Wieacker, Franz. *History of Private Law in Europe with Particular Reference to Germany*. Oxford: Oxford University Press, 1995.

Wieacker, Franz. *Privatrechtsgeschichte der Neuzeit: Unter Besonderer Berücksichtigung der Deutschen Entwicklung*. 2., Neubearb. Aufl. Göttingen: Vandenhoeck u. Ruprecht, 1967.

Wilson, J. Dove. "Baldus de Ubaldis." *The Yale Law Journal* 12, no. 1 (1902): 8–20.

Winkel, Laurens. "Recht Als Wissenschaft, Geschichte Der Juristischen Methode Vom Humanismus Bis Zur Historischen Schule (1500–1850)." *Tijdschrift Voor Rechtsgeschiedenis* 75, no. 4 (2007): 416–7.

Winroth, Anders. *The Making of Gratian's Decretum*. Cambridge: Cambridge University Press, 2004.

Winterberg, Hans. *Die Schüler von Ulrich Zasius*. Stuttgart: W. Kohlhammer Verlag, 1966.

Witt, Ronald G. *"In the Footsteps of the Ancients:" The Origins of Humanism from Lovato to Bruni*. ACLS Humanities E-Book: Brill, 2000.

Witt, Ronald G. *The Two Latin Cultures and the Foundation of Renaissance Humanism in Medieval Italy*. Cambridge: Cambridge University Press, 2012.

Witte, Jr., John. *The Reformation of Rights: Law, Religion, and Human Rights in Early Modern Calvinism*. Cambridge: Cambridge University Press, 2007.

Witte, Jr., John. "A Short History of Western Rights." In *God's Joust, God's Justice: Law and Religion in the Western Tradition*, edited by John Witte, Jr., 31–48. Grand Rapids, MI: Wm. B. Eerdmans Publishing Company, 2006.

Wohlhaupter, Eugen. *Aequitas Canonica: Eine Studie aus dem Kanonischen Recht*. Paderborn: F. Schöningh, 1931.

Woolf, Cecil N. Sidney. *Bartolus of Sassoferrato: His Position in the History of Medieval Political Thought*. Cambridge: Cambridge University Press, 1913.

Zorić, Vladimir. "Banished with No Force: Exile and Metonymy in Cicero's Pro Caecina Oratio." *Diacritics* 40, no. 4 (2012): 72–103.

Index

www.ingramcontent.com/pod-product-compliance
Lightning Source LLC
Chambersburg PA
CBHW071322230926
51849CB00002B/287